KEITH RICE
Grocer and General Stores

TINTINHULL POST OFFICE - YEOVIL - SOMERSET

The Other
British Isles

By the same author

Britain Beside the Sea
Coastal Walks in England and Wales

The Other British Isles

A JOURNEY THROUGH
THE OFFSHORE
ISLANDS OF BRITAIN

Christopher Somerville

GRAFTON BOOKS
A Division of the Collins Publishing Group

LONDON GLASGOW
TORONTO SYDNEY AUCKLAND

Grafton Books
A Division of the Collins Publishing Group
8 Grafton Street, London W1X 3LA

Published by Grafton Books 1990

British Library Cataloguing in Publication Data

Somerville, Christopher
  The other British Isles: a journey through
  the offshore islands of Britain.
  1. Great Britain. Islands. Description & travel
  I. Title
  914.104859

  ISBN 0-246-13317-1

Photoset in Linotron Goudy by
Rowland Phototypesetting Limited
Bury St Edmunds, Suffolk
Printed and bound in Great Britain by
William Collins Sons & Co. Ltd, Glasgow

To all the young people of the islands
– seed corn of the future.

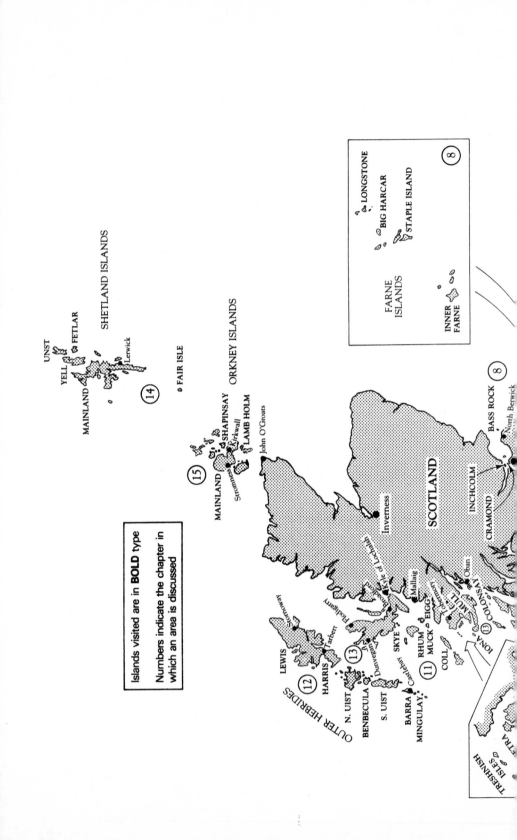

Islands visited are in **BOLD** type

Numbers indicate the chapter in which an area is discussed

SHETLAND ISLANDS

UNST
YELL
FETLAR
MAINLAND
Lerwick
⑭

ø FAIR ISLE

ORKNEY ISLANDS

SHAPINSAY
Kirkwall
LAMB HOLM
MAINLAND
Stromness
John O'Groats
⑮

FARNE ISLANDS

LONGSTONE
BIG HARCAR
STAPLE ISLAND

INNER FARNE

⑧

SCOTLAND

Inverness

INCHCOLM
CRAMOND
BASS ROCK ⑧
North Berwick

Kyle of Lochalsh
Mallaig
Oban
MULL
COLONSAY
IONA ⑬

RHUM
MUCK EIGG
SKYE
COLL
⑪

LEWIS
Stornoway
HARRIS
Tarbert
Dunvegan
Rodel
⑫
⑬
N. UIST
BENBECULA
S. UIST
BARRA Castlebay
MINGULAY

OUTER HEBRIDES

TRESHNISH ISLES
ETRA

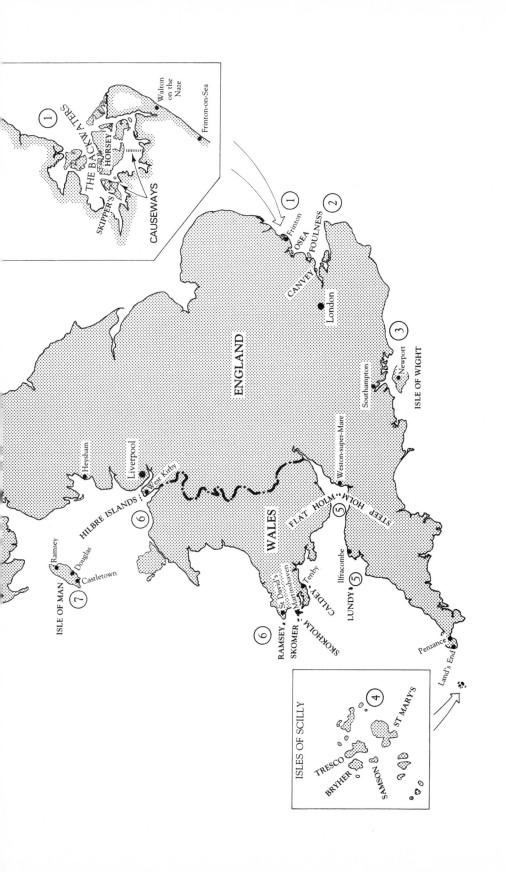

Contents

Acknowledgements

If I set down a list of all the people of the other British isles who opened their houses to me, encouraged me, put me right on my mistakes, played me their music, told me tales and sent me on to their friends and neighbours – it would just be a list of names. What I owe them can't be expressed in that way.

However, I must record my special thanks to Loganair Ltd, who generously allowed me to fly with them at a much reduced rate.

As for the individuals – they appear in their proper places in this book. I can never repay their open-hearted kindness, but I shall never forget their hospitality. I only hope they will feel that I have done justice to them and their islands.

Looking forward

If ever I meet Laurie Sparham, I shall buy him a big drink. It was his photograph that sowed the seed for this book. The picture appeared on the front page of the *Times Educational Supplement* of 3 January 1986: a grainy, smudgy shot of the old schoolhouse on the island of Stroma in the Pentland Firth. I kept that page, liking the grey bleakness of Mr Sparham's photograph. And when I came to plan a new book, it was that picture that bobbed up in my mind.

I had no idea at all what I was taking on when I decided to travel right through the islands that lie off the coast of mainland Britain. Islands had always fascinated me with their remoteness and air of being slightly out of the world. Everyone I spoke to about the project turned out to have just the same feeling about islands. 'Oh, I'd *love* to do that,' they said when I mentioned the Outer Hebrides, or the Scilly Isles, or Shetland. I looked in libraries, in bookshops and on friends' shelves for other travellers' tales of the islands. Plenty of people had written of walking through the Hebrides, sailing round the Orkney islands and mooning romantically over Skye. No one, as far as I could discover, had attempted a journey round the whole range of what I soon came to think of as the 'other British isles'. I spread out the Ordnance Survey maps, and went island-spotting. After a thousand I stopped listing potential destinations, and began gasping at the size of the job I had taken on. In the end I got to fifty of them; enough to make a fair cross-section.

In February I began the travelling; not with the glories of the Western Isles, but among the wind-blasted, ice-cold marsh islands of Essex. That was the start of nearly two years of walking, sailing, flying, bicycling, hitch-hiking; of wild exhilaration and crushing sadness; of fiddle tunes and Gaelic songs; of unrepayable, unforgettable hospitality. Again and again the islands sprang their surprises – Arab stallions on a bleak Essex island of mud, clan chiefs at their kitchen tables, Shetland towns more Norwegian than Scottish, ravishingly lovely scenes of atrocious mass murders. Before the journey I would never have believed that whole communities still lived many miles from a motor road, or that old men still clambered cliffs forty miles from land to catch gannets for the pot. At one time or another I found myself shearing sheep on Ramsey, stormbound on Rhum, serenaded in Fingal's Cave, bullied into the Boston Two-Step on Shapinsay . . .

But all this lay hidden in the future on that frozen February morning in the silence of the muddy Walton Backwaters.

1. Skipper's, Horsey and Osea

THE MARSH AND MUD ISLANDS
OF ESSEX

'Rendezvous Birch Hall Farm 1030 hrs.' That was the brisk message scrawled across the postcard from Harry Hawkes of Skipper's Island. There's no telephone on Skipper's: no mains electricity, for that matter, or gas, or roads, or fresh water. A flat blob of mud and raw scrub on the lonely expanses of the Walton Backwaters behind Walton-on-the-Naze in north-east Essex, Skipper's Island has slipped the attention of the everyday world. Few people know of its existence. Fewer still suspect that anyone could be spartan enough to live there – let alone a solitary man of seventy.

Harry Hawkes met me at the farm in his mud-spattered Land Rover. He was tall, square-built, with a hawk's downward-hooked nose. He checked his letterbox, and filled three plastic containers from the farmyard tap. Then we boarded the Land Rover and jolted down to the edge of the marsh.

Two causeways connect Skipper's Island to the mainland, reached from the sea wall by humpbacked runs of gap-ridden duckboard on stilts. The chief causeway is a curving, tilting ridge of gravel, pebbles and concrete blocks, consolidated between weed-green wooden stakes through which each tide seethes. All parts of the causeway are smeared and surrounded by gleaming, milk-chocolate-coloured mud, covered at high tide but revealing itself as the water goes down in piled banks like stinking cottage cheese, then at a lower level flat, slimy sheets in which gull and wader prints are caught and fixed like fossils until the next tide washes them away. Tough grey grasses and sea purslane leaves make wig hats for the mud banks, holding the whole structure of the marsh together. It was high tide now, both causeways under several feet of water. Harry Hawkes threw me the end of a muddy chain to steady his home-made ferry – several stout baulks of timber, a steering oar and a small outboard engine fixed on top of three ex-USAF fibreglass aeroplane fuel tanks. Just one of a string of examples of Hawkes's ingenuity at making do, essential qualification for life on Skipper's Island. Clambering aboard, we puttered across a couple of hundred yards of water. In front was the low shore of Skipper's, with a collection of boats moored beside another Hawkes invention, a long jetty on spindly legs leading high above the mud and on to the island.

There is only one house on Skipper's Island. Like the ferry, the jetty and much else, it was made by Harry Hawkes, using 2000 feet of African hardwood that cost him five bob a foot and endless trouble in transporting it to the island. The roof is curved, the windows resemble portholes. Hawkes built it to form the living quarters of a gigantic houseboat he began work on, a fifty-foot monster that would have cruised the Backwaters like a pike in a puddle.

Fed up as a young man in 1938 with his job with Mobil Oil and life in London – 'Couldn't stand London! Bloody awful place' – Harry Hawkes joined the army as a private soldier. Commissioned just after the outbreak of the Second World War, he spent most of his war service in the Middle East, and stayed on there in the peacetime army. He retired in 1970, on his fiftieth birthday, having commanded a parachute battalion. He'd come first to the Backwaters in 1954, wildfowling, and had fallen in love with the area. When the owner of Skipper's Island, Fred Williams, asked Hawkes if he'd like to look after the island for him – nothing paid, just for the interest and for something worthwhile to do – Harry jumped at the chance. Williams, a dedicated naturalist, had granted the Essex Naturalists' Trust a lease in perpetuity of Skipper's Island at a rent of £1 a year. Hawkes became its unpaid warden, his duties boiling down to maintaining the island in as natural a state as possible.

Skipper's Island is a naturalist's paradise. Enthusiasts squelch and slide over the muddy causeways, or buzz across on Harry Hawkes's fuel tank raft, to wallow among the breeding shelduck, redshank and oystercatchers, the owls, harriers and buzzards, the pigmy shrews and short-tailed voles. Forty species of lichen thrive in the soil, on tree trunks and on the rotting wooden posts of old jetties. The rough grass is rich in butterflies, richer still in moths – five-spot burnets, feathered ranunculus, footman, day-flying Mother Shipton. Pride of place goes to a moth so rare that Harry Hawkes forbade me to reveal its name. It possesses a pair of smart white wing-flashes that aid identification when Hawkes and his guests go moth hunting by torchlight. This moth lays its eggs in the hollow stems of a plant only found here in the Backwaters and in one other place in Kent. Sea hog's fennel is its local name, but medieval herbalists knew it as sulphurwort. The 16th-century herbalist John Gerard described it: 'I have digged up rootes thereof as big as a man's thigh, blacke without, and white within; of a strong and greevous smell, and full of yellow sap or liquor, which quickly waxeth hard or drie, smelling not much unlike Brimstone . . .'

Lepidopterists can be ruthless when it comes to rare moths. Harry Hawkes surprised one raider climbing into his boat with an armful of yellow and green sea hog's fennel, in hopes that some moths' eggs might be inside. Hawkes put the thief through such a blistering tongue-lashing from the shore that he shamefacedly threw all his booty overboard.

Hawkes took me up the 30-foot observation tower in the centre of the island, a shaky climb up slippery old ladders. From the top at high tide Skipper's Island looks like a large bush set in a sea. The thorn and bramble thickets that cover the island once teemed with rabbits – enough for the pre-war owner Captain Leigh Pemberton to shoot bags of up to 1000 in a season. Myxomatosis in 1956–7 wiped out the lot. A sea wall completely surrounds the 146-acre island, breached in a couple of places by the 1953 East Coast sea surge that brought death and havoc to the entire eastern seaboard of England. Because of those two gaps in its defences, Skipper's Island becomes two-thirds salt water at each high tide. Where freshwater pools lie protected by the sea wall, a marsh and salting environment has grown, ranging from completely saline and wet to half-salty dry ground. Here the waders, ducks and geese congregate in their thousands. On this February day there was constant bird movement, low-slung bodies cutting through the sky at every point of the compass, some formations nearly a thousand strong, all veering this way and that at the same split second.

Harry Hawkes, showing me his tiny kingdom, leaned nonchalantly over the open hatchway in the observation tower's top deck. One visitor, stepping back up here to take a photograph, was exceedingly lucky not to have killed herself.

'I was drinking tea at the back of the house with a friend, when he suddenly said, "Good God, Harry, someone's just fallen off your tower." I shot out there, and they had indeed. Thirty feet down into brambles. She – was – a – mess. Cut to ribbons. Had obviously broken her femur. Luckily the chap I was with was feeling strong, so between us we carried her on a divan to a boat and managed to get her away to hospital. Another thing altogether if it had been low tide.'

Inside the wooden house there's a place for everything, and most things in their places. The approaches to the island are well covered by a telescope on a tripod, mounted at the picture window that looks out to the jetty and causeways. It's a snug, handy house, built and furnished entirely by the hand of Harry Hawkes. While a couple of miles away to the east there are whole regiments of folk his age toddling out their lives in Frinton, he has to turn to and work, not just for little comforts but for every convenience that most people take for granted. He has to generate his own electricity; 'that bloody great machine', jarring away in its own shed, cost him as much as his whole house did. He clears his own drains, pipes in his rainwater supply, mends sea walls, patches up causeways and jetties, cuts back scrub, services a dozen boats and plays ferryman and host to any visitor who wants to get across to Skipper's Island. Hawkes thrives on it, tremendously hale and fit-looking, eternally enthusiastic. He'll turn his hand to anything, have a go at any job. The house is surrounded by what he calls 'kit'. Kit means old marine engines, peeling ancient boats up on blocks, sheds crammed with lengths of wood and tools, a tangle of water and power lines on the grass, bits of obsolete army gear, ammo boxes, jerry cans, the engine from a scout car that saw service at El Alamein. There's a small Ferguson tractor, bought by a previous owner of the island back in 1948 – and second-hand then. Second World War pontoons, acquired by Harry Hawkes as a cheap job lot, lie like beached whales on the grass.

'I know the ideal is to lead a simple life with no machinery, nothing that's not natural. But it doesn't really work out. Chopping your wood, sawing it into pieces with a bow saw – living like that takes so much sheer bloody toil. You need machinery to keep going: tractors, generators, boats, engines.'

Harry Hawkes is nothing if not self-sufficient, tidy-minded and soldierly. Yet his one-man settlement is as cluttered as a Pacific island village encumbered by the detritus left behind by wartime American marines. The problem is simply one of waste disposal. Nothing heavy or unwieldy leaves Skipper's Island unless it's an absolute necessity. Try manhandling a block of iron weighing half a ton along a six-inch plank high above a bath of mud, and you'll soon see why. When a machine rusts solid or can't be coaxed into going again, it is just laid aside for attention – one fine day. Not just machines, either. Harry Hawkes made his own splatchers, special overshoes to enable him to scoot around over the sloppiest, most quaking mud. He wore them once, but found that they filled with mud. They're on a nail in the shed, waiting until he gets round to modifying the design. He used to go trawling and drift-netting for grey mullet and Dover sole on the Backwaters, using a forty-foot net from his old side-winding trawler. Trawler and net are laid up now, against the day that Harry Hawkes hears of a fit, retired man, preferably an ex-soldier, who might like to go out with him on clear nights, trawling the Backwaters. The enormously long list of repair and maintenance jobs pinned up in his porch, he acknowledges, will never be ticked off. With work always either in hand or in prospect – usually both – self-contained, content to use any of the products of the industrialized world to help him maintain his hardy existence on Skipper's Island, Harry Hawkes leads a better-balanced life than most.

'Brothers usually have one pretty well summed up, and mine always said I was a bit of a loner. And I *am*. I hate all that wasted time over social chit-chat, saying the same things to the same people a thousand times a week. I don't know what loneliness means – I never get lonely. I was cut off for five days last winter – may have been more, but five at least – by ice floes piling up on the causeway. It was like the bloody Antarctic. Luckily I had a good stock of books, and I'd had to put off some guests, so I had enough food for about nine meals. I loved every minute of it. When I leave this island it'll be in a box, six foot three by eighteen inches.'

Horsey Island, just across the water from Skipper's and twice the size, is the biggest island in the Backwaters, connected to the mainland by a causeway across a muddy gap appropriately known as the Wade. It looked forbidding in the half light of the following dawn, a gleaming sea of mud with a single strip of roadway embedded in its surface. Part of the causeway lay under six inches of water, part under cold, oozy mud. Mud plains extended on both sides into the wastes of the Backwaters, watercourses trickling through their smooth-sided grey canyons. There was an alien look to the electricity cables snaking haphazardly over the mud. I threw in a pebble. *Plup*, said the mud, settling back instantly into an unwrinkled membrane.

Here, in his seventh 'Swallows and Amazons' story, *Secret Water*, Arthur Ransome almost drowned Titty, Roger, Bridget and Sinbad the kitten, caught on the causeway by a rising tide. It's still a wonderfully exciting chapter to read, with brave Titty trying to choke down her anxiety for the sake of the younger ones, as the water closes inexorably in. The episode was illustrated by one of Ransome's scratchy little sketches, showing the Swallows striding out across a sloppy causeway identical with today's rough crossing. The Swallows, or Walker children, had been marooned on Horsey Island in typically breezy style by their father, quite happy to leave his ewe lambs on their own to make out as best they could for an unspecified time of trial. Daddy's brisk farewell to his five children is: 'Goodbye, all of you. Use sense. Watch the tides. John and Susan in charge.' His greeting, after several days of abandonment: 'Hullo, John. Good man.' Poor sensible John, terribly serious and conscientious, racked with anxiety throughout the adventure over the filling in of Daddy's blank map of the area. John did sterling psychological duty all through the 'Swallows and Amazons' books, working out Ransome's own *angst* over his sad relationship as a boy with his critical, disapproving father. John is infinitely preferable, at least in my view, to the hearty, larky Nancy Blackett in her red stocking-cap, waking the camp at dawn with a war cry and jabbing blood out of other people with a pin during blood-brother ceremonies that nobody wants except her.

Nowadays, as when *Secret Water* was written half a century ago, Horsey Island holds the feeling of a place at the edge of things, poised somewhere on an undefined margin between land and water. It covers about 300 acres, most of it penned in behind sea walls. If you get a sheep in front of you on the wall top, as I did that early morning, you can find yourself driving the silly thing for miles before it has the sense to run down the side. Sheep do well on Horsey Island, nibbling away at the huge, flat pasture fields. Joe Backhouse, who with his mother owns and farms the island, has an agreement with the Nature Conservancy Council not to plough more than fifty acres on Horsey. Extensive ploughing would deprive hundreds of thousands of birds of their food supply.

Horsey is an incomparable bird refuge, especially for wildfowl. Later on that chilly morning, looking out of the Backhouses' kitchen window into the next field, with Joe's help I spotted godwits, golden plovers, starlings, lapwings, fieldfares, brent geese, gulls, moorhens and curlews digging in the rain-softened earth, all within a grassy patch of about ten square yards. Walking round the sea walls I used binoculars I'd hardly picked up since my teens, and strained my eyes sore. Trying to hold the binoculars steady on birds in flight proved impossible. I just couldn't swing the things quickly enough. The increasing February cold, nipping at my fingers, didn't help matters. The enormous dun and black blankets of saltings at the margin of the island rang with bird bubble and squeak, peepings and pipings. Terns came overhead on long, pointed wings. A short-eared owl sulked on a fence post, thoroughly upset by my scrutiny. I followed the flight path of two herons, and glanced down to be transfixed by the sight of five fat seals wallowing like great slugs on a mud bank just offshore. They lay watching me watching them, rear flippers cocked up behind. One was a pup, with pale fur in patches on its back; the others wore mottled coats that gleamed with reflected light. Waddling down the mud slopes to the chill water of the Backwaters they looked clumsy, but as soon as they had slipped into the channel they entered a state of grace. They were dignified swimmers, holding their glistening heads high like very fat, bald old men with several chins apiece, staring fixedly in my direction. Diving, they either made a tremendous splash or simply vanished in a single ripple. They were a joy to behold, but it was too cold to stand still any longer.

Joe Backhouse enjoys the birds of Horsey Island, which is the reason he doesn't plough and profit. He has lived out here in the isolation of the Backwaters all his life, based in the ramshackle, cluttered farmhouse in the centre of the island. Dogs sidle into the kitchen to lick your hand under the table, or curl up in the armchairs by the Aga. Joe has little time for gushers and sentimental sighers. He shrugs off any suggestion of a romantic side to island life, or of hardships nobly borne. The causeway presents no difficulty, if you have the sense to read your tide table properly. He and his mother see more people than any other family he knows. People love to come to the island, so the Backhouses are never lonely – shades of Harry Hawkes. He'll admit that island farming is more expensive than on the mainland – concrete costs twice as much, transport can be a problem; the salt mud of the Wade chews up as many as three or four second-hand Land Rovers a year.

The farm's most profitable operation is a romantic's dream if ever there was one – breeding Arab horses. It has worked to greater and greater success for the best part of forty years. Buyers come from all corners of the world to cross that clarty causeway and look over the Backhouse stock. At least, the hardier customers do: the more fastidious send their Eton-educated aides to get muddy in lieu. The best of the horses can fetch many thousands of pounds. They are beautiful creatures, squirrel red with white nose blazes and flowing black manes and tails. They graze contentedly on the salty grass of the farmhouse fields, while their foals in the sheds share feeding buckets with the Horsey Island sheep. The Arab horses move over the cold Essex marshland as the seals do in the Backwaters currents – slowly, gracefully, perfectly controlled.

The Backhouses acknowledge that, in spite of the efficient early warning system now operating, Horsey Island could still be vulnerable to flooding, especially on a spring tide after several days of strong north-westerly gales. At such times the North Sea is banked up hard against its eastern shores. If the wind shifts round to the east as the spring tide is on the make, the North Sea comes slopping back across the basin towards Britain. When it happened in 1953 the waves came right over the tops of Horsey Island's tall sea walls. The water stopped twenty yards from the farmhouse, which saved the Backhouses; but they lost almost all their sheep and cows, a devastating blow from which they might never have recovered had the entire East Coast not been declared a national disaster area and enormous compensation paid. Most of the horses survived, which persuaded the Backhouses to get their breeding operation into full gear.

In one night the 1953 flood disaster wiped out the work of fifteen years. Nancy Backhouse bought Horsey Island shortly before the Second World War when she and her husband were looking for a farm by the sea. Horsey just happened to be one property in the estate agent's sheaf. Those were the days when Arthur Ransome was still active in the area. *Secret Water*, a great success on its publication in 1939, details just about every nook and cranny of the island and its creeks and inlets and neighbouring marshes. The story grew out of Ransome's own holiday jaunts to the Backwaters with his children and their friends. He, like his creation Commander Walker, would maroon his young charges on Horsey and retreat to his yacht in Hamford Water while the youngsters careered about in muddy freedom all over the secret world of the island.

'Arthur Ransome was a nice old boy,' Nancy Backhouse said as she ferried me in one of her bucketing, splattered Land Rovers back across the causeway through the Wade, 'but that book has brought an awful lot of strangers here. Ransome enthusiasts come from all over the world, literally all over – Canada, Australia, Japan – to Horsey, in order to stand on the exact spot where the children camped and so on. Perfectly charming, of course – they all ring up before they come – but they're all rather, you know, *odd*.'

Fifteen miles south of the Backwaters, the long tongue of the estuary of Essex's River Blackwater curves inland and is swallowed at Maldon. Lodged here in the very throat of the river lies Osea Island, marooned each low tide in a plateau of glistening mud. Familiar by now with the pre-dawn bleakness and mystery of Essex island causeways, I still stood entranced by the babel of duck and geese noises that burst into earshot as the smoky orange sun rose behind Osea, and by the zig-zag line of the causeway marching out into the estuary mud, the only solid thing in all that shining, quaking plain.

'Osey or Osyth Island, commonly called Oosy Island, so well known by our London men of pleasure, for the infinite number of wild-fowl,' wrote Daniel Defoe three centuries ago, 'that is to say, duck, mallard, teal and widgeon, of which there are such vast flights, that they tell us the island, namely the creek, seems covered with them, at certain times of the year, and they go from London on purpose for the pleasure of shooting; and indeed often come home very well loaden with game. But it must be remembered, too, that those gentlemen who are such lovers of the sport, and go so far for it, often return with an Essex ague on their backs, which they find a heavier load than the fowls they have shot.'

Agues and wildfowl were the two chief attributes of the Essex marshes. Defoe noted how few old folk were to be seen hereabouts – the ague, or malaria, would soon make away with anyone not young and fit. The sovereign remedies were boozing and opium-taking, neither doing anything to strengthen local constitutions against local conditions. Essex men, reported Defoe, would work their way through anything up to a couple of dozen wives, going inland to the healthier uplands for a fresh mate as soon as the last one had succumbed to an ague.

But Osea Island was always a mecca for wildfowl and wildfowlers. Sporting Squire Kemble of Runwell Hall recorded in late Victorian times seeing 'the sky darkened with wild-geese covering a space of half-a-mile by a quarter-of-a-mile as thick as manure spread upon the ground, and making a noise which I could only compare with fifty packs of hounds in full cry.' Punt-gunners went after the brent geese in winter, in hopes of killing several dozen with a single well-placed shot. These days about 40,000 dark-bellied brent geese winter in the Blackwater estuary, one of the largest concentrations in Europe, not so much in danger from sporty squires or rustic punt-gunners as from the polluted food they pick up on the Blackwater's unsavoury shores. The Essex farmers shoo the brent geese off their fields with gun and bird scarer, forcing them to take slimmer pickings along the tideline – one washed by the poisoned and polluted North Sea. The brent numbers are steadily falling, year by year. The fallout from the Chernobyl nuclear power station accident in 1987 reduced their ranks considerably. Osea Island may yet prove their salvation, however, if the Nature Conservancy Council's deal with Osea's owner comes good. They plan to make it just about worth his while to switch the cultivation of Osea's couple of square miles from the present wheat, barley, peas and potatoes, into grass, a giant larder for geese.

David Cole, the man at Osea's helm, loves the island passionately. He bought it in 1970, sold it to Cambridge University in 1977, found he couldn't bear to be without it, and bought it back again in 1986 after ten years of flying visits and sadness as he watched his manor house deteriorate, unlived in, and his farmland run down. The reason for my dawn raid on Osea was a breakfast date with David Cole, shakily arranged over a bad telephone line and destined to be unfulfilled, since when I arrived at the manor house I found he had left the island the previous night – a common hazard when fixing meetings with island inhabitants. 'Time and tide – especially tide – wait for no man' might be the motto of every island dweller. David's son Martin, though, was happy to sit in weak winter sunshine and chat about the joys and sorrows of island life. More joys than sorrows, he feels.

'In summer, for example, we can get the boat out and go off to Maldon – it's a five-minute trip – have a curry there, and come back by moonlight down the estuary. Or go off by boat to a party on shore. You really get the feeling of *going* somewhere when you set off from Osea by boat. Maybe once a fortnight the tides are right to spend a whole weekend on shore, but you very soon learn to organize yourself so that there's a well-stocked larder. I love it here. This part of the world is very subtle – the attractions are to do with atmosphere, blends of sky and water. It's a waste of time to look for features in the landscape: there aren't any. It's a sailor's area. People are very keen to keep the wooden boat tradition going, and especially under sail.'

Martin Cole is a keen sailor, like his father. You need to be, to get the best out of an area stiff with creeks, outlets, rivers, marsh and estuary. On hot summer days Osea Island draws visitors by the hundred, with the Blackwater full of boats moored just off the island and the pebbly little river beaches of Osea lined with sun-worshippers. Up to fifty people are living on Osea then, but during the winter the population shrinks to a stable half-dozen or so (the Coles and their island workforce). In the various cottages of 'the village', a cluster of Edwardian beamy small houses behind the manor house, lives a diverse selection of people whose only binding thread is their freedom from a timetable imposed by a nine-to-five job. There's a BBC producer and his wife and small daughter, until recently taken to school in Maldon by boat. There's the English correspondent of a Norwegian tabloid newspaper, who spends his time combing the downmarket English papers for naughty titbits to send home. There's a shifting, semi-stable population of writers, artists, photographers, thesis-scribblers; all wanting that ultimate ungetatability that Osea offers for sixteen hours out of twenty-four. They are reachable only by way of the amiable postman who bikes across the causeway every day – the best part of his round, he vows.

Their sewerage arrangements must be the most extensive per capita in use anywhere in the known world – a great cavernous system under the island brought to light a few years ago by questing operatives from Dyno-Rod, but laid down during the First World War when tiny Osea had nearly 2000 inhabitants. Motor torpedo boats were based here, striking as far away as the Baltic. At least one Victoria Cross was won from Osea Island by these dashing young men. While at rest, the MTBs were serviced in a huge concrete dry dock, which now lies smothered under brambles near the manor, together with a torpedo-testing tank and other relics of those war years – crumbling, greening barrack houses, blockhouses, storehouses. Rusty rails run out of the sea and cross the beach to plunge into the prickly bushes of shrubby seablite that cover the low sea walls of Osea. As my island journey unfolded I was to find many traces like these, specialized detritus of war abandoned to disfigure islands large and small from Essex to Orkney. This broken concrete and stained iron never failed to look strange and deadly, no matter how beautiful the surroundings. Some of those sturdy wooden torpedo boats have stayed in the Osea area, too, tucked away up side creeks along the Blackwater estuary, their 3000 hp Rolls-Royce engines long gone, houseboat homes for a generation of modern water gypsies.

Osea Manor was built as 'Rivermere', a home for gently-born, beyond-the-pale Edwardian drunks and junkies, 'gentlemen suffering from the insidious and baneful effects of Alcohol and Narcotics'. For a time just before the First World War, the island was full of reforming alcoholics. The scheme was hatched by Frederick Charrington, a member of the brewing family, who bought Osea in 1903 after experiencing a Pauline conversion from the trade. He had witnessed a drunken man outside a pub, enraged by his wife's demands for money to feed the children, knock her flat in the gutter with a blow. Charrington, horrified, had looked up to see his own name emblazoned across the top of the pub. 'That blow,' he was fond of saying, 'knocked her into the gutter, and me out of the brewery.' Refusing to touch any job or money tainted by malt and hops, he bought Osea in hopes that enterprising speculators would build alcoholics' homes where the sufferers couldn't get at the cause of their misery. Needless to say, human ingenuity undid the best efforts of philanthropy. The Blackwater fishermen did a roaring trade in smuggling booze out to Osea. A ridiculous game of 'hunt the bottle' developed, with staff and inmates vying to find bottles hidden in caches under bushes and down rabbit burrows, or attached to buoys out in the mud. The scheme collapsed. But Osea Island had well and truly got its hooks into Frederick Charrington. 'When I first took possession of it, I felt like Robinson Crusoe,' he said. 'It's truly beautiful.' As succinct an explanation as you could want of why people buy islands.

Wonderful stories have gathered like Irish mist around another of Osea's previous owners, a man with a taste for humiliating his employees – the more senior the better. The unwilling guests, knowing full well what bizarre rituals awaited them once trapped across the causeway, dared not refuse the boss's kind invitation. In-house party games are said to have included 60-year-old company directors wrestling naked in the mud for ping-pong balls; swimming round the pier between two courses of dinner, under threat of a forfeit of next year's pay rise; classical Greek lessons given by the gowned and mortarboarded owner to guests sitting on schoolroom forms in shorts and caps; nude chases through the shrubby seablite at the business end of an electric cattle prod; senior executives dressed in Robin Hood outfits shooting each other with bows and arrows under the appreciative eye of their host. Stories like these, apocryphal beyond doubt, tend to accrete round the owners of islands. They only reflect what most landlubbers feel about island-dwellers: must be barmy enough for anything.

Islands, like any other piece of coastline, don't stay unchanged in shape down the years. Tidal action burrows and moulds, nibbles away at soft parts, builds up spits and banks. Ebb tides suck round Osea, slicing off portions of its crumbly clay cliffs. North Sea pollution doesn't just poison the brent geese on Osea's tideline; it also kills off the vegetation – grass, seablite, sea purslane – that holds the surrounding saltings together. This is especially noticeable at the eastern or seaward tip of the island, which stretches out in a flat apron of saltings, a dun-coloured, salty, half-watery world beloved of brent geese and curlews. Martin Cole has seen these saltings slowly disappear over the last ten years or so, through pollution and sea erosion. 'Talk to people who knew the Black-water before the war,' he told me, 'and they'll tell you that in *their* parents' time you could hardly row a boat in the estuary, the weed was so thick. None here at all now.'

Walking back through the drying puddles over the causeway, I could only spot a few tufts of bladder-wrack clinging to concrete blocks in the mud. Barking of geese and wheeping of curlews still rang all around, though, and the bicycling postman took a great sniff of salty air as he passed me half-way across. 'Magic, mate – eh?' he called over his shoulder, grinning conspiratorially.

2. Canvey and Foulness

BLEAKEST CORNER OF THE THAMES

Joos Croppenburgh, 'a Dutchman skilled in the making of dykes', certainly started something when he financed the building of a sea wall all round Canvey Island back in 1620. Although it took another three centuries for development to get going on any scale, the Dutchman's enclosure made it possible to think of Canvey as a single block of land. Today's Canvey Island lies where London's eastern outskirts finally shred away, a popular place with East Enders for a weekend's letting the hair down. But in Stuart times this was a world as remote to most Londoners as any Hebridean isle.

Until Croppenburgh got to work, there were six separate islands out here off the marshy northern or Essex shore of the River Thames, only interconnected at low tide when the dividing creeks dried out. Shepherds, with little three-legged stools strapped to their buttocks for instant ease of squatting, kept their flocks grazing on the excellent salty grass and made cheese from ewes' milk; but each year at the spring tides the sheep had to be hustled back on to the mainland as the Canvey islands disappeared under water. The 200 Dutch workers who moved across the North Sea to build Joos Croppenburgh's sea walls stayed on Canvey thereafter as a distinct community, remembered today in road names – Derventer Avenue, Baardwyk Avenue. The Canvey Island they created, however – a dead flat triangle of grazing marshes lying well below sea level – has all but vanished under as motley a collection of houses, bungalows, caravans, ramshackle shops, shady dance halls and dubious niteries as you'll find anywhere around the shores of Britain, jammed up against a potentially explosive cocktail of gas, oil and chemical storage depots. 'BOOMING CANVEY!' chirped a headline in the local paper. One hell of a boom, if anything goes wrong.

The Lobster Smack, an old weather-boarded pub crouching in the shadows of both sea wall and oil storage cylinders, made a good starting point for the walk I'd been promising myself for years, the fourteen miles or so right round Canvey's rim. Moored against the jetty just below the pub was the *Texaco Stockholm*, her rusty superstructure towering enormously over the low-slung roof of the Lobster Smack. From the top of the sea wall I got a view packed with contrasts – the wide, quickly-flowing, muddy Thames dotted with tankers and freighters, parrot-cage buoys dipping and bobbing with the tide; beyond these a long green shore on the Kentish bank of the river, a huge sky stretching above; nearer at hand a great stark run of thin-legged jetty festooned with pipelines and cross-bracing, in front of the eastern outposts of a four-mile industrial-opolis of oil refineries, white cylindrical storage tanks, pipework, tall metal chimneys and funnels dribbling sickly orange, bile-coloured and vile-smelling smoke. These places, their flaring burn-off points and jetties harbouring tankers full of chemicals, gases and explosive liquids, lie all together on a cast-off corner of the Essex mainland only separated from Canvey Island's own storage terminals by the few murky yards' width of Hole Haven Creek. The area is a marshalling yard for unglamorous things we couldn't do without but would rather not have in our own back yards, thanks very much.

Geometric shapes in bright primary colours, assembled in such quanti-ties, are grimly fascinating, more than can be said for the tightly-squeezed parcels of pre- and post-war housing with which almost the entire interior of Canvey Island has been filled, sea wall to sea wall. In the 1890s, with a population of only about 300, Canvey was touted to Londoners by would-be holiday entrepreneurs as 'a wild and forbidding place, bleak and deserted', just right for a breezy week of rough-and-ready farmhouse accommodation away from all the crowds. The East End trippers re-sponded in their thousands, but Canvey's building boom couldn't really get under way while ferry and causeway remained the only routes on to the island. Once the swing bridge was built over Benfleet Creek in 1931, everything just went pop. Houses, shops, bungalows, pubs, amusement halls all proliferated like mad, a rash of spots on Canvey's plain face. Canvey Island shops are hangovers from this era, shabby, cheap, dusty and gimcrack, friendly places called Phil's, Michelle's or Bob's. A lot of hardboard has gone into their construction, and not an ounce of style or sophistication.

As the building boom continued, Canvey's green acres shrank to a scrubby apron on the western end of the island. All round the perimeter, just inside the sea wall, caravans settled like snowflakes. But they didn't melt away. Around the small indentation of Thorpe Bay they sit in well-drilled lines, each with its miniature telephone pole and few square feet of sterile grass. Walking round Thorpe Bay, I spotted no model later than about 1970. Most were rich in art deco curves and chrome trim: Sun City for outmoded caravans on the shores of Thorpe Bay, with its crescent of sand, a thin wedge of startling yellow above the grey pebbles and grey, slimy rocks of the lower Thames estuary. Can this tropical, buttery-yellow sand be natural – or have municipal spades deposited it here? People are happy to bathe from Thorpe Bay, anyway, less than a mile downriver of those storage and refinery plants and their throat-catching, stomach-churning smells.

Beyond Thorpe Bay the concrete bar of the sea wall ran on, twenty feet above the greasy, gently-heaving Thames. Some amateur artist had chalked drawings all over the inside surface of the wall – victims skewered by bloody daggers, anatomical studies of an optimistic sort: and, in contrast, a delicate study of a young girl's head. On top of the wall the button-shaped Labworth Café was for sale. Just inland lay a shabby collection of night spots, pool halls and dance dives. The Monico looked especially dilapidated, its once-smart curves of brick now stained and pock-marked, posters flapping on its billboards advertising faded 1960s pop stars still flogging their old hits round the halls. For me, though, magic oozed from every crack in the Monico's façade. Across its stage in recent years had raved Canvey Island's own rhythm'n'blues kings, Dr Feelgood, in their creased old suits, thin ties and wide-boy hairstyles, back in the 1970s before it all got too much for them. No one on the live show circuit played guitar more wildly than Wilko Johnson of Dr Feelgood; no one sang morning-after lyrics in a more gravelly grunt than Lee Brilleaux. Something in this seedy music called irresistibly to my polite, well-brought-up, English graduate's soul, and still does.

I hailed a young man coming down the Monico's fire escape. Was the Monico still in business? Unshaven and red-eyed, he looked nervously around. It might be, he allowed himself to say in a 'who-wants-to-know-eh-John?' tone of voice. His tousle-haired mate, unseen by me until then, got slowly out of their car (pillarbox red, sharp, with home-made gofaster flashes on sides and back), leaned his elbows on its roof and stared coldly at me from eyes as veined and pale as lychees.

Had Dr Feelgood played there? Yes, said the unshaven man, a long time ago. Why? What was it to me? Oh, nothing – just interested, that's all. Both men stared at each other, then at me. Must be Old Bill, I could hear them thinking. Well, never mind. Thanks, anyway. Goodbye.

I walked away and round the corner. The red car revved extravagantly and came screeching past, both men looking at me out of the rolled-down window. The car swerved into the kerb a hundred yards ahead and stopped, the engine still running, the occupants talking hard and glancing back at me. So why was he asking all them questions, eh? I turned away, feigning interest in the old posters on the Monico's boards; then walked as casually as I could back up to the sea wall and on. The red car followed. Oh God. What on earth had I interrupted? What could they have been up to in the darkened Monico? I stared rigidly out at the tankers in the Thames, exuding innocence. The red car crawled below me, then suddenly shot off down a side turning and roared out of sight among the houses. My heart bumped with relief. I wasn't tough enough to take on the world of Dr Feelgood.

Out at the eastern end of Canvey Island the sea wall cut back on itself, leaving a trail of saltings narrowing out to a point of windblown sea purslane. Further east, Southend-on-Sea's long sprawl of skyscraping blocks and Victorian terraces ran away and out of sight along the Essex shore. As I turned back to stroll along the northern edge of Canvey, the atmosphere changed immediately and completely. As if by magic all those closely bunched houses disappeared, and a different world stretched open and remote beyond the wall. Sailing boats lay at anchor in the narrow waterway of Hadleigh Ray, overlooked by the grey stubs of Hadleigh Castle's ruined towers. Curlews, oystercatchers and larks began to make themselves heard. The wind whipped over the skirt of marsh, filling my nostrils with fresh salt. It was all bleak, lonely and lovely. I walked six long miles around Canvey's western shoreline and saw nobody – unless you count the occupants of cars and lorries on the A1301, nose to tail as they crawled over Benfleet Creek and off the island. Some of the meadows here can have changed hardly at all since Croppenburgh's men brought them into being. Bizarre is too mild a term for the contrast between the empty green pastures of this end of Canvey and the chimneys and storage tanks of Hole Haven filling the horizon ahead.

The *Texaco Stockholm* was still there by the jetty as I completed the circuit of the island, the Lobster Smack lying like a tiny white matchbox in her gigantic shadow. Tired after the walk, I savoured a pint in the beamed, smoky bar of the old smugglers' haunt by the sea wall. The internal walls of the Lobster Smack are several feet thick in places, separated from the low ceiling by a strip of latticed window about eighteen inches high. 'Two dabs! Two plaice! Two sprats!' shouted the landlady among the smartly-dressed lunchtime drinkers – no red-eyed, shady Feelgood characters here. A guidebook to the Canvey Island of 1897 found the little inn 'perhaps the quaintest in all Essex . . . No one need expect comfort there, but the keeper purveys for all comers with a rude hospitality which is amusing.' Thirty years later W. L. Gadd came here in search of source material for his cranky and massively detailed book *The Great Expectations Country*. By then the Lobster Smack had become a popular venue for boating and picnic parties, but was still Gadd's choice as 'the most solitary tavern on the lower Thames'. Gadd found rich pickings for his book at the Lobster Smack. It was Charles Dickens's Ship Inn, where the convict Magwitch was hidden to await a suitable steamer for escape to the Continent. The old-fashioned bedroom that Gadd found, reached by a narrow, crooked staircase from the kitchen, where Pip lodged while minding Magwitch, has been turned into an upstairs bar; but atmosphere still lies thick on the Lobster Smack.

What may one day happen to Canvey Island if things go disastrously wrong is something Canvey-dwellers prefer to push to the back of their minds. A recent study declared them at three times the national average risk of death from accident. An IRA bomb in 1979, which caused the spillage of 130,000 gallons of aviation fuel, highlighted the problem. Unbelievably dangerous combinations of explosive material lie here, ready to go up. In the 1960s a series of huge underground methane gas storage tanks was constructed next door to the oil terminals. The idea was fair enough: to freeze a ring of earth 130 feet deep and the same across, scoop out the unfrozen earth in the middle and pour in liquid methane, which takes up only one six-hundredth of the space it needs in its gaseous state. Sealed in by permafrost in this way, 21,000 tons of the deadly stuff can be stored without risk of explosion. But soon the permafrost had begun a steady outwards creep, closer and closer to the oil tanks alongside. Permafrost cracks the earth, and the cracks fill with liquid methane. If you don't thaw the frost, it creeps on. If you do, you thaw the liquid as well – which suddenly, as the critical temperature arrives, expands six hundredfold. Boomtime! Underground heaters gradually stabilized things, and the methane silos were filled in with nice safe sand. But those methane years had been nail-biting ones for local residents.

Then there's the flooding threat. During the East Coast flood disaster of 1953 the sea surge overtopped Joos Croppenburgh's walls and literally engulfed Canvey Island. Fifty-eight people lost their lives here in those desperate hours of darkness and panic. Afterwards the sea walls were redesigned, strengthened and rebuilt. But England's eastern coast continues to tip seaward a few centimetres a year, as the west coast rises with the gradual general tilt of this section of the earth's crust. It could happen again. It probably will – and, when it does, the Thames Flood Barrier at Woolwich will come into operation, guarding London from the swollen Thames. All that water, driving up the estuary, will have to break in somewhere. Canvey's sea walls are as vulnerable to such freakish tides as are the Backhouses' defences up on Horsey Island in the Backwaters.

'Yes, we know the floods will be back again,' John Hughes acknowledged as he walked his spaniel on the sea wall behind the Lobster Smack. 'Stands to reason. And if the floods don't get us, the bloody terminals will. Have you seen those signs on the roads – Yellow and Blue Routes? That's supposed to be our escape plan if something happens. Huh! All those roads meet at the roundabout up there at Waterside Farm. It'd only take one clever bugger to turn his car over there to block us all in. Everyone tearing off the island, emergency services trying to get on – can't you just imagine it? What a bloody circus. For years we've been asking for alternative roads off Canvey. But will they listen? What do you think?'

John jerked his thumb out over the sea wall towards the Thames.

'Listen, I'll tell you something, mate, since you're interested. There's a World War Two ammo ship on the bottom out there. *Montgomery*, I think she's called. She's down there, with practically all of her cargo. If she ever goes up, we can all stop worrying for good, know what I mean?'

On Foulness Island, ten miles out to the east where Thames meets North Sea, explosions are a fact of everyday life. You couldn't really get a more off-putting name for an island than Foulness, and everything I heard about it in advance of my visit enhanced its grim reputation.

'Not *Foulness*! God-forsaken hole. Overrun by the army. They won't let you on for a start, and there's nothing there anyway. And the wind . . .!'

Thus kind friends. Mention of Foulness does have that effect on people, those who have heard of it. A strange effect, since one can be almost certain that they have never set foot on Foulness. The island, a weapons testing area since the First World War, is run with clench-tight security by the MOD from their desolate old barracks at Shoeburyness. ('*Shoebury-ness?* The armpit of Essex, mate . . . what they meant when they invented the word "boring" . . . a dump.') It took a series of tedious phone calls to the echoing offices of Shoeburyness to get myself a pass on to Foulness Island. The patient officer at the other end of the line wanted to know what kind of a camera I was going to bring with me. I told him it was a miniature one that fitted in my buttonhole. A prickling silence followed. I cursed myself. Facetiousness had cost me the trip. Then a reserved chuckle came down the wire.

'You mustn't tease our Security Officer, you know.'

At last my visit was agreed – subject to certain conditions. Mr John Stevenson, the Secretary (Admin), would arrange a pass for me. He would accompany me at all times. He would tell me what I could and could not photograph. He would tell me where I could and could not go. I began to realize that they meant what they said about security. There wasn't much encouragement, either, in the few descriptions of Foulness I managed to unearth. 'Depressing' was a word that figured largely. So did 'dreary' and 'bleak'.

Studying the Ordnance Survey 1 in 50,000 map, though, Foulness looked fascinating. There on the west was the long minor road straggling north-east out of the sprawl of Southend-on-Sea, crossing bridges between islands that looked to be three parts water, finally petering out on a blunt arm of sea walls and vein-like watercourses with its outermost finger buried in an enormous sheet of mud and sand. Not a single contour line showed. A few buildings clustered round a church at Churchend, and out at the furthest sea wall stood a pub – surely the loneliest in Essex. Running almost the entire length of Foulness, but half a mile offshore over the Maplin Sands, was a six-mile footpath marked 'The Broomway'. Other names around the marshy skirts of Foulness added fuel to the imagination, too: Clark's Hard, Smallgains, Great Shell Corner, Fisherman's Head, Horseshoe Corner and Wakering Stairs.

I met John Stevenson at the police check-point north of Shoeburyness on a grey winter's morning, with sleet showers driving up the Thames estuary on a cutting wind. Camera duly checked and pass endorsed, we drove slowly over the bridges on to Havengore Island, New England Island and finally Foulness itself. All looked identically flat, grey and wet, devoid of colour. The island road passed the Atomic Weapons Establishment ('*Very* restricted,' murmured the Secretary (Admin) at my side, 'even *I* can't go in there without an escort') and Churchend Battery ('I'm afraid you can't photograph the gun, but do by all means have a look through the gap . . . nothing there? . . . they'll have taken it away, then'). MOD wastelands lay on every hand, that soul-deadening combination of concrete posts, chicken wire and small, windowless brick boxes on acres of rank ground. Skeletal towers stood on the sea walls, target-holders for gunfire. Fields of fire run at every angle on Foulness Island – along the sands, out to sea and over fields and roads. Most of the eastern side of the island is under restriction at one time or another. On the west are atomic secrets, on the north what are chillingly termed 'environmental' ones. I asked what that meant, but John Stevenson couldn't really say.

To explain the workings of the more conventional departments of Foulness whizz-bangery, he handed over a couple of glossy brochures, beautifully photographed and laid out, of the kind expensive London companies use to publicize themselves. The Directorate of Proof and Experimental Establishments (DPEE) runs Shoeburyness and Foulness to test weapons for all three armed services, but other customers are welcome if their credit is good. Anyone (approved of) can hire the facilities on Foulness to test almost anything that goes bang. Sophisticated equipment and expert advice come as part of the package. You can fire shells into the sea at high tide, and fish them off the sands at the ebb. You can fire bullets at your bullets to see how they stand up to rough treatment. You can spatter a cast-off Sea Harrier with small-arms fire, then patch it up as you would on the battlefield. You can set enormous fuel fires raging, or touch off explosions that will touch off complaints from Clacton-on-Sea to the Kentish coast. The wide open spaces of Foulness – 7000 acres of land and 30,000 of firm sand – are just right for this type of thing. Foulness may be a name unknown to holidaymakers, but it draws nods of appreciation in defence department offices and armaments company boardrooms all over the world.

We drove on slowly, past heaps of battered, bullet-riddled aircraft bodies, their rubbery intestines coiling drunkenly out of great jagged holes. No, unfortunately, it wouldn't be a good idea to photograph those; nor the Rugwood Towers and their dangling spherical target. For such sophisticated, high-tech experiments, the MOD's jetsam looks remarkably clumsy and ramshackle – piles of scabby old breeze blocks, cobbled-together scaffolding, home-made gun mountings. Bits and pieces lie where they have fallen, many too dangerous to pick up. The impression is of an enormous playground after a particularly untidy set of children has gone indoors. It was only when we dropped down on the weather side of the sea wall and crunched in the freezing wind over a beach of cockle-shells that Foulness began to look anything other than outlandish.

The Broomway turned out to be the roughest of causeways, marked out in medieval times by sprigs of broom, running parallel with the shore. Until the bridges were built it was the only way to get on to Foulness Island. The tide comes in here at a brisk walking pace, so a stroll along the Broomway is not to be undertaken lightly. Foxes come up the old road along the sands, however, to raid the pheasant chicks on the island. When human intruders get past the military defences and walk, swim or sail on the sands, they are chased off in short order by a hovercraft kept on standby for just that purpose. Wandering up and down beside the wind-whipped waters of the estuary of the River Crouch, the Secretary (Admin) expounded on over-zealous MOD police, foxes, hovercraft, explosions and wild geese. We began to relax in each other's company as the escort/intruder relationship softened, and I took some innocuous photographs as we chatted.

To be a Foulness islander is to live under another form of government, to accept another set of rules from those that apply the far side of the Havengore bridge. The army colonel in charge of the Shoeburyness operation has complete powers of say-so. If you break the speed limit, then you won't drive any more on Foulness – not for a month or so, anyway. If he says a road is closed, you don't get past the barrier. Every single building on Foulness, with the exception of church, rectory, school and village hall, is owned by the MOD. All the islanders are lease-holders, and the housing list – a very long one – begins and ends in John Stevenson's hands. A few days before my visit he had completed the installation of a young Foulness islander in one of the houses. All over the island I watched him carry this good news before him like a peace-offering into post office, shop and pub. It's tremendously important to the 250 islanders that children should continue to be born and live on Foulness. The single school at Churchend had thirteen children under eleven on its roll in 1987, split between two teachers. The Education Department keeps trying to close it down, and probably will unless numbers rise. But there's not much work on the island if you aren't a farmer and don't work for the military. Teenagers and young adults have been leaving Foulness steadily since the war. Those that remain almost all work in one or other of the secret establishments on the island. It's one of the biggest concentrations of private residents in MOD territory in England. Some of the time it's a damn nuisance living with the bangs, the inconvenience, the closed roads and arbitrary changes of routine. Mostly, though, Foulness islanders count their blessings.

'Some days I can't leave my house, that's true,' said Sue, drinking a lunchtime half-pint in the bar of the George and Dragon at Churchend. 'All four roads can be closed all at the same time, and I'm caught in the middle with firing lines all round. Yes, that's a nuisance. And you can't sneeze on this island without everyone else asking if you've caught a cold. But I'd rather have that and be able to live like we do. You've got to admit that it's the MOD who have kept this place from becoming another horrible, overcrowded Canvey Island. No one can get on or off here without permission, so there's no crime. We all leave our houses unlocked. Our cars, too. In fact, you can always tell who's a stranger by looking to see if they've got their car door locks down. There's no vandalism, no graffiti, no rubbish left lying about. If you see a crisp packet, it's probably your own. And where else in the whole of England could you let three young girls out in the morning, and not have to worry about them all day?'

John, her husband, nodded his agreement. Sue and he lease their farm from the MOD. They enjoy poking fun at 'Shoebury' – the blanket name used by the islanders for all powers-that-be – and telling stories about the weird and wonderful experiences that come from living side by side with secrets, like the time John went out fishing at dawn on the shell bank off Foulness Point, and turned round to see two frogmen emerging silently from the waves.

The fierce east coast weather causes many more problems to the islanders than the MOD. In bad winters, all life shrinks to the single common aim of keeping the road clear of snow – 'digging off' and 'digging on' the island. And John can remember, as a small boy in 1953, looking out of the window one night and thinking the lawn had been suddenly covered in snow. It hadn't: this was the night of the flood disaster, and the farmhouse was completely surrounded by water, the moonlight turning the lapping waves white. John and his family eventually escaped by rowing boat, leaving the cups and saucers, set out for next morning's breakfast, bobbing up against the downstairs ceiling. 'There were hayricks floating off along the flood, with sheep on top of them,' John said, 'and a plank floating by with a rabbit on one end and a stoat on the other – my dad saw that. Only two people were drowned on the island, but I'll show you what that flood did to this place.'

He fetched old photographs from behind the bar, showing the church on its little knoll like an island in the sea, houses with water up to their roofs, ricks floating and trees drowned up to their top branches. All the Foulness islanders are convinced it will happen again one day, in spite of improved sea walls.

Along the road in the hamlet of Courtsend, the King's Head would be a developer's dream – if such folk were allowed anywhere near it. The pub itself was a single wooden room on the side of a Tudor farmhouse. Shortly after my visit John Nicholls, the landlord, a born-and-bred Foulness islander whose family roots in Foulness go back many generations, gave up the lease and the King's Head ceased trading. But on this bitter winter day I found a pub that had changed hardly at all in a hundred years. Old chaps from the Foulness farms gathered on the blue-painted benches round the big, ancient, red-hot stove, to revile the MOD, the outside world and the modern way of going on. Foulness accents cut the smoky air, a thicker and twangier version of rural Essex speech, closer to Norfolk in sound according to Sue, almost impenetrable to the outsider. Some of these old men knew Foulness before the military took it over in 1915. In spite of their tough talk against Shoebury, it's that well-guarded isolation that has kept the wheels of Time so static out here on the tip of the island.

To sit by that blistering stove and listen to the memories and opinions of a community completely free from modern influence, less than an hour from central London, was miraculous; as it was to walk around an island just six miles from Southend's packed promenades and see not a single ice cream stall, caravan, beach chalet or bucket and spade. Whitsun Bank Holiday, August school holidays, the Easter weekend: they just don't impinge here at all. Neither can the mountains of money available to smart, rapacious London developers buy one acre of Foulness for marinas, weekend houses or executive 'exclusive waterside village' schemes. If the MOD decides, as rumour whispers that it may, to pack up its equipment one fine day soon and find another playground, then the whole lot might be up for grabs. Meanwhile, encrusted with military excrescences, shaken by big bangs, hedged about with regulations, Foulness inviolate clings to its solitude, safe for the present in its wired and locked time-warp.

John Stevenson, dropping me back at the gate, couldn't really say if change was in the air. If it *was* – then he, personally, hoped that the Nature Conservancy or some such body would buy up the island. Of course, there was always the threat of a re-heating of those old plans to build a gigantic airport out on Maplin Sands, but he couldn't see that as a serious proposition.

Oh – and would I please hand in my pass? And submit my film to the Security Officer in due course – just for checking.

3. The Isle of Wight

Q. What's brown and steaming and comes out of Cowes?
A. The Isle of Wight ferry.

For thirty years that was the sum total of my knowledge of southern Britain's largest island, along with the fact that the world's population could fit on it if they all stood still. And if they all jumped up together, the shock of their landing would tilt the Earth off course and send it crashing into Jupiter. From fields near school in the Isle of Purbeck we used to watch speck-like paddle-steamers ploughing out beyond Bournemouth towards the Isle of Wight. Boys with boating fathers painted a dream picture in my mind of forests of yachts pitching round an island in green seas, cheering crowds, duckings and capsizings, genial madness, all in a frame labelled 'Cowes Week'. I hated sailing. My father, on the rare occasions he took me out in small sailing dinghies, hauled ropes and handled tillers with characteristic economy and efficiency, but I was cack-handed and afraid of the sea. The very thought of Cowes chilled me to the marrow. I was amused to find traces of that boyhood aversion still active when I telephoned my Aunt Rachel Millen and fixed up an Easter jaunt to the Isle of Wight.

Close on seventy, Rach is a spring of gaiety. Her salty sense of fun carried us breezily through a day that might have become a disaster. The Isle of Wight was still rubbing the sleep of winter out of its eyes, and most doors were locked against us. We couldn't get in to see Osborne House or St Mildred's Church at Whippingham. The island's bus drivers, ferrymen and shopkeepers seemed to be having a communal bad day, short on temper and charm. The weather turned nasty, too, but Rach didn't. She approached the outing with panache from the start, driving me from Southampton railway station to the ferry with a fine disregard for traffic lanes, pointing out blocks of the waterfront that she had seen bombed into ruin during the war.

The long arm of Southampton Water glittered under an unseasonably clear blue sky – too clear, as it turned out – as we crossed the Solent in company with ships like floating chemical works, ships like tower blocks, huge container carriers, strings of barges and slab-shaped, matt grey naval supply ships. The waterfront of West Cowes lay overseen by the pepperpot roof and shaven lawns of the headquarters of the Royal Yacht Squadron, the Isle of Wight's equivalent of Boodles or White's Club. The lovely building was originally a fort built against the threat of the French by Henry VIII. Most of those schoolboy yarns of Cowes Week high jinks had begun and ended with pink champagne in the RYS, but I wonder now how many of the seadog hero fathers had ever really got past those pearly gates. Membership of the Royal Yacht Squadron is (or used to be, according to Rach) the ultimate social thumbs-up for a yachtsman.

'My father joined that club,' Rach said as the old castle slid by below, 'but he wouldn't fly their burgee. You could be a very bad sailor and still do that. He flew the Royal Cruising Club's burgee instead – that was a club where you really had to be known as a good sailor who could handle any conditions. *Sailing* snobs, as opposed to social ones. Mind you,' she murmured, 'I'd have loved to spend Cowes Week in the Royal Yacht Squadron. Dancing and parties . . . but no one's asked me. Yet. By the way, did you know that your grandfather used to sail in a model of HMS *Ajax* here? He sank in her, in the middle of the Solent.' A block off the young chip, perhaps.

The ferry inched on into the mouth of the River Medina, above houses rising straight from the water. An old ship's figurehead, a blowsy madam with a fine cutwater, gazed skywards from a veranda over the river. We disembarked and trudged up the road towards the main treat of the day, a tour round Osborne House. Prince Albert bought up the Osborne Estate for £26,000 in 1845, and rebuilt the house into what became the only place where the convention-ridden royal family could really relax and, for a couple of months at least, lead an untrammelled domestic life. They all came over every year, for Cowes Regatta and for Christmas. The young princes and princesses adored their little Swiss cottage in the grounds, a kind of celestial Wendy House among the trees overlooking Osborne Bay. Here they could get down to cooking the kinds of messes every child loves to concoct, in the miniature cottage kitchen, while Mama daubed away at her oil painting and Papa sketched in another pinnacle on his plans for St Mildred's at Whippingham. Rach and I had planned to spend most of the day rubbernecking at Osborne, but we found a large-bellied, portentous security guard blocking the entrance gate.

'Not open till Friday,' he said firmly, pointing to the notice. Of course! Britain's monuments need their hibernation, too. The Monday before Easter was asking a bit too much. 'Mr Underwood would have obliged you, I'm sure,' said the guard, 'but the Duchess of Kent happens to be coming tomorrow. Security, you know. I'm sorry, but you won't get any nearer than this. We're in a securitous state.'

I begged Mr Underwood's telephone number, and called him from the box down the road. 'Sorry,' said Mr Underwood down the line from Osborne House. 'It's the Duchess of Kent, you know. I can only suggest you come back on Friday.'

I gave Rach the bad news, and in return she told me a story of how a skinhead on the Tube had defended the honour of an elderly friend of hers. 'Fack off,' he had grated to a drunken couple annoying her with their behaviour. 'Can't you see you're upsetting this old dear? Just fack off, oright?'

Down the road at St Mildred's there was a disappointment, too. The church stands on a green ridge overlooking lines of yachts moored midstream in a shining bend of the Medina. There's something distinctly odd about St Mildred's. Bavarian pinnacles rise from an Italianate tower. Plain Norman arches fight with finicky Victorian over-elaboration. The more you walk around the outside of the church, the bigger and more bossy it looks. One wonders if the masons smiled to themselves as they carried out the Prince Consort's design. What it looks like inside we couldn't tell, as the doors were locked. But down on the banks of the river at the Folly Inn we found the doors open and welcoming.

In the yachting season the Folly is a humming hive of jampacked freshwater admirals, but there was plenty of elbow room this early in the year. Below the floor of the inn are the ribs of an ancient ship in the mud bank, the original alehouse on this spot. After lunch, walking on along the muddy bank of the Medina, we passed more rotting ship bodies in the ooze and came to the Wight Marina. Here among the yachts lay *Ryde Queen*, retired after 50,000 trips between Portsmouth and Ryde, a stylish old paddle-steamer stuck fast in a muddy morass, fairy lights slung between her masts, soldiering on in reduced circumstances as a restaurant and night-spot. Her paddle covers were picked out in flaking green and yellow paint, her funnel in red and black stripes. Under a lowering grey sky she looked derelict and sad, slowly dissolving, barred perpetually from her natural element by a hundred yards of sticky bog.

'I'm a born lager lout,' asserted Rach as she strode zestfully through the mud patches of the path. 'I went on holiday with friends before Easter one year, and they said they'd given up drink for Lent. Ha! I told them they'd better arrange a dispensation and take an extra week after Easter.'

We beat the rain into Newport by a short head, passing the old warehouses by the river and racing through the streets to catch the bus back to the ferry at East Cowes. The bus driver, chewing lean jaws on a mouthful of bad-tempered bile, wasn't in the mood to accommodate idiots who left their money behind in his tray. 'Change!' he snarled up the aisle after Rach. 'Look left before you get off,' he rapped at a youth about to alight at Whippingham. 'Yes – looked *right* – bloody fool,' gritted the driver, rolling his eyes theatrically to heaven and revving angrily. Rach nudged me and pulled a face at the driver's hunched back. Back at the Red Funnel ferry terminal, the left-luggage operative couldn't dredge up a smile or even a word as he shoved out my rucksack across the counter. Rach looked a bit glum as the ferry swung us across the Medina to the jetty at West Cowes. But she revived over a cup of tea, and waved cheerily from the saloon window as I shouldered the pack and stood watching her off.

Bands of thickening rain came sheeting into my face as I put my head down and slogged the five miles back down the west bank of the Medina to Newport at the centre of the island. It was a pelting rainstorm, a real soggy soaker, by the time I stamped dripping into the warm haven of the Quay Hotel. Later I walked up the street to a big hotel, in search of a chat. I wanted to find out how island youngsters enjoyed themselves on a rainy March evening. I found out, without benefit of speech, when the hotel juke-box began to play. This was something special, a video machine high up on the wall that gave pictures as well as a very great deal of sound. The teenagers at the bar, clutching glasses of lager, watched inscrutably as rock stars sneered, postured and leaped across the screen. Spotting me scribbling away at my diary in a corner alcove, the landlord came across and stood shaking his head and grinning. 'How can you do it?' he said wonderingly. 'Writing away there with all that row going on.' I saw his point when I was reading over what I'd written, sitting up in

31

bed at midnight in the Quay Hotel – one line of gibberish after another.

The weather forecast next morning sounded bad: a series of deep depressions rolling in across the island from the Atlantic. I pulled on my boots and made an early getaway by way of the old quays of Little London in the centre of Newport. Here the freighters would berth after sailing down the Medina from Cowes. 'Oh, yes,' said the district nurse with pale blue hair who came by, 'ships used to come over the Solent with wood, barrels of beer, all that sort of thing. Quite big ships. I well remember them back in the 1950s. Nowadays – well,' she pointed to the tall brick warehouses on the quayside, 'they're really doing a lot to Little London, trying to bring it back to life.' The warehouses, crumbling hulks a few years ago, are now swish penthouse apartments, each with its cheesecloth vertical venetian blinds and rubber plant in the window, garage under and fine view over the swan-bobbing waters of the Lukely Brook to the newly opened Quayside Arts Centre. Someone has had the sense to retain the elaborate cast-iron window grilles of the warehouses with their motifs like spread ears of corn. Given that it will never again be economically viable for the big ships to make their way to Newport, this discreet gentrification is probably the best thing that can happen to what had become a sadly run-down corner of town. Newport, with its watery quarter and granaries, its wide streets and mellow brick buildings, its feeling of the sea and ships not far away, reminded me of those quiet East Anglian coastal towns – Southwold or Woodbridge.

With rain threatening, I had to hurry away from the blue-haired nurse and make my way by side lanes and half-marked footpaths north to the skirts of Parkhurst Forest and the Isle of Wight's most desolate secrets. Across the Yarmouth road stood a ghetto, rank on rank of identical small brick Home Office houses, their neat gardens lying like confetti on a wasteland of starved grass. Beyond snaked the Wall, twenty feet high, stained concrete topped with a continuous, slug-like grey tube of unclimbable design, bleak in the extreme, encircling many acres of misery.

'Twenty-five or thirty years, some of them in there,' said the pleasant young warder at his front door. 'High risk category, all of them. This is the Albany here, and Parkhurst's just along the road. The Albany's quite new, but Parkhurst – that's a terrible old place.'

To tuck three prisons away in the heart of the smiling isle is a practical arrangement, but its implications sear the mind. The Albany, Parkhurst and the lower security Camp Hill hold thousands of prisoners, many shut in after unspeakable crimes, to suffocate their human emotions and instincts for what in real terms is the rest of their lives. I walked up the road to Parkhurst, past great walls of puce brick broken every few hundred yards by low doorways. A dip in the ground gave a partial view inside, of immense wet slate roof ridges, the tops of chimneys, aerials and cupolas, and row after row of tiny windows criss-crossed with white-painted bars. There was plenty of green grass on view, all of it cut to regulation length, flayed and naked like a convict's skull. The only sound from inside the citadel was a very faint and far-off high-pitched shouting from a single voice, a parade-ground bawling-out beyond the surveillance cameras on stalks and the arc-light poles. Thousands of men sat in their bare little rooms thirty or forty yards away from me, making no noise at all. The unearthly silence was broken by a shrill screaming from the grass desert in front of the wall where a young woman, one of the warder's wives, was yanking cruelly at the choker chain of her Alsatian puppy while she cursed it. I was glad to get away and strike out for Carisbrooke and another old prison of a different kind.

The tall Norman keep of Carisbrooke Castle looms in the centre of the island, its curtain wall snaking up and down over humps of earthworks on a swell of downland above the village of Carisbrooke. Trees break up the outline of the castle, whose graceful shape and weathered grey tones seem – so unlike the two ugly sisters back at Parkhurst – to be part of the landscape, blending in naturally. I can't believe that Parkhurst would ever harmonize with its surroundings like Carisbrooke Castle, no matter how many years its raw bricks were left to weather. King Charles I came to Carisbrooke on the run, hoping to be helped on his way abroad from the shambles of his Civil War defeat. He had the Governor of the Isle of Wight, Colonel Hammond, in mind as an ally. But Hammond, mindful of the power of his Parliamentary masters, held on to the royal refugee. Charles walked round the castle walls, played bowls on the little green laid out for him and waited with dignity for his inescapable fate. Two of his children, Elizabeth and Henry, also knew Carisbrooke as a prison when they were sent here shortly after his execution. Poor Elizabeth, a delicate, pale and pious teenager, was soon dead of a fever she caught playing bowls in a rainstorm on her father's lawn.

I began to worry about rainstorm chills myself as I slogged up the sticky chalk track high above Carisbrooke and over the downs. Already the next ridge but one was sliding behind a milky, opaque sheet of rain, and out in the Channel there was a lot more of the same. A light grey sky turned dark, and the vanguard of the rain marched up the slope to engulf me. This was rain with a vengeance, turning the track into a whey-coloured river of liquid chalk, infiltrating my supposedly waterproof trousers and anorak. It blew and lashed me along into the miry ways of Brighstone Forest, where some wag had been fooling around with the footpath signs. With a thick mist now blanketing the trees, I got thoroughly lost. Brighstone Forest had caught the full force of 1987's October gale, the Great Storm that had devastated millions of acres of south-east England. Trees still lay where they had fallen, their roots in air, flints from underground spattering the plantations like shrapnel. The forest looked like a scene out of Flanders Fields – splintered trunks snapped off at head height, exploded craters of earth and holes full of muddy water. The effect was enhanced by thousands of long plastic sheaths guarding ranks of newly planted trees, creepily like the crosses of a war cemetery. Through the mist I dimly made out a man astride a pile of logs on a trailer – a most phlegmatic man, steadily working on as the rain splashed down, pearling his sweater and plastering his hair. We gestured a conversation above the roar of his tractor. Awful weather, eh? Sure is. Clearing up after the storm? Yes – and look what the bugger did to these trees. All flattened down, like that. Is this the way to the road? Yes, straight on. Good luck!

That stoical man directed me wordlessly, forward to a footpath that plunged down through the mist to the road. There was a pub. And a fire. The landlord was horrified when I came squelching through his saloon bar door on to his nice carpet, but by the time I had spread sodden clothes all round his fireplace he had resigned himself to the inevitable. He even called me a taxi, and waved me on my way to Freshwater Bay.

Mr Plucknett, the taxi-driver, had been an island councillor, a man who could trace his family back several generations on the Isle of Wight.

'I left the island as a young man,' he said as we swooped along the coast road over chalk cliffs and below downland slopes. 'Had to, to get on. But I was glad to come back. The youngsters today, they don't want to leave. They seem very wedded to the island – it's their friends, you know. But unemployment's about four per cent above the national average, and in the so-called prosperous south of England, that's bad. A lot go on the dole in the winter, then find tourist work in the summer – always lots of that about. Things have certainly changed since I was young. There are a lot of mainlanders on the Council now, and they're rather too keen on funny ideas. Too much infilling. Any gap anywhere and they want to pop in a building. This new dual carriageway at Newport, too, and all the talk of computerizing the traffic lights – all totally unnecessary. We don't need it. But it's a lovely island. Look at that over there. You could go to Spain, Portugal, Greece, and see nothing better than that, eh?'

'That' was the white curtain of cliffs rising on the far side of the tiny semicircle of Freshwater Bay. With a broad green stripe of grass across their back they sloped up and away to a dark blob on their summit. 'The Tennyson monument,' explained Mr Plucknett as he dropped me off. 'You'll be blown about a bit before you get up there, mind.'

The wind became a force to conquer, step by step, as I hunched my shoulders and plodded up Tennyson Down. The rain had swept away to soak walkers elsewhere, but sea-level clouds were racing towards the island like smoke, shredding and re-forming on a rising gale. I struggled on and up to anchor myself 500 feet above the sea by the monument, a tall Celtic cross in granite. It was put up on the highest point of the western edge of Wight as a beacon to sailors and a towering memorial to the Poet Laureate who loved to walk up here in a billowing cloak and broad-brimmed hat. How he kept the hat on, I can't imagine. The wind pushed and shoved, blurring my eyes with tears so that I could hardly read the monument's inscription. Alfred, Lord Tennyson had certainly needed somewhere remote to get away from the pointing fingers of Victorian visitors. After the dear Queen, he was the Isle of Wight's chief tourist attraction. The cloak and hat can't have contributed much to the anonymity he craved, though.

He lived below the down at Farringford, just outside Freshwater, from 1853 for the next fifteen years, always in fear of a chance meeting with his camera-wielding neighbour Julia Margaret Cameron. This formidable lady, a lawyer's wife, was a fanatical amateur photographer who would entice victims into her hen-house studio for long sessions of sitting still. Tennyson became her special prey – she originally moved to the Isle of Wight in order to have her hero close at hand, and she pursued him relentlessly to capture him yet again, even up here on his favourite morning walk. The poet seems to have submitted with a reasonable grace, though complaining that her pictures made him look like a dirty monk. Eventually all the fan worship got too much for Tennyson, and he left the island to look for another refuge among the Surrey hills.

Below the Tennyson monument there was activity on the cliff edge. A burly, bearded coastguard stood by his blue Land Rover chatting to a sadly smiling young man. 'Seen a black border collie?' asked the coastguard as I came up. 'Answers to the name of Maktar. No? Oh, dear.' The young man kept smiling bitterly. His dog had disappeared a couple of hours before during a walk. Probably gone over the cliff, said the coastguard. A couple of chaps were down on the beach now, having a look, but there wasn't much hope. Looking back from the next shoulder of downland I could see the two distant figures hunched against the wind, waiting forlornly on the edge of those 500-foot cliffs, not expecting anything.

Now the sea was visible on both sides of the narrowing neck of land. I fought the wind all the way to the apex of the triangle, where the Isle of Wight cuts the English Channel with a white prow of chalk. There was a surprise at the end: a neat terrace of suburban brick houses, coastguard cottages, grimly on duty in this high and wind-blasted spot. Beyond them the sliver of downland that marked the island's western corner was as ugly as could be, a military dustbin of concrete blockhouses, concrete walls, concrete roads, rusty security fences, metal boxes and galvanized metal sheets. Britain had tried to get her space race entries off the starting blocks from here, testing the Black Knight and Black Arrow rockets that proved such dismal flops. This end of the Isle of Wight has always been a defensive stronghold, guarding the narrow channel between island and mainland; but nowadays, with tourism the mainspring of Wight's economy, it's a sad thing that this superb and dramatic downland walk should have such a squalid climax.

There was reward, anyway, once I had edged past the barbed wire and stood, buffeted by fists of wind, looking down on the Needles. The three chalk blades rose straight up, nearly the height of the down itself, out of a pale green sea, their bases slimy green, their sides dazzling white. A red and white striped lighthouse stood at the seaward end, its light enclosed in a kind of vast wire mesh basket with a little round helicopter pad on top. The gale-driven waves thrashed at the Needles, sheeting up spray:

a transfixing sight. The lighthouse is one of the dwindling number still manned by keepers, but automation will soon put them ashore, leaving electronic equipment to carry on the good work. During southerly gales of Force 8 and upwards, the wind bounces off these cliffs and scoops up and over in a wild vortex. Local coastguards doubt the ability of a helicopter to land on the pad in such conditions, just the circumstances in which something will be bound to go wrong with the automatic equipment. For the time being the keepers soldier on, imprisoned between wind and wave.

More rainstorms were beating in from the west, lit in silver pools on the sea by apocalyptic shafts of sunlight leaking between the clouds. I could have stayed there shivering until darkness fell, but a Dutch couple came up, wanting me to take their photograph against that Turneresque background. By the time I had steadied their camera long enough to squeeze off half a roll of film – long enough even for Julia Margaret Cameron to get Tennyson to watch the birdie – dark was creeping up on the downs. I walked round the edge of the cliffs at Alum Bay, streaked vertically with different clays and minerals in startling colours that glowed even in the thickening dusk – black, yellow, ochre, crimson, cream and salmon pink. Victorian curio craftsmen exploited the potential of Alum Bay sand to the hilt. Their essays in 'marmortinto' or sand pictures can be found on boarding-house walls and in antique-shop windows here and there in the island, some built up layer upon layer into remarkable 3-D effects. Phials of Alum Bay sand sell by the thousand to today's visitors. In the gift shop below in Totland Bay the keyrings marked GENUINE ALUM BAY SAND were made in Hong Kong. Are containers of the stuff collected at Alum Bay, shipped out all the way east to be graded, sorted and packed into little Isle-of-Wight-shaped plastic holders – and then shipped all the way back to the Isle of Wight again? I wonder.

A car drew up beside me on the way down into Totland Bay. It was the young dog owner from Tennyson Down, offering me a lift. Grief had streaked his eyes red. No, the dog hadn't turned up. He and his wife were on holiday from Surrey. He'd just taken Maktar up on the down for a run in the fog, and had seen a notice warning of the dangers of the cliff edges. Looking round for Maktar, he'd actually seen him, out of the corner of his eye, slip over the drop; thought he'd heard a whimpering, but couldn't tell where it was coming from; had rushed down to call the coastguard. Maktar was only two years old, such a lively dog, full of beans. The young man couldn't take in the suddenness of it. He dropped me in Totland Bay, and drove away still smiling in shock.

I never did find out whether Maktar had made a miracle return from the dead, as next day's weather forecast sent me scurrying on round the coastal path of West Wight. Wintry showers turning to snow, said the weatherman, and Force 8 winds set to rise. As it turned out, sunshine bathed my afternoon ferry ride back to the mainland, but the morning's walk was a *tour de force* of wild weather, beginning down at Totland Bay's tiny pier and deserted beach. The gale roared in the pine trees and drove the waves in to batter against the sea wall, throwing curling feathers of spray twenty feet into the air. The green Solent was striped into lanes of foam by the wind, and a fishing boat out beyond the Needles stabbed its bows with alarming violence into the rollers. Across the water the curving gunports of Hurst Castle were half hidden in white horses.

'Welcome to Totland Bay' smiled the sign over the pier entrance. 'Warning!' snapped the notice in the pier kiosk window, next to a picture of a ravening Alsatian. 'Burglar Alarm fitted. Trespassers will be prosecuted. *High Voltage Electric* is switched on in these premises when closed. You Have Been Warned.' I enjoyed that evocation of The Electric as a demon, filling the pier with its deadly power. It was the wind that delivered the all-pervasive power this morning, pushing me up the cliff path and over the headland to arrive breathlessly outside Fort Warden's redoubtable walls.

This western section of the island's coastline is punctuated by forts, high up on the brows of the cliffs or standing defiantly out in the sea. They were built, some in the reign of Henry VIII, others in Victorian times, to guard the narrow seaway between the Isle of Wight and the mainland against threatened French invasions. What you see of each fort is only the tip of a military iceberg. They burrow hundreds of feet down and back into the chalk and sandstone. Magazines, storehouses, guard rooms, latrines, shell hoists, tunnels and branching roadways honeycomb far beneath the outer edges of the island, a pitch-black, labyrinthine underground city of damp concrete and flaking iron, never seen or even suspected by most visitors. All now disused and decommissioned, the old forts are great stimulaters of unlikely dreams and schemes. People buy them up for holiday homes, for camps, for hotels, for concert halls roofed with great domes. The dreamers pour in money as if mesmerized. Penthouse flats are established here, cafés there; but all with a strong whiff of impermanence, butterfly whims settling for a few moments among the grim reality of iron and concrete twenty feet thick. Fort Warden is now a holiday village run by the Mecca organization, a group of chalets tucked away out of the constant sea wind inside the ramparts of the old battery. I was shown round by Bob, the deputy manager, a genial Midlander who had settled in the island after being demobbed and stayed on to work in the tourist trade. Bob left his account books lying on the table to give me a tour round the shabby old chalets, soon to be replaced, and down rusting iron stairways into one of the magazines that underlie the fort.

'We don't let kids down here – too dangerous,' said Bob as we negotiated trailing electricity cables and piles of damp rubbish in the dank bowels of the magazine. 'Look at this wall.' He slapped it admiringly. 'Solid concrete. God knows how many yards thick. You'd need dynamite to shift all this stuff.' The tunnels leading to the gunports were mouldy, the ports themselves filled in with breeze blocks. 'Here's the hoist that took up shells to the guns. Cables still there, as you can see. This was where the gun stood. Storerooms over here. Built in the 1860s when they thought Louis Napoleon might be going to come over. Built to last, too. This fort was garrisoned right up till the end of the war, then in the fifties some chap bought it up for a holiday camp. Made shower rooms down here, a bowling alley – utilized everything. It's all got terribly run down since then. We'd like to do it all up again for the visitors, but you can see the amount of work involved.'

The magazine stank of mouldering iron and damp earth. We climbed up to the fresh air and stood on the ramparts of Fort Warden where the wind squeezed tears from our eyes. Bob pointed down the cliff. 'There was a searchlight battery down there to light up the Solent. Clever thing – they turned the light inland and reflected it off a moveable steel mirror. Enemy could fire like buggery at the reflection without ever getting near the searchlight.' Bob smiled, with a Midlander's pleasure in clever machinery cleverly used. He walked me back to the gateway, pointing out the fort's parade ground, dry moat and ivy-hung power room. 'Retiring next year,' said Bob as he shook my hand. 'Looking forward to my ducks and hens and a bit of garden. Ah – spotted I was from the Midlands, did you? Thought I'd lost the accent.'

I struggled on, shoved by the wind, past grim grey Fort Albert rising in a square block out of the sea (nowadays those fortress walls imprison rich yachtsmen in luxury flats); past Fort Victoria and its red-brick magazine arches. Soon the wind began to slacken, and I walked down into Yarmouth. In the Middle Ages Yarmouth was the most important town in the island, trading widely, the headquarters of the Governor, site of one of Henry VIII's castles. By 1800 it had declined to a ramshackle place, a rotten borough sending two MPs to Westminster to represent a population of fewer than a hundred. The painter George Morland, a rake and raver who befriended smugglers and scandalized polite island society, was staying at the George Hotel in the town to keep out of sight of his creditors when suspicion over French spying activities began to centre on him. He was arrested, largely on the strength of a drawing of his that looked just like an outline of the island. Hooted by a mob on his progress under armed guard through the streets of Newport, Morland was let off with a caution. The 'map' turned out to be a sketch of his pet spaniel.

Waiting in Yarmouth for the ferry over the racing Solent to Lymington, I went into the beamiest, quaintest hotel I could find. The beef sandwich they served me reeked of carrion. I swapped it for a ploughman's lunch. The bread roll was rock hard, staler than a schoolboy joke. The lettuce curled brownly. Oh, well – this was Wight out of season, after all. Aunt Rach would have enjoyed the expression on the landlord's face as I handed in the gamesome beef. Bloody tourists – not even Easter, and they're complaining *already*.

4. The Isles of Scilly

AN ATLANTIC DREAM

A sense of being off duty, on holiday in a carefree way, rarely touched my travels from Essex to Orkney through the other British isles. But going to the Isles of Scilly was different. Three of us spent the week there – my wife Jane, my youngest daughter Mary, and me. Mary, still three months away from making her entrance on to this world's stage, played an unobtrusive but significant part. She put her unseen (but occasionally felt) foot firmly down on the twenty-mile walks and bicycle rides, the late-night yarning in bars and the marathon early-hours writing sessions in hotel rooms that became standard practice for me as I moved north through the English, Welsh and Scottish islands. Jane and I progressed with stately slowness by bike, boat and foot round the Scilly Isles, stopping every few hundred yards for breathers on wayside rocks and benches as our little invisible minder dictated. So the working trip became a holiday, throwing a holidaymaking, rose-tinted slant on everything I saw and did.

Somewhere in the twenty-eight miles of deep blue Atlantic between Land's End and Scilly lies fabled Lyonesse, the sea kingdom overwhelmed by a raging sea, site of the last battle between King Arthur and black-hearted Mordred. These days the clattering helicopter from Penzance makes short and unromantic work of those ten leagues of sea; but before air travel came on the scene they were a stiff challenge to the traveller. In stormy winter, with the boat service reduced to once a week, helicopters and planes grounded by gales, Scilly can quickly become one of the most inaccessible places in Britain. But at 500 feet on a blue April day, the roughest thing in sight was the foam collar round the base of the lonely Wolf Rock lighthouse nine miles out from land.

The Scilly archipelago was all one block of land until recently – in geological terms – perhaps until or even after the last Ice Age. It split up into separate islands as the sea level rose and drowned the connecting valleys, leaving a shallow lagoon between the islands no more than a few feet deep. In certain tide conditions, and if you don't mind getting wet, you can actually make a round walk between the five principal islands of the group. Looking down from the helicopter we knew we were approaching Scilly when the profound blue of the deep Atlantic suddenly became a clear Caribbean turquoise. The five main islands turned slowly below on their green disc of lagoon – St Martin's, Tresco and Bryher on the north, with their pinched-in waists and hilly ends; in the centre the larger, irregular blob of St Mary's; away to the south-west tiny St Agnes and the outlying teeth of the Western Rocks at Scilly's boundary with 3000 miles of landless ocean.

The attractions of the Isles of Scilly are plain to see for even the most casual visitor – mild climate, white sand beaches, clear light, clean water, tame green farmland shoulder to shoulder with rocky granite moors, deep-sea rollers dashing spray over jagged rocks, seabirds and seals: English-speaking island paradises reassuringly near and at the same time satisfyingly far; Lyonesse for the taking. Their isolation still safeguards the Scillies from the worst of the West Country's seaside overcrowding, in spite of their small size – St Mary's, the biggest, has a coastline of not more than ten miles, and only about five miles of A road. On St Martin's, Tresco, Bryher and St Agnes, driving is not even an option: you bicycle or walk. Good footwear is far more use than a car in Scilly. Travelling between the isles is by boat, buzzing across the lagoon in one of the hard-worked launches. And there's no need to lock your front door behind you when you set out. Various factors combine to keep visitor numbers down: the high cost of the helicopter and plane flights; the three- or four-hour sea crossing aboard *Scillonian III* in waters that even in summer can become suddenly and startlingly rough; the few hotels and guest houses, always booked up; absence of arcades and fun palaces; the impracticality of making a cheap day trip so far offshore. Scillonians are friendly people, in consequence, quick to recognize regular visitors, apt to stop and chat. People who come frequently to Scilly feel a strong commitment and sense of belonging. They ask tenderly after their island friends, clucking sympathetically over misfortunes, smiling with pleasure over births, marriages and snippets of good news. They know exactly how many years they have been coming – 'Only twenty-six, I'm afraid! Now my sister – this will be her thirty-third year. Is that right, dear? Thirty-three, or thirty-four?'

The outcrops of rock around the islands, especially the Western Rocks in the Atlantic approaches, have been notorious among seamen since ships first sailed these waters. From the time of the Phoenician tin traders and the first Bronze Age settlers in Scilly 4000 years ago, vessels of all sizes and sorts have impaled themselves on the rocks and split themselves open in the coves and bays, unavoidably during ferocious storms or in thick fogs, inexplicably under open skies and in calm water. The most famous and terrible of all, the wreck of Sir Clowdisley Shovell's fleet in 1707, sent four ships and 1650 men to the bottom, along with their Admiral and a vast treasure of plundered Spanish gold. There are three lighthouses in the archipelago, including the Bishop Rock light down on the Western Rocks, the tallest in Britain, 175 feet of tapering granite tower rising straight out of the sea and visible as a warning finger on the horizon from everywhere in the islands. But the ships go on making mistakes, losing their way and blundering on to the rocks.

Looking at the photographs in the museum on St Mary's, the half-submerged freighters, the tangled masts and yards of last century's merchantmen rammed into the cliffs, broken hulls lying on beaches, was a salutary reminder of teeth only just hidden behind the smile of Scilly. So were the museum's accounts of life in the Isles of Scilly two centuries ago and more, when the Duchy of Cornwall leased them to absentee landlords. Several thousand Scillonians lived in abject poverty, cut off from mainland help, eking out existence by piloting passing ships, fishing and subsistence farming. They ate boiled limpets off the rocks when the winter gales set in and the fishing boats could not go out. They starved when the potato crop failed. They sickened in the damp and cold of their granite-walled huts, avid for the next shipwreck and the firewood, the shoes, shirts and building timbers that would float their way. The sufferings of the dispossessed and evicted Scottish clansmen of the same era were to become all too familiar to me when I reached the Hebridean islands, but here in Scilly their contemporaries were living lives of equal misery and brutishness. It took an iron fist in an iron glove, a relentless will wielded by a most remarkable dictator, to lift the Scillonians out of the trough they had lain in for so long.

When Augustus Smith took on the vacant lease of the Scilly Isles in 1834, he set himself a single-minded task of improvement that very few men would have taken on. At thirty years of age, a member of a rich banking family, Augustus could easily have fallen into the kind of idle, self-pleasing life that his social contemporaries enjoyed. But he was a true reformer to his finger-tips, a young man burning to take barren soil and force out of it a fruitful crop. The overpopulated, isolated Isles of Scilly, with their poverty-stricken families, their unschooled children and empty meal tables, neglected by their mainland landlords, gave him the opportunity he was looking for. His preliminary fact-finding trip convinced him of that, and once he had assumed the title of Lord Proprietor of the Isles of Scilly (paying the then enormous sum of £20,000 to the Duchy of Cornwall as an earnest of his intent), and got the reins of power into his hands, he drove the islands and their people like an energetic coachman. Nowhere in Scilly was free from his attentions or failed to feel the weight of that tremendous will. Individual islanders either went along with his ideas or were made to leave.

The reforms he railroaded through, bitterly resented by some inhabitants, spelled the end of the life they had known and a sudden and immediate change of course. Only one family member could succeed to the tenancy of house and land. Boundaries were redrawn to create holdings of land that could realistically be expected to support a family. No one was allowed to marry unless he had a house to move into. All Scillonian children were to go to school: parents paid a penny a day when their offspring attended, twopence when they did not. Subletting land was forbidden. So was smuggling. And these 'do nots' were accompanied by a host of positive measures – a postal service from the mainland introduced, piers constructed to enable ships to come and go with cargoes, new houses and public buildings put up, agriculture improved. All boys were taught navigation as a matter of course; this measure resulted in Scillonian seamen soon becoming recognized as among the best in the world.

Augustus Smith never shrank from the most autocratic of decisions if he felt that the greater good of the populace would be served. The tiny island of Samson, lying a mile across the channel south of Tresco and Bryher, was cleared of its inhabitants in 1855 because the water supply became foul each summer, and the fifty-odd islanders could no longer support themselves. In another move, almost all of the Scilly pilots were 'persuaded' to leave their respective islands and settle on the most southerly, St Agnes, to put them nearest to the Western Rocks and the greatest area of demand for their services. Troublemakers and questioners were likely to find themselves on the next boat to the mainland. Augustus's methods earned him the nickname The Emperor, and the absolute respect (though by no means the universal affection) of the subjects of his Atlantic empire. Some of those subjects, natives of St Agnes, were bold enough to knock him down one day, bundle him up in a sail and leave him at the mercy of the tide – though common sense reasserted itself in time for his bonds to be cut before he could drown. The Emperor was an unstoppable force. By the time he died in July 1872, after a reign of almost forty years, Augustus Smith had created from a desert of depression a going concern with enough momentum to continue in prosperity.

He had also created for himself on the island of Tresco the baronial granite residence of Tresco Abbey in the grounds of a ruined Benedictine abbey, and had surrounded it with a remarkable garden of sub-tropical plants, culled from the ends of the earth over the long years of his reign. To quote from the Isles of Scilly guidebook, the gardens contain 'Citrons, Bananas, Mexican Yuccas, Chilean Puya, New Zealand Ironwood, Burmese Honeysuckle, Himalayan Ginger, Australian Scarlet Bottle-brush, Madeira Lily-of-the-Valley trees, Aloes, Dracaenas, Indian Fan Palms, Chinese Paper Plants, Prickly Pear, Cinnamon, Musk, gigantic Ice-plants and Mimosa' – to name but a very few. Many of these were added to the gardens by Augustus Smith's successors at Tresco Abbey, but the inspiration was his: a vision of lush growth and beauty on a foundation of bare, barren granite hillsides, a horticultural parallel of his social engineering. And in his gardens as in his wider empire, Augustus planted and planned for the future. Today, a hundred years on, as one looks round the Scilly archipelago from helicopter or hilltop, there's no mistaking Tresco, its bushy green spine of trees standing out from the gorse and heather of the other islands' stony hills. Walking along the Tresco lanes, fleshy spikes of exotic leaves and startlingly shaped and coloured flower heads rear from the roadside and cluster in the trees.

Augustus Smith was lucky to have the creation of his garden lovingly recorded throughout all its later stages in the water-colour paintings of his sister, Frances le Marchant, showing the slow blooming of the desert from the 1860s onwards. Jane and I were on Tresco for the April awakening of the garden, and we also saw, in a slide show one night in the Tresco reading room, its summer glories. Along with the slides went a funny commentary by the photographer, Frank Naylor, now retired from his job as gardener at Tresco Abbey and still head over heels in love with every one of his exotic charges. As a teenager in 1928, Frank had been talent-spotted working on a Lincolnshire estate by the third-generation ruler of Tresco, Augustus Smith's great-nephew Arthur Dorrien Smith. 'The shooting wasn't too good,' said Frank to his audience in the reading room, 'so he poached the gardener instead.' It took another seven years for young Frank Naylor to take up Major Dorrien Smith's offer of a job on Tresco, but once he'd signalled his acceptance the Major moved quickly. 'Take the next train south,' he commanded, and after a long journey and sickening sea crossing Frank found himself in a heaving punt off Tresco, unable to gauge the right moment to leap for the beach. 'For God's sake, boy,' exploded his new employer, 'jump off when the wave goes back, and run like hell.'

These were days when, apart from the Major's friends, very few visitors came to Tresco: when the garden staff was big enough to make up a football and cricket team to play the island's farm workers. Frank's stories and spicy side comments ranged far and wide over his half-century of service. 'The blackbirds and starlings love to take nectar out of the plants. They get themselves dusted gold all over with the pollen. I get these bird fanciers running up to me, all excited: "Oh, Mr Naylor! I've just seen a golden oriole!" – "I should think you have, dear," I say to them, never letting on. We do get some funny comments from the visitors. When the *Torrey Canyon* was wrecked on the Seven Stones back in 1967 and all that oil got spilt – do you remember? – well, I was pumping out some sludgy mud from the bottom of the pond, all black and sticky, and one visitor said to me, "Ooh, Mr Naylor," she said, "that oil has got everywhere, hasn't it?" I said, "Yes, it certainly has. We've had an exceptionally high spring tide, you know." Then there was the time that Prince Charles came here. He had just hurt his finger and his arm was all done up in a sling. Well, I saw him coming along the path, so I just went up to him and said, "Hello – have you come about that job for a single-handed gardener?" He took it well, as a joke, I will say.'

The jokes dried up, though, as Frank showed us his slides of the hundreds of rare trees and plants killed off by a deadly week of frost in 1987. He murmured the names of the victims like a roll-call of dead friends: '*Metrosideros* . . . how lovely they were . . . I was very, very fond of them. Look at these, now . . . beautiful, aren't they? All gone – all dead.' Kew Gardens, long-time allies and colleagues of the gardeners of

Tresco, are providing new seeds to restock the gardens, but some of those gaps in Frank Naylor's beds and banks will never be filled again as he knew them in their prime.

From this lush paradise of plants Jane and I set out, as our holiday week went on, to explore some of the other isles of Scilly. The first evening, though, while Jane slept off the journey, I braved a spitting sky and a swelling sea to join a boat-load of race-goers. It was the first gig race of the season. In the days of sail six-oared Scilly gigs would race each other out to passing ships, right of pilotage going to the crew who could get their man first on to the deck of the client. What goes on today, competitive racing among island and mainland crews, lacks the right spirit, according to Eddie, the elderly Tresco man in our accompanying launch. 'It's not fun, like it used to be,' he growled. 'When I was a young man we used to race in the gigs for the fun of it, and maybe a bottle of beer for the winners. Nowadays they're all far too serious, mainlanders and islanders alike. It's all done for cups and medals. No one really enjoys it like we used to.'

I don't know how much fun the six crews racing that evening were getting out of it, but there was no question about their commitment. The gigs were slim things, low slung and long; open rowing boats that disappeared entirely behind each swell. The six oarsmen in each gig, most stripped to the waist, tugged in a furious, back-breaking rhythm at their two-handed sweeps, while the coxswains lurched back and forth in sympathy, bellowing themselves scarlet. The oldest boat was *Bonnet*, painted lime green, built back in 1830 for serious business and raced with equal seriousness by a crew from St Mary's. The gigs covered the two-mile course from St Agnes to Hugh Town jetty on St Mary's in a few minutes of high excitement, the crews heaving heroically through icy drizzle and half light. The varnished wood *Endeavour*, a mainland gig powered by a St Mary's crew, just got the better of the dark blue *Royal*, crewed by mainlanders. A spatter of partisan applause came from the little crowd of Scillonians on the jetty. One or two crew members, once past the finishing line, collapsed over their oars, chests heaving – it was the first race of the season, after all – but most had made their way up the slipway to the pub by the time that the venerable *Bonnet*'s unsynchronized crew had thrashed and splashed their way into last place.

Over on St Mary's, capital island of the Scillies, we decided that there wouldn't be enough time to go on a Vic's Tour. This was a poor decision. We learned later that Vic's Tour – a trip round the island in an ancient bus, with side-splitting commentary on local places and people – is one of Scilly's great traditions. Instead we bicycled along the narrow lanes, one behind the other on a wobbly hired tandem with slipping gears. The fields of St Mary's were small and square, surrounded by thick head-high walls or tall, bushy hedges to keep out the salt wind and spray. The Scilly daffodils had been picked, packed and sent off to the mainland markets the previous month, and the little fields were full of leaves left in place to feed the underground bulbs. The lanes twisted past tiny ponds, sheltered by elm hedges. It was a charming scene, but not twee – the granite walls, farmhouses and outcrops gave force and weight to this gentle landscape.

The island of Samson, we hoped, was going to be different. No one had lived on Samson since Augustus Smith cleared it of its inhabitants in 1855. There was a superb white sand beach and sandy isthmus in the centre of the island, a flat-crowned hill at either end, the whole less than a mile long. We hired a tiny boat with an outboard engine to land us on Samson as castaways for a long day. By the time we had steadied this brute's tendency to fling up its nose and break into an ear-splitting and nerve-jarring snarl, we were across the lagoon and bumping our bow into the white sands of Samson Flats. Not alone, alas. Behind us a long green launch had been quietly catching up, and now followed us into the deserted bay. A landing ramp was put out, and twenty-eight bird-watchers from Bournemouth tramped up the sands beside us. They staggered under tripods, cameras and binoculars. A laconic young man in a wide-brimmed hat was in charge. They formed up behind him and snaked away through bracken and bramble towards the gull colonies on South Hill. There was something biblical in this scene of elderly figures bowed under great weights, plodding across immemorial sands after the stern young leader.

By dint of some skyline creeping Jane and I managed to have the north end of the island to ourselves. We wandered past clumps of miniature blue flowers where sulphur-yellow spiders hurried across our hands. Black rabbits, descendants through Heaven knows how many generations from the original pairs introduced by Augustus Smith, scampered among the quarrelsome black-backed gulls on the slopes of North Hill. At the summit was a grooved granite box a couple of feet square, sunk into the peat – a kistvaen or burial chamber for a Bronze Age corpse folded into a sitting posture. We sat by the kistvaen in glorious isolation until the vanguard of the Bournemouth bird-fanciers came filing over the crest of South Hill, then scrambled down through the bracken and along the sands to the boat. Petrol was seeping out of the valve on top of the outboard engine that I had forgotten to close, but there was enough left to chug north across the shallow lagoon to the quay on Bryher island. We nosed and butted our way clumsily back and forth by the moorings, finally managing to fasten rope to ring under the amused gaze of a crowd of local boatmen.

Preconceptions are silly things to carry around among the islands of Britain. For some reason I had pictured the Isles of Scilly as thoroughly geared up for tourism, oriented towards the holiday trade to the exclusion of all else. In fact, as we began to discover the further we explored, island life is as close to the bone here as anywhere. Scillonians, whether natives or incomers, have to diversify their livelihoods in order to survive, especially in the 'off-islands', as Bryher, St Martin's, Tresco and St Agnes are known. On Bryher the café owners were doing up their barn for self-catering accommodation, as well as running a farm and growing flowers. From the island's sandy road we saw evidence of struggles to survive: overgrown walls, fields of weeds next to fields of daffodil bulbs, tumbledown buildings and back yards full of lobster pots, oily boat engines and empty crates. Beyond the small areas of hedged fields rose stony hillsides where nothing could be made to grow. Across the low-lying waist of the island the landscape changed to a barren western coast where in the well-named Hell Bay the waves came pounding in foam over the rocks. In summer the tourists come to stay in the Hell Bay Hotel and in the cottages of the islanders, but from autumn onwards life contracts again to the boat service, fishing and farming.

To send or receive goods costs a third as much again for the inhabitants of Bryher and the other off-islands as it does for the folk on St Mary's – hence the difficulty of setting up businesses on the smaller isles of Scilly. There are other problems for families, too. Bryher's little primary school closed down in 1972, and the island's children have to travel each day across the water to school on Tresco. Bryher has no doctor, no library, no rubbish disposal or airstrip. Yet there's great competition for houses on the island when they come up for sale, both from outsiders keen to settle and from young Bryher men and women who have trained and qualified on the mainland and want to get back to their home island to work and raise a family. Price tags on Bryher houses reflect the competition – £200,000 was the latest talking point in the Vine Café. Self-employment and self-reliance go hand in hand here, with uncertainty for the future a constant background. This hard fact of life came home to us as we turned away from the rugged outline of Bryher and motored slowly across the lagoon, back into the well-ordered world of Tresco.

The rough landscape of the other islands appears at both ends of Tresco. To the north the shore path runs through a sweet-smelling natural garden of campion, honeysuckle, violets and wood-sage on to a slope piled with granite boulders, from which Cromwell's Castle sticks out into the water, a round tower as damp and dark as a well inside. A bare plateau of heather, riddled with the pits of old tin workings, drops to black cliffs with their feet hidden in white foam. Walking here on a day heavy with sea mist and hearing the long double moan of the foghorn on Bishop Rock, we could have been on the wildest island in Britain. The southern end of Tresco has none of this rocky grandeur; it spreads out into a dry wilderness of rabbit-infested scrub, nettles and brambles, rising to shaggy dunes where granite outcrops perch in layers like stony cottage loaves. The influence of the Smith dynasty lies lightly on these extremities of Tresco, in contrast to the island's central green and pleasant saddle of fertility.

The taming of Tresco is seen at its most remarkable in the sub-tropical gardens of the Abbey, but everywhere there is the same order, the same efficient neatness. The small granite houses are clean, their gardens immaculate. Field walls are clear of brambles and overgrowth, hedges are clipped in regular lines, roadways are well surfaced and tidy at the edges. Rubbish is marshalled strictly into a couple of old pits. There's an air of purposefulness, not to say preoccupation, about the people as they dig crops, drive tractors or mend boats. Everyone seems to be going somewhere, to do something when they get there. Visitors are easily recognized by the slowness and aimlessness of their sauntering. I soon learned to make an appointment if I wanted a good long chat with anyone on Tresco; every single islander is busy during working hours. It's the antithesis of the laid-back pace of life on Scottish islands.

All this industry, this green fertility of landscape and sense of prosperity, springs from the maintenance of Tresco as a privately owned and run estate, exactly as it has been since the reign of Augustus Smith. The Tresco Estate owns all the island houses but one. Nearly all the native islanders and the incomers work for the estate, on the farm, in the woods, in the gardens or in the expanding and highly successful tourist business. In return for their forswearing of cars and dogs, their neat upkeep of the island's appearance and their general co-operation, they are guaranteed house, a job and security, and a place in what most of them – particularly those who have come here from lucrative but pressurized jobs on the mainland – clearly regard as an earthly paradise. Awkward customers soon leave, their house and job refilled with little trouble. There is no shortage of applicants.

I had been hoping to bump into one incomer in particular, having read a brief paragraph about him in a newspaper article which described him as a 'medical man from Salisbury' who now worked as a gardener at Tresco Abbey. The 'medical man' had in fact been a clinical toxicologist in charge of a department at Porton Down, the Wiltshire research establishment where the effects of chemical weapons are investigated. Seeing this slim, bearded, deeply tanned man forking over the soil of a flower bed, and thinking of the job on which he had turned his back, brought home the other-worldly nature of Tresco as nothing else could have done.

'I always wanted to live on this island,' he told me, 'ever since coming here on holiday twenty-six years ago. So it's like a dream come true for me. The most important thing about living here is to fit in. When I arrived as an employee three years ago, it was made very clear to me that many other people could have been chosen in my place: that it wasn't so much a question of what skills I had to offer, but of how I would fit in. I gave up a salary seven times what I earn now – but what's more important, a big salary or the quality of the life you lead?'

'Feudal' was a word that cropped up sooner or later in conversation about Tresco with any Scillonian from the other islands. 'Very pretty, yes, and no worries about security – but I couldn't live there, not under that feudal system, tugging their forelocks and scared to put a foot wrong,' said a woman on the Bryher boat, dismissing Tresco with a scornful flick of the hand. I saw no forelocks tugged on Tresco, but it's certainly true that there's more than a pinch of anachronism in the island's mixed economy. The independence of the piecemeal way of life on the other Scilly islands carries its risks with it, of failure, unemployment, poverty, bankruptcy. On St Mary's the Duchy of Cornwall has sold off many of its houses to occupiers, some of whom have sold them on again, diluting the population with second-homers and absentee owners. On Tresco there are no such dangers to the social fabric. But the picture, even here, is slowly changing. About forty of the estate houses have been discreetly converted into holiday places, some on time-share, others as rentable flats. Upmarket, clean as whistles and tastefully done up, they have quietly established tourism as a major factor in Tresco's economy. The visitors they attract are just those most likely to blend in with no fuss — bird-watchers, botanists, elderly retired couples, middle-aged professionals with children of beach-and-bicycle age. 'Such a *privilege* to be here' was a comment we heard from several visitors. That feeling of privilege, of having a foothold on hallowed ground and walking warily in consequence, is shared by all Tresco's holidaymakers, and goes a long way to explain the caution of estate workers, especially incomers, over discussing too revealingly their thoughts about the finely stratified social order of the island.

'My view, for what it is worth,' wrote the 'medical man from Salisbury' to me long after my visit to Tresco, 'is that it is very difficult for any managing director of a business, in this case a working island estate, to make both business decisions and decisions concerning the welfare of his employees and their families without appearing to be autocratic. It is inevitable that in trying to meet the needs of individuals there will be conflict with the overriding requirement of running a profitable business. Without an overview, some decisions may seem to be arbitrary and insensitive.'

Robert Dorrien Smith, the present ruler of Tresco on lease from the Duchy, pulled more of the threads together for me when we chatted in the sunshine on the terrace of Tresco Abbey.

'Mr Robert', as he is styled by the island workers, runs a tight ship with an eye very much to the future. A Union Jack flies over the house when Robert is in residence, but there's nothing showy in his manner. Still a young man, he has been taking decisions affecting other people's lives and livelihoods since his father died suddenly and left him, untrained and unprepared, holding the reins and a bright red balance sheet at the

LUNDY

above: heat haze over Rat Island, with another batch of visitors disembarking from MV *Oldenburg*

right: the Old Light stands high and dry on the crest of the island

below: demolishing the old signal cottage to improve the visitors' view of the castle

ISLE OF MAN

Above: the Millennium Way
runs along the flank
of Carraghan, with the
delectable East Baldwin
valley dropping away to
the left

Right: lush vegetation
smothers the stone stile
that leads to the Church
of St Runn
Below: site of the meeting
of Tynwald in 1428

BARRA
Above: Loganair's Twin
Otter unloads passengers
and baggage on the wide
white cockle sands of
Traigh Mhor

Right: the view from
Castlebay out to where the
MacNeil stronghold of
Kisimul Castle rises from
the water

MINGULAY
Left: ruins of the abandoned
clachan by the beach

SOUTH UIST
Left: shell artistry all over a derelict bus

BENBECULA
Below: the extraordinary landscape of the island, half water and half peat bog. The mountains of North Uist dominate the distance

LEWIS
Top: the peat badlands, with a peat-cutter's hut marooned in the waterlogged waste

Above: herding sheep along the Pentland Road

HARRIS
Left: the old road to Rhenigidale snakes tortuously up the hillside

Below: Rhenigidale, the settlement about to be joined to the outside world. The school house, made redundant by the new road, stands up the bank on the left of the picture

age of twenty-one. Reserved and private by nature, he had to follow in the footsteps of a flamboyant father. Between the need to make the Tresco estate pay its way and the equally strong desire to retain the peaceful beauty of the island, Robert walks a tightrope, well aware of being the focal point of onlookers' criticism. Journalists are always alert to the copy potential of the feudal paradise under its Old Etonian ruler, and he's used to the twists they give to his explanations of how the island works.

'The point about the island,' Robert said, smiling warily as he watched me jotting notes, 'is that it runs successfully. Practically everyone on Tresco works for the estate, and practically everyone contributes in one way or another. This is just about the only self-supporting, privately owned island in Great Britain – I think I can claim that fairly. St Mary's, for example, is in a bit of a mess now: seven hundred cars at the latest count, council houses sold to tenants who then quadruple the sale price, dentists from Birmingham buying in and only visiting the place a couple of times in the year. The councillors on St Mary's can't have any clear idea of how things are going to go there, but I can be pretty sure what's going to be happening on Tresco in five years' time. In fact, together with my managers, I run what amounts to a continuous Five Year Plan. Tourism has to be carefully controlled, but it's definitely the way we have to go, along with agriculture, the flower business and so on. We managed to show a profit last year for the first time, which has to be a good thing. My first responsibility is the hundred and fifty livelihoods of the people who work here.'

This businesslike approach, and the limited number of houses available, means that estate workers are expected to keep up to the mark in their jobs; otherwise they can find themselves out of work and home in short order. 'But that's what one would expect in any business,' Robert pointed out. 'Retired people who worked for the estate aren't bundled off the island, far from it. But the situation can arise where you have Mrs Tiggywinkle, aged eighty-two, living in a four-bedroomed house. She would be asked to move into something smaller to make way for a younger couple with children. But we're building some houses for old people, and starter homes for people who are going to be starting a family. Tresco has to change with the times – it's just a question of degree.'

As I left Tresco Abbey a film crew was arriving to conduct yet another interview with Robert. 'I wonder if *they're* going to stab me in the back?' he muttered under his breath as a pair of lynx-eyed young producers bounced on to the terrace. In the entrance hall of the house hung a portrait of Augustus Smith, plump of jowl and thunderous of frown, in his Freemason's apron, the very spit and image of an autocratic emperor. Times have changed a long way since he ruled the Isles of Scilly. His great-great-great-nephew grapples with problems of financial survival and public presentation that the old bulldog would not even have recognized.

And change goes on in Scilly. Even as Jane and I were flying out of Tresco on the helicopter, a new luxury hotel, aiming both at moneyed holidaymakers and the conference trade, was opening on the hitherto unexploited island of St Martin's. 'Beyond Land's End, where romance begins,' sighed the brochure, 'a venue to inspire creative decision making.' And there were fears that the entrepreneur who had recently bought up Land's End might be planning to leapfrog those thirty miles of sea and bring a lot more of the same to an unreceptive Scilly. Anne Oyler, a farmer on Tresco and the island's representative on the Council of the Isles of Scilly, told me across her kitchen table, 'That would be the very last thing we want to see. But I'm quite optimistic about the future of the islands. You have to be. Have you been to Samson? Have you felt its atmosphere? There's times I've been on Samson, or on St Agnes looking out west, and I've felt a million miles away, even from Scilly. These islands are magical, there's no other word for it.'

The faintest whiff of exploitation by outsiders is enough to unify all the islanders, independent or not, along with their besotted long-term visitors, in a solid protective barrier. They are all utterly determined that Scillonian magic will never be bottled and sold across a tourist counter, whatever the inducement. It's a brave shout in the face of the future.

5. Steep Holm, Flat Holm and Lundy

THE OTHER CHANNEL ISLANDS

If you're looking for a thrill in a small boat among tumbling waves, you can find it in the narrowing strait where the Bristol Channel swings from east to north, with Wales to the left and England to the right. Here the tides are squeezed inwards and upwards to reach the second highest level in the world. Only Canada's Bay of Fundy beats the Bristol Channel for record tide levels. Incoming waters meet outgoing ones, pushing the River Severn's contrary tides up and over each other. One effect of this constriction of racing water is the spectacular Severn Bore, a tidal wave that can reach ten feet high as it surges upriver. Another effect, less well known but equally dramatic for anyone in the thick of it, is the unexpected tossing and pitching of a boat on a windless day. Bad sailors think twice before making the five-mile journey out from Weston-super-Mare or Barry to the little twin islands of Steep Holm and Flat Holm that lie right in the middle of this tidal fairway.

Our outward trip from Weston to Steep Holm aboard the open-decked *Weston Lady* wasn't too bad. Fifty of us chugged out on a sweltering May day – gull fanciers, amateur botanists, wartime gun emplacement freaks and plain ordinary trippers. Steep Holm is many things to many people. The mid-channel twins are physically as unlike as could be: Flat Holm a level pancake, Steep Holm a green hump. Flat Holm belongs to Wales, Steep Holm to England, though there are only a couple of miles of water between them. Both islands are slabs of limestone, knobbles on the honeycombed and chambered floor of the Severn estuary. Both have experienced down the centuries the common lot of Britain's offshore islands – Bronze Age subsistence farming hard in the face of the storms, Roman and Viking intrusion, monkish settlements of the Dark and Middle Ages, a dash of smuggling and wrecking, a messy sprawl of fortifications against the 19th-century French and 20th-century German threats of invasion; nowadays a new importance as refuges for wildlife.

Between devotees of the two islands there is a sometimes-voiced, ever-present rivalry. Look at our wild peonies, say the Steep Holm botanists – the only wild colony in the British Isles. Ah, replies the Flat Holm Society, but what about our unique cholera hospital, and our lighthouse? All very well, sniff the Steep Holm historians, but it was *our* island where Viking raiders starved to death in 914 AD. Not so, assert the Flat Holmians – it was us. Look at the *Anglo-Saxon Chronicle*. All written down there in black and white. Hah! retort the Steepholmians. That may be the version *you've* seen, but three others say it was Steep Holm. And so on, and on – all good fun, but with a definite edge. The day-visitors from Barry and Weston let these claims and counter-claims flow over their heads. It's enough to be out for a few hours among the racing tides of the Bristol Channel, the everyday world reduced to a strip of hills on the horizon, with seabirds and wild flowers to enjoy and a jumble of forts, ancient cannon and other military remains to be scrambled over and speculated on before the boatman returns.

Weston Lady crunched her bows hard into the shingle beach below Steep Holm's eastern cliffs, and we began the zig-zag climb to the top of the island. My two teenage children, George and Ruth, had come along for the ride and the day out, and were restless after the hour-long crossing. But island magic gripped them immediately, with the discovery of a just-hatched lesser black-backed gull chick on a nest beside the path. The chick's twin was still in the egg, visible through a hole in the shell as a tiny beak chipping hopefully away. 'Ahhh, it's sweet,' murmured the children, on their knees and rapt above the damp, stripy bundle of the chick. The mother gull stood guard on a nearby wall until we were well up the path, then flew down to settle on her brood with an indignant chakker.

The path wound up the face of the cliff along the course of a narrow-gauge railway, made of iron and with irony in its construction. Captured in the First World War from the Germans, the rails and sleepers were laid on Steep Holm in the next war, first to build and then to supply the searchlight and gun posts that defended the Bristol Channel against the railway's original makers. At the top we found the grey stone barracks put up in the 1860s when an earlier French invasion threatened. These days the barracks serve visitors with food, drink and souvenirs, house a gull research station and provide a dormitory for anyone staying on the island. We picnicked in the beating sunshine outside the barracks, looking across to Weston-super-Mare and its backdrop of Mendip Hills. Then we walked on round the summit path, through green thickets of alexanders and elder, sycamore trees and the overgrown privet bushes first planted seven centuries before by the monks of Steep Holm. Every hundred yards or so we stumbled across another derelict military emplacement: semi-circular redoubts of concrete and brick, square concrete bunkers, rusty cannon splashed with gull droppings. 'It's rifled – here, feel the grooves,' said George, rummaging at arm's length inside the muzzle of one cannon. These muzzle-loaders would have been hellish things to operate in a proper bombardment of an invasion fleet, with each tightly-fitting shell having to be screwed laboriously down the full length of a red hot barrel. Luckily for their crews they turned out to be completely unnecessary, rusty white elephants that never had to fire a shot in anger.

The cliffs fall from the top of Steep Holm 200 feet and more into the estuary. Round on the west side we looked over to the flat stepping-stone of Flat Holm, its white lighthouse tower sticking up from one end. Beyond were the Welsh shore and distant mountains, an immense view. But the children were keen to get back to the landing beach. George had brought his sea rod and a slice of none-too-fresh raw cod, and was determined to catch a whiting from the rocks. Ruth was for sunbathing. So we dropped back down the railway path to sea level. George stationed himself carefully between cliff and pebbles, and cast out into the roughening waters of the falling tide, while Ruth waded out cautiously into the current. Bathing from Steep Holm is a thoroughly bad idea. Tide-rips and cross-currents wait just offshore to sweep the strongest swimmer helplessly away. But Ruth enjoyed her paddle, while I went off to help build a wall with the warden, Rodney Legg.

Steep Holm was bought from the Wharton Estate in 1976, for the extremely reasonable sum of £10,000, by the Kenneth Allsop Memorial Trust. The money was raised on appeal and the island bought, in the words of the slate plaque above the beach, 'to preserve the memory of the writer & naturalist, Kenneth Allsop, 1920–73'. Allsop, born in Yorkshire and brought up in suburban London, became one of television's star presenters in the 1960s – *Tonight* and *24 Hours* were two of his best-known programmes. He was also a passionate lover of and writer about natural history, a conservationist at a time when the widespread destruction of wildlife was only beginning to be noticed. Steep Holm's preservation as a nature reserve in Kenneth Allsop's memory is an admirable ideal, but the more I chatted to Rodney Legg as we piled rubble into the wall, the more I learned of the problems faced by the Trust.

'Most of these wartime buildings are scheduled monuments of one kind or another,' Rodney said. 'They all need to be preserved, and I feel it's a sort of duty to the men who built them to maintain them properly. But where do the priorities lie? There are six Victorian batteries on the island, ten guns, several World War Two searchlight posts, generator housings, Nissen huts – all in disrepair. Then there's the priory ruins being excavated, the farmhouse and walled garden falling to pieces on top, the cottages and the old inn here, which we're hoping to do up as a better warden's house than the barracks. Visitors have to be kept safe, too; one old man gashed his leg badly, falling down the steps by the beach, so those had to be replaced. And this wall' – he slapped the stones with a rubber-gloved hand – 'it's to stop visitors falling over on to the rocks. That's a sample of the repair work, but on top of that there's the wildlife to be managed – birds, plants, the Muntjac deer I brought over a few years ago. Steep Holm is wonderful for birds – we have peregrines nesting here, and you'll have seen the gull nests everywhere.

'This kind of project needs money as well as voluntary help. We rely entirely on the visitors and their landing fees. We get no government grants of any kind. The Allsop Memorial Trust members, thank goodness, are wonderful with their help and their labour. They come and stay on the island – people who prefer to do rather than to talk. The whole place would be self-funding if we didn't have such a surfeit of buildings to maintain. As it is, with all the inevitable emergency things that need doing as they crop up, it's hard to stick to any proper plan.'

Rodney Legg can only come to Steep Holm when time permits – in his other, mainland life he's kept busy as a writer. He gets some quiet amusement out of the tunnel vision of visiting specialists whose world revolves exclusively round one of the many wildlife facets of the island. There was the lecturer in botany from Cardiff University who came across with a party of students. Up on the top of Steep Holm she was talking away when an unusual butterfly, a speckled wood, landed on the alexanders. Rodney pointed it out. 'Oh, they won't be interested in *that*,' snapped the lecturer. 'There are plenty of *butterflies* on the mainland. It's the *plants* we've come to see!' Rodney sees the island as a place where the many parts of nature can interact under the eyes of, but not disturbed by, interested visitors: 'I think Steep Holm does echo Ken Allsop's principles – a place which offers a challenge for human beings, and a better place for wildlife to thrive. There's just too much to do, and not enough money to do it with.'

The sun had gone behind the summit of the island by the time we had finished our section of wall. *Weston Lady* came butting and sliding sideways across the now agitated Bristol Channel, digging up spray with her bows. We tossed back to Weston-super-Mare, jostled by high, sandy-brown waves. The little girl on the seat opposite was sick all over her shoes, a lurid pink outflow. The young woman beside us stared, groaned, turned pale green and sank her face in her hands. The passengers smiled bravely at each other, or kept their eyes fixed ahead on the distant hotels of Weston. The three of us, though, were smugly unaffected. No whiting had fallen to George's lures, but he had dug out a wartime machine-gun barrel from a cave by way of compensation. Ruth was well paddled and sunned. And I kept my stomach in order by staring back over the heaving stern to watch the sun set directly over the bushy crown of Steep Holm.

Where Rodney Legg and the Kenneth Allsop Memorial Trust struggle for time and money to carry out their plans for Steep Holm, Dr David Worrall and the Flat Holm Society have it, comparatively, on a plate. Round on the Welsh side of the Severn estuary next day, having swapped my children for a pair of binoculars, I met David Worrall at the Flat Holm Project's office in the old police station near the dockside in Barry. David is a lucky man, and knows it. He runs the Flat Holm Project for South Glamorgan County Council, who have not only leased the island as a local nature reserve from its owners, Trinity House, but are backing their initiative with a lot of money. To David Worrall and his employers Flat Holm is a unique educational tool, something to be carefully nurtured and put at the service of a public that ranges from school parties to research students, from ornithologists to local historians, as well as any casual yachtsman stopping by for a quick look. We motored the five miles out to Flat Holm in the brand-new *Lewis Alexander*, £60,000 worth of boat paid for by 'Glam', as David calls the County Council. We sat in the cabin, shouting a conversation over the tinny howl of the engine.

'We're very lucky in having supportive employers like Glam, who really want this project to succeed,' David roared at me. 'Otherwise they wouldn't have bought this boat. And the Flat Holm Society are excellent supporters, too – about 150 of them. I've already got a score of volunteer wardens who'll relieve our full-time warden whenever he needs a break. They'll turn their hands to anything – clearing scrub, cutting paths, restoring the buildings, raising money. They got enough money together to equip this boat with all its electronic gear. There's a hell of a lot to do on the island – you'll see when we land – but there's both the will and the money to do it.'

We landed on the island jetty and walked to the farmhouse, now restored as a warden's house and visitor centre. Here we were joined by the Flat Holm warden, Will Sandison, a companion to rival David Worrall in enthusiasm, and the three of us set out to walk round the island. Flat Holm is flat – dead flat, a circle of rock 500 yards across, flanked by low cliffs. It was farmed from medieval times up until 1941, when the Harris family was evacuated to make way for the military. Since then the fields and meadows of Flat Holm have run wild, covering the island with nettles, brambles and elder bushes. Half-hidden in this low, jungly covering stand the island buildings, a bricks-and-mortar compendium of Flat Holm history. Some, like the farmhouse and the Victorian barracks, are being cleaned up and put back into use as accommodation and resource centres for the visitors. The rest crumble gently into ruin. David showed me the elegant building put up in 1896 as an isolation hospital for cholera victims. Sailors coming home with the disease from 'vurrin parts' were shunted off out here in the estuary, to get better or to die. The cholera hospital is a fine building, with a neat little porch and ornamental tiles on the roof ridge. But the roof gapes in holes, and the walls are beginning to crack. 'Half a million pounds would put it right,' David murmured, 'but I couldn't ask the Flat Holm Society to take on major repairs like that. Now what I'd *like* to do is have an exhibition on cholera in that end – the disease, the hospital, the whole story – and maybe a teaching room on the other side. But I'm afraid it won't get done.'

As we strolled on round the edge of the island we came across circular gun pits in the ground. Rifled cannon of identical pattern to those on Steep Holm lay in the brambles. 'Look at this superb workmanship,' said David, stroking the rounded and bevelled edges of masonry. 'Those Victorians – such craftsmen. Flat Holm was one of a whole string of forts across the Bristol Channel, from Brean Down near Weston across by Steep Holm and Flat Holm to Lavernock Point, over there behind Barry. Built in the 1860s, but they were useless, really. People called them Palmerston's Follies – he was Prime Minister then. They could never have stopped French ironclads.

'These here were Moncrieff guns. Heard of them? They had spring-loaded carriages. Invented by a Scotsman – Moncrieff Disappearing Carriages. The gun popped up to fire, and the recoil pushed it back down again into the gun pit. But those rifled barrels were no good as muzzle-loaders. They had a firing test somewhere else, and the gun exploded and blew everyone in the pit to bits. So the guns were taken out of service. No use at all, but what a great idea for the carriages.'

Victorian ingenuity showed up again in the water catchment area at the south-east corner of the island. A great tiled wall like a skateboard park sloped down and curved inward to a drain hole at the bottom. Tanks in the cliff below stored the rainwater as it flowed down the drain. The whole thing will be cleaned up and put into use again to serve the accommodation due to be installed in the old barracks just above. 'Twenty-six miles of grouting to be done there,' said David. 'We've worked it out, because it's us who have got to do it all.'

Cutting back across the middle of the island we walked through the heart of the Flat Holm gull colony. In the mid-1970s there were 8000 pairs of herring and lesser black-backed gulls nesting on Flat Holm, with a comparable number across the water on Steep Holm. Since then their numbers have plummeted – due to pollution of the estuary, according to Rodney Legg; from botulism, says David Worrall. The drought summers of 1975 and 1976 killed millions of shellfish, and their rotting bodies started an epidemic among the gulls. But the black-backs are still well in evidence on Flat Holm. Gull nests lay on all sides, their brown mottled eggs on view. The parents wheeled above, diving down with high-pitched screams to zoom just above our heads. One had drawn blood from David with a passing beak-swipe the week before. Will the warden held up a dry nettle stalk as a decoy. I looked nervously up and kept ducking, holding my arm aloft – better a pecked finger than a pierced eyeball. But David strolled nonchalantly on, hands in pockets, talking about the shelduck, the rare wild leeks and the butterflies which have all found refuge on Flat Holm. In the centre of the island he stopped. 'Right, then.

You win the Smart Alec Visitor Award if you can tell me what that is.'

Looming out of a bramble bush was a strange-looking item about four feet tall, made of square blocks of grey metal sheeting mounted on slug-like puddings of concrete and a rusty grid base. On top was a flattened rhomboid of metal, which turned stiffly when pushed. The whole thing was thickly smeared with gull guano. I racked my brains. No inspiration.

'That,' said David impressively, 'is the Marconi monument.' He and Will smiled at my dropped jaw. In May 1897 Guglielmo Marconi, as a 22-year-old, had come to Flat Holm to see if his pioneering wireless communication invention would work over water. His epoch-making message, the rather prosaic 'Are you ready?', had gone from this spot across to a receiver three miles away on Lavernock Point. The Marconi monument, David Worrall told me, was created in the 1970s by a local designer, Tom Bird, to commemorate the historic achievement. It was helicoptered across to the island and successfully installed. But the helicopter crew, untutored in modern design, mistook the iron transporting frame for an integral part of the sculpture, and left it in place under the monument. The thing sits there in the centre of Flat Holm, designed by a Bird, freshly redecorated every day by birds, an object of – well, *interest* to the warden and his visitors.

Back at the farmhouse, a young PhD student had just come in from a morning's experimentation, shifting gull progeny from one nest to another to see if big eggs always produced thriving chicks. Will pointed over the scrub and elder bushes. 'All the other half of the island we're going to leave alone as semi-scrub, managing it carefully of course, for the wildlife. But this end I'm intending to cut right down and then graze with sheep and maybe some goats, get it back to the original limestone sward that was farmed for centuries. I'm looking forward to the work. I don't mind living out here at all. I'm married, but my wife lives close by on the mainland, and soon she'll be joining me for a month or two. It's a two-year contract – to start with, anyway,' said Will, grinning at David. Energy and optimism are this pair's middle names. There's only one cloud on the horizon: the as yet shadowy plans for the building of a Severn Barrage.

From the top of Steep Holm one can see, miles away to the south, the square box-shapes of the Hinkley Point nuclear power station on the Somerset shore. If present plans go ahead there will soon be a third one alongside. There is an alternative: to generate electrical power from turbines, using the enormous force of the Severn's tidal surges. The scheme for the barrage envisages a gigantic wall, pierced by turbines, running along the same line as Palmerston's Follies – Brean Down to Lavernock. ('Rodney wants a causeway built from the barrage to Steep Holm,' says David Worrall. 'Of course, they do need the money over there.') Steep Holm would be left on the seaward side of the barrage, but Flat Holm would be caught inside the wall, 'an island country park in a great watersporting lake' as David puts it. The whole tidal, sea-flavoured character of the island would be bound to change. The prospect causes heartache and anger among many Flat Holm Society members, but it doesn't really worry their forward-looking project director. For him Flat Holm is a challenge, a place of boundless opportunity where local people can indulge their Robinson Crusoe fantasies while he, Will Sandison and their eager volunteers set about opening the visitors' eyes to the richness of the island.

The narrowing throat of the Severn estuary all but swallows the twin morsels of Steep Holm and Flat Holm. But Lundy Island rises magnificently free, twenty miles west of Morte Point where the lower lip of the Bristol Channel turns down into the long peninsular chin of England. Seen on a clear day from the high ground of this corner of North Devon, Lundy's far-off cliffs catch the morning sun and gleam in a tiny line on the sea horizon – an Atlantic island, rather than a British one, alone in a great disc of water.

On the day of my visit, however, heat haze lay thickly over land and sea. Lundy was hidden in a soft white blanket. I had a scramble to reach the MV *Oldenburg* in time for her morning sailing from Ilfracombe, scurrying on board with one minute to spare. *Oldenburg* doesn't wait for stragglers. In contrast to the open boats that serve Steep Holm and Flat Holm, she's a trim little ship of 300 tons with three decks, capable of carrying more than 250 passengers, built originally to ply from the German coast to the Frisian Islands and Heligoland. Her shallow draught makes her lively in any kind of a swell. The week before, according to the crew, everyone had been horribly sick during the two-hour trip out to Lundy in a Force 6. But today was flat calm. Slowly the island shaped up out of the haze, a three-mile bar of grey rock under a cap of green, lying north and south, the towers of St Helena's Church and the Old Light standing tall, granite cliffs gleaming in the sun. There's only one landing place on Lundy, down at the south end in the shelter of Rat Island. *Oldenburg* rattled out her anchor, and the island boat ferried us ashore in batches to trudge up the steep path to Lundy's cluster of houses at the top. Now the position was reversed: the mainland lay hidden in the haze, and the substantial world had shrunk to the green back and grey flanks of Lundy.

Granite forms Lundy's character, first and last. You leave the soft, warm sandstone of Exmoor to land on what might be a chunk sliced off the Cornish coast. There's a hard edge to the island, its granite buildings, granite field walls and granite cliffs. Your boots crunch and ring on granite scars and outcrops in the thin skin of turf and heather, which sparkles with crystal brightness. The island is a single bar of granite, cooled magma from a subterranean upflow fifty million years ago. A land bridge stretched to the mainland until it was drowned by rising sea levels caused by the melting of Ice Age glaciers. Perhaps across that bridge, perhaps later, primitive people came over to Lundy to make what they could of life in such isolation. Bronze Age settlers left hut circles and flint tools. Christian missionaries came at the start of the Dark Ages, and left their inscribed gravestones. The Norsemen named it Lundy, or Puffin Island. The Norman de Marisco family held it from the Conquest for two centuries, until William de Marisco got on the wrong side of Henry III and was hung, drawn and quartered. King Henry then set his own stamp on Lundy by building a stumpy granite castle, which 400 years later proved loyal to the crown – the last Royalist stronghold in the kingdom. Pirates and brigands used Lundy as a base for operations. Owners came and went, not all of them upright citizens. One diverted transported convicts from their New World destinations to work for him on Lundy; another used the island as a gambling counter one night at the tables, and lost. A rich and wild history, played out far from mainland rules and restrictions, punctuated down the years by the shipwrecks for which Lundy has always been a powerful magnet.

The granite beneath the grass made short work of my flimsy metal tent pegs as I tried to hammer them in. Camping and misery are synonymous in my personal dictionary, but every bed on Lundy was booked up. Under nylon was the only way I could spend a night on the island. An hour's solid cursing had the tiny one-man tent up, after a fashion, on a patch of pineapple mayweed whose sweetly acid smell didn't quite make up for its lumpiness. Then I set off along the three-mile track to the northern tip of Lundy. The island is quartered by three stone walls, and runs from smooth grazing and hay fields in the south end to a wilder landscape as the cliffs converge towards the north. Heather, bracken, sedgy moorland and granite outcrops weathered into bizarre shapes fall to the white tower of the lighthouse on the north end of Lundy, sheltered under the cliffs above a confused length of tide-rips and races. Walking back along Lundy's west side, I followed a sheep path above cliffs that sloped in green and then plunged in grey, 400 feet down to the sea. A deeply indented, savage succession of stacks and pinnacles, carved by the Atlantic surge of wave and wind. *Oldenburg* had left Lundy an hour before to take the day visitors back to Ilfracombe, and there was no one else in sight. In spite of the sunshine the Old Light looked bleak, a stark granite tower above a stern, small-windowed keeper's house. It came as no surprise to learn that the Old Light had been designed back in the early nineteenth century by the architect of Dartmoor Prison. These days the warning lights of Lundy shine only from the north and south ends. The Old Light, too high up to be seen by shipping in fogs, lives on in retirement as a holiday home.

In the graveyard beside the old tower I found the gravestones of those early Christian settlers standing on end against the wall, their inscriptions weathered beyond deciphering. More recent proprietors of Lundy lay here, too, their stone crosses and tombs smothered in bracken – William Hudson Heaven, Hudson Grosett Heaven and Walter Heaven. Father, son and grandson, they ruled as lords of Lundy from early Victorian times until the end of the First World War. William Heaven bought the island, built houses, made roads, planted trees and cultivated as much of the land as he could. Hudson Heaven was Vicar of Lundy and built the church of St Helena. Lundy in their day was known as the Kingdom of Heaven. The Harman family followed them as rulers of Lundy, and lie beside them in the overgrown graveyard – Martin Harman, his wife Amy Ruth, and their son Albion Pennington Harman, who died in 1968. Next to these memorials are others: to Edith Gade, 'known as "Cheerful"', and her husband Felix Gade, 'known as "Giant"'. The Heavens and the Harmans between them steered Lundy through more than a century of family ownership, into the arms of the Landmark Trust. When Lundy came up for sale following the death of Albion Harman, the Landmark Trust had been in existence for just a couple of years, its aim to buy up and maintain as holiday homes places that were in danger of disintegration. Lundy fulfilled that qualification. The buildings were in disrepair, the roads and walls full of holes, the fields neglected. The Landmark Trust saw its opportunity, initiated a public appeal to buy the island, turned it over to the National Trust and then leased it back. Twenty years of hard labour followed, gradually restoring the buildings, revitalizing the pub and shop, introducing their own employees as a permanent staff who would work the island up into an attractive prospect for tourists and long-stay holidaymakers.

All but one of Lundy's buildings lie in the southernmost quarter of the island, most of them packed into a tight little huddle, 'the village'. Here are the old schoolhouse, the fridge and radio rooms that have been done up for visitors; also the generator houses and farm buildings that keep the island running. The Marisco Tavern is the social centre of Lundy, a stone-flagged, cool granite building which also incorporates the island shop, restaurant and Trust offices. The walls are hung with lifebelts, marked with the names and dates of the wrecks they came from – *Maria Kyriakides*, 27.3.29; *Amstelstroom*, 18 July 1948. In spite of these *mementi mori* it's a cheerful place. Singing evenings, heroic Christmas feasts and social gatherings all take place here, fuelled by the sweet and powerful 'Puffin Purge' bitter brewed in the tiny brewery across the lane. Day visitors and holidaymakers drink and eat in the tavern, as do the twenty or so people who make up Lundy's all-year-round community: the tavern manager, the shopkeeper, farmer and farm manager, foreman and builder, engineer and domestic staff who look after the holiday houses. All but one are incomers, employees of the Lundy Island Company through which the Landmark Trust runs the island.

It's a relaxed and co-operative group of people, but as a community it has its limitations. There is no provision on Lundy for retired people, so a whole elderly generation is conspicuously absent. Lundy as an island cannot support itself – there's no fresh-water spring capable of serving a community, no doctor, no social services in the mainland sense. The multitude of rabbits all over the island prevents any self-supporting agriculture from getting established. Fresh vegetables, furniture, canned

66

food, all the basic necessities have to come over those twenty miles of sea on board *Oldenburg*. And, most destructive of all to a small society, Lundy has no school. Families with school-age children find it impossible to stay. When I met the Landmark Trust's agent, John Puddy, for an evening drink in the Marisco Tavern, he told me about the difficult decisions he and his wife will soon have to face over the schooling of their daughter.

'Emma's only eight months old now, still a baby, but we've got to think about it. We could teach her at home till she's eleven, but then she'd have to go off, perhaps to a State boarding school in North Devon. Not having a school here is one of the main drawbacks to establishing a proper Lundy community. A family with two young boys has just left because the parents couldn't see any other solution. As employees of the company it's hard to think of ourselves as a real village. Most of us look on Lundy as a place to work. It's a bit like having an overseas posting – do your time, and then leave. You can't retire here. We can't plan for the next generation – only till the end of our jobs. It's a holiday island, pure and simple.'

John Puddy has certainly done his best to make the island a going proposition. When he was appointed agent in the early 1980s, his first act was to go to the opposite end of Britain, to Fair Isle in the Shetlands, to have a look at how their wind generator worked. Then he came back and put one up on Lundy. He's experimented with hardy Scottish cattle. They stood up well to the harsh conditions of a Lundy winter, but the dealers of Devon were more than suspicious. 'When we took the cattle across on the boat to market, they took one look and said, "What's *that?*" It's not too bad for the Scottish islands, because they're competing with mainland farmers who have the same sort of problems of bad weather, bad land and so on. But out here we're in competition with those rich Devon farmers and all their advantages. It doesn't work out.'

When John and his wife came to Lundy in 1980 there was no electricity and many of the buildings were falling down. The Landmark Trust's pioneers lived in an unhealthily claustrophobic atmosphere, particularly in the winter when the island shut down and very few visitors came. These days Lundy has electricity from its own generators, water from its own rain catchment areas. Most of the buildings have been done up to a very high standard. More than anything, though, it was the purchase of *Oldenburg* in 1985 that made it possible to develop the new life of the island.

'That boat has made all the difference,' John said with enthusiasm. 'Beforehand we had the *Polar Bear*. A good boat, but she could only carry twelve passengers, and she might take five hours to do the crossing. In rough weather that was no joke, I can tell you. Day trips weren't really on. But the *Oldenburg* is a part of the island, a vital one. She's expensive to run and maintain, but she only loses about as much money as *Polar Bear*, and she's had a major effect on Lundy's economy. Turnover has increased tremendously. We had about 12,000 visitors last year, paying £10 a head here and £10 back, and spending in the shop and tavern. Now we've got the *Oldenburg* I think the island's future is probably secure.'

Walking back to the camping field I looked out to the horizon to see a faint dusting of lights around Ilfracombe, and the single flash of the North Foreland lighthouse beyond. I crawled into the tent at midnight, and didn't wake up until the sparrows began scratching their claws on the roof above my head. Another hazy, burning day. The Lundy workers were as busy as bees by eight o'clock, roaring around on tractors, sweeping and cleaning the tavern, drilling the chimneys off the old signal cottage beside the castle that had been condemned to demolition for spoiling the view from the village. I forced the tent off the mayweed and into its impossibly small container, and walked down on to a path along the east cliffs that wandered through the thickets of rhododendrons, sycamores and oaks planted back in those days of Heaven. Gigantic foxgloves grew horizontally in long green spikes out of the banks, reaching into pools of sunlight where they turned up their tips and sprouted a burst of purple bells. Sika deer rustled and crashed away in the rhododendron bushes, showing an occasional flash of brown back. Out at sea *Oldenburg* appeared out of the haze, a dark, purposeful dot trailing a white arrow of wake. I climbed up to a pond in a roughly hewn bowl of the cliffs, where goldfish were swimming lazily in a group just under the surface, warming their spines. Nearby stood a little hut with a plaque in its wall to Felix 'Giant' Gade. Felix had been agent to the Harman family, a tall, energetic man dedicated to Lundy. His daughter Mary still lives on the island, working for the Lundy Island Company at anything she is asked to turn her hand to. Mary has seen all Lundy's changes through the forty years she has stayed here, by far the longest-resident inhabitant. Back in the Marisco Tavern she took a few minutes away from her kitchen duties to chat.

'I was born on the mainland, but came back to Lundy at two weeks old. The only time I was away was when my children were school age. Before the war there were very few visitors – just those who rented a couple of cottages from the Harmans. There was more arable land then, and the visitors would be roped in for potato picking and harvesting. Everyone lent a hand. The Bideford shopkeepers, grocers and butchers and so on were marvellous to us; they allowed us credit all the way through the winter, and we'd kill a few sheep in the spring to pay off the debts.'

Henry Williamson, author of *Tarka the Otter* and many other books set in North Devon, was living near Bideford then. It was Williamson's magical evocation of Lundy in the opening chapters of *Salar the Salmon* that first made me aware of the island. Mary Gade knew him well. 'Oh, Henry was a great friend of my father's. They looked rather similar, tall and eccentric. It was always a question whose jacket was tattier than whose!'

The war years on Lundy were Mary Gade's happiest. 'During the war was the best time ever. There were no people. For a long time it was just my parents and me, though the government did give us a Fordson tractor and sent Land Girls over to help. We had a potato mountain – they were dyed purple and fed to the cattle. The Royal Navy had a watching post in the Old Light, and they and the lighthouse keepers were very good friends to the island, helping us and mucking in with the farm work. We lived a very isolated life then; my daughter was three and a half before she went to the mainland for the first time. I remember how amazed she was to see the buses and trains.'

In those days the island women did every kind of job – working the boats, tending the animals, digging and harvesting. Mary herself has worked as a farmhand and a boat-hand, waitress and chambermaid, cook and gardener, construction navvy and tractor driver. She regrets the domestic flavour of her work for the Lundy Island Company today.

'I enjoyed it most,' she said decisively, 'when life was harder. We had no modern amenities, and we had to work hard to survive. But we were closer to the animals, to the land. These days it's not so sociable on Lundy. There seems to be no time any more for that sort of thing. But there's no doubt that things were run down at the end of the Harmans' time. Islands swallow money, you know. If you want to be a poor man – buy an island.'

Oldenburg had disgorged its new load of day visitors by the time I had strolled down to the southern end of Lundy once more. They came straggling up the cliff road, looking forward to lunch in the Marisco Tavern. Four hours' grace before the homeward trip. I found a sunny niche above the landing beach, put my back against a rock and basked like a lizard in the sunshine.

6. Caldey, Ramsey, Skokholm, Skomer and Hilbre

THE LITTLE ISLANDS OF WALES

On the upper margin of the Bristol Channel the little islands cluster off the south-west tip of Wales. Each has its seabirds, and each has its saints – some of them lost in Dark Ages mists, and some of them still struggling on through the fogs of our own dark age.

Thirty miles due north of Lundy lies Caldey Island off the southern Pembrokeshire coast. In 1987 Caldey hit the headlines. The monks of the island's Cistercian monastery had appealed to the Pope through their Abbot General to be allowed to stay on Caldey. Monastic involvement with the island stretched back fourteen centuries, but now it looked as though the end might be in sight. No young men had applied to join for several years, and the resident Brothers, fewer than ten of them, were not getting any younger. None was under fifty; most of them were well into their sixties and seventies. Three miles off Tenby, in the face of Atlantic gales, Caldey was a tough place to live, liable to be cut off for weeks at a time in winter. The monks had diversified in order to keep going – they ran a farm and a guest house, made perfume and chocolate, welcomed visitors on retreat, allowed day trippers to swarm over the island. But the demands of monastic life itself had not changed. Its rigours, both physical and spiritual, were proving too much for the youngsters so badly needed by the community. They came, they saw, they found themselves conquered by those demands – and they left, carrying all that youthful energy back to the mainland with them.

Caldey is a lovely island, in some ways the epitome of the universal island dream. Approaching in a leaping open boat from Tenby, I marvelled at the beauty of Caldey's long profile: two miles of rocky cliffs, yellow beaches, wooded slopes where the red-tiled roofs of the monastery buildings peeped over the treetops. Calm and green, it looked the ideal place to retreat and pull up the drawbridge after you. Practical life was very much in evidence as I landed, though. The jetty was an ingenious piece of do-it-yourself, made of three concrete barges left over from the D-Day landings, jammed together in a corner of Priory Bay. On the jetty a bearded monk was catching boxes of supplies thrown up to him by the

71

boatman. Day visitors in luminous Bermuda shorts were clustered round the tea room and packed into the perfume shop. Caldey perfume is no longer made from flowers picked on the island, but it *is* still made by the monks; hence its great appeal, though it smells pretty good as a bonus. Fern, Gorse and Island Bouquet were selling well, as was Caldey For Men. The bars of monk-made chocolate glittered in their silver and gold wrappers. I tried some and found it smooth and delicious, far tastier than anything on the mainland so modestly priced. I admired the quality of the monks' workmanship, while at the same time feeling rather priggishly uncomfortable about their servicing of Pride and Gluttony. That didn't stop me filling a bag with a good helping of both to take home.

Caldey has a long history of human occupation, perhaps the longest in West Wales. The monastic influence is a long-lived one, too. Saint Pŷr, the first recorded monk to settle on the island, arrived in the first years of the 6th century AD, probably before Columba left Ireland for Iona. Saint Pŷr is a shadowy figure, with only a dubious legend to flesh him out. The story goes that he drowned after falling into a pond, dead drunk. Not an auspicious beginning, and the Caldey community has had its share of problems in this century. Around 1900 the island was offered for sale as a drying-out retreat for alcoholics, on much the same lines as Osea Island in Essex. It was bought and the buildings restored by a Harrow schoolmaster, the Revd Donne Bushell, who turned it over to the Benedictine order in 1906. The monks renounced their Anglicanism before the First World War; their Abbot was a strange, colourful man who seems to have been both a wild spendthrift and a fierce taskmaster. Fifteen uneasy years of Catholicism followed, until in 1928 the monks left Caldey to set up a new monastery at Prinknash in Gloucestershire. They sold Caldey Island to the Cistercians who live there today.

Brother Robert, the present-day community's Abbot, met me with a hard handshake in a quiet, panelled room of the monastery's guest house. Brother Robert wore a black and white habit, greasy with work stains around the cuffs, and was magnificently bearded. 'They'll like you at the monastery,' the Tenby boatman had told me on the way over, 'they go in for beards up there.' Several times during our chat Brother Robert threw back his head and roared with laughter, his eyes disappearing in wrinkles of amusement, his beard pointing to the ceiling. He's a humorous, direct man, though forgetful enough to have urged me to send him a postcard a few days before our meeting to remind him to turn up. I suspect he is quietly amused at the electronic gadget that plays Handel's 'Thine is the Glory' to fill in gaps in telephone communications with his office.

There had been a tremendous response to that appeal for a stay of execution in 1987, he told me. Hearing of the monastery's ageing community and its 'romantic' island setting, hundreds had applied to join. 'A lot of completely unsuitable people applied – Buddhists, for example, and married men. A lot of people attracted to the romance of a quiet life on a beautiful Welsh island. They had absolutely no idea,' said Brother Robert, smiling and shaking his head. 'You don't come here to lead a beautiful life full of beautiful thoughts. It's real, and hard. However, we did get ten who eventually started as postulants, and six of those became novices. Those six have now been whittled down to three, of whom one is going to be professed next September. They will boost our community up to ten, and they'll also do a lot of good in lowering the average age; at fifty-six I'm the youngest, and these three men are between thirty and fifty. But young men in their twenties – well, they just don't seem to be able to face themselves nowadays. It's my biggest fear for the future of this community.'

The Caldey monks live close to nature, inevitably on such a small island, and they find their moods changing in tune with the seasons. 'In February everyone is low and depressed. You look outside and see no leaves on the trees, no flowers, no animals, and you think – eeeugh! Then in spring it's – bang! Where are all the visitors? Let's get up and go! At the fruitful time, when everything's dropping off the trees and plants, I find I just want to drop off, too.'

Brother Robert sees cycles of recurring discipline and licence in human history, which directly affect the number of applicants to join the order at any given time. He pointed to the discipline of the late Victorian era following on from the naughty early 19th century, the drift to permissiveness of the Edwardians, the tightened belts of the thirties and the post-war relaxation. 'I was young during the war; those were my formative years,' he said, gripping his beard and stroking it through his palm in reflection. 'I think I'm probably therefore more in tune with that optimism, that sense of being British and In The Right, that we were encouraged to believe in by all the propaganda. It gave me a belief in myself.'

It's the lack of self-belief in today's young people that upsets and saddens Brother Robert; not self-belief in an arrogant sense, but a willingness to face up to the truth about oneself. He told me of one young novice whose veneer of sophistication and contemptuousness of the simple teaching of the older monks had driven them all to despair.

'This young man complained that we were not teaching him anything. We tried to tell him that we were teaching him all we knew, but he dismissed it all as rubbish. I can hear him saying it now – rubbish! Some of the other Brothers wanted me to confront him, to break him, but I could see it was all just a front. And when I did point out to him that he really knew nothing, he burst out: "But that means I can't trust myself! Or God!" I said to him, "God you can trust. But yourself – well, no." And I saw that young man literally collapse in front of me, deflate before my eyes. He was looking inward at his own emptiness for the first time. I told him to hold on, and just to reflect on what I'd said – that this was the realization he had to come to, that he was only an empty vessel, before he could begin to let God in to fill the void. But next day he was gone. None of the young people who have wanted to join us has been able to face their own emptiness; yet it's only when you do that, that you can really begin to make sense of this life. It doesn't get any easier, either – just a bit less incomprehensible. We all try to slide it off on to each other: it's *their* fault, *their* wrong attitude. But in the end you have to be honest and look at your own emptiness to begin to find God.'

Life on a small island intensifies that self-examination. There are all the distractions of the visitors, the perfume and chocolate business, the telephone, the constant intrusion of the outside world. They dilute the severity of life in the Caldey Island monastery, to some extent, while at the same time making the prayer and inward searching more powerful and painful by comparison.

'There are parallels between island life and monastic life,' Brother Robert observed as he got up to sort out a flood in the guest house fridge; another hour, another demand. 'Both look like places of escape, but in fact they are places where you have to face up to yourself, because there's no running away.'

It was the simplest and profoundest summing-up of island life that I heard anywhere in the other British isles.

This was not the moment for the normal courtesies. 'Door!' shouted Derek Rees as he sheared through the last connecting string of wool. The shaggy mat of fleece peeled away on to the floor of the shed, and an enormous naked ewe sprang up and out from between his knees. 'Open the f—ing door, man, quick!'

I wrenched at the half-height door, jammed fast on a wedge of sheep-shit and greasy wool. The ewe, maddened by her five minutes' tickling with the electric shears, charged round behind Derek and slipped over. Her little pointed hooves scrabbled frantically in the slough of dung and wool clippings. 'Door, Chris, for Christ's sake!' yelled Derek as Arnold Boorman staggered in with another struggling giant clasped to his sweaty chest. I gulped, and yanked at the door. It scraped back, and the shorn ewe slalomed out on her side. In the yard she jumped up, none the worse for wear, and released all her pent-up emotions in a catapulting spring, clean over a four-foot fence, to join the head-shaking, bleating, disgruntled crowd already stripped of their disguise by Derek and his shearing gang. In the sunlight the knock knees, fallen arches, skinny ribs and sagging bellies of the sheep were mercilessly exposed to view.

'You want to whip that bloody door open quickly, Chris,' advised Derek, straightening his bare, glistening torso and sweeping half a pint of sweat from his forehead with the back of his hand. 'Let them see the light as soon as I let them go.' Arnold lit two cigarettes and slotted one between Derek's lips as he bent again to start unzipping the fleece from his thirty-sixth sheep of the day. I was learning, lesson by lesson, the realities of my allotted job as doorman and tally keeper at the summer shearing of the Ramsey Island flock. At such cathartic times in the island calendar any pair of hands, however clumsily inexperienced, is better than none. 'You'll get sworn at – everyone does,' Sue Ward, the island's manager, had warned the previous evening when I had volunteered to help round up the 210 Ramsey sheep. Never mind. Such curses are more satisfyingly earned than many a honeyed word elsewhere.

Ramsey lies a mile off the most westerly point of Wales, south of St David's Head. The sheep have free range over Ramsey's two-mile length, the ledges of its cliffs and the slopes of its two miniature mountains.

Peddling life insurance to Ramsey Island sheep would be a thankless task. Security is theirs already. No butcher's block awaits them at the end of their span of usefulness to man. Instead of the slaughterhouse, they are shipped off to an old sheep's home in Warwickshire, to nibble out their declining years in the dignity of retirement. The terms of the Trust that administers Ramsey on behalf of its owners stipulate that nothing shall be killed on the island: not a sheep, not a bird, not a rat or rabbit – and there are plenty of those. Ramsey is designated a Site of Special Scientific Interest, too, and is under a covenant of the National Trust. It's also part of the Pembrokeshire National Park. The island may enjoy isolation, lying on the far side of a water barrier, but many watchful eyes are bent on these 700 acres in the sea.

It's as hard today to make a proper living on Ramsey as it has ever been. The several thousand island rabbits, their lives protected, put paid with their incisors to any possibility of arable farming. Ramsey wool can be turned into profit, but Ramsey mutton cannot. The little herd of red deer, introduced under a different régime a few years ago for venison farming, now wanders unharmed across the island. As for tourism – there is only one substantial jetty on Ramsey, a concrete wall joining an offshore islet to the island. The ferrying boats are small. And the churlishness of one or two previous tenants has given local mainlanders the idea that Ramsey is still a no-go area.

There is an illustrious precedent for sour temper on the part of Ramsey inhabitants. Saint Justinian, if the stories about him can be believed, was the most intractable of the lot, a 5th-century Breton of noble birth with an unpleasantly imperious streak. When he arrived to inspect the island, he found one Honorius and his sister already in residence along with their maidservant. The two women had to be banished to the mainland before the saint would agree to live on Ramsey. The demons that so regularly tormented island-dwelling saints in the Dark Ages had their work cut out to get the better of Justinian. On one occasion, having taken on the appearance of boatmen, they had the saint in their power in the middle of Ramsey Sound. Justinian, however, realizing that not even the wild, heathen Welsh could look quite as ugly as this trio, leaped to his feet in the nick of time, reciting the 79th Psalm:

May the groans of the captive reach you;
by your mighty arm rescue those doomed to die!

Pay our neighbours sevenfold, strike to the heart
For the monstrous insult proffered to you, Lord!

The boatmen saw that the game was up, sprouted black wings and
beaks, and flew away like a flock of crows. The demons got Justinian in
the end, though, through the agency of three of his monks. Enraged by
their leader's accusation of idleness, they seized him and cut off his head.
The saint kept his cool, even in this extremity. He calmly picked up his
severed head and walked with it across the sound to his burial place on
the mainland. The three murderers were paid out for their crime with
the affliction of leprosy. From the spot where Justinian's head hit the
earth sprang an unquenchable spring of water – the same spring that
feeds the island's farmhouse today. If the saint's prayers had been a little
less effective, his headless walk could have been made dry-shod. It was
Justinian who had prayed for the rocky isthmus joining Ramsey to the
mainland to disappear, so as to leave him in even greater isolation.

Whether or not due to the prayerfulness of Justinian, the notorious
Ramsey Sound has always been a problem for would-be dwellers on the
island. On the Friday evening before my weekend visit to Ramsey, I
walked a circuit of the mainland cliffs overlooking the channel. It was
calm, sunny weather, yet as a background to the walk there was a
continuous churning and roaring from the tide in the sound. Tide is too
mild a description. In the centre of the channel between island and
mainland, a curving highway of white water forged irresistibly northwards
at twenty miles an hour or more. I watched two canoeists charging the
jets of foam between the Bitches, a reef of rocks just off Ramsey. Tiring
of the buffeting, they allowed their little craft to fall away into that
central tidal race, and in a couple of minutes had been swept a mile
through the channel and were fluorescent orange dots in the widening
sea. The race was flanked by comparatively calm waters, yet even
in those I could see whirlpools, contrary rips, surges and eddies round
just-submerged rocks. Ramsey islanders' accounts of winter in the sound in
the days of oar and sail tell of crossings that took all morning to conquer
that mile of water. Down the centuries Ramsey Sound, capable of violence
at any season, has meant a constant struggle for the Ramsey farmers to

get their produce to market. The island has never supported a farming community, just a single farm doing the best it can. One by one the farmers have tried, failed and withdrawn to lick their financial wounds. Today, though, as a privately owned nature reserve beginning to court the tourist trade, Ramsey Island is grasping at a new kind of lifeline.

On Saturday morning Bob Millidine and his sister Tricia were waiting for me in a big inflatable boat by the lifeboat ramp at St Justinian's, a couple of miles west of St David's. Bob and Tricia, a young couple from Kent, had been appointed as wardens of Ramsey a few months before. Sue Ward, the manager of the island, came down to join the boat, and we roared out to smack our way across the race and into the calm water by the Ramsey jetty. A steep path led up to the square white farmhouse overlooking the sound where the Millidines live, and around which all the social and working events on Ramsey revolve. There was just time for Tricia to put a cup of tea in front of me before a landing party arrived looking for lunch. In the kitchen we sliced, buttered and piled up enough sandwiches to feed a Harvest Home. The visiting party ate, drank and moved on, to be replaced by Derek Rees and Arnold Boorman, who had come over with their dogs to help gather the sheep for the Sunday shearing. The big kitchen table was ringed with brown faces, and with brown hands holding cigarettes and mugs of tea. 'We'll clear them off the south end first,' Derek advised, 'then bring them all in from the north.'

We fanned out from the farmhouse in twos and threes, working down across the southern end of the island. The Ramsey sheep form several social groups and stick to their own particular friends, Sue Ward told me as we tramped over the heather and bracken. They would follow their leaders manageably enough if we hung back, influencing their course from afar rather than trying to chase them. Sue has been a sheep farmer for more years than she cares to reveal, and is wise in their infuriating ways. Her appointment as manager of Ramsey was the fulfilment of a lifelong love affair with islands that began with childhood visits to nearby Skomer. She never stopped dreaming of working an island farm one day. If the present owners hadn't bought Ramsey in 1981, she would have done so. All the same, she is realistic about island life. 'The weather is so frustrating,' she said as we slowly steered sheep in single file along the cliff edge. 'There are always things to do, but often one simply can't get on with them because of the weather. Rain never falls vertically here; it comes at you horizontally. And everything takes twice as long. That's what a lot of people who try island life fail to realize. If there's a breakdown with a piece of farm machinery, you either have to go to the mainland for the part, which is half a day wasted, or you make it yourself. You can't just pop out to the shop. It's all a matter of planning and foresight. Ramsey won't provide the three of us with a living through farming, though, as you can see – look at what these blessed rabbits have done.' She kicked at a bare patch of brown, matted grass, nibbled down to the rock.

'Did you know that there's supposed to be a Curse of Ramsey? Yes – several owners have met untimely deaths. I don't believe in that sort of thing myself, but I do think that islands have personalities. Ramsey's is benign, I'm sure of it. The reward of this job for me is just being here. One day I'd love to come and live on the island permanently. But,' she murmured cautiously, 'who knows? I'll have to see how I get on as manager. Come on – mustn't let those sheep split up.'

Gradually we urged the sheep into a single group at the northern end of the island. They disappeared behind a rocky knoll, followed by Derek Rees and his young dog, Spot. Then the fun began. I was stationed in one of the many gaps in the stone wall that runs most of the length of Ramsey, with orders from Derek to walk the sheep gently down to the yard once they appeared. I stared up the slope towards the knoll, and waited. Half an hour passed in the level sunlight. I was watching Arnold running across the slopes of the knoll to head off a breakaway party of sheep, when the main body came suddenly into view 300 yards below me. Derek and Sue came running behind them, shouting and waving frantically. I couldn't make out a word at that distance, but was soon enlightened. The ovine vanguard went streaming through a gap in the wall that I'd failed to spot. I threw off my coat and ran like a madman over tussocks and heather, faster than I'd run since school, to try and turn them back. The island's red deer herd had joined the rout, bounding off alongside the sheep – a beautiful sight, but I had no eyes for it. With red-hot lungs and flailing arms I got to the gap in the wall. The onrushing sheep skidded to a halt, staring at me with horror. They bucked round and went wobbling back again on their little black chorus-girl legs, their overloaded wool coats bouncing. Spot ran and snapped, Derek ran and cursed, Sue ran and saved her breath. The sheep flooded into their proper path, and went jostling down through the gate and into the yard by the shearing shed. We slammed the gate after them, wedging it shut with planks, and leaned exhausted over the top of it to admire our captives. Ten or so had got away with the deer, but most were safely gathered in. The over-enthusiastic Spot, who had ignored Derek's orders throughout, got the tongue-lashing that I felt I should have shared. 'Too bad about those escapers,' said Sue. 'We'll pick them up in the morning. They'll probably come to the shed anyway, once we start shearing. Sheep are very inquisitive animals.'

Later on we lay drinking beer on the grass of the farmhouse garden, while the fulmars in their cliff nests chided us for our noise and laughter. The stories came out, one after another, staple stuff of island talk.

'I'll tell you a funny story, now,' Derek Rees began, peeling open a fresh can of lager. 'Rob Davies – you know him – he had an old ewe that was always leading breakouts. Well, one day she'd got out through a gap and was in the field along with about twelve others. Rob happened to have his rifle with him that day. He waited till all the others had come back through the gap, and then he just lifted the rifle and plugged that ewe, smack between the eyes, and she fell over dead right in the gap. Rob said to me, "I had to go off to market, you see, so I left her lying. She just filled that gap nicely."' Derek's creased, sunburned face broke across in a grin. 'I thought that was rather an expensive move. A couple of boulders would have done the job.' Our laughter sent the fulmars barking round in circles over our heads.

Derek had to go off the island to meet his wife, but he came back to Ramsey with her at one o'clock in the morning over the pitch-black sound, long after I had reeled away from the living-room party to find my bed. Next day we got down to business. Bleating and jostling in their heavy coats, 198 Ramsey sheep went in at one end of the shearing shed, and came tittuping out naked at the other. Stripped to the waist in the sweltering shed, Derek notched up a personal tally of 66 fleeces. Three other shearers came across to help and accounted between them for 126 more. Sue Ward sheared the remaining six. I know these figures, because I marked them all down throughout the long day, in purple wax marking stick on the shed wall. The number of curses, of half-throttled sheep and trodden-on toes, of cigarettes smoked and beers drunk, went mercifully untallied. I got into Bob's inflatable for the trip back to St

Justinian's tired beyond telling, smeared with wool grease and dung, my head ringing with baas and beers, my fingers purple to the wrists. Two days of sheer delight.

From my bed-and-breakfast place on the mainland I phoned home, and found myself on the road ten minutes later, back to earth with a bump. Jane was ill, and I was needed. Out of the window went my plans to travel among the cluster of islands off the south-western point of Pembrokeshire – Skomer, Skokholm and Grassholm. Island journeying, with its boat, train and plane connections and its enormous distances between objectives, doesn't easily allow for such changes of plan. When at last I found myself free to make that Pembrokeshire trip again, a whole year of travel through the islands of Scotland and northern England had gone by. I never did voyage the seven miles out to remote Grassholm and its great gannet colony, though I saw it from the cliffs of Skokholm and Skomer lying white-topped and remote across the sea. But with a feeling of anticipation too long delayed I got myself at last within range of the other two islands.

Skokholm Island was familiar ground to me long before I set foot on it. I had battled the winter treacheries of Jack Sound in an open boat, rebuilt the island farmhouse with timber salvaged from a wreck, herded goats and studied the Manx shearwater in its burrow, all in a single night's luxurious read of Ronald Lockley's *Dream Island*. I couldn't put the book down.

Lockley had lived on Skokholm between 1927 and the Second World War, and this was his account of his early years here, the passionate testament of a young man in thrall. If ever there was a love affair between man and island, with all of love's strifes and struggles, it was between Ronald Lockley and Skokholm. Like a lover he cut all former ties and plunged headlong into the adventure, buoyed up by dreams, hopes and curiosity. For thirteen years he worked like a demon to keep things going on Skokholm. He marketed the island rabbits, plundered a wreck for materials to make the farmhouse habitable, knocked up furniture out of driftwood, sold shellfish in home-made pots, made one bucketing trip after another in his tiny boat *Storm Petrel* in ferocious gales through the tide-rips and rocks between the island and the mainland. His accounts

81

of these terrifying journeys, full of snapped oars, white mountainous seas and vomiting companions, had my landlubber's heart pounding as I lay reading in bed.

The high-voltage energy of the man sparked and crackled from the pages of *Dream Island*. In spite of the title of his book, Ronald Lockley was no dreamer. During his time on Skokholm he established Britain's first bird observatory, and made pioneer first-hand studies of puffins, rabbits and the Manx shearwaters that colonized the island. Lockley's wife, Doris, was more than a match for her livewire husband. She had gladly spent her honeymoon among the nesting gannets on Grassholm, seven miles out in the Irish Sea, during which the happy couple, as Lockley records, submitted to repeated peckings and drenchings in regurgitated fish oil – not every young bride's honeymoon dream. But all was wonderful to the young Lockleys. The honeymoon gave rise to one of the purpler passages in a book not starved of them:

> All night long the north wind soughed and sighed, saying, 'It is well, I blow softly; no other wind dares me. Sleep thou, thy boat is safe, the moorings are listless in the calm water . . .'

Ronald and Doris cut replaceable turf trapdoors in the roofs of the shearwaters' burrows on Skokholm so that they could watch the progress of the eggs. Lockley described the abandonment of the shearwater chicks by their parents, their hazardous night crawl to the sea over terrain patrolled from daybreak onward by hungry black-backed gulls, crows, buzzards and herring gulls. Such observations shed light in dark corners of the bird world. *Dream Island* was published in 1930, and by the time the Lockleys left Skokholm had become a classic of its kind.

Ronald Lockley lives in New Zealand today, but his influence is still strong on Skokholm Island. The first thing I saw on the dusky red sandstone cliffs was the skyward-gazing figurehead from the wrecked coal boat *Alice Williams*, still in position where Lockley had placed her sixty years before: 'Alice Williams herself, the serene and lovely figurehead of the schooner, dressed, as she was first conceived, in the fashion of the eighteen-fifties.'

On a plateau of green ground above the island's landing place, the kitchen and dining room building still displayed *Alice Williams*'s brass-bound wheel where Lockley had set it over the hearth; though there was no sign of his ingenious arrangement of chains by which a turn of the wheel would lower a kettle on to the fire. The nearby farmhouse that Lockley had restored was full of his handiwork. The timbers that he saved from *Alice Williams* survived in its ceiling, beams, floors and fireplace surround. On the wall was a coloured photograph of the man himself sitting modestly on a wall, taken when he came to visit Skokholm in 1988. 'He's well over eighty,' said Michael Betts, one of Skokholm's two wardens, 'but he was marvellous. Came straight up and introduced himself, and wanted to know everything that was going on. And once he started on the stories of his time here – we heard the lot. And I mean the *lot!*'

It was a thrill to see so many bits and pieces described in *Dream Island* still in use and valued for their association with Ronald Lockley; still more of a pleasure to see how the spirit of his enterprise is kept vigorous on Skokholm. The island is run as a nature reserve by Dyfed Naturalists' Trust, which maintains a careful year-round study of the shearwaters, black-backed gulls, puffins, guillemots and other seabirds. The two wardens, Michael Betts and Susan Barclay, encourage natural history enthusiasts to stay for a week at a time in the farmhouse and to take part in the work – counting, controlling, replanting, repairing burrows, adding to the sightings of birds of passage and rare visitors. On the day of my visit Michael and Susan were playing host to a party of young ornithologists. The youngsters, in their early teens, trudged in wordless absorption along the island paths, laden with tripods and binoculars, going to their vigils in crevices and on cliff tops, immersed in their work. Life on Skokholm is free of modern amenities – no electricity, no roads, no flush lavatories. Water is pumped up from springs, and jealously hoarded. At night the Tilley lamps glow in place of the television. The young visitors love it. There was only one drawback this week. They had already eaten their way through the entire stock of chocolate in the tiny shop run by Susan.

Visiting Skokholm is no casual spur-of-the-moment decision. You have to apply in writing to Dyfed County Council for a permit, and day visitors are allowed out to the island in strictly limited numbers on Mondays only. Michael Betts took a dozen of us on a leisurely tour of the island. Skokholm measures only just over a mile in length, slightly less in width. It slopes up from east to west, its covering of bracken and bright yellow ragwort giving way to a barren, bird-trampled carpet of brown flattened grass riddled with Manx shearwater burrows. A magical moment came when Michael silenced our chatter with a finger to his lips, and we stood still to hear a sulky grumbling coming from under the grass we were standing on – the complaints of female shearwaters disturbed by our footfalls over their heads. 35,000 pairs of Manx shearwaters breed on Skokholm, raising a spectacular cacophony at night as they come in from sea feeding to their burrows. The shearwaters' feet are perfectly adapted for swimming, but sited so far back on their bodies that they can only shuffle slowly on land. The black-backed gulls kill as many as they can get hold of. Black-back numbers on Skokholm have gone down dramatically in the last few years, thanks in part to a programme of egg-smashing carried out reluctantly by the wardens, but they still wreak havoc. The young ornithologists had collected dozens of shearwater corpses and laid them out by the side of the path for Michael's inspection. He showed us one, a bedraggled slab of feathers and cleanly picked bones.

'They don't mess about, the black-backs,' said Michael. 'They make an efficient job of it, but grisly. They get the shearwater in their beaks and shake it until it literally turns inside out, then eat the muscle and soft parts. See these feather stubs on the outside, and the feathers themselves inside the body here? It all looks a bit mind-boggling. And the rabbits – the black-backs just swallow the young ones whole. Ulp! Ulp! You can see them flying off with two little furry feet sticking out of their beak. Visitors don't like it. They've been known to run after the gulls, throwing stones and shouting, "Put it down!"'

On the cliffs at the western end of the island we looked down on the broken water of Wild Goose Race. A grey seal put her head out of the water at the foot of the cliff and lay there staring up at us, waving her flippers underwater to keep in position. We followed Michael to the newly whitewashed lighthouse, now stripped of its keepers, fully automated and – according to local opinion – incapable of detecting the thickest of fogs at thirty yards. Then we sauntered back towards the boat by way of the light railway track laid along the back of Skokholm when the lighthouse was built. 'It was a horse-drawn railway,' Michael told us as we stumbled across the rusting rails. 'Sugar was the horse's name. He became quite famous. Whenever the boat arrived with more materials or people to be pulled, he would go and stand in the middle of the pond where he knew he couldn't be got at. So when he died, that's where he was buried – in the pond.'

One problem above all was plaguing Skokholm this summer: lack of water. No rain had fallen for months. The water supply was getting dangerously low, and the burrowed-out surface of the island was tinder dry and powdery. Next morning, a mile or two north on Skomer Island, the warden greeted each newly landed party of visitors with a plea not to smoke and to stay away from the crumbling edges of the cliffs. Skomer's water deficiency was even worse than Skokholm's. Streams had run dry for the first time in memory. The level in the well was right down, the water in imminent danger of turning foul. 'It's a crisis,' said the warden, looking worried. Walking the cliff-top circuit of Skomer, I could see why. The bracken was turning brown, the bird-trampled grass hanging in lank mats on the slopes. Through binoculars I watched puffins waddling to and fro outside their burrows, their outlines wavering and trembling in the heat haze pouring up from the dry ground. All colours were bleaching away to a washy blend of pale brown and pale grey. A blazing sun burned me red raw during the day, and caused the hulking young black-backed gulls in their brown plumage to stand wheezing feebly with beaks half open and tongues extended, for all the world like panting dogs. The old farm buildings in the centre of the island, roofless and semi-derelict since farming stopped in the 1950s, stood starkly out against the dry rock ridges and blue sky. Skomer lay crushed in inertia under the arid heat. The island is twice the size of Skokholm, but now it was shrinking, the parched turf withering back from the underlying volcanic rock.

It was too hot for continuous walking. On the northern cliff I flopped to the turf and looked down at the crag of the Garland Stone rising out of the water below. Seals were playing in the falling tide, corkscrewing over and over, chasing each other in sinuous white streaks under the surface, popping up their heads to stare with round black eyes at the passing pleasure boats and their reciprocal rows of round black camera lenses. I envied the seals their sleek wetness, their energy and grace. Up on Skomer the humans trudged and lumbered under their tripods and knapsacks, sighing and sweating. Skomer, like Skokholm, is a nature reserve, but only a few hundred yards from land. Boat trips run out to the island several times a day, and hundreds of visitors walk the paths and watch the birds. Those that stay on overnight in the converted cowsheds of the old farm experience a thrill that the day trippers never know – the arrival at dusk and during the night of a hundred thousand pairs of Manx shearwaters from their sea feeding grounds, the world's biggest breeding colony. They shriek, groan, exult and squabble all night, raising hell on Skomer. It's a rare place where silence falls as humans arrive.

The shearwaters, the puffins and the thousands of Skomer rabbits have reduced the top covering of the island to a tunnelled tissue of fragility, shorn of its vegetation. The reserve wardens and their volunteers have built several 'exclosures' on Skomer, square areas wired off against the rabbits, to show how the island would look if it was not nibbled bare. Even in this waterless summer the exclosures were luxuriant with greenness, squashy mattresses of tussocky red fescue grass four or five feet thick. I could willingly have climbed over the rabbit fence and wallowed like a seal in that soft green sanctuary.

'The *what?* Sorry – never heard of them.'

That's the reaction nine times out of ten to a mention of the Hilbre Islands. I only found them myself by chance, unfolding the last section of the Ordnance Survey map of Liverpool and seeing one of those boxed-in sections that means 'included, but off the map'. These three modest shelves of sandstone – Little Eye, Middle Eye and Hilbre – lie in Liverpool Bay a mile off the north-west corner of the Wirral peninsula, surrounded on all sides at low tide by the enormous expanse of sands that chokes the wide mouth of the River Dee where England stares across at Wales. The map shows them as tiny fingers of rock parallel with the Wirral's shore, sitting in line astern on a plate of flat outcrops. As I walked out to the Hilbre Islands from West Kirby against a strong sea wind, their smallness was emphasized by the vastness of their surroundings – a long spine of Welsh hills on the far side of the estuary, rising to the distant peaks of Snowdonia; a huge sky, clear blue out west over the Irish Sea, heavy with grey towers of rain above the southern horizon; a thin bar of green sea flashing with white horses on the skyline. Sand was everywhere, dominating everything, smelling strongly of shrimps and seaweed, ribbed and streaked with water; dozens of square miles of flat brown carpet in which the three little sandstone knolls were almost lost.

I kept to the dog-leg course laid down in the Hilbre booklet guide – straight out to Little Eye, then a sharp right turn to squelch and slide over sticky sand and rock past Middle Eye to Hilbre, the biggest of the three, a couple of hundred yards long. The angled course is a safeguard against hidden gullies and the power of the tide, which can rise fast enough to trap and drown unwise explorers. The route is only open between high tides when that far-off bar of water comes dashing in to swallow the sands. The path was well marked by the boot tracks of walkers who were already scrambling on the rocks around Hilbre, tiny dots in an empty disc of sand and sky. Little Eye's few yards of sandstone sparkled under a cap of grass. Middle Eye was spotted with pink tufts of thrift and yellow patches of birdsfoot trefoil, across which three young children were running and yelling happily into the wind while their parents shivered in cigarette smoke down in the lee of the rocks.

Beside Middle Eye the sand was patterned by parallel wheel tracks with horseshoe prints between them. They led on across the weed and sandy rock plates to the southern end of Hilbre Island, where a red-painted pony trap stood with its rear door open. 'Waiting for my passengers – late, damn them,' complained blonde Elaine as she leaned against the trap, clutching her coat round her. 'Seen the grey seals? Over there on the Hoyle Bank.' Through the binoculars I could see a dark mass of animals, twenty or thirty of them, clustered in a crowd on a long sand spit by the water's edge. 'Not as many as there usually are,' Elaine said. 'You can hear them singing sometimes – what a beautiful sound that is. I love the Hilbre Islands. Been doing these pony trips for years with old Guinness here.' Guinness stood patiently in his blinkers, shifting his hooves in the pools of water. Elaine shuddered with cold. 'Freezing bloody cold, eh? But I'd rather be out here than in some office. No, thanks!'

I left Elaine and Guinness to their windy vigil, and climbed up on to the green back of Hilbre. A track led among the wooden bungalows owned by a handful of well-to-do Wirral families who spend their weekends out here; six hours in the sea alternating with six hours in the sand. West Kirby's houses ran along the shore a mile away, but on Hilbre the sense of isolation was complete. It took time to notice the signs of activity – the netted Heligoland bird traps like fruit cages, the coastguard observation tower, the bird observatory and warden's house and outbuildings. Hilbre's position out in the estuary has always drawn people to the island – Neolithic farmers, Roman watchers of the approaches to Chester, Dark Ages hermits, medieval monks, wreckers and pirates. These inhabitants left their artefacts behind: flint and bronze tools, pottery and beads, grave slabs and a Celtic cross. Hilbre is dotted with buildings, too. One was the 18th-century Seagull Inn that served sailors and fishermen, travellers and soldiers waiting for boats to Ireland. Another was the telegraph station of the Trustees of Liverpool Docks. The Victorian adventurers of the Mersey Canoe Club built their clubhouse on the northern end of the island beside the lifeboat station, and set off in their sailing canoes on jaunts as far afield as Scotland. For a lonely slip of rock, Hilbre's life has been a remarkably lively one; and these days, as a nature reserve of Wirral Borough Council and the headquarters of the Hilbre Island Bird Observatory, it sees tens of thousands of visitors every year.

I found Vicky Seager in the old telegraph station, surrounded by Girl Guides from Hoylake. Vicky was three months into her appointment as Hilbre Island custodian and Dee Estuary ranger, and still wondering how she was going to find the time to unpack and get her house shipshape. Certainly not today – not with a dozen eager children scrambling behind her like puppies over the sandstone plates of Hilbre and perching in a row on a ledge in Lady's Cave to hear a tragic tale of love and death. 'A long time ago . . .' Vicky began the story of the drowned lover, while the Guides stared down at her with their mouths open. After the story the children scattered over the rocks, shrieking in mingled terror and delight as tickly live prawns were put into their palms. 'You can tell it's a prawn and not a shrimp by this serrated ridge along its head,' Vicky instructed the Guides. They squealed until the rocks rang. 'Jesus God!' shouted Kate, a freckled Irish imp. 'I'll tell yer mam ye said that,' her friend said, giggling.

When the Guides had gone, I walked round Hilbre with Vicky and her black spaniel. Life on Hilbre Island yields moments of pure magic: winter dawns when the whole Dee estuary lies in curling lines of frosty pink and grey; flaming Atlantic sunsets that set the sky on fire over

Liverpool Bay. It's a hard life by any mainland standards. Drinking water comes from the roof in rainstorms, electricity from the diesel generator, heating from a driftwood fire. There's always too much to do, instructing visitors, reading the tide gauge for the Mersey Docks and Harbour Board, keeping the islands and sands clear of litter, setting up visitor accommodation, working with the Bird Observatory volunteers, writing reports, mending and making, acting as an auxiliary coastguard. Vicky has to be always alert, always energetic and hospitable. Tall and athletic, she never strolls when she could be striding, or strides when she can run.

'I never yearned to live on an island, nothing like that,' she said over a cup of tea in her kitchen. 'It's pure luck that I'm here. I did a couple of years as a Ranger on the Wirral Country Park, and then this job came up. I jumped at the chance. I might get as many as a thousand people coming across on a Sunday. They're all over the place, and I don't have time to even think. Then at five o'clock they all melt away – it's amazing how quickly they disappear – and I'll have the islands to myself again.'

On the wall of the Bird Observatory were pinned clippings of local newspaper stories about Vicky, fruit of the journalistic invasion she had to deal with when she took up the job. 'Lone Ranger Vicky Faces Up To A Cold, Hard Life Out On The Rocks' ran one headline above a photograph of Vicky holding an armful of driftwood for the fire. For a week or so the journalists couldn't get enough of the Girl Friday story. Then they, like the Sunday trippers, faded away and left her to get on with her work. 'They were all keen to dig up dirt, speculating on the danger angle, a girl alone on the islands. But in fact my only threat is from drunks who might come across and get stranded by the tide,' said Vicky. 'And if I can't deal with a few Liverpool drunks – well . . .' She smiled, modestly.

Before the evening tide began to cover the sands we walked back by Middle Eye and Little Eye to the shore at West Kirby.

'If the present rate of erosion carries on, the islands won't be here in a thousand years' time,' Vicky told me. 'I'd like to really get things going on Hilbre. I've got a whole lot of plans for improving the accommodation, getting a proper visitor centre going and so on. But so far I haven't even had time to unpack my things. Dave Phillips, the warden I took over from, told me to give it seven years and then get out before I started to crack. I don't know – I'll see how it goes. There's no time limit on the job. I'll know when it's time to go, though. The islands will kick me out.'

7. The Isle of Man

MILLENNIUM WAY THROUGH
THE HILLS

There was a traditional royal welcome waiting for me in the Isle of Man – mist. The island's legendary wizard king, Manannan Mchir, veils his kingdom in this way whenever more earthly royalty pays a call, and this evening in early June he had pulled out all the stops. For four hours the ferry from Heysham had cut through white vapour, mooing sadly on her foghorn. There were long banks of mist rolling off the cliffs and fellsides behind the ferry port of Douglas. But as I disembarked under the eye of a white-helmeted policeman, the sun came through and shone full tilt on a great white phalanx of hotels along the promenade. Weather changes in the Isle of Man come suddenly. As I boarded the bus north to Ramsey, I hoped Manannan Mchir would pick me out quickly as a humble commoner. Mist was the last thing I wanted for the two-day walk I'd planned through the hilly heart of the island.

Thirty miles from north to south, ten from east to west, the Isle of Man is the perfect size for a good walk. The island lies fifty miles to the west of the Lancashire and Cumbrian coasts. 'Man' means mountain, but the mountains of Man are no rearing monarchs of rock. They swell in manageable slopes, filling the centre of the island with green peaks and ridges, beckoning rather than overawing the walker. The Millennium Way long-distance footpath I meant to follow, from Ramsey down to Castletown on the southernmost point of the island, had been established in 1979 to celebrate the thousandth anniversary of Tynwald, the Isle of Man's parliament. On the map it looked splendid, rising from the flat lands of the northern Ayre district to skirt the flanks of Man's tallest peak, Snaefell, running for miles over lonely moorland where the contour lines made a brown haze, dropping again to low land as it neared Castletown – twenty-five miles of good hard plodding. From the bus window I looked out at a slice of the country I would be walking the next day; long slopes rising to ridges, rough central ground in contrast with the tidy, walled farmlands below on the coast. The last of the mist shredded away, and buttery yellow sunlight lay over the landscape. Man looked good enough to eat.

On a bench on Ramsey's waterfront later in the evening, I leafed through the *Isle of Man Examiner* and read of death. The island's annual TT races for motor cycles had ended the week before. 'It's T-Terrific!' blared the headline over the centre spread about the first fun-fair in living memory to visit the island and entertain the TT crowds. Thousands had had a whale of a time, including the chortling toddlers pictured on roundabout chairs. The owner of the fair had been more downbeat when interviewed. 'I've never seen so much red tape,' he was reported as saying. 'It was the first time I've been met on arrival by a tax inspector.'

There was news of a more sombre kind in the *Examiner*. The TT, though drawing tens of thousands of fans to the island from all over the world, has always been notorious for its crashes and fatalities. The competitors race, not round a purpose-built circuit, but over winding mountain roads where hairpin bends, bridges and gateposts lie at the end of every straight stretch. That element of danger and uncertainty gives the TT its magic; also its potential for disaster. This year the races had claimed the lives of five riders and two spectators, as well as the usual toll of broken bones and other injuries. The *Examiner* carried reports of the inquests on two of the riders, both in their thirties, both married men with little children. Their bikes had been examined, and no faults found. It was just human error. When the racers first began using the mountain circuit back in 1911, the winning average lap speed was 47 mph. It took until 1957 for 100 mph to be reached. These days the bikes, enormous things with enormous sponsorships behind them, streak round nearly half as fast again as that. I asked the man next to me on the bench what he thought about the TT and the deaths.

'It's terrible, of course,' he said, 'and the professional riders aren't the only ones who get hurt. After the races we have what we call Mad Sunday. The mountain road's closed in one direction, so visitors can take their bikes along at any speed they want. They've been watching their heroes all week, you see, so they're out to show what they can do.' Fired up by what they have seen during the week, the boys and girls from Blackpool, Frankfurt and Adelaide tear round, some only in their teens and not properly in control of their machines. They wobble off on the bends, crash through walls or headfirst into gateposts, fly off down the mountainside. The island's Noble's Hospital is busier during TT than at any other time. But the Isle of Man couldn't do without the TT, not with regular tourism steadily on the decline and the public jetting off to the sunny coasts of Spain. 'We used to see the visitors pouring off the boats in their thousands at this time of year, all coming over from the Lancs cotton towns,' said my neighbour, 'but now it's hundreds, if that. It's the expense. That's the most expensive stretch of water in the world. Bringing a family of four and a car over here costs far more than going abroad on a package. The visitors won't do it. That's why you'll see so many hotels and shops closed down all round the island.'

In the morning, before I set off along the Millennium Way, I walked along Ramsey's seafront to see the closed hotels for myself. There they were, like rotten teeth in a white smile, shabby and boarded up, windows dusty and front gardens overgrown. Some had already been cleared away, replaced by gleaming new blocks of flats and retirement houses. With a top income tax rate of twenty per cent and a mild climate, the Isle of Man serves as paradise for well-off or retired mainlanders. There's no raping or mugging; very little crime of any kind. People leave their doors unlocked, and can look to the quiet hills from their own back gardens. Tynwald runs the island's affairs independently of mainland pressures, and Tynwald runs a conservatively tight ship. The birch was wielded here until recently on unruly teenagers. Dope smokers and street louts are hustled into jail with no messing. Tolerance of a certain amount of bad behaviour from young visitors, as reluctantly practised on the Costa del Sol, forms no part of Tynwald philosophy.

There is no guidebook to the Millennium Way. The tourist office had a skimpy leaflet. The Town Hall had the same leaflet. The library had nothing. The one useful description of the route comes at the back of a book on the coastal footpath* which I found by chance in the Ramsey bookshop. This showpiece among footpaths, this celebration of landscape and history, goes untrumpeted and under-promoted by the island's tourist organization. What a wasted chance to entice ramblers and walking holidaymakers to Man! No wonder I saw not one other walker anywhere along the Millennium Way, on two days of clear sunshine under peerless blue skies. Solitary walkers, misanthropic ramblers, this one's for you.

A mile out of Ramsey I found the first waymark on the Millennium Way and climbed up a stony track under chestnuts, beeches and sycamores, a sheltered tunnel where the sunlight slipped through the leaves in bright

---

* *Isle of Man Coastal Path* by Aileen Evans, Cicerone Press, 1988.

splashes. The track led up and out over the brackeny flank of Sky Hill. A tremendous view opened up to the north, over the eight or nine miles of Ayre to the topmost point in the island. Larks sang their heads off. The bare back of North Barrule, a long fell with a pointed head, rose into increasing prominence as the view went on widening – all of Ayre laid out below, Ramsey a scatter of white dots, wooded glens carving their way to the coast. Exhilaration took over as I passed the thousand-foot mark, and stayed with me for fifteen up-and-down miles of sunny walking.

The Millennium Way forged uphill between banks of foxgloves and gorse, a sunken track expanding and contracting as it rose over Sky Hill and on towards Snaefell. A royal road, and not just in walkers' terms. This was the Regia Via or Royal Way taken by successive Kings of Man as they processed from their landing at Ramsey down the length of the island to hold meetings of Tynwald at Castletown. Tynwald is an ancient institution, a parliament still based on the procedures laid down by the Norsemen who annexed Man in the 9th century. The name itself is Norse, from *thing* (an assembly) and *vollr* (a field). The Norse chieftains would build an altar to Thor on a mound in the open air, and after prayers to the gods would settle disputes, hear complaints and make new laws. Much the same process goes on today when Tynwald holds its annual ceremony at St John's on 5 July, the date of Old Midsummer Day. The twenty-four Keys, or good men and true elected to parliamentary office, assemble in the church of St John the Baptist along with the Bishop, the Governor, the Captains of the island's seventeen parishes, the coroners and clergymen. Everyone processes from the church to take their allotted stations on Tynwald Hill, a four-tier mound built with earth from every parish in the island. Prayers are said, coroners are sworn in, laws passed in the last year are read and three hearty cheers for the Queen given. Then the assembly processes back to the church, and the rest of the island makes whoopee. Tynwald is no mere ceremonial creation, however. The laws it passes, the decisions it makes are every bit as binding on the Manx people as those of Westminster. When people moan about the government in the Isle of Man – as they do – it's Tynwald they are referring to.

Words are the weapons these days, but back when the Manx kings rode along the Regia Via things were rougher. The route from Ramsey to Castletown lies along the uplands for a very good reason. From this stony road between its earthen banks there were uninterrupted views over the surrounding countryside where attackers might be lying in wait. Sky Hill, nowadays a high haven of tranquillity and birdsong, was the scene of a battle and crushing defeat for the Manxmen in 1079 AD, when the Norse chief Godred made a successful bid for the crown of Man. Godred was a veteran of the Battle of Stamford Bridge, and knew what he was doing when it came to strategy. He posted half his force in ambush above the flooded Sulby River three miles to the west, and then advanced with the rest of his men up Sky Hill where he knew the Manx warriors were waiting for him. The islanders leaped down to attack, following the retreating enemy all the way into the jaws of the trap on the Sulby River. When they were well and truly caught, Godred showed great statesmanship by letting his captives off the usual Norse penalty for losers. He ruled the island until his death in 1095, and his descendants followed suit for the next two centuries until the last of them, Magnus, finally fell in step with the march of history and ceded power to the Scottish king Alexander III. The Isle of Man became a political football between Scots and English until 1403, when the Stanley family were given the island and ruled it as Lords of Man for the next three centuries and more. All these immensely powerful men's footprints – or hoofprints – lie stamped on the mud and stones of the Millennium Way, history in the travelling.

I climbed on, passing a stone pen full of sheep, all miserably bleating as they stared apprehensively through the gate at the mobile shearing stalls in the yard on the other side. Three tall lads stood glugging at pop bottles while their father sat on the floor of the stalls, trying out his three electric shears one by one. 'Come on and give us a hand,' he shouted when he saw me at the gate. 'Have a go, if you like.' I thought of Derek Rees on Ramsey Island a couple of weeks before, his fleeces dropping to the floor every couple of minutes in neat woolly squares; and of what havoc I might wreak on the tender skins of the sheep with those razor-sharp prongs, crossing each other with the speed of barbers' clippers. 'No, thanks,' I called back. 'Got to get on.'

Now the purple top of Snaefell stood up over the ridge ahead, more than 2000 feet of mountain, sprouting tall radio masts from its crown. The Millennium Way led on and up, grass and gorse yielding to heather and bright green leaves of blaeberry as it rose to the crest of the ridge, then plunged dramatically down into the shadowy bottom of the valley of Block Eary. Bare moorland tumbled away in all directions, pock-marked with grassy humps where old-time Manx shepherds had built their shielings, summer dwellings where they lived for months at a time while their flocks fattened on the mountain grass. A lonely and beautiful place, watered by a burn running in the valley bottom under the towering flank of Snaefell. The Way curved away west here, but I couldn't resist the challenge of that great green slope shooting away and up for a thousand feet into the sky.

Blaeberry clumps make efficient snares for hiking boots, as I quickly discovered. My pack, as light as air on the downward slope, began mysteriously to gain weight as I stumbled up the mountain. The sun came nearer, too, and raised a pair of fiery red stripes along my arms. It couldn't get at my legs through my jeans, but they were having problems of their own. It's a mistake to stop and gasp awhile when you're climbing straight up Snaefell. The slope below never looks as satisfyingly lengthy as you think it will, and the legs don't like the restart one little bit. It took an hour to sweat that thousand-foot slope in the full sun. But at the top was a double reward. They say you can see six kingdoms from the top of Snaefell – the kingdoms of Man, Ireland, England, Wales and Scotland, and the Kingdom of Heaven. Only the first and last were on view today; the others were hidden behind a purple band of heat haze round the horizon. Man stretched out on all sides, falling away from Snaefell to the lower peaks, the moorlands, glens and coastline. Mist was still rolling over Douglas like thick smoke, but all the rest of the island lay for inspection like a relief map, animated by tiny cars and motor bikes crawling on invisible roads. The Kingdom of Heaven looked good, too, blue and burning.

The other reward came in a tall glass in the cool, dark bar of the Summit Hotel. Canned Tetley's, to be sure, but distilled essence of nectar to a parched throat. 'You've done what?' gaped the man in the pink T-shirt. 'Climbed up? From down there?' He stared at my pack, and down at my boots. 'In those boots?' He looked round at his friends, shaking his head. It could have been admiration, or deep disgust. I rode down from the summit on board one of the creaky wooden carriages of the Snaefell Mountain Railway, winding in a gently falling curve to the station half-way down the mountain. The man couldn't take his eyes off me. Incredulity was written all over his face. I could hear him thinking: 'He could have ridden up! Could have done the whole thing without lifting a leg! Look at him . . . red as a tomato and all in a muck sweat. Some folk . . .' As I hoisted the pack and walked off, I could see his face at the carriage window, eyes still fixed on me, still incredulous and a touch indignant. I think I rather spoilt his day.

Back on the Millennium Way I walked on round the flanks of Carraghan, hoping not to meet the Red Lady. To see the old witch in her red cloak and pointed hat brings unimaginable frightfulness. But only curlews and sheep were on the mountain with me. Away on the left opened the deep and delectable East Baldwin valley, fertile green fields hemmed in with stone walls hundreds of feet below, farmhouses and trees drowned in dark blue shadow. The Way became a stony track, shedding height for mile after mile. I passed a circular stone wall like a sheep pen – the site of a Tynwald held on the fellside beside the Regia Via in 1428. All the island's great and good had gathered under Carraghan to settle a kingdom's affairs without bloodshed, while over the sea to every point of the compass other powerful men were hacking each other to pieces in fruitless attempts to achieve the same ends. Perhaps the Manxmen didn't know how lucky they were with their settled, reasonable system. More likely they did, and felt contempt for the self-destructive aggression of the rulers across the water.

The path went on down from moorland into farmland. At Crosby the pub had a complete pre-war Norton motor cycle on display in the bar. One wall had been removed and the Norton mounted in the gap in a glass case, lit by lurid green lights. There was a photograph in the case of a smiling, elderly man astride the bike. The Norton had been painstakingly restored by an islander, and the original TT rider invited over to admire the rebirth of the machine on which he'd gained glory back in the thirties.

With evening coming on I caught the bus to Douglas. The hotels along Loch Promenade on the seafront ran away in a mile-long curve. Among the Belvederes, Wellingtons and Eskdales the choice was enormous. Few had 'No Vacancies' notices in their windows. On the corner of the promenade a whole block of them stood boarded up, neon signs dangling, waiting to be demolished to make way for a '125-bedroom luxury hotel and leisure complex with business centre, offices, shopping, car parking and serviced residential apartments', another throw of the dice for the tourist authority. Cheap'n'cheerful bed and breakfast hotels have just about had their day in the Isle of Man. But what the customers are looking for, those that do decide to spend their money on Man rather than Marbella, still baffles the office of tourism. The *Isle of Man Examiner* was running articles urging Tynwald to approve the building of a vast £9 million Aqualeisure Centre for water fun – daredevil rides, slides and chutes – to attract the mass tourist market, while at the same time the inexpensive mass-market B & B places were being axed in favour of grander accommodation, and the cost of getting over those 50 miles of sea was rising all the time. It's hard for an island so steeped in history and natural beauty, and so attractive to influential tax exiles, to humble itself in the mass market-place.

Bushy Brew's Pub in Victoria Street had no doubts about its market. '18? Got no ID? Then Frag Off!' advised the sign in the window. Bushy's goes straight and hard for the young tourist. Its corporate image is a cocky fox, randy and irreverent. 'Only Dick 'Eds Drink and Drive', he winks on the posters, jerking a scornful thumb over his shoulder at a drunken teenage motorcyclist struggling to get a leg across his machine. Bushy's brews its own beer, has discos and live music, and runs a van shaped like a beer bottle. No image problems there.

Next day's walk, ten miles from Crosby down to Castletown, was mostly on lanes and roads. The Millennium Way made the most it could of field paths and short stretches of green lane among the farmlands of southern Man. If the Regia Via had really taken all those twists and turns, the Kings of Man would have had a puzzling ride to Tynwald. Two ancient sites enlivened the steady miles of trudging in the sun. The first, at the top of the hill out of Crosby, was the church of Saint Runn, alias Saint Runius, aka Saint Ronan. The small stone building stood in an overgrown graveyard, its walls full of blocked doorways eight centuries old. Oil lamps swung from the beams inside, and the aisle was floored with ancient bricks. The altar was a venerable slab of stone laid on top of a table. Beside it two pre-Norman Celtic gravestones leaned against the wall, inscribed with roughly cut crosses. The font and piscina were massively carved, roundish stone blocks, who knows how old? There were no church notes to say; no guides to these treasures of Manx history. The noticeboard at the church gate tantalized with its lack of information. Three bishops were 'possibly buried here', it told me – Lonnan,

Connaghan and Runius. What these men did, and why they ended up here, there was no way of knowing.

At least the second ancient monument, half a mile down the road, had some legend attached to it. In the middle of a wheat field stood a small cluster of stones, three of them upright and roughly squared, the whole pile caged in by a barbed wire fence. This was Saint Patrick's Chair, though it's doubtful if the saint ever really visited the island. The stories say that he preached the Gospel to the heathen locals from this spot. It's certainly the right setting for open-air conversions, with the buttresses of the mountains rising on the north to call attention upwards to the heavens. If you sit on the stones and rest your back against one of the crosses inscribed on the uprights, you will never feel weariness again. If you say the Lord's Prayer at the same time, you'll never be lonely. I was rather enjoying the loneliness, but I could have done with the weariness antidote with Snaefell still taking its toll of my calf muscles. I would have tried it if it hadn't been for the barbed wire.

The Way wound on through the quiet lanes past the whitewashed church and cottages of St Mark's, the granite and slate house and barns of Ballamodha Mooar. In Silverdale Glen the Silverburn trickled beautifully under the trees, sparkling down to the old mill where a little waterwheel turned a merry-go-round loaded with children, while their grandparents boated on the mill pool and drank cups of tea in the café in the mill building. This was the well-scrubbed face of tourist Man. Beyond stood the overgrown square stone towers of Rushen Abbey, once a seat of enormous power for the Cistercian monks who had a firm grip of the medieval purse-strings of the island. The Abbot of Rushen paid no taxes. As many roads led to Rushen Abbey as did to Castletown, linking the Abbot to his holdings among the warehouses and fishing fleets of Castletown, the farmlands and ore mines of Man, and the sea routes to his valued trading partner, Ireland. One of the packhorse bridges built by the monks crosses the Silverburn nearby, a double-arched span with a cobbled roadway and narrow waist. In its shadow I watched a dipper bobbing among the stones of the burn, flicking like an old cine film from black to white as splashes of sunlight caught him.

Castletown, when I reached it across the meadows, was lovely, a striking end to the walk. Right in the centre stood Castle Rushen, stone Norman solidity overlooking the harbour where kings, bishops, lords and chieftains embarked and disembarked. Water forms the backbone and shield of Castletown: a wide bay in front, bending south to the low promontory of Langness; arms of sea and river penetrating the heart of the town. Wharfs and bridges, quays and bollards abound. There's a good, salty, old-fashioned feel to the place. The police station across the road from the castle gate still has its *Dixon of Dock Green* blue lantern over the door. In the upstairs bar of the Ship Inn they were talking Manx. I sat near to listen, thrilled to be hearing a language officially considered dead, not worth teaching in school or keeping alive at home. Four men sat round a table, laughing and joking in the rising and falling, rhythmic tongue. Full of long-drawn *ooohhs* and *emmms* and *sh* sounds, it has the quality of singing rather than speech, with (to my ear) strong dollops of Gaelic and a dash of Welsh. There was a marked contrast between the slow, throaty speech of the men and the much quicker, lighter chatter of the two elderly women at the next table. So much so, that I asked them about it.

'Bless you, love – it's *Welsh* we're speaking,' chuckled Helen, tickled to death. She and Pat, exiles both, were enjoying a natter in their native tongue while Pat's husband sat in on the Manx conversation. 'He's very interested,' Pat said, 'oh, yes. Goes to the Manx language class on a Monday night and practises it here on a Thursday.' Pat, from Wrexham, and Helen, from Bangor, both retired to the Isle of Man a couple of years ago. Pat loves it. Man's retired folk all do. They talk about the island carefully – 'it's so peaceful . . . friendly . . . lovely' – as if frightened that a wrong word will shatter their dream. But Helen is an iconoclast. She pines for the mountains of Snowdonia, for the North Wales sense of community. The island is too slow for her liking, the boats to Heysham too inconvenient ('I just *don't know* why they don't go to Liverpool any more'), and the Manx people too superstitious. 'If you go in at a house door, now, you have to come out at the same door, did you know that? Otherwise it's bad luck. And they won't call the rats by name – they call them "long-tails"! Ridickalus! I thought they were talking about cats, at first. I said to this woman, admiring her cats, you know, "Ooh, what a lovely pair of long-tails you've got there." She was *furious!*'

Mrs Jelley, my landlady for the night at The Rowans on the bay, was yet another immigrant, but a long-term one. She'd come over from Kerry in the south-west of Ireland during the hungry thirties, her mother dead and her father left at the age of forty to bring up eight children. At one time Mrs Jelley had owned the whole row of houses along from The Rowans, but she'd got out when tourism began to slump. They'd not really had a season since 1979. The families just weren't coming to the island any more, they were all away in Spain. TT fortnight was great, but apart from that you could forget it. Was I American, myself? Canadian, maybe? Where would I be from, then, with an accent like that? I didn't sound like any Englishman she'd ever met. Had I seen the TV advert for the island? A horse bus trotting up and down Loch Prom! It was a disgrace. There was more to the Isle of Man than Douglas, after all – I must have seen that for myself, with the walking I'd done. That tourist board wanted shooting, sure they did.

In the morning Mrs Jelley's friend, a local builder, gave me a lift over to Douglas. Sure it was no trouble at all. He was from Ireland himself, over here for twenty-six years. Never been to Ireland, had I not? I must go there. I'd have a wonderful time, he could guarantee it. At the jetty in Douglas there were two big boats waiting, one each side. You could step left aboard Mona and be in Ireland by teatime, or step right on to Tynwald and be in England by noon. I looked at the faces lining the rails of Mona, off to their guaranteed wonderful time. Then I stepped right. Ireland could wait. The northernmost of Snaefell's six kingdoms lay waiting just over the horizon. A thousand miles, heading north all the time. Across the top of England first, to the tiny islands of the north-east coast. Then back again to the west and up through Scotland's great chain of islands to the cold seas of Shetland, to Orkney and the end of the journey.

8. Coquet Island, the Farnes, Bass Rock, Cramond and Inchcolm

ROUND THE NORTH AND INTO THE FORTH

A string of islands runs up the Northumberland coast and round into the mouth of the Forth estuary, almost as far upriver as Edinburgh. They are small blobs of land, each a mile or so offshore, where seabirds nest in their hundreds of thousands and the wind whips across all year round. Apart from Holy Island off Northumberland and tiny Cramond in the Forth, both at the far end of causeways, these islands of the north-east coast can only be reached in small boats that pitch out over choppy waters to steps or jetties slippery with weed. It's impossible to plan a visit more than a day ahead, even in summer. A wrong combination of wind and tide can set up a swell on the calmest of sunny days that the local boatmen won't risk, for fear of damaging their boats against the landings. It's a case of early morning telephone calls to the boatmen, more often than not resulting in a regretful 'I'm very sorry, but the trip's off. Wind's getting up, and there's a swell.' In the course of several journeys over two years to the north-east I managed to set foot on five of the islands, and was reckoned lucky.

Coquet Island, the southernmost of the chain, lies so low off the old Northumbrian coal port of Amble that I could only fix its position from the lighthouse on its southern point. Coquet stands just a few feet high, a roundish block of sandstone a quarter of a mile long, topped with a flat wasteland of bird-trampled grass and nettle patches, surrounded at low water by a skirt of rock platforms on which perch the terns, black-headed gulls and puffins. The island is covered with seabirds. Ten thousand pairs breed every year on these fifteen acres of bare ground – 500 pairs of common terns, 2000 of Arctic and Sandwich terns and about twenty of Britain's rarest seabird, the pink-breasted roseate tern. There are 4000 pairs of puffins, and nearly the same number of black-headed gulls. There are eiders, shelduck, oystercatchers – an ornithologist's dream, maintained in its richness by the Royal Society for the Protection of Birds, which manages Coquet Island as a reserve. Before 1972, when the RSPB took over, there were few birds on Coquet; they had been scared away by visiting boat parties. Nowadays, with just one warden in residence along with the three lighthouse keepers, no one disturbs the birds. Landing is strictly banned. It took me a lot of explanation and arrangement by phone and letter to the RSPB to fix up permission to go out to Coquet Island for a couple of hours and be shown round by John Osborne, the warden.

In the end, Gordon Easton of Amble agreed to make a special trip out to the island. On a bright and breezy morning we set out from the harbour in his little boat, which he normally uses for ferrying supplies out to the Coquet lighthouse keepers. Gordon brought the boat cautiously in to the island jetty, where John Osborne was waiting to grab ropes and help me ashore. John, dark-haired, young and slim, was well into his five-month stint on Coquet, and gearing up for the breeding season's round of hard work. We walked a circuit of the island, on turf stamped by the birds into a dry yellow plateau and riddled with the tunnels and burrows of the puffins. My clumsy boots broke through more than one crust into underground hollows, sending puffins scrambling into flight a few yards away.

'This puffin erosion is a big problem,' John said, kneeling down to finger the dusty surface. 'I'm experimenting with planting thrift and perhaps some marram grass to hold it all together. And there's these nettles' – he waved his arm over the straggling nettle beds by the lighthouse – 'they've grown up on ground that was used as gardens in the last century when the lighthouse keepers had their families living with them. Nettles are too thick for the terns to nest. I'll be cutting and spraying them, monitoring each area to see how effective I've been. I've all this trampled grass to scrape up and burn, too, to let new growth up from underneath. There's a lot of work.'

There certainly is. As well as trying to control and restore vegetation, John has to conduct a bird count (taking an average of occupants of several carefully-marked squares of ground), ring the chicks and write reports. This day his hands were covered in yellow and purple stains from another of his experiments, sexing terns by daubing the edge of the nest with dye which would stain the breast feathers of the females as they scrabbled the nest materials together. Then there was his weight-gauging experiment. 'Look at this,' said John, picking up what looked like a large pebble in front of his canvas observation hide. The pebble was a dummy, a skin of moulded fibreglass, which opened to reveal an electronically operated balance inside. 'I put this between two nests, and remove every other potential perch in the area. The tern comes to sit on the dummy and triggers the balance. The weight's recorded in the hide there.'

We walked on, sending a great screaming army of black-headed gulls into the air from their nettle-bed nests. They hovered in lines, head to wind, cursing us. The brown eider ducks were more phlegmatic, sitting on their five or six green eggs even when John Osborne bent down to scratch their heads. He's been fascinated by birds ever since his boyhood in Gosforth, and has been wardening for the RSPB for several years. They posted him to Coquet Island for a season's duty even though he would rather have gone to Orkney, but being on his own for months at a time doesn't worry him. Nor do the tough conditions he lives in. He has a tiny two-room wooden hut up against the wall of the lighthouse compound. 'There's no electricity in the hut – I've got a gas stove and a Tilley lamp. I get my drinking water from the compound, and washing water from my rain butt.' The water lay in a greenish pool at the bottom of the plastic butt under John's home-made filter.

Inside the hut was a narrow bed, some photographs and charts on the walls, and the table at which John writes his reports and bulletins with the help of his little portable computer. It's not too lonely. Friends come over from the mainland to visit, and John has an inflatable boat to take him ashore when the wind is light enough. But the island can be cut off for weeks when bad weather sets in. The lighthouse keepers come in and out by helicopter. 'I get on all right with the keepers,' John said guardedly. 'They work a month on, a month off, so there's some variety. We tend to respect each other's privacy. They'll come in for a cup of coffee, and I go into the compound for water and to use their toilet, and for a chat. But on the whole we keep to ourselves.'

Without written permission from Trinity House I couldn't go into the compound, talk to the keepers or climb the lighthouse tower. Looking over the wall, I surveyed the keepers' tiny kingdom: high walls to keep out the wind, small lawns shaved like snooker tables, immaculate flower beds and lettuce rows – the meticulous neatness of self-contained men marooned away from their families. I was glad to be outside the compound in the sun and wind, watching the roseate terns flapping overhead and Gordon Easton's boat butting out to Coquet Island to pick me up.

On the return trip to Amble harbour a dolphin accompanied us, chasing the boat and arching its back clear of the water while glancing up at us with a calm round eye. I waved over the stern to the fast-receding John on the island jetty. He lifted a hand before coiling the mooring rope and trudging back up to his hut under a cloud of birds.

Just south of Berwick-on-Tweed and the Scottish border, Holy Island leans out from the coast in a cutlet-shaped curve. I had explored and written about Holy Island only a year before,* and for that reason did not revisit. But the nearby Farne Islands, only glimpsed on that occasion from the top of Holy Island, were now fair game. The Farnes rise 25 miles north of Coquet Island off the fishing village of Seahouses, like a fleet of surfacing submarines. Slab-shaped outposts of the great dolerite wall of the Whin Sill that runs across north-eastern England, the Farne Islands are low, treeless and windswept, uninhabitable except by hermit monks and their latterday successors, the National Trust wardens. Dark Ages mainlanders peopled the islands with devils, 'demons clad in cowls, riding upon goats, black in complexion, short in stature, their countenance most hideous, their heads long'. There is something demonic – certainly something strange and other-worldly – about these hard, bare shelves of rock in the sea. They shift behind spray clouds, and disappear one by one as the tide rises. Twenty-eight islands dwindle in number down to fifteen. Rocky causeways between them surface and vanish. Even the local boatmen are wary of the Farnes when a gale is on the way.

'Aye, well,' said Billy Shiel to his brother Jack at the door of his booking shed on Seahouses harbour, 'ye'll go – but not the whole day, mind. It's not too bad just now, but ye'll keep a tight eye on the weather?'

'Aye, aye,' muttered Jack. The radio was offering a forecast reminiscent of the Isle of Wight – Force 8 and rising. Rain fell in drifting curtains. Thirty of us got aboard Billy's boat *Glad Tidings*, while Jack started up the engine and swung out of the harbour. Trips around the Farne Islands have been bread and butter for thirty years to Billy Shiel and his employees. The three on *Glad Tidings* this day knew more about the birds, seals and wild flowers of the islands than any guidebook. 'Shags,' said Will, pointing, 'see the crests on their heads?' The dozen schoolchildren around him shrieked with glee as *Glad Tidings* dug in her bows and

* See *Britain Beside the Sea*, Grafton Books, 1989.

105

shipped a bath-load of spray. The children had come from Cumbria for the Farne Islands trip, and were determined to milk it of every possible pleasure. 'Abigail's being *sick*! She's going all *green*, look!' They sighed with delight when a string of grey seals popped up their heads off the tip of the outermost island, Longstone, and lay floating and staring at the boat. The other group of students aboard Glad Tidings were ten years older, undergraduates from Newcastle University's psychology department. In contrast to the children, all neat and weatherproof in brightly-coloured raingear packed for the trip by prudent parents, the students shivered in sopping denims. They hadn't expected rain. Will produced a roll of plastic sheeting and threw it over the lot of them. Under the plastic they passed round a half bottle of whisky, and were soon giggling as merrily as the children.

The Farne Islands are grouped in little clusters with evocative names: the Harcars, the Wamses, the Wideopens. Grey seals breed around the islands, along with eighteen species of seabird. We cruised between rock stacks whitened like wedding cakes. Fifty thousand birds wheeled overhead, cut through the water, bobbed up beside the boat and sat on the stinking rocks – fulmars, puffins, guillemots, shags, cormorants, black and white eider drakes, V-tailed terns, kittiwakes screaming in unison. 'I was nine yesterday,' confided Michael, his back to all this immense activity, the worksheet under his arm dissolving in the rain. 'And I was sick in the car.'

From Longstone Glad Tidings followed the route rowed in a stormy September dawn in 1838 by Grace Darling and her father William, keeper of the Longstone lighthouse. Will the boatman spun out the famous story to the children: the paddle-steamer Forfarshire wrecked on Big Harcar, the nine survivors huddled on the rock, the brave pair taking off a few before returning through the storm for the rest, the bodies of the 40-odd victims floating in the morning tide. The children nodded politely. They had heard it all before from their teacher, back in the classroom preparing for the trip.

The sea was too rough for landing on Staple Island, but Jack Shiel got the boat alongside the jetty on Inner Farne. We scrambled out and up the path to the little cluster of buildings at the top. Here on Inner Farne Saint Cuthbert had lived as a hermit for eight years, wrestling with the demons in prayer and solitude, until in 684 AD he was dragged unwillingly

106

away to become Bishop of Lindisfarne. Cuthbert managed to get back to his beloved Inner Farne after two unhappy years on the mainland, to die shortly after his return. Other hermits lived and died on the island in the following centuries, and there was a monastery from 1255 until the Dissolution 300 years later. The buildings – a tower, two chapels and a monastic guest house – survived further centuries of tenancy by mainlanders harvesting the rabbits, seals and seabirds. The National Trust took over the Farnes in 1925 to safeguard them for future generations. The old monastery buildings now house an exhibition and provide accommodation for the six wardens who live on Inner Farne from March until December each year.

'I wouldn't say we were hermits, no,' grinned David Richardson, the chief warden. 'We can be cut off by gales for a week or more, but with 40,000 visitors a year we're not exactly lonely. We only get one week's holiday in our nine months' stint, so it's important to be able to get on with the other wardens. But we're far from being solitary people. On an island this size, only about 16 acres, you couldn't get away from the others even if you wanted to.'

David and his colleagues, along with the three wardens over on Staple Island, have plenty to do. As with John Osborne on Coquet, there are the common warden's tasks – ringing, counting, monitoring, noting the birds, keeping an eye on the seal population. The Farne wardens also have to maintain the buildings and play host to the visitors. The boats bring them their food and water. When Saint Cuthbert had trouble with the Inner Farne water supply, he produced more by praying for it. The National Trust wardens have to rely on collecting rainwater from the roof in butts. Having run down through a thousand gull droppings, it's only fit for washing in. As for the demons of Inner Farne, David Richardson hasn't seen one. 'They do say there's a ghost here, though,' he told me. 'She's supposed to be a lady who comes and sits on the end of your bed. That's the kind of supernatural being none of us would mind seeing once in a while out here.'

Seabirds dominate the island with their noise, and with their sheer weight of numbers. I walked a careful path among thousands of blackcapped Arctic terns and fat eider ducks to the southern cliffs, to stare down the sheer dolerite walls at the nesting colonies of guillemots and kittiwakes. No need for binoculars here. The birds were nesting, squabbling and flapping their wings right beside my boots on the cliff edge. A fight broke out beside my left toe-cap as one kittiwake tried to usurp the place of another. The intruder was forced away by the occupant of the ledge, beak ajar and stabbing. Kittiwakes swooped in to their twelve-inch holdings with beakfuls of grass and sea campion, dropping their cargoes and stamping them into the structure with webbed feet. Further out and down, the black-jacketed and white-shirted guillemots stood packed together on top of a tall rock stack, necks stretched up and beaks together as if community singing.

The psychology students wandered up and stood in a loose group while their bearded tutor embarked on an open-air lecture on the sexual habits of the kittiwake. They are faithful birds, he told his audience, meeting their mates at the same place every year to go through the same old ritual. While the female is out fishing, though, the male stays home and plays around with his neighbours' wives. Male kittiwakes are both philanderers and jealous husbands, keen to make sure that their own seed is the latest to hit the target. 'You'll notice that male kittiwake down there – see? – mounting a female. It's a bit late in the season for fertilization,' commented the tutor, 'they're just fooling around. Now here's something that will interest you. Researchers recently got ten couples to take part in an experiment on the effect of separation of human partners on sperm count. It turned out that the male human's ejaculation contained a far higher amount of sperm when the couple had been apart; *but*' – the tutor paused for effect – 'only in copulation, not in masturbation. And copulation was found to be far more frequent after separation,' the tutor smiled. 'How extraordinary.'

Not a single student eye was on the tutor's face. The girls and boys looked sideways at the seabirds and at each other, some pink of cheek, torn between academic sobriety and a desire to giggle. 'Now,' said the tutor, 'this closely parallels kittiwake behaviour – pairs copulate more frequently when the male or female has been away from the nest looking for food. Questions?'

The students eyed each other. Someone snorted with suppressed laughter. A lone voice spoke up, tinged with defiance. 'Have there been any studies to show whether birds enjoy doing it?'

'But how could you measure that?' countered the tutor. 'The smile on the beak of the kittiwake?'

A dam of laughter burst all over the cliffs, causing the students to double up and the lecturer to smile benignly in his beard. They were still sniggering when Jack Shiel came up the jetty to call his charges back to harbour.

North of the Farnes and over the Scottish border, a dozen small islands are scattered in the Forth estuary. Some are low humps covered in derelict forts and gun emplacements, others are lonely rocks where only seabirds get a foothold. Opposite each other at the outer edge of the estuary stand two islands which (weather, tide, swell and time coinciding favourably) can be landed on from a boat. The Isle of May, in the middle of the seaway, tempted me most. History and legend, lighthouses, old buildings, birds, caves, a long boat trip – the May had it all. But I was destined not to land. I made three carefully planned attempts over two years to reach the May, and was frustrated each time by a running swell making the landing place on the island too dangerous to approach. Opposite the May, however, a couple of miles out from the red sandstone resort of North Berwick, the Bass Rock proved an easier nut to crack. There was only one false start before I got the phone call I was hoping for from the North Berwick boatman, Fred Marr: 'It doesn't look too bad just at the moment, so if you can get yourself down to the harbour by 11.30 we'll be going out to the Bass. Can't promise to land you, though.'

Fred Marr's *Sula* was a big open boat with benches for 70 passengers along her sides. Fred and his son Chris, both patriarchally red-bearded and blue-eyed Vikings, weatherbeaten and rock solid, had her packed with passengers in a trice. They spun her round and pointed her towards the Bass Rock lying dead ahead. The Bass looked tremendous, a sheer-sided chunk of volcanic detritus rising and rising out of the Forth to a domed top 350 feet up; a great block of weight and mass packed into a circumference of less than a mile. A white lighthouse clung to a ledge in the southern face, with a faint path zig-zagging above it to the top.

Fred Marr steered *Sula* close in under the western cliffs of the island. Everyone on board craned back, pointing cameras and binoculars up the sheer rock faces. What we had all come out to see, the main attraction of the Bass, covered the upper flanks of the rock like a snowstorm and

109

streamed out in a thick, swirling pennant from the top – gannets, fifty thousand of them. The Bass Rock is the gannet's only stronghold on the east coast of Britain. They covered the ledges in parallel rows like a white blanket of corduroy, and filled most of the grassy top of the rock. 'They only nest on the top because they can't find room on the ledges,' Fred told his open-mouthed boatload. Expert in gannet lore through half a century of experience, he gave us a lecture full of dry asides as *Sula* coasted round the teeming, screaming cliffs of the Bass. 'There's a long breeding season, nineteen weeks, and the young gannet stays on the nest for three months being fattened up by the parents. They're so heavy when they leave the nest that they can't really fly. They just tend to flop into the sea and float there for a couple of weeks, living off their body fat. Those that learn to fish survive, but many of them starve to death. About seventy per cent don't make it to adulthood.'

The gannets swirled in circles along their flight paths above our upturned faces. I couldn't see how they avoided mid-air collisions. Every square yard of air seemed to hold a gannet, swooping, gliding or flapping. Fred Marr broadened his lecture, describing the use of the Bass in past centuries as a prison for Covenanting ministers and Jacobite revolutionaries, a fortress against the Dutch and a lighthouse post. These facts failed to interest us. It was the sheer weight of gannet numbers, their noise, stink and movement, that mesmerized everyone. We landed at a slimy little jetty, stumbling ashore as the boat swayed up level with the steps. Then we trudged in a line up the zigzag path, with hardly a glance for the attractions of the Bass – fortress and lighthouse, clumps of rare purple tree mallow, the ruined chapel of Saint Baldred, a 7th-century hermit. Wonderful views unfolded themselves to all points of the compass as we climbed: Fife and the snowy Grampians fifty miles north, the Lammermuir Hills to the south, Edinburgh and the whole of the Forth estuary eastwards. We spared them the briefest of inspections. At the top of the Bass we scattered ourselves on grass tussock, concrete pathway and rock outcrop, slaves to gannet fever. I leaned on the rusty rail by the path, and for the next few hours was a shameless voyeur.

The gannet has a pair of cold, pale blue eyes in a buff-coloured head, a thick, dagger-like grey beak, white body and wings, black wingtips and black webbed feet with pale green stripes down the toe ribs. It's a big bird, three feet long, with a wing span nearly twice that. Coming in to land it spreads its webs and folds its wings into a downward and backward curve, shivering with braking power as it drops into its own few inches of space. Those that undershoot on landing trample clumsily over their packed and crossly jabbing neighbours to their own spot. Birds that have stayed on the nest to guard the egg greet their incoming mates demonstratively. The two partners clash heads, rub beaks together and intertwine necks in a display of recognition that to me, in spite of scientific objectivity, looked suspiciously like affection. The lovers only break off canoodling to swear and jab at too-close neighbours. The arriving birds were bringing in beakfuls of grass and seaweed, which were manoeuvred into position in the nest structure with tiny quivering movements of the beak. A square of polythene from someone's sandwich wrapping blew through the colony, to be grabbed and then released by one gannet after another. The slippery stuff was useless for nest-building, incapable of staying put. Birds took off to go gliding out over the sea. A mile away, white specks against the blue, they went plunging down after fish. Added to the movement of the colony – shuffling, repositioning, bickering, landing, taking off, greeting mates – were the churring, throaty bark of their squawks and the fishy reek of unguessable gallons of gannet guano. This overwhelming overdose of gannetry blurred all my senses after an hour or so, but the herring gulls on watch at the fringes of the colony stayed razor-sharp in concentration.

Under most of the nesting gannets was a single, large, green-brown egg. The gulls stood just out of stabbing range, shifting from foot to foot, watching their moment. I saw a gannet on the cliff edge take off, leaving her egg unprotected. In a flash a gull was in there, whacking its axe of a beak into the shell and sucking out the yolk. The mother gannet's sortie took less than half a minute, but that was about twenty-five seconds too long. She returned to squat on the broken shell until its flat, empty shape made her uneasy, then took off again and did not come back – her one breeding chance of the year thrown away in a few seconds off guard. Another gull nearby was watching over a brace of stolen eggs in a hollow as solicitously as any gannet mother. Five other gulls were standing casually about, looking anywhere but at the thief, waiting for their chance to steal its booty. I watched gulls flying overhead with their beaks forced painfully far apart as they gripped a gannet egg. One was harried by another until it dropped its prize, which went rolling down the cliff and exploded against a stone in a shower of yolk. The disappointed pirate returned to peck its attacker, then went into a long, furious tantrum of screeching.

I longed sentimentally for the gannets to rise up in a body and set about these cold-hearted baby snatchers with their horrible jarring cackles. But human interference was partly to blame for giving the gulls their opportunity. Back on *Sula* at the end of our stay on the Bass Rock, an elderly lady was spluttering with indignation about the behaviour of a sallow young Italian photographer in the party. 'Went right up to the gannets, he did, and just lay there taking his blasted pictures. I saw the gannets leaving the nest, and the gulls coming in for the eggs. So thoughtless! I shall report him when we get back to North Berwick – I shall.'

The Italian slumped into a corner of the boat, staring sulkily in front of him above the battery of expensive cameras across his chest. Fred Marr, coming round to collect the money, gave him a talking-to, but the young man either didn't understand or was pretending not to. He sat and sulked in his corner, refusing to look up even when a grey seal put its head out of the waves and gravely saw us off from the island. All that evening, scrub my hands as I might, I still carried round with me an oily, fishy stink of Bass Rock gannet.

The name of Cramond Island had enticed me for years; probably an echo of that lovely hymn tune 'Crimond'. Half an hour out of central Edinburgh, dropping down a leafy lane between the old stone houses of Cramond village towards the causeway, I thought my dream of an island paradise in the Firth of Forth was coming true. But I had failed to hoist on board the true effect of two world wars on this landscape. Rosyth naval dockyard lies just upriver of the islands of the inner Forth, and all of them – Inchgarvie, Inchmickery, Inchcolm, Inchkeith and even little Cramond's quarter-mile – had suffered a plague of iron and concrete. Gun emplacements, searchlight batteries, pillboxes, blockhouses and garrison barracks were crowded on to their few acres. Positioned where they are, right across the throat of the Forth and barring the way inland, the islands have been under attack in one form or another often enough in the past. The hermits and monks of Dark Ages Scotland who settled on the Forth islands took a series of hammerings from Norse invaders, and after the Norman Conquest the English carried on the tradition. A thousand years of attacks like these left hardly a scar on the islands. But the ugly detritus of the 20th-century version of war still stands there glowering on every island in the inner Forth. It has been worth nobody's while to clear it all away and free the overloaded islands.

As the tide went down the Cramond causeway came slowly to light, a concrete jetty followed by a crumbling tarmac roadway in the estuary mud. Not very inviting, and neither was the giant's toast-rack of concrete trestles accompanying the causeway. On each side of the roadway lay banks of millions of mussels covered with billions of barnacles, all slimed with gluey grey mud from which a faecal and chemical stink was rising. I ought to have been prepared for this at least, on the tideline of a great city, but that magical Cramond fantasy still held sway. The island itself looked fine, a green back with a wooded cleft turned to the mainland. Following a narrow path up to the rocks at the summit of the tiny island, I disturbed small blue butterflies among the great drifts of rosebay willowherb – that pink-faced lover of bomb sites and harrowed ground. From the top of the rise there was a good view upriver to the dinosaur head of one span of the Forth railway bridge poking over the trees, downriver to the cranes and breakwaters of Leith docks, and beyond them Inchkeith Island lying in the fairway. Things were quiet enough out here, a mile into the estuary, for oystercatcher pipings to come up clearly from the drying mud expanses, though in the background was that eternal hum, almost an animal noise, that tells you a million people are just over the skyline. Cramond was beginning to live up to expectations, until I came to where the island dropped away into the water. Concrete covered this whole end of Cramond – pillboxes square, oblong and semi-elliptical; circular gun mountings with racer rails still embedded; stark huts with steel window shutters swinging open. Kev's, Kelly's and Tosh's aerosol signatures were smeared far and wide. At the far end stood the shattered walls of a house where the Cramond herdsman of another age used to quarter himself in summer, tending his beasts and making a good thing on the side out of the Cramond oysterbeds. What he would think today of his peaceful few acres passes imagination.

Cramond has proved a poor haven for fugitives. Back in 1004 a rival of King Malcolm III, one Constantine, thought the island would give him safe hiding; but the King's brother got across the causeway and murdered him on Cramond. The saddest story, however, belongs to Tengmalm's owl, a handsome fox-brown little bird only nine inches tall, with a splendid pair of white eyebrows. Tengmalm's owls have very occasionally veered far enough from their native mountain forests of Europe's extreme north to find themselves in Britain, but no one had managed to get their hands on one until December 1860, when Philip Lumley took his son James duck-shooting on Cramond Island. The herdsman had abandoned Cramond for the winter as usual, leaving behind mounds of grain scattered across the island where his beasts had been feeding. Mice had found the grain, and birds of prey had arrived for the mousing – among them a Tengmalm's owl, blown or carried by some freak air movement or navigational aberration across Europe to the Firth of Forth. The Lumleys, poking about in the herdsman's empty buildings out of curiosity, opened the stable door and spotted the owl sitting on a rafter. It made a dash over their heads for the open door, but Philip Lumley managed to knock it down into a stall, and his son grabbed it before it could get away. They took it home with them and kept it alive for a week. Then they invited Mr Hutchinson, the gardener at Cramond House and a keen amateur taxidermist, to come and have a look at their captive. Like any good Victorian naturalist faced with a rarity, he lost no time in wringing the owl's neck and stuffing its corpse; after which Mr Hutchinson kept his Tengmalm's owl proudly in his collection for the rest of his life.

Round on the northern side of the Forth estuary later in the day, after a bumpy ride in a small ferryboat, I viewed Cramond from the abbey ruins on Inchcolm Island. What happened to the murdered Constantine's body on Cramond is anyone's guess, but Inchcolm in its day was considered such holy ground that Danes defeated by King Macbeth at the nearby Battle of Kinghorn paid hugely – in gold – for the privilege of burying their fallen chief and comrades on the island. It's hard to overestimate the tremendous mystical pull exerted by the other British isles. From the 6th-century Saint Colm onwards, an unbroken line of hermits each added his stone to the cairn of Inchcolm's reputation for sanctity. In 1123 the incumbent hermit played host to an influential guest when King Alexander I found himself storm-bound for three days on Inchcolm. In thanks or deliverance from the storm, Alexander saw to the building of the monastery here.

These ruins are hardly ruins at all. They stand magnificently on a saddle of low ground between the two humped wings of Inchcolm. Some walls are crumbled, as one would expect, but most stand solidly under stone-tiled roofs; barrel-vaulted cloister buildings round a grassy courtyard, a great central Romanesque tower, an octagonal chapter house with ribbed vaulting and the stone triple seat where the abbot and his priors handed out decisions and judgements on all monastery matters. The Inchcolm community was well battered by English raiders, who stole not only treasures but the monastery deeds and records as well. Trying to prove their ownership of far-flung lands without these documents was one of the biggest headaches for successive abbots of Inchcolm.

I stood on top of the tower and looked down over the buildings to the little ferryboat lurching away from the jetty. Every rock ledge above the bay held a lesser black-backed gull, every current of air half a dozen of the same. There were only a few pairs of black-backs when Hunter Brown and his wife came to Inchcolm Island as custodians in the early 1980s, but they have multiplied to become a thorough nuisance. 'You're seeing them at their worst,' Hunter told me as we watched them from the flat ground by the ruins, the one gull-free spot on the island. 'The trouble is the school parties. The kids chase them and torment them, and they don't like it when they're rearing their chicks. Just now they're a bit on edge, you know? You have to be careful when you move anywhere on Inchcolm at this time of year. They'll divebomb you close enough to draw blood from your head with their feet.'

Later on, walking on Unst in the far north of the Shetland Islands, an infuriated bonxie came nearest to taking off the top of my head; but the Inchcolm black-backs got close enough. 'You'll find a tunnel right through the top of the island,' Hunter said. 'Built to carry stores from one side of Inchcolm to the other in the war. They had a string of searchlights on the islands – I well remember seeing those as a boy, lighting up the whole of the Firth of Forth at night.' Inchcolm's wartime ness, unlike Cramond's, is dwarfed into insignificance by the size and impressiveness of the abbey ruins. What's left – blockhouses and pillboxes among the nettles – is now under gull guard, fiercer defenders than the wartime garrison ever had to be.

I found the brick-lined tunnel running through the spine of the island, dark and damp. Two fur-coated gull chicks shuffled furtively out of the far end as I approached, but the mouth of the tunnel was as far as their parents, uncles and aunts allowed me to go. They pinned me back into the entrance, smacking the air around my head, chakkering and screaming into my face. There was a continual *splap* of droppings hitting the leaves of bushes, and whoosh of air over wing surfaces. I had to turn back, jacket streaked white and dignity destroyed. An easier fate than the Inchcolm oystercatcher chicks are up against the moment they can walk. The black-backed gulls circle round. One instant's distraction of the mother bird is all they need.

9. Islay and Jura

THE EMPTY ISLES

Twenty minutes out of Glasgow airport and 5000 feet up, I looked down at a tiny ferry crawling at the head of its thread-like wake across the Firth of Clyde towards the curve of Rothesay at the edge of the Isle of Bute – traditional home-from-home for generations of holidaymaking Glaswegians. Beyond squatted the mountainous, lumpy landscape of Arran: then a stretch of deep blue sea and a different, remoter island world. Away on the horizon, wavering through the blurry window of the Loganair Short 360, rose the three tall, bare peaks of the Paps of Jura, and further out still the lower hills and white crescent beaches of the Isle of Islay. Here the long scimitar shape of the 500-mile Scottish island chain descends to its southernmost tip, free of all firths, bays and sea lochs of the mainland. On Islay, the kingly island from which Macdonalds once ruled all the Hebridean world, I hoped to find a fitting place to start the great straggle north by plane, boat, bicycle and foot, through both Inner and Outer Hebrides, that would lead me up and out to Britain's remotest islands of Orkney and Shetland.

In Islay's living rooms, television news comes from Belfast rather than Glasgow. Islay is very much an island apart, out on a limb of loneliness. From the aeroplane it's a wrinkled green and grey cloth thrown down crumpled in the sea, bare and empty looking. The impression of emptiness strengthened as John Barford from the Islay Hotel drove me in his jerky old Land Rover the five or so miles from the island airstrip to Port Ellen. Scrubby peatlands ran away from the road to rise into low hill ridges. The few patches of cultivated land stood out in sharp green contrast to the dark, dun-coloured moorland and hill landscape that lay on all sides, empty of all but an occasional solitary human figure.

Port Ellen, down on the south end of the island, was brought into being on a tide of whisky. A number of distilleries sprang up nearby in the nineteenth century, and the little town was built to service them, a respectable settlement of whitewashed houses, a couple of pubs and a handful of shops sited prettily around the tiny, almost circular Loch Leodamais. Until the 1960s Port Ellen was a prosperous place with jobs for everyone in distilling, fishing, crofting, the tourist trade or those one-

and two-man making and mending industries so vital to island life. But today there are unmistakable signs of slump – boarded houses, dusty windows, barred and nailed doors, a harbour nearly empty of fishing boats; above all, in the talk of Islay folk, a kind of shrugging acceptance of down-at-heelness. Islay has been down in the dumps of several years of recession linked to the fluctuating fortunes of the whisky business, as John Barford explained to me. The ten or more years that good malt whisky needs to mature in barrel meant that Islay was behind the rest of Britain, living as she was off stocks piled high in boom times, in feeling the economic pinch of the early 1970s. In the 1980s, reality struck hard, at a time when mainland confidence was rising. When John and Lesley Barford bought the hundred-year-old Islay Hotel in the winter of 1986, it had been suffering from a decade of neglect in the hands of hard-up owners. The fine moulded ceilings had been crudely painted over, or hidden above plasterboard partitions. Tourism in Islay was in a trough, with less and less work for the school leavers who so often become island leavers with hardly a backward glance at their home. Fatalism had settled gently over this most lovely and well-favoured island.

To shake the Loganair gremlins out of my legs I walked up behind Port Ellen into a long, slowly rising lane between stone walls. Flags grew in yellow sheets along the boggy banks of small burns. The bones of the underlying rock stuck up through the thin green skin of sheep-nibbled grass, bracken and heather. There wasn't a sound to be heard, apart from the ever-present Hebridean anthem of quietly moaning wind. As the lane climbed, the yellow flags gave way to white cotton-grass, wet hollows of streamsides looking as if someone had burst a feather pillow all over them. A standing stone many thousands of years old raised its fifteen-foot, lichen-green finger from the hillside. The larks were the only noise-makers, until I stepped off the road and into lapwing territory. The nests full of chicks were too cleverly hidden among the rocks for my eyes, but their positions were well advertised by the parents flapping overhead, hurling abuse in creaking calls as they divebombed me, slapping their square-tipped wings threateningly together just above my head.

I climbed on and up, for a grandstand view over Port Ellen and out across the bay to the club-shaped peninsula of the Oa. A heavenly view, in marked contrast to the effing and blinding that went on later in the public bar of the Islay Hotel. A family of three was just coming out of the bar as I walked in, father tight-lipped, his teenage daughter grinning behind her hand. Father wanted to know if the hotel had a *respectable* bar. It wasn't the furnishings that had upset him. I was hoping to get an hour's quiet chat with the locals about the island, but they were all locked into fishing stories – The Day The Effing Eel, Its Effing Head Severed, Bit My Effing Finger, and other juicy tales. Someone brought in a skate he'd caught, sliding its glistening, blue-white corpse out of a plastic bag and waving it under the nose of the shrieking barmaid. 'Good for the willie, this is!' shouted the fisherman – 'makes you effing randy!'

In Port Ellen I hired a little Vauxhall – three years old and 100,000 miles already on the clock – to get me around the long miles of winding road that skirt the great trackless spaces of Islay. It rattled, buzzed and spluttered throughout our brief relationship, but it loyally carried me over terrain where no small saloon should have been asked to go. Early next morning I drove north to Kildalton to see what my guidebook promised would be the finest Celtic High Cross in Scotland, up at the far end of one of the remotest roads in the island.

In Lagavulin Bay a smallholding was tucked away down a pot-holed track, showing all the signs of breadline farming. A water butt stood against the house wall, a few hens scratched in the dust, a flimsy belt of wind-tattered shelter trees leaned wearily behind the croft. The farm's riches lay in its view, across the bay to the silhouetted ruin of Dunyvaig Castle, craggy walls on a craggy promontory, ancient stronghold of Clan Donald, Lords of the Isles.

The Macdonalds ruled not only Islay, but a vast slice of the Hebridean island chain, from the 12th century for the next 300 years. The founder of the dynasty was Somerled, the Summer Traveller as his Norse name styled him. After defeating King Godred of the Isle of Man in a great sea battle in 1156, when Somerled must have been getting on for sixty years old, his power base was secure and he set about extending his influence northwards and eastwards as a great and independent ruler. Somerled was murdered after eight short years at the top – the usual fate of Scottish chiefs, as I came to learn during my island wanderings – but by that time Lagavulin Bay was established as the chief anchorage of the clan's navy. Dunyvaig Castle was built in the late 1300s as a statement of Macdonald power and might. It contained within its defences a repair dock where ships could be drawn up safe from attack. Clan Donald acknowledged no master but their chief. The people whose own bards declared them to be the very flower of courtesy, strong, wise and gentle, tended to strike their neighbours and rivals as arrogant, pig-headed folk whose noses should be bloodied as often as possible. They lost Dunyvaig along with the Lordship of the Isles at the turn of the 16th century, but it took the hated Campbells another hundred years to topple them finally from their pre-eminence in Islay.

Two large hares were playing catch-as-catch-can on the side track up to Kildalton Chapel. I stopped the car and sat watching them romping along the ruts, quite unconcerned by the bright red Vauxhall. Wildlife on Islay is prepared to accept you on its own terms in a way inconceivable in any English setting. Later that morning, down on the rocky shore at Loch a'Chnuic, a pair of oystercatchers intent on feeding allowed me half an hour's peeping tommery from a range of about five feet, without even a pipe of alarm.

Kildalton High Cross was astonishing. The blue stone cross, the only undamaged one of its kind in Scotland, stands nine feet high in the graveyard of the roofless, ruined chapel, complete in all its superb elaboration after 1200 years of existence. Only the extreme remoteness of its setting on an extremely remote island could have ensured its survival for so long. Weathering has taken off the finest edges of the carvings incised in the stone by the Celtic craftsman from Iona who made the cross, but the details can still be clearly made out – a Virgin and Child, David apparently cuddling but in reality killing his lion, long-winged angels, four headless lions with lashing tails, intertwining tracery and bosses standing out proudly. It is a wonderful piece of work, beautiful and forceful. I came down the track from the chapel on a wave of exaltation. Laphroaig malt whisky shook me back into real life again, by way of elevation of a different kind.

Laphroaig Distillery stood on another of Islay's rocky bays, its white buildings shining against the green and blue of grass and sea. A quiet and uplifting place to make Uisge Beatha, the water of life. Islay's present-day economy owes a good deal to whisky distilling. Islay malt whisky has a devoted discipleship all over the world. Admirers come across from the United States just to visit the true fountainhead. There are eight distilleries on the island, five of them in intermittent operation. Each has its own water source, the purity of which adds that little dash of perfection to the world's best whisky. Islay malt doesn't slide over the tonsils like mother's milk; it injects the tastebuds with a tangy shot of peat smoke. Laphroaig's whisky is famous for the peatiness of its flavour, a rich taste that can make the unwary gag on their first sip like fainting ladies in an Ealing comedy. The thick, tarry, sweetly acid reek of peat smoke that wafts round the distillery buildings rises to a throat-stopping crescendo in the kilns where the malted barley is infused with that unique taste.

John Calder showed me round the process, in company with a bearded American in a white vest and a kilt who was hitch-hiking through the Western Isles. Mr Calder showed commendable practicality in his attitude to temperature control on the malting floor – 'Ach, if it's too cold we close the windows, and if it's too hot we just throw them open.' Over the open hatchway of a great vat of fermenting, bubbling, yeasty stuff called 'wash' I took an incautiously hearty sniff, and reeled back with eyes full of tears and a larynx seemingly shut down for good. 'The wash,' said Mr Calder, 'yes, that's kind of a strong smell. The yeast is attacking the sugars and turning them into alcohol, praise the Lord.' Attacking was the *mot juste*. Normal service to the lungs was only just restored by the time we reached the long row of tall copper stills where the magic takes place. Whisky could just as well be beer up until this point in the process, but as the temperature in the still creeps up the real thing begins to make its appearance. First come 'low wines', weak stuff not fit for drinking. 'Feints' come at the end of the process, at high temperatures. 'You'd hate yourself in the morning after a night on the feints,' was John Calder's comment on this high-octane rocket fuel. In the middle, between low wines and feints, slides out the true whisky, a colourless but far from odourless spirit that needs at least ten years of maturing in oak barrels, bought second-hand from American bourbon distilleries, before it takes on that familiar golden colour and rich flavour for which the appreciative public pays through the nose.

Islay's malt whisky distilleries have been in the doldrums since the 1960s, when the optimism of those dream years of economic boom led the distillery companies to produce enormous quantities of the liquid gold. In the pinched, lean and competitive seventies they found they couldn't sell half of the stocks they had in bond. Distilleries closed, people were laid off and the industry nose-dived. So did the production of peat for the smoking of the barley, and the transportation side of the business. Hundreds of Islay people cut the distilleries' peats or drive the lorries that bring in the peat and barley and take away the whisky. Now modern technology is slowly replacing men with machines, even in this very traditional and old-fashioned industry. Mechanization happened years ago on the farms of Islay, it's happening in the distilleries, and now it's just beginning to make its presence felt out on the peat diggings where for many centuries everything has been done entirely by hand.

Beside the road from Port Ellen to the airstrip, five or six small figures were at work in a wide, flat landscape. Here the peat runs in an unbroken blanket for two miles from the shore to the hills. The green covering of grass and heather lies in sharply stepped and angled ridges and ditches a few feet tall, legacy of past peat diggings. The men at work this day, however, were pioneers of a method which may see Islay's traditional peat cutting completely outdated by the turn of the century, and the ridged landscape just another historical curiosity. Their machine was burrowing under the top covering, forcing a mixture of peat and turf – mostly peat – into small, sausage-shaped cylinders. These were laid out to dry on the ground in neat rows, looking from a distance like a carefully ploughed field, while the green blanket of grass, cut into long strips, subsided gently on to the next layer of peat a few inches down. Tractors, trailers and elevators loaded the dried peats into lorries, to be taken off to the Port Ellen maltings that deliver ready-malted barley to several of the island's distilleries.

Peat cutting here has been the subject of a bitter argument between the cutters and conservationists. Many wild geese feed on the peat lands in this part of the island. Greenland white-fronted geese, in particular, rely on the nutrients packed into the parts of the bog-cotton and white beak-sedge under the surface of these peat mosses. Conservationists claim that peat cutting for the Islay distillery companies is threatening this food supply. They recently tried to stop a contractor building a road to the peat workings. Mainland protesters, some from south of the border, came over to the island, got in the way, hectored the islanders about their traditional way of life and made a thorough nuisance of themselves. That's how most Islay people see it, anyhow. When the celebrity conservationist David Bellamy was brought over to speak to a public meeting in Bowmore, he was booed off the stage and then off the island. Some of the islanders were dismayed by the bad manners and failure to give the fellow a fair hearing, but most have not a good word to say for what were described to me as 'interfering outsiders trying to tell us what to do'. The new peat-cutting machines haven't helped matters, burrowing out more peat in a single day than a hand cutter could manage in a month.

'No good, those machine peats,' said Davie and Thomas, stacking the family peats a hundred yards away on their father's hand-cut bank. 'Too much turf in them. But look at these here. First peats from the top of the bank, and not a piece of turf in them.'

The long bricks of the hand-cut 'first peats' lay stacked on the grass, brown and crackling dry. Davie, a pink-cheeked sixteen-year-old, stood down in the bottom of the cutting, throwing up chocolate black peats to his elder brother, who piled them roughly behind him as they came flying through the air. These were 'second peats', cut out of the second layer down in the bank, purer than the first peats, darker and denser. Later they would be stacked more neatly in criss-cross 'windows' to let the breeze dry them off. On the fire they would burn slow and hot. In the corner of the bank lay the tools that had cut the peats: a great heavy iron spade with a sharp point, a wooden-handled digger five feet long for peeling back the surface layer of turf, a right-angled cutter. They were as massive, practical and old-fashioned as a steam locomotive fireman's shovel. The boys' father, who had inherited most of the tools from his own father, hadn't been in work since he was laid off from the Port Ellen maltings in the early 1980s.

'I left school last year,' said Thomas, 'and I've been on the dole as well since then. But I'm leaving Islay. Going to Glasgow to take a training, maybe an apprenticeship, or college. There's just nothing for young people in Islay if you're not fishing or farming.' He pointed across the scarred acres of old peat workings to the hills. 'Glasgow will be a hell of a lot different to this! I'll miss the island, I know I will. You might tell your friends you won't, but you will. Here you can do what you want. No one bothers you.'

I spent the afternoon doing what I wanted, which was wandering along the cliffs at the Mull of Oa. The stubby Oa peninsula leans south-west from the underside of Islay, the remotest place on the island coast. The one narrow road in the Oa soon declines to a rutted track through a series of gates before reaching Upper Killeyan, a farm isolated in a sedgy hollow thick with flags and ragged robin at the very end of the peninsula. Beyond it fall the cliffs, plunging 300 feet seaward in pink, black and yellow curtains of rock and scree. A great disc of sea stretches out to where Ireland's cliffs curve in a faint line up on the horizon and down again. A stark tower, banded in dark and light stone, stands on the edge of the Mull of Oa like a lighthouse – neither Scottish nor Irish, but American. It was built as a memorial to the 266 soldiers and sailors drowned off the coast of Islay in two separate troopship wrecks in 1918. A herd of goats was nibbling the turf around the base of the tower as I came up over the rise of ground. They sidled off and out of sight, to reappear a few minutes later on a ledge 200 vertical feet below that looked no more than a crack in the cliff face. I was happy to stay on top, edging round the sheer-sided gullies with body and mind in neutral. Hours and miles seem to slip magically away in the Oa, in solitude as heady and savourable as an Islay malt.

Solitude was the keynote, too, at Loch Finlaggan the following morning. Lying well off the road in the north-east of Islay, the loch is looked down on by the deserted and boarded-up farmhouse of Finlaggan, its range of outbuildings and barn all ruinous. There was activity on the shore of the loch, however, as a gang of builders knocked an abandoned cottage into shape as a soon-to-be-opened visitor centre. Loch Finlaggan holds the very spirit of medieval Islay on its two tiny slips of islets, but up until recently the grass and sedge were allowed to run riot over what remains of the seat of power of the Lords of the Isles. Here in this remote valley between rocky hills the Macdonalds dispensed justice, summoned their vassals, feasted their allies, planned the downfall of their enemies and invested their clan chiefs. Whatever the shape of the islet buildings may have been – only the broken remains of a chapel and another barn-like structure stand among the nettles and weeds – they saw decisions taken in the three centuries before 1500 that affected the lives and livelihoods of all Hebridean islanders from Islay to Lewis. In 1493 Clan Donald was cut down from its high eminence when King James asserted his authority and took the rule of the isles under his own hand. But for those preceding 300 years the Macdonalds were gods in their own island heaven, this insignificant loch of Finlaggan the wellspring of their imperious will.

To reach Eilean Mór (the Great Isle – all of a hundred strides from end to end), I pulled myself across a thirty-foot gap by wire-guided boat. Two cheerful Danes in cycling shorts were with me in the nutshell dinghy, whose every movement threatened to pitch all three of us out and up to our necks in peaty water. There was a baling bucket in the boat, and I could well see why. We landed soaked through on Eilean Mór, and forged through the nettles to the chapel ruins, the Danes slapping their bare legs and swearing Scandinavian curses that would have made a battle-crazed Macdonald green with envy. 'What iss history of thiss, plizz?' they demanded. How to summon up the grandeur of the Lordship of the Isles from this overgrown medieval builder's yard? I didn't even know the facts very well myself. 'A lot of fighting,' I hazarded. The taller of the Danes laughed loudly, baring big white teeth and bunching an enormous fist. 'Fighting? Good, good!' he roared.

I lingered by the ruins, looking out at the little green pimple in the loch, Eilean nan Comhairle, the Council Isle where the dies of Macdonald decision were cast, until a shout from the Danes hurried me back to the boat. It was already half-way between the island and the shore, rocking wildly as the Danes laughed. 'Goodbye, goodbye,' they bawled across the widening gap. 'It's bin very nice to mit you.' My expression of dismay at finding myself marooned made them roar even more loudly. 'Jost jokking! Jost jokking!' bellowed the fighting fan as he returned the boat to the island with one heave of his great piston of an arm. Back on shore, the Danes leaped on to their bicycles and pedalled powerfully away up the hill and out of sight, trailing dusty clouds of glory. They must have ridden like supermen, for I saw no sign of them on the road to Loch Gruinart, my last destination in Islay, where the deposed and land-hungry Macdonalds notched up their most terrible victory.

By midday I had forced the groaning Vauxhall up into the north-west corner of the island, to the shores of Loch Gruinart where cattle munched seaweed. The mud flats of the sea loch were spread between white gashes of sand dune as a gleaming dinner table for thousands of wading birds. The breeze carried the thin cries of redshank and snipe, lonely sounds in a lonely place. The roofless stone shell of Kilnave Chapel stood above the loch on a grassy slope, its graveyard full of crosses. Ducking through the four-foot-high doorway, I came into the bare interior of the church, a tiny cell whose stones were bearded with pale green tufts of lichen. The roof was open to the sky: the thatch that once covered it had been the death of thirty Macleans from Mull when fired by the torch of an avenging Macdonald.

The loss of the Lordship of the Isles in 1493 had left everyone in the Hebrides, not only the Macdonalds, dissatisfied with their holdings of land. It was the beginning of centuries of bickering over ownership, sometimes granted and sometimes withheld by successive Kings of Scotland as they chose to strengthen or weaken alliances with the various clan chiefs. In 1543 the Macleans and Macdonalds found themselves on opposing sides of a rebellion. James Macdonald supported the King, and when the rebellion collapsed was rewarded with land in Islay which the Macleans regarded as theirs by right. Hostage-taking, raiding, murder and treachery followed, spread over succeeding decades in true clan style. Things finally came to a head more than half a century and two generations later when Lachlan Maclean arrived in Islay on a Thursday in August 1598, with an army of supporters from Mull, intent on kicking out Sir James Macdonald, grandson of the unrebellious James. The two forces met the next day in the gently sloping fields at the southern end of Loch Gruinart, with Lachlan Maclean's men holding the advantage of the slope. Sir James Macdonald knew a trick worth two of that, however, and outflanked the Macleans with a pincer movement that soon had them in desperate trouble. Lachlan Maclean, taking a drink from a well with his helmet off, was shot through the back of the neck with a crossbow bolt and died with his face in the mud. The archer was the Dubh Sith or Black Fairy, a stunted, hairy little native of the Isle of Jura who had had his offer of service spurned with contemptuous laughter by Maclean before the battle. Hiding in a rowan tree beside the well and waiting his moment, it was the Dubh Sith who had the last laugh.

The Macleans fought on after the death of their chief, but the position was hopeless. The Macdonalds, fired to fury at the sight of Sir James laid low by wounds (in fact he later recovered), chased their enemies from the field and all the way up the lochside to where a fleet of boats lay waiting to take them off. Here the stories differ – some say that a great storm blew up and trapped the boats, others that those on board could see what was happening on shore and made their escape while the chance was there. Either way, the fleeing Macleans found themselves at the door of Kilnave Chapel with all escape routes cut off. In the somewhat optimistic hope that the Macdonalds would respect holy ground, they crowded into the little church and waited to find out if their sanctuary had been spotted. For a few minutes the pursuers were baffled, but the suspense didn't last for long. Something – noise or movement – caught the attention of the Macdonald search party, and the game was up. They lit a torch and set fire to the chapel's thatch. Trapped inside, all but one of the Macleans choked or burned to death as their enemies exulted outside.

The lone survivor, a man named MacMhuirich, managed to break out through the flaming thatch and stagger down the slope into the loch. The Macdonalds chased after him until he vanished under the water and didn't come up again; after which they went away, satisfied with a good job well done. If they had stayed a little longer they would have seen a sodden figure crawl out of Loch Gruinart and creep away inland; MacMhuirich had managed to survive by anchoring himself underwater to some rocks, breathing through a reed that he'd grabbed during his escape dash. He must have recovered from his adventure and found safe lodging in Islay with Maclean sympathizers, for his descendants still live in the island today. This was the only happy footnote to a complete disaster for the Macleans; a catastrophe which could have been avoided had Lachlan Maclean not ignored a warning given to him by a wise woman before he set sail from Mull. She prophesied a bad ending for the expedition: but if her lord was determined to go, then he should beware of landing on a Thursday, of fighting on the shores of Loch Gruinart, and of drinking from the well. Lachlan treated these warnings as he did the proffered help of the Dubh Sith, and paid for his two misjudgements with his own life and the lives of thirty of his kinsmen – history and superstition hand-in-hand, as always in the Scottish isles.

I could have lolled on the peaceful shores of Loch Gruinart all day, watching the birds and picturing the battle and slaughter; but my time in Islay was up. The ferry was waiting at Port Askaig to carry me over to the land of the Dubh Sith, Jura of the red deer and enormous emptiness.

When the last Ice Age was receding from northern Europe, it took with it an immense weight of ice that had been pressing down the smothered land underneath. Islands like Jura, relieved of the pressure, rose up like so many sponges that had been held down by a finger. Beaches that had been at sea level rose by as much as a hundred feet, to lie as sheets of

127

pebbles and rocky caves high above the new shoreline. The western coast of Jura, with all its ins and outs of lochs and bays, runs for at least fifty miles north-east of Feolin Ferry, an unbroken succession of raised beaches, caverns and inlets, totally deserted and remote. To get to the west coast of Jura involves you in a walk of several miles over some of the roughest terrain in the Hebrides. There are no roads, no intermediate inns or even houses where you can beg a glass of water; just deer tracks through the heather and over the shoulders of hills craggier and less accessible than anything a Cumbrian or Pennine landscape can offer.

Most of Jura is composed of quartzite, sand of prehistoric sea floors baked by subterranean fires, tilted and hoisted high. Quartzite discourages plant growth. Heather, scrubby grass and bog sedges are the dominant theme, with the hard, crystalline rock always ready to break through. It makes a sharp contrast to Islay's fertile lowlands. The lowest of Jura's hard-edged ridges looks formidable, the highest a challenge you wouldn't want to take on without careful planning and a good compass. In those fifty miles of Jura's western coast, from Feolin Ferry north to the Gulf of Corryvreckan, there is not a single inhabited house. The present population of 200 have all the elbow room they want in an island of almost 100,000 acres. There are more than twenty times as many red deer as humans on Jura, and they form an important part of the island's economy as targets for visiting marksmen intent on taking home a well-branched stag's head as a trophy.

Jura has just one road, running from Feolin Ferry round the southern curve of the island and up the eastern coast for 32 miles to Kinuachdrach Farm a couple of miles short of the northern tip. Craighouse is the biggest of the two or three tiny settlements along the road. Charles Fletcher gave me a lift from the ferry to the Jura Hotel at Craighouse, shoving tins of dog food off the passenger seat to make room for me in his battered old car. All cars on Jura are battered and old. If they aren't that way when they arrive on the island, they become so after a few months negotiating the grass-grown, bumpy road. Charles Fletcher runs the most northern of the six estates of Jura, 'a little bit of this and a little bit of that. We raise cattle and sheep, do some forestry, rent out cottages on long lets in the winter and short ones in the summer. It's no good trying to set yourself to do just one thing here. You have to diversify to keep going.'

There are between 50 and 60 people in employment on Jura, the maximum number of jobs the island will support. They work on the estates, mend the road, drive people and goods around. Each of the estates has employees who double up as stalkers during the deer-shooting season, taking parties up into those wild hills for as much rough treatment as they're prepared to put up with.

'We get mostly continentals coming to shoot the stags,' Charles said as he ground round the sharp bends of the road. 'They pay per stag shot, about £180 a head, plus VAT, and they might shoot between five and twelve each. That's between August and October. From November to February it's the hinds. It's a funny thing, the difference between the continentals and the English. Your average continental wants to shoot a good stag with an enormous great head of antlers, a huge head to take home, without a lot of trouble or having to do very much or walk very far. The Englishman – we joke about this – he wants to walk about twenty miles, crawl on his belly through one bog after another, go hungry and thirsty all day, and shoot a miserable little hind at the end of it. Then *he's* happy.'

In spite of the isolation, the vast empty spaces and the tiny population, life on Jura has its racier side. Phoning home that night from the Jura Hotel, a scribbled line of handwriting inside a folded tariff card caught my eye. I unfolded the paper, and read: 'Hi there. Our names are M—— and K——. We are the "chambermaids". If you are young free and single with a good time in mind. Give us a wink!! We are upstairs most days!! See you soon!!'

Unwinking, I survived the night, to catch Charlie outside the hotel early the next morning on his return from the school ferry run. Charlie is Jura's own Mercury, taking messages, people, letters and parcels up and down that long road. His busiest time is in the early morning and evening, when young children from all parts of Jura have to get to the island's primary school at Craighouse, and their older brothers and sisters must catch the ferry to their secondary school at Bowmore in Islay: 140 miles of to and fro for Charlie. Sometimes he drives a battered old minibus, sometimes a battered old car, depending on numbers. Today his partner had allowed the bus battery to run flat, and Charlie was not at all pleased. Conversation was intermittent all the way north for sixteen up and down, in and out, left and right miles to Ardlussa, the home of Charles Fletcher, where I planned to start a long day's walk to the northern tip of Jura. Charlie couldn't take me any further, partly because he had a return journey to make, partly because he feared for the suspension of his well-worn Ford car. I soon learned why.

Ardlussa House looks out through beech trees to a splendid view down into Ardlussa Bay. These woodlands of pine, birch and beech, splashed with purple rhododendron bushes, came as an oasis after the long miles of stark moorland. Woodpeckers were hammering away deep in the woods. The single-track road, grass tufts bursting up through the tarmac, dipped and climbed under the trees between battalions of foxgloves. Then it entered an open glen, shed its smooth surface and became a stony track where I stubbed my boot toes again and again on upstanding rocks. Cars like Charlie's tend to leave their exhausts behind on this section. Tractors are a better bet, but none came by as I trudged north warily past fat-shouldered brown bulls lying across the road in dopy domestic stupor among their harems. The green flank of the glen, spotted over with pale pink orchids, dropped away to the Sound of Jura stretching across into the mouth of Loch Crinan and the Kintyre peninsula's backbone of blue shadows. The view held me enchanted for five stumbling miles until the road dipped shorewards above the grey house of Barnhill.

Barnhill lies under a green slope rising to tall sea cliffs. These days the house, its walls weatherbeaten to a salty grey, does duty as a holiday cottage, approached from the road by a track paved with small boulders, as forbidding to modern cars as it was to George Orwell's motor bike back in 1946. Orwell had come to Jura to escape the demands of the London journalism that he felt was getting in the way of the novel he wanted to write. He was determined to live a life of self-sufficiency at Barnhill, but the novel made too many demands on a constitution being steadily weakened by tuberculosis. Barnhill stretched him beyond his strength. There were always peats to be cut, vegetables to be grown, fish to be caught and stores fetched by boat or tractor and trailer from Craighouse. The motor bike was too often in pieces, writing too often interrupted by the work that needed to be done to maintain a household without any modern services. Orwell finished 1984, pounding his typewriter in a bedroom at Barnhill in a race to beat the dwindling of his energy; but the TB gained on him until it became impossible to go on living on Jura. He left the island in 1949, and died on the mainland the following year.

At Kinuachdrach the road finally wound to a close. In comparison with lonely Barnhill, Kinuachdrach was a cosmopolitan centre of activity. A gang of geese hissed me into the farmyard. Hens stepped importantly around the outbuildings. Goats lazed in the shade of a tractor. A party of brightly-stockinged walkers was setting off up the glen from the bunkhouse beside the farm. Their citified pale faces contrasted, not to advantage, with the red cheeks and clear skin of the farmer's daughter who courteously put me on the right path. Loud bursts of laughter rocketed out of the windows of Kinuachdrach farmhouse, where a midday ceilidh was well under way. I followed a deer track over a couple of miles of moorland that looked quite straightforward on the map. It didn't take into account the squelchings through peat bogs, the scrambles up slippery glensides or the trips and stumbles over stones. Where Jura fell away into the Gulf of Corryvreckan I was glad to sit in the heather and munch a sandwich above the famed and feared Corryvreckan whirlpool. The wrinkled flanks of the Isle of Scarba, all strata steeply curved at the same sweeping angle, rose from the sea a mile away, a dramatic guardian of the strait. The tide was only just past the full, so the scene below was peaceful. A two-masted sailing boat passed serenely over the spot where, misjudging the tide, George Orwell all but drowned himself and three young companions in August 1947. When winter gales are blowing in from the west to meet a flood tide, Corryvreckan becomes an unnavigable confusion of white water crashing in all directions at once. From the hilltop where I sat I could hear a faint roaring, the only hint of the power held in check below.

The whirlpool takes an annual toll of Jura's 5000 red deer. Not content to stay on their native island, the deer try to swim the narrow sound across to Islay, some of them getting caught midstream by the tide and swept the length of Jura. I had hoped to spot the deer in one of the deserted glens on the outward walk, but apart from half-glimpses of dots on the skyline I had had no luck. I had retrodden the long road almost back to Ardlussa when the moment arrived. I was in that state well known to weary walkers, putting one foot in front of the other with an empty mind, when I had a sudden feeling of being under observation. Looking up, I saw a herd of ten hinds – not an antler among them – watching me from a slope about thirty yards away. Every neck was stretched high, every ear cocked, tension and grace combined. I raised my camera, and the watching heads rose another notch. I pressed the button and the little mechanical noise, a tiny sound in all that wide space, acted like magic on the herd. All ten turned and trotted over the skyline, starlets too shy to be photographed.

On a triangle of grass below Ardlussa, after more than twenty miles of hard walking, I pillowed my head on my knapsack and drifted off. Charlie's taxi, rattling up, woke me an hour later. Back at Craighouse a hilarious bunch of shirt-sleeved Islay businessmen was lurching in the road, putting down their final shots of Jura Distillery malt whisky before setting off in a minibus for an evening's sea fishing. 'Here, take this,' said the distillery manager, handing me a giant measure of malt. 'They'll only spill it all over themselves.' Raising the glass to toast the occupants of the departing minibus, I provoked an almighty cheer – the loudest noise I had heard all day.

I would have climbed the Paps of Jura next morning, if the Jura adders hadn't been holding a sunbathing convention on the south-facing slope above the Corra River. They lay out basking on the warm rocks in the heather, stripy olive-brown old school ties coiling away into cover as my descending boots spoilt their day. The three Paps, well over 2000 feet of scree-sided bare quartzite, towered on the skyline, beckoning me to an ego-boosting scramble. These great cone-shaped peaks dominate all views in the south of the island. The week before, during the annual Bens of Jura race, runners had completed a circuit including the three Paps and four other peaks in a little over three hours. Wonderful views from the top of Beinn an Oir at over 2500 feet, said Mr Wright of the Jura Hotel – Mull, Colonsay, Arran, the Kintyre peninsula. My desire for that view survived the first close encounter with an adder as I was stooping down with cupped hand to drink from the Corra River. The adder had the same idea in mind and wasn't happy to find a rival on its patch, though it didn't stay to make its point.

I inched uphill away from the river, watching every step, and almost put my boot on another sunbather. This one, vivid in black and brown zigzags, stayed where it was, defending its rock bed with a hiss like a Kinuachdrach goose. I stepped back, saying something short and hard, and took a long look at the surrounding heather. Two more in view at least. I thought of John Hillaby in *Journey Through Love*, picking up an adder: 'grasping neck and tail resolutely, stretching her a bit and tossing her into the bracken'. The smooth operator! In my case discretion conquered valour with no trouble at all. Sherlock Holmes couldn't have inspected a trail more assiduously than the one I scanned back to the road. The Paps still beckoned, but I was more than happy to let them alone. The rough track over the spine of the island to Glenbatrick would do nicely.

At first sedgy, then stony, the path wound over the ridge past a string of lochs, then down the far side through the high-sided pass above Glenbatrick. The hillsides of the pass looked as though they had been sprinkled thickly with flour – millions of quartzite boulders rubbed off by the retreating Ice Age glaciers, still perched where they came to rest 10,000 years ago. The view ahead opened up between the curving flanks of the glen, down over a shallow triangle of sea to the rocky, pebbly shores of northern Jura. The Glenbatrick River tumbled from fall to fall below the path. First making sure that the bank was adder-free, I knelt to take a drink and found myself staring into the amber-coloured eye of a tiny frog, sitting on a stone in midstream. Held in place either by paralysing fear or by an unfounded confidence in his smartly speckled brown-and-silver camouflage, he sat tight and let me take photographs, gulping silently, before diving into the pool with an athletic sitting jump and swimming away into shelter below the bank.

A single house stood on the shore at Glenbatrick, facing a spectacular view out over a chain of islets to the north shore's long line of raised beaches and square-mouthed caves. In front of the house ran a semi-circular cove of white sand, behind it the curve of a raised beach like a crescent rampart, now green with grass and bracken. The house is the only survivor of a farming and fishing community that lived here until roadlessness caused it to melt away. Through the windows I made out a curious mixture of old and new – an ancient kitchen range alongside modern heaters, candlesticks beside Camping Gaz lanterns; a pair of brand new water-skis propped up in a cobwebby corner. Glenbatrick is kept on by its owners as a base for sailing, deer-stalking, bathing and water-sporting, the only way to extend its existence. The nearest house is five rocky, mountainous, moorland miles away. Glenbatrick transport is by boat. For perfect solitude and a perfect view, Barnhill has nothing on this.

Loch Tarbert, the sea loch that faces Glenbatrick, runs east into the centre of Jura, failing by one mile to cut the island in two. There are many Tarberts and Tarbets in western Scotland. The Isle of Harris has its Tarbert; so does the Kintyre peninsula. The name comes from the Gaelic for a place where things can be carried across land from sea to sea. Jura's Loch Tarbert is flanked by caves, crags, sheer rock faces and those great sheets of pebbles that cover the raised beaches. The only paths are deer tracks. On the map it looked to be about five miles from Glenbatrick to the eastern end of Loch Tarbert, where Jura's road runs a mile away and where I hoped to be picked up by Charlie the taxi-driver on his return school run. In practice I must have walked twice that distance, sliding over pebble beaches, slipping over seaweed, scaling rock cliffs in vain hopes of a short cut. There were otter prints on the white sands, deer slots in the peaty wet ground. A couple of times I stepped from firm grass straight into sinking bog, well above the knee. Every level green sward turned out to be a quaking morass of grass tussocks among trenches of soft bog.

On the brink of a burn, washing off the peat dirt from my latest plunge, I noticed a stone under a jet of water whose striped surface was wavering like smoke. Hundreds of tiny pollywogs a tenth of an inch long were anchored in nose-to-tail lines, wriggling in the flow as they maintained station. As my fingers divided the little jet of water and made it fall with unequal force on different parts of the stone, the leaders of each queue clung on grimly while the tail-arse charlies went sliding down the slope of the stone to be whirled away to new holds further down the burn. I spent a happy ten minutes by that jet, altering pollywog destiny with a twitch of the finger. Then it was up and on, slipping and scrambling, racing the clock over bog, heather and seaweed to my rendezvous with Charlie. The full glass of Jura had had to be drained in one short gulp. Loganair would be waiting at the airstrip over in Islay to whisk me back to Glasgow and the next step northward.

10. Mull, Coll, the Treshnish Islands, Ulva, Staffa, Iona and Colonsay

THE CRUISE OF THE *LORNE LEADER*

Main Parts:

DON ....*Skipper*
MIKE...........*Mate*
KIRSTY ....*Cook*
NOVA ....*Cook's mate*
         (pressed on voyage)
NORMAN .....*Musician*
ANN ....*His mate*
EWEN..........*Ship's boy*

Walk-on, Stagger-off Parts:

JOHN AND	CALUM........*Teacher of Glasgow:*
JUDITH........*Newlyweds*	*cousin to* DON
RICK...........*Man of Ludlow*	KEN............*Naval engineer*
BRIAN.........*Golfing fiend of*	CLARA ....*Yachting journalist*
Sunningdale	DAVID.........*Old* Lorne Leader *buff*
ROBERT ....*Doctor of Australia*	SELF ....*Interested spectator*

The first thrill of the *Lorne Leader* adventure came when a packet of sealed orders dropped through my letterbox. Beautifully printed on expensive paper, they gave off just the right whiff of enticement: a wooden-hulled, gaff-rigged Brixham trawling ketch, a mixed bag of a dozen passengers, a young skipper with an impressive string of qualifications, a clutch of seductive photographs of the boat in full sail passing the green and blue outlines of Hebridean islands.

Calum Hind, cousin of the skipper Don Hind, gave me a lift north from Glasgow in his car. Calum, a teacher in the city, had earned his berth on the forthcoming cruise already, through hours of scraping rust off the boat's pig-iron ballast. As we drove through pelting rain and ground-level cloud up the Argyllshire glens, Calum told me the story of *Lorne Leader*. Built at Brixham in Devon in 1892 for the Lowestoft

135

trawling trade, she was sold to Swedish owners before the First World War, and spent the next half-century and more fishing and training sailors in the Baltic, where Don Hind found her in 1985. Don, from a tough working-class Glasgow background, had drifted away from the city to sea, first on oil tankers and then as instructor and master of various sail training vessels. As master of the *Arethusa* he had taken groups of London approved school and Borstal youngsters across the Channel until the job held no more pleasure for him. *Lorne Leader* was the answer to his prayer, though one that had to be worked hard at. She was thoroughly overhauled and refitted to give passengers as much comfort as goes with a smallish boat and the heavy seas of the Western Isles. Don and his wife Gilly ran the whole enterprise from top to bottom. Now they were waiting for us and their other passengers – or guests, as they think of them – up at Craobh Haven a few miles south of Oban.

Lorne Leader lay at the end of the floating jetty, a long, low hull painted dark blue, two thick masts rising from the deck with traditional ratlines and running rigging, a spoked wheel, a brass bell, rows of belaying pins along the bulwarks. How many mutineers' skulls had been stove in with a belaying pin in my childhood sea stories! On deck, only the nylon of the sails and a big inflatable dinghy with an outboard engine bore witness to the 20th century. Just lying moored there, the rain leaping off her deck, she generated excitement. By the time her complement of guests and crew had claimed bunks, squashed too-big cases into too-small lockers, bumped heads on the deck beams and introduced themselves, reserve had been banished. You can't sleep with a stranger's snores six inches above your own nose, or eat with his or her elbows digging into yours at a big communal table, and keep your distance.

Calum set the tone for the cruise, sitting down straight away to a hilarious game with Katrina and Jamie, the Hinds' two youngest children, involving hurling rubber pigs across the table and making free with the insults. Before sailing, Gilly Hind and the two small children went ashore, leaving ten-year-old Ewen Hind as ship's boy for the duration. Ewen was made for the job. He climbed around the rigging like a spider all week, played tin whistle, wrestled with his big cousin, masterminded navigational decisions and directed conversations, the cheerful asset any ship's boy should be. Ewen had leaned over thousand-foot cliffs on St Kilda, seen seals and sea otters, eagles and red deer within the past week.

136

He had taken responsibilities and performed athletic feats that would have left most ten-year-olds for dead. Ewen's father, at the same age, couldn't even have imagined such freedom.

Don Hind's story unfolded in chunks as the cruise got under way. He and his sister and five brothers went through what Don, with masterly restraint, calls a 'heavy-duty upbringing' on the fringes of the Easterhouse housing scheme, one of Glasgow's toughest. Lessons at school were interrupted by intruders with iron bars entering the classroom to fell gang opponents at their desks. Gang membership was compulsory in Easterhouse in order to ensure personal safety on the streets, but somehow Don and his brothers kept clear. They paid the price of non-membership in bootings and beatings. That Don should have survived free of police trouble is unusual enough, but to emerge to run an enterprise like *Lorne Leader* takes extraordinary qualities of character and determination. Birds, beasts, flowers, geology, tides, weather, engineering, doctoring, practical psychology – all these are grist to Don Hind's mill: a born leader, and an enviably well-balanced man.

There was no time that first evening to do more than slip out for a couple of hours as the rain cleared, to an anchorage in an inlet of Seil Island where we watched the seals bobbing in the water and listened to tunes from Shetland and Sweden on deck until the midnight air got too cold for the musicians' fingers. Norman and Ann were the music-makers, along from Edinburgh for the week with their great array of concertinas, tin whistles, harmonicas, bodhrans and other things that go bump and squeak in the night. There was a swift change of heart in those who protested at first that they couldn't play – had never played – wouldn't dream of playing. The cutlery locker was raided for spoons, and impromptu knock, knick and knack bands began to get steam up for the island pub ceilidhs we had been promised along the way.

Unless ye become like little children, ye shall not enter even the lowest reaches of sailing competence. Next morning, under way up the Sound of Mull, we began to learn what it meant to have placed ourselves in a realm in which Don Hind was king and the rest of us were mere serfs. At first with age-long patience, then with crisp decisiveness in his directives ('orders' would be too harsh a word) Don brought us up out of the pit of darkness through the vale of travail into the light of only partial incompetence. I don't know exactly what we all were, in the normal world beyond the Western Highlands – a doctor, certainly; a computer programmer; a couple of teachers; a trainee journalist – but here on board we had to lay aside all customary competence and expertise, and become open clay to be worked on by Don and *Lorne Leader*'s mate, Mike. The 'Hornblower' books had filled my head from an early age with sailing scenes rich in 'Avast hauling! Belay that rope! Luff her up and slacken off the foretops'l!', and here it was in action.

Lorne Leader was gaff-rigged, meaning that the mainsail was framed between two wooden spars, gaff on top and boom underneath. The mainsail had to be hauled up by hand, like all the ship's sails. In teams of two and three we learned to pull down with full weight on ropes apparently hempen but in fact of plastic fibre, while the blocks and pulleys squealed and the mainsail gradually rose to a satisfyingly tall and broad sheet overhead. The lines and lines of halyards (pulling the sails up) and sheets (tightening them across), a baffling cat's cradle of ropes at the start of the cruise, began to take on names and characters as we got to know them. So did the sails. Above the mainsail was the topsail, lashed to the mast and shaken out by Mike, who would climb up the web-like ratlines to do all jobs aloft. At the back of the boat rose the mizzen-mast with its rhombus-shaped mizzen sail and, in good wind, triangular mizzen staysail: at the front, over the long bowsprit, the staysail, jib and flying jib – all these triangular as well. Various combinations of sails were set as wind, tide and direction dictated. One of the best moments of each day came when the jib was set. I used to look forward to this manoeuvre. Stowing the jib at night involved rolling it into a long sausage and tying it round with scores of lengths of green garden twine. In the morning we would haul the grey nylon sausage into position. Then, with a flick of the wrist, Mike would shake out the sail with a ripping noise as the pieces of twine burst apart more quickly than the eye could follow, upwards and downwards from a starting point a third of the way up the jib, and flew away to float into the sea.

My working partner was Robert, an Australian ear, nose and throat doctor, over in Europe for a year's specialist training in treatment of cancers. Together Robert and I hauled on the ropes and grabbed flapping armfuls of sail until our palms began to feel – if not horny, at any rate not quite as soft as they had been. Robert's confident calmness was quickly spotted and exploited by Don, who was getting him to oversee jobs and take initiatives on the first day while the rest of us were still wondering which of five identical parallel ropes was the one to pull. One hands-on experience, and Robert knew. I wouldn't at all mind having Robert for my doctor.

All afternoon we hauled, made fast and stood by as *Lorne Leader* tacked up the Sound of Mull with the mountains of Mull to port and the mainland ranges to starboard, little more than a mile apart. At evening we came to Tobermory, Mull's tiny main town, colour-washed houses curved round the bay under a steep backdrop of tree-covered hills. There's no more enchanting sight than Tobermory at sunset. We tied up alongside *Coll*, one of Caledonian MacBrayne's smallest ferries, and clambered across her deck to reach the quayside and the Macdonald Arms on the waterfront. We were only intending to play a few tunes in the back room for our own amusement, but once *Lorne Leader*'s contingent started dancing the Dashing White Sergeant with the local boys and girls among the stools and tables, the evening began to catch fire. Norman had quit us the evening before, called away to his sick father by a radio message, and Ann was left to carry the tunes on her concertina. The Tobermory folk couldn't resist her. There was an hour or so of traditional music and dancing; then the customers began to dredge up requests from shelves far to the back of their memory banks. From jigs and reels we slid unresistingly down through blues and boogie, aided by a guitar I somehow found in my hands. Three local girls – we christened them the Tobermaries – began to shriek out Gaelic songs, dipping and swaying with their arms round each other. It was well into the next morning by the time we had lurched back to *Lorne Leader*. I sat later still on deck, watching two swans crashing up and down the bay like little tugs, and hearing the cries of a colony of gulls on some far-out rock.

Poor Calum. As soon as *Lorne Leader* left Tobermory he was in trouble. The wind was Force 5, enough to raise a swell on the unsheltered water beyond the land as we made west for the Isle of Coll, twenty miles away. Calum's face turned white and filled with creases, his chaffing Glaswegian wisecracks died out to a miserable silence, and he sank to his knees to become a fixture by the lee rail. *Lorne Leader* rose and dipped over the waves: Calum's head rose and dipped over the rail. He sat all day in thrall, under a weight of sickness that crushed him out of our companionable circle, a ghost-faced man apart. We passed and re-passed his hunched figure as we hauled on halyards and made fast to belaying pins, smothering complaints from our own queasy stomachs in the concentration of hard work. Any rope that needed coiling or sail that wanted tying had half-a-dozen eager volunteers hurrying forward, thankful to be distracted. Calum couldn't even raise the energy for a smile, let alone take part in any activity. He was in good historical company. Dr Samuel Johnson had had exactly the same trouble in the same stretch of sea during his journey to the Western Isles with James Boswell in 1773. Calum just had to sit and hang on until we anchored in the shelter of Loch Eatharna on the eastern side of Coll.

Coll and Tiree lie further west than the rest of the islands of the Inner Hebrides. On our passage over from Mull we passed three intriguing shapes away to starboard – mountainous Rhum, spiny-backed Eigg and the little rocky button of Muck. I gave them many a glance under my hauling, bracing, tying arms. In a couple of weeks I would be seeing them at close quarters. To port were the flat wafers of the Treshnish Islands, with unlikely conical peaks of basalt rising from the biggest of them. The fertile green back of Tiree lay hull-down on the horizon. The eastern face of Coll lay low and barren-looking, bare grey volcanic rock rubbing through a thin sheet of grass and heather. The map showed only one road, a short loop with a protruding thread. 'Wonderful beaches,' said Ann, who had camped on Coll. 'All on the west side – you must see them.' We descended in a flock on the guest house by the pier and hired almost every bicycle they had, boneshakers of all sizes and states of repair. Mine was an upright, black-painted grandpa model, with a hard, narrow seat that slipped backwards on every hill, forwards on every slope. This seat was what you might call anatomically divisive. Others in the group had children's bikes, or bikes with no gears. Every bike rattled and squeaked. Setting off, seven of us crouching over diminutive handlebars, elbows and knees sticking out, we raised some grins on the faces of Coll folk who saw us go by.

Arinagour is Coll's only village; a fine church with a pinnacled tower on the ridge, a low street of cottages, the Coll Hotel, the Coll Trading Company (everything from booze to bathsalts) and, amazingly, the Coll Bistro. Coll's population of about 130 is well served. Away from Arinagour houses are widely scattered, singly or in pairs, behind bright little flower gardens walled in against the wind. There are no tremendous hills; just a landscape of stony outcrops, grass and heather. While the others biked on down the road to the beaches, I lagged behind and turned off to climb the 300 feet of Ben Hogh, Coll's highest peak and a viewpoint over many miles of mainland, island and Atlantic. By an abandoned croft at the foot of the hill a boggy stream flowed, its damp margin bright with flowers. With the help of *Lorne Leader*'s flower book I laboured to identify birdsfoot trefoil and bog asphodel (yellow), marsh lousewort and bog pimpernel (pinkish), bloody cranesbill and bell heather (purplish) and cotton-grass (white). The book came in handy again down on the machair. This is wonderful stuff, a lush sward of grass and wild flowers that establishes itself along these west-facing island coasts, building up on top of the lime-rich shell sand blown inland and shaped by the Atlantic winds into meadows and dunes. Cows and sheep love the machair, and thrive on it. As well as grass, they munch a floral salad of clover, buttercups, daisies, plantains and orchids. Pyramidal, early purple and spotted orchids were the ones I managed to identify, but you could probably quadruple that number. All these plants were freckles of colour on a basic theme of yellow from the omnipresent flat spikes of lady's bedstraw. The tyres of the bike crushed clover, heather and wild thyme, releasing warm, spicy smells. Standing on the curve of cream-coloured sand in Hogh Bay, with dunes on either hand, machair at my back and green Atlantic rollers sheeting spray over the rock headlands of the bay, I drank in exhilaration in great gusts.

Down at the southern end of the island stands Breacachadh Castle, a dark block blending with a dark background of seashore rocks, expressing the grim fortitude of its Maclean builders as it has done for 500 years. Grim fortitude is the requirement of today's guests at the castle, young people going through hell to be tempered for glory. Breacachadh's owner, Major Nicholas Maclean-Bristol, runs a training school for overseas development workers renowned for its toughness. Press photographers love to capture the 'galloping Major', yomping inexhaustibly with flapping kilt and streaming hair over Coll's rocks and bogs in the rain, followed by a train of sodden youths in the last stages of exhaustion and misery.

Just up the bank from the old stronghold stands the one built new by Coll's Maclean laird in 1750. Its appearance is unusual to say the least, a square Georgian mansion top-heavy with Victorian corner turrets, splendidly out of place and out of sympathy with the low and subtle landscape of machair and weatherbeaten rock. Dr Johnson called it 'a neat new house' in his *Journey to the Western Islands*, but he had been rather ruder about it in private to Boswell: 'there was nothing becoming a Chief about it: it was a mere tradesman's box.' Johnson and Boswell had been blown in to Coll by a tremendous squall on their journey from Skye to Mull. In his account Johnson dismisses the storm in a few lines. He was lying below, seasick, and so was spared the sight that scared Boswell half to death, 'a prodigious sea, with immense billows coming upon a vessel, so as that it seemed hardly possible to escape. There was something genuinely horrible in the sight. I am glad I have seen it once.' On board the ship with Boswell and Johnson was Donald Maclean, the son of the laird of Coll, who managed to pilot them all in to safe harbour in his island and entertained the travellers for several days until the storm relented sufficiently for them to get away. He was an impressive young man, very concerned for the improvement of his land and tenants. Dr Johnson was delighted by Young Coll's hospitality, and by the good relations he observed between the islanders and their laird's heir.

'Wherever we roved, we were pleased to see the reverence with which his subjects regarded him. He did not endeavour to dazzle them by any magnificence of dress: his only distinction was a feather in his bonnet; but as soon as he appeared, they forsook their work and clustered about him: he took them by the hand, and they seemed mutually delighted. He has the proper disposition of a Chieftain, and seems desirous to continue the customs of his house.'

At that time, with the smashing of the clans at the Battle of Culloden less than thirty years in the past and all their traditional systems in full disarray, the notorious clearances were beginning to depopulate the Highlands and islands. Clan chiefs were obliged by law to send their sons to be educated in the south among the civilized peoples. The wearing of tartan was proscribed, as was the carrying of weapons. Clan lands were confiscated, and the chiefs' traditional powers of jurisdiction among their people withdrawn. The clan leaders, stripped of their ability either to command or to help their clansmen, began to change into fine, flowery Edinburgh gentlemen. Money, once an unimportant part of their lives, now became a necessity, in huge quantities, to service their drinking, gambling and party-giving habits.

With the emotional ties between clan leader and clansman now cut, neither party felt towards the other the obligations and the affection which had kept the old clan system viable. So the chiefs began to sell off their lands to rich incomers – English lords, self-made men or canny lowland sheep farmers. The new lairds felt even less sympathy than the old for their tenants. There was no profit in Gaelic-jabbering clansmen. But the hardy, fat and sturdy Cheviot sheep, big, white and Roman-nosed, would thrive on the best of the clan lands and could be turned to good account in the market. Better still, they needed only a few shepherds to look after them.

Out went the new lairds' agents, the factors, to deliver the eviction notices to the clansmen. A year was a generous allowance. If they were not clear by then, in came the bully boys, torches in hand, to burn the thatch, throw down the timbers and smash the possessions of the tenants. Tens of thousands of men, women and children, of all ages and states of health, at all seasons of the year, were put out of their homes in this way between 1770 and 1870. Most went to the poor, stony land by the shore and eked out existence there, turning ignorant hands to fishing, eating shellfish off the rocks, planting a few potatoes and some corn in 'lazybeds' heaped up out of seaweed. Droves of dispossessed people emigrated to Canada, to America and Australia. Their old settlements crumbled into their component stones, and the rich land went under the sheep. Even today the islands are suffering from the effects of the clearances. Their populations fell below a critical level and have never recovered. The first and most powerful aspect of the islands to strike me was their emptiness.

Young Coll and his father had about a thousand tenants on their small island, scraping a livelihood out of growing oats, grazing cattle and gathering seaweed on the shore. Coll was an overpopulated and under-resourced island, but neither old nor young laird had any intention of jumping on the clearance bandwagon. Young Coll was a beacon of hope for the future, full of energetic plans, building roads, prospecting for lead seams, introducing the cultivation of turnips. Johnson and Boswell fantasized together about building a statue to Young Coll. Boswell decided that they would 'have him as a pilot; we will have him as a fisherman, as a hunter, as a husbandman, as a physician'. Johnson, in his character-istically peppery, detached way, summed up Young Coll as 'a noble animal. He is as complete an islander as the mind can figure. He is a farmer, a sailor, a hunter, a fisher: he will run you down a dog: if any man has a *tail*, it is Col. He is hospitable; and he has an intrepidity of talk, whether he understands the subject or not. I regret that he is not more intellectual.' The noble savage, no less. With all his talents and good qualities, and with so many expectations invested in him by his people, it must have been a shattering blow to the island of Coll when, making the short journey between Ulva and Mull the following year, young Donald Maclean was drowned.

Next day *Lorne Leader* went slowly south with a light wind behind her, past the extraordinary shapes of the uninhabited Treshnish Islands. Garrisoned by Macleans in times past to guard the Mull approaches, Don said as we went by. The Treshnish looked like a flotilla of submarines, flat basalt slabs with central cones like conning towers. Laval flow created formations like these all over the Hebridean islands, squeezing its way up into cracks and chambers of already existing rock. Then it cooled into basalt. As the softer surrounding rock wore away through millennia, the basalt stayed standing in the shapes into which it had been moulded: plug, spire, column, or, in the case of the two chief Treshnish islands, Lunga and the Dutchman's Cap, central towers. I wanted to get ashore and climb up one of those towers, but we had to use the wind while it was there. *Lorne Leader* ploughed on south to an anchorage in a narrow bay between the islands of Ulva and Gometra, near the spot where Young Coll had met his death.

A scramble with Dr Robert up the steep basalt ledges in the face of Ulva was followed by a riotous evening playing lubricated Trivial Pursuit at the big saloon table below decks. After two days on the Stugeron seasickness pills and off all food and drink, Calum Hind was getting up steam again, and he wiped the floor with the rest of us. Do you know how many sides there are to a scalene triangle, or which is the only one of the ancient Seven Wonders of the World still standing? Calum did. 'Christ Almighty,' said Don, 'I preferred you when you were sick. Tomorrow we'll find some rough weather and shut you up again.' It was just as well that this threat never came to pass, as rough weather would have denied us a landing on Staffa, for me the high spot of the entire cruise.

In the towers of the Treshnish Islands the basalt had shown a little of what it could do, but Staffa is basalt's masterpiece in the Hebrides as a

144

whole. This tiny, flat-topped block of black rock six miles or so off Mull cast a spell over everyone in *Lorne Leader*'s inflatable as Don Hind took us close inshore under the columns of basalt. Trapped rocks and gas bubbles showed in the bottom of Staffa's three layers. The top layer overhung the sea a hundred feet above us, bulging out like a black, petrified brain. In between, insulated during the cooling process and therefore able to crystallize, the hexagonal columns stood twenty or thirty feet tall, all parallel, hundreds of black pencil shapes packed tightly together. In some cliffs the columns were vertical; in others they all bent sideways together at the top, or in a flowing curve at an oblique angle. A pile of rectangular basalt blocks formed Am Buachaille – the Herdsman – just offshore, looking exactly like a large heap of carelessly stacked peats. Trying to write about Staffa, one reaches for the similes – pencils, brains, stacked peats – in vain, aware that two centuries of writers have overdrawn this literary account. 'A dread loneliness seems to lurk in every nook and cranny,' wrote Thomas Nicol in 1931, in one of any number of florid passages in his book *By Mountain, Moor and Loch to the Dream Isles of the West*. 'At each step new wonders are revealed and the grandeur of the whole structure is on such a vast scale that you cannot comprehend its meaning. When one attempts to describe it, words fail . . . Staffa stands as a wonderful example of Nature's craftsmanship veiled in solitary grandeur, a lone isle guarded by the great Atlantic swell.'

Square-mouthed caves run into the sides of Staffa. Don nosed the inflatable into one of these, where a colony of shags was nesting. At first sight just small black versions of the cormorant, the shags revealed themselves at close quarters as handsome birds decked out in iridescent green plumage. Their nesting sites were untidy bundles of collected seaweed on narrow ledges in the side of the cave. Six or seven shag families perched one above another, the whole rock face slubbered from top to bottom with greeny-white shag shit. 'Kind of a shag tenement,' observed the fast-recovering Calum. 'Outside lavvie, too.' The mother shags on guard over their bundles of fluff threatened the approaching dinghy with staccato barks, each one accompanied by a sideways flick of the head. As we got nearer the mothers abandoned their perches and hobbled down the tenement stairways to dive into the translucent green water of the cave, where we saw them swimming ten feet below the boat.

As Don guided the inflatable into Fingal's Cave past snorkelling divers and boats full of sightseers, Ann took out the concertina she'd brought with her and sent Phil Cunningham's haunting and beautiful air 'Miss Rowan Davies' echoing up into the black shadows of the cave's roof. 'Like the nave of a cathedral' said all the guidebooks, and that's the only description that fits – 200 feet long, 50 feet high, flanked by rock pillars and with a mouth rising to close at the top in a cathedral's pointed arch. The green water, so clear that the sandy bottom showed twenty feet down, slopped us up against the back of Fingal's Cave. At high tide in stormy weather the waves thunder and vibrate in the cave to produce what some listeners describe as cannon shots, others as melodious tones: hence the Gaelic name An Uamh Binn, the Cave of Melody. I thought, as anyone visiting Fingal's Cave must do, of young Felix Mendelssohn coming to Staffa during his Hebridean tour in 1829 and receiving inspiration in the cave for his Hebridean Overture. Ann put an edge of realism on this highly romantic picture. Felix was indeed overcome, but not solely by the glories of Fingal's Cave. There was a heavy swell running at the time, and he spent most of the trip pouring out his feelings with his head over the side of the boat. Calum enjoyed this part of the story. When they got back to land again, Mendelssohn staggered to the piano to try out the tune that had forced its way into his mind through his sickness, only to be sternly chided by his host for attempting to make music on the Sabbath.

Half a mile of green plateau makes up the top dressing of Staffa. This is a wonderful place of orchids, vetches, ragged robin, thrift and clover: machair raised a hundred feet above the sea, the flower heads of all the species twice the size and brightness of familiar mainland versions. What causes this well-being among the plants of Staffa I don't know, but their beauty set the seal on the enchantment of that still, pearl-grey morning. Dr Robert lay full length on the sward, shooting the flowers with his close-up lens. Others of the *Lorne Leader* contingent went off to photograph the puffins doing sentry duty outside their burrows, or lay out on the cliff edges and gazed westward towards Tiree. I did one, then the other; then wandered round the rim of the cliffs, whistling 'Miss Rowan Davies', drugged by the loneliness, the strangeness and beauty of Staffa, until it was time to be picked up.

Other islands in the Inner Hebrides gave off this exhalation of beauty n isolation, but none more poignantly than Staffa. It was rather a pity that our next port of call should be Iona, Saint Columba's holy isle. Still dizzy with Staffa, I wasn't really in the mood to appreciate what many people see as the jewel in the Hebridean crown. For nearly a thousand years Iona was a sacred object of pilgrimage, the place to which Scottish kings were brought for burial. From Iona came the itinerant preachers, the converters of heathens, the artists and craftsmen, the bands of monks setting off to die in droves under Viking swords while establishing their communities all over Britain. Iona was the nerve centre of the great Christian invasion that established the faith in these islands, its touchstone and fountainhead. The tall, square shape of the Abbey still dominates the eastern side of the island above the Bay of Martyrs where we anchored for the night. Behind the Abbey a little museum held the grave slabs of nearly fifty kings. All this was too sombre and historical for that light afternoon, with Iona's few tourist shops packed to the doors and Glaswegian children shrieking over a football game on the grass outside the Abbey. I gave the whole of Iona's heritage a few minutes' half-attention, then headed for the bookshop and a frivolous hour among slightly-foxed volumes of 18th-century Scots folklore and the reminiscences of crackpot island lairds of richly merited obscurity.

Returning late in the day to *Lorne Leader*, I felt guilty at my failure to drink deeply from the fountain of Iona. I did eventually make my way back, taking time out from a different journey a year later through Skye and Mull. Then some magic did rub off. But for the present Iona was to me a missed opportunity.

A deathly pallor had been stealthily invading Don Hind's healthy, weatherbeaten complexion as the week's excesses began to take their toll. Like a good host, Don had been keeping the rest of us company as we sang, drank and randied into each morning's early hours, slaves to the *Lorne Leader* effect. The little bar under the counter in the saloon was well stocked with bottles and cans, the shelf with books of sea shanties. All normal habits of rest and recreation were suspended by tacit agreement. Ken, Rick and David were notable stayers-up, raising the deck beams with tuneless gusto till first light. On most evenings the *Lorne Leader* revellers were joined aboard by islanders drawn like moths to the boat's bright flame of good cheer and music. At anchor off Iona, we scooped up the survivors of a ceilidh ashore and danced reels and two-steps

147

with them on deck. When Don's endurance ran out just before dawn, he imposed a unilateral curfew in self-defence.

Colonsay, the final stopping place on the cruise, yielded another outlandish crop of pushbikes. This time I went off alone, wanting to savour the island in my own good time. Like the other remote islands of the Inner Hebrides, Colonsay lies angled north-east and south-west, under the heel of Mull and above the left shoulder of Jura. As on Coll, there was a circuit of road to follow, a seven-mile circle among more rock outcrops, meadows full of sedges and yellow flags, white crescent beaches and aprons of flower-studded machair. Colonsay felt warmer than Coll, though: more sheltered and intimate. The island is rich in trees; sycamores, their trunks thick with moss, grow in sheltered valleys. Pedalling over to the west coast through a rocky pass I watched buzzards on reconnaissance flights above the hills. Then I dumped the gearless, lampless, almost brakeless bike by the roadside and climbed one of the outcrops to look over more unspoilt miles of machair, beach and headland, all bounded by green ocean. Kilchattan churchyard lay below, stocked tragically full of headstones of wartime sailors whose bodies had fetched up on Colonsay beaches, some named and others inscribed simply 'A Sailor'. I biked slowly on through a slowly revolving succession, more varied than on any of the other islands, of rock outcrop, cornfield, woodland, loch and meadow. Colonsay's hills kept dissolving in solid belts of rain that came drifting in, five minutes apart, from the Atlantic; then they reconstituted themselves as milky white outlines hardening to purple, grey and green. This was bliss.

Our last evening on board *Lorne Leader* wouldn't have disgraced a Burns Night. All week a stream of the most delicious meals had come steadily off the erratic paraffin stove in the tiny galley. They were created by Kirsty, the New Zealand-born cook with the face of a well-travelled goddess who rolled her own cigarettes and wielded *Lorne Leader*'s flower book like a Bible. Now, tied up at Colonsay's jetty, the boat rang to a pipe tune from Norman's flute (he had made it back in time for the finale) as Don pranced around the big table, holding aloft a dish of steaming haggises, Kirsty's finest hour. Ritually stabbed to death by Don's knife, the haggises mingled their spicy entrails with the obligatory nips, neeps and tatties – whisky, turnips and potatoes – while Calum recited as much as he could remember (it was rather a lot) of Burns's 'Tam O'Shanter'.

Three Essex island causeways over the mud

clockwise:

SKIPPER'S, HORSEY, SEA

FOULNESS
Above: the Secretary
(Admin) ponders the bleak
shapes of military rack and
ruin

CANVEY
Right: the Feelgood
Connection – dark deeds at
the shabby old Monico
nitespot

ISLES OF SCILLY
Above: Robert Dorrien-
Smith, the ruler of Tresco,
on the terrace at Tresco
Abbey

Right: extravagant garden
growth at New Grimsby,
Tresco

LE OF WIGHT
ove: Fort Albert glowers
t over a storm-whipped
lent

STEEP HOLM
Right: a clutch of black-
backed gull eggs under
inspection
FLAT HOLM
Below: the warden, Will
Sandison, outside the old
cholera hospital

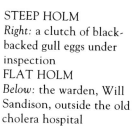

CALDEY
Above: fine buildings of the island's monastery

RAMSEY
Left: Derek Rees puts his back into the sweaty business of sheep-shearing

SKOKHOLM
Right: shearwater burrows riddle the tinder-dry, hone combed turf

HILBRE ISLANDS
Below: Little Eye's wafer layers of sandstone make a swirling landscape. Hilbre squats on the horizon

SKOMER
Right: looking down on the Mew Stone, with Skokholm lying low on the left

OQUET
ft: John Osborne, the
arden, and a skyful of
itated terns

ARNE ISLANDS
low left: the rock stacks of
aple Island, beslimed with
illemot guano

BASS ROCK
Below: every square yard of
the gannetry holds a bad-
tempered tenant

CRAMOND
Left: causeway to the island, flanked by a giant's toast-rack of concrete trestles

INCHCOLM
Below: view from the roof of the Abbey tower over the narrow waist of the island

ISLAY
peat-cutting methods – ancient . . .

and modern

Right: Lorne Leader
tacks up the Sound
of Mull: in the
foreground, Don Hind
(right) and his cousin
Calum. There were no
smiles from Calum on
the lively passage to
Coll next day

JURA
Far right: the Paps, seen
from the banks of the
Corra River

TRESHNISH
ISLANDS
Above: the Dutchman's
Cap; or, less romanti-
cally, a basalt plug

COLL
Right: green Atlantic
rollers pound the
unsullied sands of Hogh
Bay

STAFFA
Right: Ann Ward sends the air 'Miss Rowan Davies' echoing round the nave of Fingal's Cave

ULVA
Below: Dr Robert wins the scramble to the top of the cliffs. Gometra in the background, and beyond again the misty Treshnish

No one cared how the evening would unfold, provided that Don could be shovelled into bed in time to save his reason. As it turned out, the focus of that last night's entertainment proved stodgier than porridge, though a fund of malicious delight when seen through the distorting mirror of Calum Hind's humour. A dour student of geology from Dundee, over on Colonsay to study rock formations, came on board shortly after midnight to nail us all to our benches with a two-hour lecture on plate tectonics, continental drift and the formation of basaltic plugs. What should have been an evening of sentimental musical pleasures died stillborn under the Dundonian's harsh tutelage. The lecture grew in vehemence and volume as he warmed to his subject, eyes glittering and arms thrashing. Everything in the entire wide world was either of geological worth, or it was 'rrrubbash'. Everything good was 'mega'; everything bad was 'chrrrahp'. The formation of Coll had some mega primary rock; the south side of Rhum was fu' o' chrrrahp. Don sneaked off to bed. Knowing little of geology, I stayed up and began to be interested. The following morning, though, the lecture crumpled into farce as Calum passed it through his filter of comedy. The harmless Dundonian became a grotesque dolt, a humourless obsessive, a master of boredom. Any mention of Dundee was guaranteed to raise a snigger. Calum replayed the conversation for all it was worth.

Calum:	Where are you from?
Dundonian:	Dun – *DEE*.
Calum:	Who do you support, Dundee or Dundee United?
Dundonian:	*Foot* – ba? That's *rrrubbash*. Got nathang tae dae wi' jae – *olo* – jeh. (*Long pause: then, suspiciously:*) Ah suppose ye're frae *GLAS* – ga.

Gasping with feeble laughter born of sleeplessness, we made a bad job of hauling halyards as Don steered us through the Corryvreckan whirlpool between Scarba and Jura. I remembered looking down on Corryvreckan from the hillside above Kinuachdrach a couple of weeks before. Now, as then, slack water had robbed the monster of its power. Craobh Haven lay ahead, though it was touch and go as to whether Don would live long enough to see the marina again. Grim-faced, unsmiling and unshaven, eyes like two badly poached eggs in saucers of tomato sauce, Don clutched the tiller like a drowning man his straw, the pallid Phantom Helmsman

149

calling down Heaven knew what curses on his over-active guests. Lack of sleep had drained him of every last drop of the milk of human kindness. The following day, while we in our different corners of Britain were sleeping off the ravages of the week, Don Hind would be setting off with the next group of amateur sailors, patiently initiating them into the joys of gaff-rigged sailing.

11. Eigg, Muck and Rhum

THE COCKTAIL ISLES

From the moment I began to plan my island journey, I knew I'd be visiting Eigg, Muck and Rhum. Ever since I heard those three names together for the first time at the age of ten, they had brought to mind an irresistible picture of a yellowish-brownish drink foaming in a tall glass, the kind of morning-after pickmeup that Jeeves was so adept at mixing for a hung-over Bertie Wooster. I had to wait another thirty years for my first sight of the 'cocktail isles', their distinctive shapes rising out of the sea to the north as *Lorne Leader* tossed her way outward from Mull to Coll. Caledonian MacBrayne's ferry timetable dictated the order in which I was to visit them; and so, bug-eyed from twelve sleepless hours on the train, I found myself soon after the end of the *Lorne Leader* adventure standing on the deck of the Mallaig–Eigg ferry *Lochmor*, watching the wedge-shaped Isle of Eigg playing peek-a-boo with a clinging rainstorm a mile away across the water. Sheer basalt cliffs, their tops hidden in cloud, fell hundreds of feet down into the sea at Eigg's northern end, diminishing gradually as they ran south towards a flat strip of sand and grass by the jetty at Galmisdale. Groves of broad-leaved trees gave this end of the island a soft, lush look in comparison with the wrinkled and stony moorland rising northward.

Lochmor hove to off the jetty, and a little motor boat buzzed out to meet us. Stores first, tourists a long second: that was the Eigg boatmen's practical attitude. I wasn't handed down from *Lochmor*'s side into the boat until every last box of bananas, bag of potatoes and sack of mail had been transferred.

Angus MacKinnon, my host and a born-and-bred Eigg islander, was waiting on the slipway to meet me, a broad-shouldered, short man in ex-army sweater and trousers and a clanking pair of hobnail boots, built like a bull, with thick white hair swept back from a lined, impassive face. We rattled north along the winding, single-track road under grey crags in Angus's battered old Land Rover, shouting an introductory conversation above the grinding row going on under the bonnet. Eigg vehicles are without exception old, rusty and dented. One headlight out and a mudguard missing seemed to be the fashion, a V-shaped dent in the boot another popular style. Angus stopped at Eigg's one and only shop-cum-post office to take on supplies and mail, exchange some gossip and give a lift to a couple of Gaelic-speaking elderly ladies and the young granddaughter of one of them. In the low-ceilinged room of the shop a line of customers waited patiently, silently, eyeing the packets and cans ranged in severely drilled ranks along the shelves. The goods brought by *Lochmor* had made their way up to the shop by this time, and the few boxes and bundles of fresh vegetables and fruit were up for grabs. On boat day you have to get in there in good time. 'Carrots?' said the shopkeeper. 'Anyone see any carrots come off the boat? See any carrots, anyone? No? Sorry, then – there's no carrots.' That's the first rule of life on Eigg – if it isn't on the island, you have to do without it.

Behind the shop lay an immense pile – almost a little hill – of old beer cans, in front of the shop a thick, glittering carpet of discarded ring pulls. As we drove towards Angus MacKinnon's home settlement of Cleadale, plastic bags, ancient car bodies and obsolete farm implements seemed to sprout out of every roadside ditch. There were tumbledown croft houses in evidence, too, roofs off and windows blank, gardens overgrown and boundary walls crumbled. We passed an old lady in a shapeless coat, sitting in the verge swigging extra strong lager from a can. The short journey through Eigg was fraught with images that seemed to belong more to some inner-city hopelessness than to a Hebridean island blessed with loveliness and seclusion.

Cleadale itself lay in a superb situation, the few scattered houses of the community facing a wide crescent beach of silver sand on the Bay of Laig, while immediately behind them like a gigantic cinema curtain hung a tremendous arc of basalt crags a thousand feet high and a couple of miles long, weathered at the summit into a line of turrets, spires and pinnacles between which a waterfall forced itself, to jet whitely down almost to sea level. I climbed up to the top of these crags later in the day and walked the length of their ridge over springy heather, looking down on to the fertile green apron around Cleadale. This is excellent land. In 1841, with Eigg's population at 546, there were more than 150 people crofting in Cleadale. Fifty years later, after clearances and voluntary emigrations had bitten into the island's population and reduced it to a little over 200, there were still 89 folk using the Cleadale fields. Angus MacKinnon, as a boy in the 1930s, saw the crofters getting loads of hay off land below the crag which has now reverted to bog. Today fewer than twenty live here, the couple of surviving Cleadale crofts worked by people getting on in years. Most of the Western Isles are in decline in one way or another; on Eigg that decline is writ large across the landscape in the shape of equipment abandoned where it last stopped working, in rubbish heaps, broken houses, good land grown boggy.

'We just don't have the young folk interested in taking on the crofts,' said Angus over the teacups late that night. 'The population of Eigg has halved even in my lifetime. It's just over sixty now, and three out of four of those are incomers. I can trace my own family back in Eigg for twelve generations at least, but the way of life my people led for all those years is over. Finished.'

To stay in Angus MacKinnon's house is to experience the old and the new of island croft life side by side. The house itself is a modern one, built by Angus just across the lane from the burnt-out shell of his father's old home. Electricity comes from Angus's generator for a few hours every evening – then it's out with the candles. There's no television, no stereo. Angus's long-horned Highland cattle munch away at the buttercups and clover right outside the kitchen window. The croft ground grows potatoes, some vegetables, a bit of corn for cattle feed. Angus's housekeeper and companion, Ann Campbell, sells a few eggs around the neighbours if the hens have put in some overtime. A little bit of this and a little bit of that pays the bills and keeps the croft going; as Angus says, crofters don't get rich – they get by, if they work hard.

In the last couple of decades, mainland escapers – some from Scotland, most from England – have been trickling into Eigg to set up small craft businesses, do building work, take on derelict crofts. 'White settlers' is the Eigg folk's name for them. Few old-established islanders think that their effect on island life has been good. The white settlers tend to be seen as pushy, too loud, too ready to jump in with both feet flailing and trample, usually unwittingly, on islanders' sensibilities. They want better roads, a permanent electricity supply, an airstrip, a regular refuse collection service, a new and better village hall. Eigg could do with these things, without question. Most old islanders recognize that the tight, insular, self-sufficient way of life is fast crumbling, infiltrated by the 20th century beyond hope of recovery. They just don't want to have the impetus towards a new and different Eigg shoved down their throats by outsiders. 'If we ourselves haven't seen the need for it, then it can't be necessary,' is the old Eigg islanders' attitude.

The eager-beaver white settlers are one thing; the 'caravan crew' quite another. These bedraggled refugees arrive from the mainland in over-optimistic hopes of a job, set up home in a caravan unlinked to any services, usually with a baby either expected shortly or just born, and stick out a couple of miserable winters on the dole until all loyalty to the romantic dream of island life has gone. The Eigg islanders, like all islanders throughout the Hebrides, view the caravan crew with the kind of half-amused, barely tolerant exasperation normally reserved for wilful children *determined* to paddle a lilo out to sea. They'll learn, if they survive that long.

Visits from officialdom are another swarm of bees in the bonnets of Angus and his contemporaries. 'In the old days we got a visit from the vet maybe once a year. The policeman might pop across, too. That was it. The islanders ran things and sorted things out for themselves. Now we get DHSS officials coming over every other day, ministry men, social services. They've just been on at an old lady over in Galmisdale. All her life she's fetched her water from the burn, washed her clothes in a tub, used an outside toilet, had a paraffin lamp at night. Now they tell her she'd be better off in a new-built house, sheltered accommodation, with tap water and a washing machine. Huh! She told them where to go.'

Against this background, it's rather remarkable that the present laird of Eigg is not more grumbled against. A Yorkshireman of strong enthusiasms – driver of power boats and vintage cars, defender of wildlife, founder of the annual Eigg Games, nostalgist for 1920s simplicities of social structure – the laird lives for most of the year on his property, which is more than can be said for most owners of Scottish islands. Since buying Eigg in 1975 he has done his best to give the fading island community a shot in the arm, putting money into forestry, sheep farming and building restoration. A new laird whose motives for owning his island are well mixed with romanticism has as much of a struggle to prove his credibility with his tenants as any hard-nosed sporting businessman using his property as an occasional slaughtering ground. The old-established Eigg people take changes of ownership philosophically. 'We've got him,' they shrug, 'so we have to make the best of him. One laird's much like another.' It's the white settlers who mutter loudest against Eigg's

154

owner, resentful of the ultimate power that, in the end, rests with one man.

Over on the south side of the island on the second day of my visit to Eigg, I wandered among evidence of the power that nineteenth-century lairds enjoyed. At Grulin, a settlement of crofting families tucked under the flank of a great volcanic whalehead named An Sgurr, there had been over a hundred inhabitants in 1841 in the two side-by-side communities of Lower and Upper Grulin. Twelve years later, with the exception of one family, they were all gone, cleared out to make way for the sheep. Almost all the Grulin people ended up in Nova Scotia, 3000 miles away. The ruins of their houses remain on the steep slope of the hillside, looking out to the Isle of Muck. Walls stand up to roof height, door-holes are still discernible. Their strongly built boundary walls and animal pens are also clear to see on the ground, even under the bracken of summer. All the ground around – reckoned the best cattle grazing in Eigg at the time of the clearances – is smothered nowadays with bracken, among whose fronds the Roman-nosed Cheviots hide from those who venture to Grulin. The Cheviot sheep were there as soon as the people had been cleared in 1853, and by contemporary accounts did well enough in their first year for every ewe to produce twin lambs; vindication of the laird's policy.

I found Grulin a miserable place to linger, a poignant combination of beautiful surroundings and tragic history. I felt the same, in spades, an hour later as I crouched on the shore below Galmisdale and worked my way into the three-foot-high entrance to the Massacre Cave. The whole mouth of the cave in the cliffs drops and narrows from an arch twenty feet high to a tiny black hole, half hidden by grass and curtains of ivy and ferns. You couldn't find a better hiding place in all of Eigg. So thought the island population in 1577, anyway, as they crowded to the last man, woman and child into the cave and sat down in its damp mustiness for what they hoped would be a short stay. I wriggled into the blackness by a faint glow-worm light, all that the dying batteries of Angus MacKinnon's old torch could produce. Several yards in from that tiny entrance, the space opened out into quite a sizeable cavern, as far as I could judge by running my hands round the walls. It's a black, oppressive chink in the cliffs, unlit and unwarmed by any sunlight, but probably just about capable of holding the 395 tenants of the 16th-century Macdonald owners of Eigg.

Macdonalds and the Macleods of Harris were always keen for a bash at each other, and a party of Macleods arriving in Eigg provided a good spark for the ever-handy tinder of clan feuding. 'The inhabitants of the Isle of *Egg*, meeting a boat manned by *Macleods*, tied the crew hand and foot, and set them a-drift.' That was the story as told to Dr Johnson in 1773, when the Massacre Cave was still full of Macdonald skeletons. But other, more savage and in many ways more likely versions claim that the Macleod intruders, whether storm-tossed seekers after haven or bloodthirsty raiders, made their stay on Eigg memorable by raping some of the local girls. The rapists were stupid or unlucky enough to allow themselves to be captured by the male kinsmen of their victims, who enacted a punishment to fit the crime by castrating the culprits one by one, and then dumping them in a boat out at sea. When the raided raiders were discovered by their clansmen, counter-retribution immediately followed in the shape of Macleod war galleys full of outraged Macleod warriors, greedy for Macdonald blood. Into the tiny cave entrance crawled the entire population of Eigg, except one aged woman whom the Macleods found but, uncharacteristically, spared during the three days they spent searching for the rest of the people. At the end of that time the Macdonalds in the cave sent out a scout, whose tracks in the freshly-fallen snow were spotted by the Macleod party as they were sailing past, thwarted of revenge, on their way back to Harris. They put in to shore and followed the tracks back to the cave entrance, where they could hear the sounds of a large number of people inside. Realizing that to try to enter by such a low entrance would be suicide, the Macleods had their revenge by the simple but effective method of lighting a fire in the cave mouth and keeping it well supplied with damp fuel. The choking smoke filled the cave and 'smorit the haill people thairin to the number of 395 personnes, men, wyfe and bairnis'.

Almost as astounding as this event was its aftermath. Eigg was not left empty for long: in its position at a meeting place of traffic between Inner and Outer Hebrides and the mainland, it was simply too important to be left untenanted. A new community for Eigg was gathered by the Macdonalds from their surrounding properties – only to be completely wiped out again in another raid eleven years later, this time by Lachlan Maclean of Mull at the head of a party of Spanish Armada sailors who had fetched up at Tobermory. This must have been the same Lachlan Maclean who was done to death at Loch Gruinart on Islay by the Dubh Sith of Jura in 1598, ten years after the Eigg slaughter. By burning and choking that Maclean raiding party to death in Kilnave Chapel, the Islay Macdonalds were just having their long-delayed revenge. Eigg was already in full swing again, thanks to yet another transplant of inhabitants from the seemingly inexhaustible reserves of Macdonald tenants.

Such terrible events stain and scar places in ways that aren't always visible. They leave behind them an atmosphere discernible even to a sceptical 20th-century visitor. Kilnave Chapel haunts one like this, and so does the Massacre Cave on Eigg. Together with the sad ruins of Grulin's settlements, and the present-day dereliction of so much of Eigg's crofting land, for me the cave cast a sombre shadow over the island. For all Eigg's beauties – and they included a wonderful morning making the Singing Sands of Camus Sgiotaig squeak underfoot while watching Rhum's peaks smoking like volcanoes under caps of cloud – and for all the hospitality of Angus and Ann, it wasn't with any regret that I boarded the motor boat at Galmisdale to rendezvous with *Lochmor* and the short sea crossing to the Isle of Muck.

The boat that collected the handful of passengers from *Lochmor* landed us on a set of slippery steps, to stumble up a stretch of pebbles after our luggage. From the outset, Muck felt different. The island's tiny teashop, opened in honour of the new arrivals, set the tone straight away – clean, efficient, bustling. Muck has only twenty-six inhabitants, but between them they had filled the shop with home-made cakes, buns, crafts, even books of poetry. I had to carry my own bags down a rushy slope and over the sands to the Port Mór Guest House, but a bell-boy in buttons would have been a more fitting introduction to what lay inside: a pine-panelled sitting room with a polished oak floor, a fully-fitted bathroom, a plainly furnished but spotless bedroom. The meal I ate there that evening with ten other guests round the big communal table would have cost a king's ransom in London – a vegetable soufflé tangy with spices, a dish of lamb covered in a subtle sauce, fresh carrots, potatoes and cauliflower, a belt-loosening raspberry and strawberry pudding.

Had I known in advance about this feast, I would have walked up more of an appetite than the three miles I covered that afternoon across the island and back again on Muck's one single-track road. Perhaps it wasn't fair to compare the low-lying, small-scale landscape of Muck with the far less fertile surroundings of Eigg's great barren basalt crags and miles of boggy moorland, all fully in view three miles away across the Sound of Eigg. But there was no denying the contrast. The farmhouse at Gallanach Bay on the northern side of Muck had the usual pile of coal for the cooker stacked outside, and the farmyard was as cluttered as farmyards usually are. But the barns were clean and well organized, the house itself was neatly painted and cared for, the silage-storing in full swing. Down on the cliffs a cleft in the rocks held an enormous scrap metal dump, all Muck's muck collected in one place, that detritus of outdated vans, sheets of corrugated iron, broken lobster pots and derelict farm equipment which had blighted so much of Eigg's living and working space. Muck looked, felt and smelt like an island hard at work, a purposeful community with a strong sense of identity founded upon a rock less than three miles long and two broad.

Like all the Hebridean islands, Muck has had its share of ups and downs. When Boswell and Johnson were touring the Western Isles in 1773, the laird of Muck and his people were doing well out of collecting and burning sea tangle or kelp for the alkaline ash that was in tremendous demand by the glass and soap industries. The island got its name from a corruption of the Gaelic *muc-mahara* or porpoise. Lachlan Maclean, the laird, was not happy with his official title, as Johnson was amused to note: 'This gentleman should regularly be called *Muck*: but the appellation, which he thinks too coarse for his island, he would like still less for himself, and he is therefore addressed by the title of, *Isle of Muck.*'

The price of kelp stood then at about £20 a ton, but within fifty years the Napoleonic wars were over and cheaper kelp could be imported from Spain. Island kelp became virtually unsaleable. Many island economies crumbled, Muck's among them. All-out concentration on kelp had led to a disastrous run-down of farming and fishing, and the 280 inhabitants of Muck were left with no way of supporting themselves. In 1826 the Maclean laird cleared all the island's tiny settlements; most of his tenants left for Nova Scotia and Cape Breton, and those that remained were ordered to demolish their crofts, take the stones and build themselves a new village alongside the old one at Keil, on the slope above Port Mór. In a few years these, too, had followed their fellow islanders into exile across the Atlantic, unable to keep going on the unfamiliar skills of fishing and potato growing. Profitable cattle replaced them. The ruins of Keil village still stand over Port Mór, a long central street with houses, gardens and corn-drying kilns opening out each side, all outlined in stones on the grassy little plateau.

From the 1830s until the present day, the island has been run as a single farm unit – first for cattle, then sheep, then dairy cattle again and crops. The population slid down and down from its kelp-enhanced 1821 peak. Today it stands at under thirty, with only four children of school age – the kiss of death, in the experience of most of the small Western Isles. But Muck is lucky. Those tidy farmlands, healthy sheep and cattle, trim houses, clean roadsides and thriving small businesses have not dropped into the island like manna from above. They stem from the most enlightened form of lairdship I saw anywhere in the islands. If the MacEwen brothers have their way, Muck's current liveliness will go on growing into future prosperity, in the face of all the odds that are stacked against such remote communities in today's world.

The following morning I found Lawrence MacEwen hard at work shearing sheep in the shed at Gallanach Farm. Shortish, toughly built, with a bristling red beard and suffer-no-fools-gladly blue eyes, Lawrence was working in shorts and bare feet, his legs and arms spattered with sheep dung. As the agitated Cheviots, Blackfaces and Jacobs came tittuping and skidding out of the pen, he grabbed them close to the head by one horn and twisted them over on to their backs between his knees, where they subsided into panting subservience. The electric clippers unzipped each fleece with great speed – down the stomach, across the flanks, up the neck and round the back, peeling off a complete square-shaped rug of wool. Tangles, knots and hopelessly matted balls of dung were clipped off with hand shears by Lawrence's assistant Judy, who then rolled up the fleece, snipping out a strip to tie up the bundle. The wool would go out on the boat to end up at market, the fine Cheviot for clothing, the coarser Blackface for carpets and mattress stuffing.

The Highlands and Islands Development Board has been helpful in providing grants and loans for equipment, but Gallanach Farm is the pivot around which Muck's economy revolves. Lambs are bred, reared and sold, tails docked, males castrated, ewes clipped and mated; cattle mated, raised and sold; root crops and silage grown and cut to feed both. Together with Muck's couple of crofts, vegetables, milk and butter are all produced to help the island towards partial self-sufficiency in food. Land is drained, oats grown and harvested. The parallel between Dr Johnson's Young Coll and Lawrence MacEwen is irresistible. Like Young Coll, Lawrence 'worked with his own hands at the principal operation of agriculture, that he might not deceive himself by a false opinion of skill, which, if he should find it deficient at home, he had no means of completing.' While I was talking to Lawrence one such deficiency arose – a broken fence, and one of the MacEwen ewes making merry among the carrots – which brought Brian, the Muck boatman, into the shearing shed as I sat there, to deliver a sharp tongue-lashing to his landlord. In no other island community I visited could that have happened: a sign of the tendency of incoming island-dwellers to question, complain and speak out, and equally a measure of the state of give-and-take that exists between the laird of Muck and his fellow-workers. Not that Lawrence MacEwen is happy with the mantle of laird around his shoulders, as he pointed out over lunch at the farmhouse table.

'Selina Scott came to Muck to make one of her TV programmes recently, and she was keen to try and make me out as a kind of tyrant. A *Kind of Kingdom* was the title of that programme, and they were looking for that sort of evidence. It's simply my job to make sure that the farm at the end of the day can pay the bills and keep the place going.'

If lairdship is a status not claimed by Lawrence, he certainly carries out most of the functions traditionally expected of a laird. Chief among these is forward planning, not just economic, but social.

'I choose those who come to live on the island, and I try to vet them pretty carefully. I get any number of applications for a house or a croft, and I always ask around for references and to find out what sort of person we might be getting. Some turn out to be alcoholic, or so unreliable that they haven't been able to get work where they live; others are fantasists with no idea at all of what their island dream will turn out to be like. One man had a police record. A lot of them are running away from debts or from personal problems. I look for someone who can contribute something new and positive to this community, which is very much in need of a balance of talents and skills. It's not easy. Women on the whole have a hard time here – the men come with some definite job to do, whereas their wives usually have to make themselves a role. Some leave and go back to the mainland. The biggest cause of tension and argument here is the choice of new people. Once they are living here it's very difficult to turn them out. I may not get on with someone personally, but if he's doing a good job for the island I wouldn't dream of making him leave.'

Muck, in common with all the Hebridean islands, can be stunningly beautiful and peaceful. The view north from the island road of the conical mountains of Rhum next to the flattened hedgehog spine of Eigg, the blue peaks of the Cuillin Hills on Skye framed between them, is heart-lifting – even more so after a scrambling 450-foot climb up on to Muck's basalt-crowned high point of Beinn Airein. There's a pristine sandy beach below Gallanach, always empty of humans and full of wildlife; a corresponding rocky bay circled by great cliffs on the south coast at Camas Mór. The interior, where it isn't tidy farmland, is all bog, rock and heather, wonderful for energetic marching. Nearly fifty species of trees, including fuchsia, eucalyptus, whitebeam, cypress and six kinds of pine, have been introduced since the MacEwens' father inherited the island in 1922. Seabirds and songbirds abound. This is the face of the island that most visitors fall in love with, the face expected always to be smiling by some of those who come back to live. But things change in the fogs of winter, or in the autumnal gales when it is not unknown for Muck to suffer several days on end of severe gale and storm force winds, blurring every view with spray, cutting off all exit routes and sealing in the inhabitants with each other.

At such times, those with the hard work habit get by the best. The MacEwen brothers lead from the front in this regard. Over at Port Mór, Ewen MacEwen built the guest house entirely with his own hands, with help from one assistant – everything from top to bottom except the electrics, the plastering and some of the furnishings. Even the lavatory skirting boards have dovetail joints. It took him the best part of eight years. A self-taught cook, Ewen can dish up a succession of meals that would put most mainland professionals, with all the resources available to them, to shame. His vegetable gardens are full of marrows, potatoes, peas and soft fruit, his cellar well stocked with wine. One morning of my stay on Muck, I drew the curtains back soon after sunrise, to see Ewen's tall, spare figure bent double in a rowing boat several hundred yards out to sea, tugging energetically at the oars as he pulled himself out to inspect his lobster pots. By sunset their contents were on the guest-house dining table, together with a princely mayonnaise. Side by side with all this hospitable labour, Ewen was building himself a house just up the hill. As far as I could tell, he never stopped working unless actually asleep.

Lawrence's wife, Jenny, takes on the lion's share of Muck's social organization, so important to the well-being of such a tiny community. She also runs the craft shop and bakes its delicious goodies; all this in addition to her partnership with her husband in running the farm. Muck islanders enjoy their social life, setting up the barn for a game of badminton or a ceilidh, inviting each other over to eat or going out for dinner at Port Mór. It's a pity that, just at present, there is no musician on the island, though sooner or later some newcomer is bound to bring that attribute along with him or her. Muck is a musical sort of place. In the village of Keil there were reputed to be thirty pipers, before they were all obliged to take their pipes and their tunes over the sea to Cape Breton.

As for the future, Lawrence MacEwen would like, by careful choice of incomers and diversification of their skills and talents, to see Muck one day a self-sufficient community, with everyone pulling equal weight. He wants to see more children on Muck, too: 'The island could probably support twice the number of people we have here at present. I wouldn't want to agree to someone coming here just because they had young children, but we'd like to get more young families in. Four children in the school is too few. That would attract more grant aid and better services, too.

'You have to try and see your own motives clearly, if you can. The buck stops with me, so I have to make these decisions. But I want to see a situation here where everyone makes decisions on their own, and those decisions are right for the island as a whole.'

During the following couple of days, exploring the coves and headlands of Muck, I came across the grassy spur of rock where the MacEwens have their family burial ground, a ring of headstones inside a Bronze Age stone circle looking out over the water to Canna, Eigg and Rhum; a tangible link through the generations for this most practical and unlairdly family. Sitting here, I thought of the optimism of Lawrence MacEwen, his determination to build up the island's small community, both physically and socially; a determination highlighted by recent events which were still clouding every conversation and reflection in the Isle of Muck. Six months before my visit, one of the island men, a father of four children, had been killed in an accident in the boat, crushed to death in the engine machinery. The islanders had just begun to put this horror behind them when they lost two more of their young men. One was a very recent incomer, the other by all accounts a gifted person with great vitality and ability, a married man with two children, just the kind of keystone of Muck's community that they could least spare. These two men had set out in moderate weather in their creel boat to set pots, and had simply disappeared. Only one body had been found. There had been no trace of the other, nor of the boat. People had to assume, in the absence of proof, that recent changes to the boat's layout had made her unstable, or that she had been top-heavy with too many creels. Not having one of the bodies to mourn and bury was bad enough, but not to know the cause of death left everyone feeling their grief was still incomplete. People were numb. Nevertheless, everyone I met on Muck brought up the subject, sooner or later, talking about it in hopes of getting another step over it – the only way for a tiny community to take such blows and survive.

At Camas Mór, the Big Bay, I scrambled round the rocks under slides of fractured stone fallen 200 feet from the crags overhead. This was a desolate, forbidding place of rock masses poised over dark water. A sheep path climbed from the end of the bay, two feet wide at best, with sheer rock rising on the right and a long fall plunging to the sea on the left. Part of the rock wall overhung the path at one point, but with the backpack off and stomach sucked in I squeezed past, to sit and catch my breath on a rock above the Muck shaggery. Ten mother shags were on their nests of scrappily assembled seaweed on ledges of the cliff face, garking threats as they spotted me. They poked their necks and twisted their heads, assessing the threat from as many angles as possible. Down on the rocks of the shore the males had their backs to me, drying wings and digesting fish in a long line of black scarecrow bodies. As soon as I moved experimentally downward, they all shuffled forward in unison, like a chorus line. I played Busby Berkeley for a few minutes, manipulating the line of shags back and forth by remote control as I bobbed up and down a hundred yards away. Then I worked my way on around the deep crevices of the cliffs until I came upon a little croft house tucked away in a valley. A narrow sheep path was the only roadway to the remote, single-storey dwelling with walls of unmortared, piled stones and roof of bracken and turf covered with netting and roped down against the weather. Inside were a rough wooden box bed, a few kitchen utensils and pieces of cutlery, a shelf with dried milk and a tin of coffee. Above the valley I found Lawrence MacEwen striding the hillside in green gumboots and shorts. The plain little house was one of the very few holiday cottages he would tolerate on Muck.

'That cottage was restored by a chap five or six years ago, from the foundation stones up,' Lawrence explained. 'Now it's a Grade One listed building, believe it or not. He lived in it for a short time – then he got married to a girl from Harris and "went bush", as they say in Australia. I like to keep a tight rein on this sort of thing. Otherwise those with a lot of money to spend come in and take these places over, and island people can't afford to live here. My attitude is: if you restore it, you can use it. Look at what would happen to the islands if our weather was like Greece. Rich men's playgrounds, every one.'

Lawrence summoned his dog and went off for yet another round-up of that fence-trampling, carrot-loving ewe. In a couple of hours' time he would be at the helm of the island boat, ferrying me out, the sole passenger, to a mid-sound meeting with *Lochmor*. Rhum was next on the menu. I had been staring at Rhum's mountainous outline rearing from the sea for several days. From Muck's low and unemphatic moorland slopes, Eigg's ridged backbone looked dramatic enough; but my eye was constantly drawn sideways, over that gap filled in the far distance by Skye's Cuillin peaks, to the tremendous cones of rock in the heart of Rhum. Streamers of cloud had flown from their 2000-foot tips, all day every day; until now, when they stood out in ominous clarity against a still, steely sky. A deep Atlantic depression had been tracking steadily east for days, and was reported to be ready to deliver a Storm Force 10 wind to the Hebrides. It did, too: but, mercifully, not until I had landed on Rhum.

When Lady Bullough sold the Isle of Rhum to the Nature Conservancy Council in 1957, she parted with a private kingdom virtually untouched by the outside world for the best part of a century. Maclean of Coll, making plans in 1825 to clear the kelp-gatherers of Muck, had leased Rhum, another of his properties, to his kinsman Dr Lachlan Maclean. This man carried out his own clearance on Rhum, in a manner that makes the Muck upheavals seem positively gentle. Three hundred people – almost the entire population of Rhum – were shipped away to Nova Scotia in July 1826, and it was said that weeping and lamenting filled every corner of the island. Soon Dr Maclean had to import outsiders from Skye and Mull into the empty isle, to look after his 8000 sheep. Dr Maclean had trouble with the bottle, and Rhum's economy slid into a terrible decline. Lord Salisbury halted the slide when he bought the island in 1845, increasing the number of sheep, improving the lot of his workers, building dams that burst spectacularly, boosting Rhum's sporting potential by stocking the lochans with trout and the glens with red deer; benevolent and, on the whole, beneficial rich man's tinkering, in short, which had the island in the right kind of trim to suit the new owners who bought it for £150,000 in 1886. The Bullough family, extremely rich industrialists from Lancashire, put down in Rhum the roots of a seventy-year sovereignty during which the island played Mount Olympus to their god-like pretensions. Even today, their name is the one that dominates their former island paradise.

What fell into the lap of the Nature Conservancy Council in 1957 was 26,000 acres of mountain, moorland, cliff and grassland: a diamond-shaped block of volcanic rock and old red sandstone, some of whose plant and animal communities had survived inviolate since the last Ice Age. There was Scotland's earliest human settlement at Kinloch, 8000 years old. There were communities of alpine plants – purple saxifrage, moss campion, Norwegian sandwort, penny cress – on mountain tops and cliff ledges where they had stayed unaffected by those early settlers' burning of most of Rhum's forests. Nesting and breeding in burrows in the mountainsides was a colony of about a quarter of a million Manx shearwaters, seabirds that spend most of their lives floating about at sea off the coast of Brazil. There were golden eagles on the peaks; snipe, merlin and golden plover down in the moorland bogs; red-throated divers on the lochans; guillemots, razorbills, puffins and shags on the cliffs. Butterflies, moths and dragonflies abounded. Bog plants throve. Red deer flourished. Rhum was a treasure trove: a little depleted, in need of sorting, cataloguing and judicious management, but a dream acquisition over which, more than thirty years later, conservationists are still rubbing their hands with glee.

To work on Rhum is just about the apex of fulfilment for conservation volunteers, a privilege to be cherished and savoured. Imagine an under-footman presented with the keys to the wine cellar, or a powder monkey invited to dinner by Lord Nelson, and you'll get the picture. Among the chosen few dozen every year are research students, scientists and volunteer workers helping with day-to-day management of the reserve and its various long-running experiments and recordings. They paint buildings, clear scrub, mend roads, count deer, plant trees, repair fencing. At the hub of this whirl of activity are nine full-time employees of the Nature Conservancy Council and their families, who live on Rhum all the year round. Altogether there are about thirty members of this little settlement, based at Kinloch where Loch Scresort provides a sheltered bay. When they are not out on the moors and mountains restoring the tree species that were once native to Rhum, reintroducing white-tailed sea eagles, tagging red deer or setting Highland cattle to graze and enrich the grasslands, Rhum's full-time inhabitants do their best to live as a community. There are ceilidhs in the modern community hall where people are expected to contribute at least a song to the evening's entertainment; lectures, slide shows and talks; indoor games in the hall. The island school at Kinloch has five children at present, and a teacher provided by the Scottish education service.

But the NCC workers wouldn't be here if they weren't dedicated, absorbed people. It tends to be an all-demanding job, taking up most of the hours in the day – and sometimes night as well. Almost all these year-round workers are men, and time can hang very heavily for their wives, as I learned on the morning after my arrival during a rather clipped conversation with Wilf Nelson, Rhum's reserve warden. Wilf, courteous but hard-pressed, kept glancing at his wrist-watch. Ten o'clock was approaching, the time when for the past thirty years Rhum's weather readings had been ritually made, and he wasn't about to blemish that pristine record.

'The wives can have rather a hard time of it,' Wilf agreed. 'They have to find something to do here, and it's a bit limited in that way. Some of them pick winkles and sell them, and there's various small craft things going on. Most of the couples on the island have young children at home, which helps. But it can be a problem. The men all work closely together, and we tend to socialize together too. In fact, during the winter months I often make a decision not to go to some social function, just to give myself a bit of a break. It can get a bit stale, with the same faces all the time.'

The Rhum community, of course, is an artificial one. There are no born-and-bred islanders here, no threads of family continuity. Workers reaching retirement age have to leave the island and resettle on the mainland, regardless of the length of time that Rhum has been their home. The whole economy of Rhum is underpinned by government money. Unlike Muck, the workforce doesn't have to fund its own future. In a community less absorbed in a common enterprise, this knowledge of financial security could lead to inertia and a lack of initiative, as to some extent it is doing on Eigg where the laird picks up a proportion of the bills. But Wilf Nelson values the underwriting of Rhum.

'The important point is that everyone in this community is on a wage. That's a vital prop. We can get on with our work with some security behind us. Mind you, if the government actually carries out its plans to privatize reserves like this, that would be another story. We'd be open to all sorts of development and commercial influences, which would be a real threat. Speaking as an individual, I for one would fight tooth and nail against that.'

The first comment on Rhum I heard had come the previous day from a young Scandinavian scrambling gratefully aboard *Lochmor* from the NCC's ferry boat. His face was covered in red blotches, seemingly a nasty case of acne. Pointing to these, he had uttered the cryptic warning, 'Bevare of ze mitchies! Oh, zem mitchies! Bevare!' Next morning, seeing the bird-watchers and mountain climbers smearing every exposed inch of skin with vile-smelling potions out of tubes labelled *Shoo!*, *Jungle Lotion* and *Buzz Off*, I got the message. Rhum's midges are notorious. According to legend – I hoped it was a legend – one unfortunate clansman who had upset his chief had been pegged out naked on a Rhum hillside as a punishment. Before the chief's tender-hearted wife had been able to secure his release, the midges had nibbled the offender to death. Small Isles inhabitants tell this story with relish, especially to visitors. Archie Cameron, a native of Rhum writing of life on the island in the early years of this century, described seeing a glassy shimmer covering the backs of workers in the fields, caused by sunshine reflecting on the wings of thousands of midges. Many of the NCC people I met were carrying impressive crops of midge bites. I set off on a walk across the island fearing the worst, but a good stiff breeze – precursor of that delayed gale still making its way towards the Isles – kept the little black devils at bay all day.

Rhum's diamond shape is cut on the cross by glens running roughly north–south and east–west, meeting at a central point in the wet moorlands under craggy mountain slopes and spines. From here Kilmory Glen goes north to the coast, where two full-time research workers have been carrying out for the past twenty years a continuing study of Rhum's herd of about 1500 red deer and their breeding, feeding and social habits. These two people know every deer individually, and must be the world's best-informed experts on red deer behaviour. Unfortunately, as is always liable to happen when journeying among the islands, my incoming path had crossed their outgoing one. So, instead of learning as it were from the deer's own lips, I had to be content with amateur observation of the stags, hinds and calves feeding by remote tributaries of the Kinloch River as I trudged the stony track over to Harris on the west coast of the island. I tried some stalking, too, though armed with nothing more lethal than a Canon Sureshot. With my behind pressed well down and belly in the heather, I crawled up a none-too-dry stream bed to within twenty yards of one hind, but she was too fly for me. One lift of her beautiful, silky face, one little snort of what sounded like amusement at the peat-stained figure clutching a peat-blocked camera and wallowing in the mire, and she was off, waving goodbye with a white flash of tail. I was glad neither Richard Hannay nor David Balfour was there to witness this failure in hillmanship.

Up from the glen swept mountains that would have dominated any mainland chain, let alone the limited compass of a small island. This was the south-eastern corner of Rhum dismissed as 'fu' o' chrrrahp' by that dour Dundonian geologist aboard *Lorne Leader*. If this was crap, it was crap on the grand scale – molten rock from the heart of a gigantic volcano, solidified into great mounds, scraped by glaciers into sharply angled mountains well over 2000 feet high, named by Norse invaders – Askival, Ruinsival, Barkeval, Orval.

The breeze that was keeping the midges away failed to dislodge the layers of dark grey cloud that covered these splendid peaks. Other visitors were up there, I knew, leaping heroically along the ridges through the clouds. I had seen them setting off from Kinloch earlier in the day, the light of battle in their eyes. I didn't feel like joining them. Instead, I turned aside and made for the as yet unclouded top of Ard Nev, apparently a short and simple climb away. Half an hour of arduous bog-squelching, up and down ridges that hadn't been visible from the track, brought me exhausted to the foot of the hill. A reasonable incline, said the map, with a little scree on the sides. A forty-five-degree slope, said my eyes, entirely covered with loose rocks. The summit of Ard Nev began to mist over as I picked my way up between the boulders, each balanced delicately on the one below, the whole structure quaking under my boots. Half-way up, the enterprise began to lose its appeal. Keeping balance was the problem. I adopted a monkey stance, and climbed on all fours to the top. The mist went on thickening, in tempo with my breathing. Eighteen hundred feet up, and no view. I turned round and came down, sideways, dislodging a rock that bounced all the way to the bottom, in an increasing company of other rocks. The mist came right behind. By the time I staggered on to the road again, after the return plunge through the ridges of bog, my knees were trembling like those of a navvy on a pneumatic drill. Richard Hannay would probably have cut me dead.

Down on the coast at Harris there were twenty red deer browsing among the ruined walls of the abandoned crofting township. On the opposite hill slope were hundreds of lazybed strips, all sweeping together in the same pattern of curves and straight lines. Fertilized by dung, seaweed and the sooty thatch of disused roofs, the raised ridges of the lazybeds and the life-long labour they absorbed supported a community of thirty houses here before the sheep took over. Watching those red deer grazing contentedly a hundred yards away, seeing orchids and marsh plants flowering at my feet, looking up towards a pair of ravens gliding away behind Askival, it was impossible also not to appreciate the richness of Rhum as a nature reserve: impossible also not to be struck by the outpouring of human effort represented by those abandoned lazybeds. Nothing feels more desolate than empty land that has once been worked and lived on, and nowhere in the islands was that feeling stronger than here at Harris.

The effect was emphasized by the extraordinary building that stood on a grassy platform above the sea, so staggeringly out of place that one's first impression was of an elaborate joke. How can you reconcile a Grecian temple – pillars, pediments and all – with a deserted island bay in western Scotland? Sir George Bullough could, and did. Cradled by the classical

169

columns of the mausoleum, he lies beside his father John and wife Lady Monica, three stately tombs looking out to sea. In the hillside nearby is what remains of John Bullough's earlier sepulchre, from which he was removed to the mausoleum. In a slit in the grass slope lies a crumbling, semi-circular mosaic, its startling colours still fresh, decorated with leaves, flowers, a Torch of Life and an intertwined 'J B': the entrance to some art nouveau tube station or very upmarket air-raid shelter. Splendid, ridiculous and touching, these are mementoes of Rhum's most extravagant and romantic lairdship, lordly gestures of immortality by absolute monarchs, placed right on top of the hard-worked field systems of the inhabitants they replaced. The contrast with the unassuming family graves of the MacEwens of Muck, which face the Bulloughs' extravaganza across the Sound of Rhum, couldn't be greater.

Sir George Bullough's grandest memorial, though, stands in red-faced glory at Kinloch, looking east down Loch Scresort. Kinloch Castle can't really be described, only experienced. Walking in through the front door, you enter the Edwardian era, miraculously preserved down to the last stair rod and candlestick. Socially, too, things are more or less as they were back in 1901 when the castle was built. In the castle itself, the nobs stay in magnificence – paying guests, these days, but in a hotel where pre-dinner drinks are served in the smoking room by a kilted, sporraned and bedirked butler (the proprietor, Iain MacArthur, in only slightly tongue-in-cheek fancy dress), and where you can sit at a Steinway grand to set your fellow guests eightsome-reeling across the tigerskin rugs and polished, inlaid floors. Round the back in the old servants'-quarters-turned-hostel, the hikers, twitchers and student field trip parties steam dry in pleasant squalor amid the fry-up pans and beer cans. Kinloch Castle stands not only as it was when bought along with the island by the Nature Conservancy Council in 1957, but almost entirely as it was when Sir George and Lady Monica entertained their shooting parties and Highland society friends at the turn of the century. Heads of stags shot by the Bulloughs stare glassily down from the walls of the two-storey Great Hall; Sir George's billiard cues stand ready beside his billiard table (made impertinent by malt whisky, I challenged Iain MacArthur to employ these superb tools in the plebeian game of pool, and was soundly thrashed for my presumption); Sir George's photograph albums are stacked in the library, full of sepia shots of Chinese criminals about to be decapitated and other delights from his round-the-world cruises in his opulent yacht *Rhouma*. I slept in Sir George's bedroom at the castle, communicating with Lady Bullough's by an interconnecting door. His lace-up stalking boots were in the fireplace with his monogrammed boot trees inside; his ewer and basin were on the washstand; his blotting paper, still mirror-marked with his correspondence, in the blotter. The silken curtains were tattered, exuding puffs of dust when touched; but they were Sir George's own original curtains. At dinner I sat in one of the swivelling chairs from the Bullough yacht, drank from Sir George's glass, ate with his knife and fork. The effect of all this constant use of a dead man's personal possessions – not a family forebear, but a complete stranger – creepy at first, became gradually easier to accept. It was like entering a museum and being actively encouraged to handle the exhibits and put your feet on the chairs. As a museum, Kinloch Castle would be overwhelming in its perfection of detail, but the life breathed into it by its function as a hotel seems to suit it.

When Victorian industrialists made money – mountains of money – they tended to lash out. Sir George Bullough's grandfather, a clog-wearing handloom weaver from Blackburn, had founded the family fortunes with a series of inventions that improved the performance of mill machinery. John Bullough had bought Rhum in 1886 on the proceeds of his father's genius, and Sir George set about making inroads into that pile of money. A team of Lancastrians was brought north in 1901 to build Kinloch Castle in red Arran sandstone, the workers being paid an extra shilling a day to please their employer's fancy by wearing kilts while on site. Unfortunately, no one was on hand to record the men's reaction when this request was first broached. The finished castle was furnished with the very best of everything Edwardian, and from it Sir George and Lady Monica ruled in the lairdly style they thought fitting, shooting stags, fishing, dancing and dining during the few months of the year they were in residence on Rhum.

Lady Bullough was not only French, but also a divorcée: frightfully scandalous in Edwardian Highland society. Some fruity stories attached to Sir George as well. He had actually inherited Rhum when John Bullough died while George was away in *Rhouma* on a transglobal cruise, reputedly undertaken on Father's orders to cool the young man's ardour after he had formed an 'unhealthy attachment' to his pretty young stepmother. George Bullough received his knighthood in the same year that Kinloch Castle was built, as a reward for fitting out *Rhouma* as a hospital ship and sending her out to the Boer War. This accolade only increased his desire – a hopeless one – to be accepted as a social equal by the people to whom he most longed to belong: the touchy, proud, Jacobite Highland lairds, most of whom had only a tenuous attachment to the old clans whose upper crust they saw themselves to be. The Lancashire Johnny-come-lately, proud of his family's emergence from 'trade' and certainly no fool, probably knew that he would never quite get into this exclusive club. He spared no expense or effort, though, to get things as right as he could. It would be nice to think that he had some fun out of it. Other stories suggest that he did; tales of London showgirls brought up by train to Oban and shipped from there to Rhum on board *Rhouma*, to enhance wild weekend parties thrown for Highland regimental officers.

Archie Cameron, then a young boy, remembers Sir George and Lady Bullough as kindly, though distant, figures. It was the hated factor – well paid to be hated, a land-bound equivalent of a ship's master-at-arms – who really drove the Rhum estate along, and who drove off the island anyone who crossed his will in any way. Archie himself was one of these, expelled from Eden at the age of sixteen for threatening to complain to Sir George about a £1 fine that had been levied on his weekly wage of ten shillings as a punishment for using a fishing boat without permission. Things began to go on the slide in Rhum after the First World War, however, and never recovered. The estate lost impetus. The laird could no longer afford to pay fourteen gardeners to look after the castle gardens. The take-over of Rhum by the NCC was probably the best outcome the island could have hoped for.

Kinloch Castle is rather an embarrassment to the NCC. It's too expensive to run, too special to knock down, and in the opinion of some of the employees is ideologically unsound, sitting ill with the NCC's open-to-all image. Wilf Nelson, the reserve warden, thinks the use of its rear section as a hostel is a good and fitting thing: the NCC's property being used by the people for the people. The NCC would really like some rich hotelier sympathetic to the Council's aims to buy up the castle and run it without too much ostentation or razzmatazz. The idea of well-heeled visitors swanking around Rhum doesn't appeal. In fact, visitors as such, in whatever shape or form, are not really the NCC's thing at all. They come a very long way second to serious students of what the island's natural history has to offer. Sir George Bullough, one feels, would fail to understand the NCC.

My fellow guests in the swanky half of Kinloch Castle were Lord and Lady Elliott – the finishing touch. The three of us sipped our drinks to the thunderous clashings of the Orchestrion, a wonderful musical toy housed beneath the staircase; a glorified, souped-up fairground organ originally built for Balmoral Castle but snapped up by Sir George when Queen Victoria died before she could take delivery. We dined at one end of *Rhouma*'s great polished lake of a dining table, under the more-than-lifesize Bullough portraits. We would have taken coffee together in the smoking room afterwards, but Lady Elliott was determined to climb Hallival in the dark and sit all night among the incoming shearwaters. This was her wedding anniversary treat, and she was damned if she was going to miss out on it. Lord Elliott groaned, softly. He had been up that bloody mountain once already today, and the shearwater caper looked rather uninviting set against a glass of malt by a roaring fire – Iain MacArthur's seductive suggestion. Lady Elliott kissed the top of Lord Elliott's head, tenderly but firmly, and went away to climb back into wet weather gear and mountain boots. Lord Elliott gave a resigned smile and followed his wife, feeling the backs of his legs ruefully. I left them to it, and went to wallow in Sir George Bullough's incredible performing bath.

There were seven settings for the control knobs. *Shower* and *Spray* did what they promised. *Wave* delivered a powerful squirt at your kidneys. *Sitz* sent bubbles frothing between your legs. *Douche* released a solid rod of water on to your skull. *Jet* did the same thing, from the bottom upwards. Sitting on the water-inlet and operating *Jet*, as I incautiously did, turned out to be a mistake. *Plunge* – that just filled the bath. After half an hour I lay back in three feet of hot water, played-out, and wished the Elliotts a happy anniversary.

It wasn't until the following evening that I heard the shearwater saga in full. The only sounds emanating from the Elliotts, in Lady Bullough's chamber next door to my bedroom, were stertorous snores, all day long. At dinner time they crawled downstairs, laden with their story. They had set off at eleven o'clock the previous night in company with a bird-watching group to climb Hallival and had arrived at the shearwaters' nesting burrows, a couple of thousand feet up, at the same time as the vanguard of that Storm Force 10 wind that had been slowly building over days to this climax. The Elliotts – not by any means in the first flush of youth – ended up spending the entire night huddled together in a survival bag that slowly filled with rain, swept by strong winds and seeing precious few shearwaters. They heard one, though – the occupant of the burrow on which they were lying, whose cries grew more feeble as the night went on, finally petering out altogether. Lord Elliott thought it had probably drowned. At first light they made their way back down the mountain in the ever-mounting gale, which turned out to be the fiercest in Western Scotland for fifty summers.

It howled all day, blanketing the sky with curving plates of rain, driving the sea outside the shelter of Loch Scresort into white waves and sending will-o'-the-wisps of spume dancing across the bay. The few yachts at anchor in the loch spent the day heeling from vertical to a thirty-degree slant, giving their occupants Heaven knows what kind of rough ride. From a turret window in Kinloch Castle I watched the biggest boat set out into this tossing sea, butting its bows into each wave in turn, half-smothered in foam as it rounded the headland and lurched out of sight. What emergency or unmissable appointment had forced the crew out into open water on such a day, I couldn't imagine. It was a taste of what island life could be in autumn and winter, for days and sometimes weeks on end.

Lochmor's rendezvous for that day had been cancelled – she could probably have made it, but the skipper had wisely decided that he could do without 200 vomiting passengers in his nice saloon. However, she had promised to battle out from Mallaig to Rhum the following day – more of a threat than a promise, I couldn't help feeling. In the event, fortified by an old wives' breakfast of ground ginger and honey, I found the four-hour crossing a tremendous thrill: the first half hour of it, anyway.

12. Barra, Mingulay, Benbecula, South Uist, Lewis and Harris

THE OUTER HEBRIDES

The Twin Otter dipped its wing, put its nose hard down and fell from 500 feet straight towards the beach. I knew it was going to happen, but it still sent my heart into my mouth. The hour-long flight from Glasgow had crossed low over the southern end of Mull and skimmed the Treshnish Islands above the basalt crown of the Dutchman's Cap, then straightened out across the deep blue Minch, the storm-bound stretch of water between Inner and Outer Hebrides. The sudden tumble from the skies over the Isle of Barra towards the beach of Traigh Mhór, the Great Sand, was a thrill included in the price of the ticket. Who needs an airfield when there are two broad miles of firm cockle-shell sand to land on? The plane thumped down and rushed on across Traigh Mhór, brakes hard on and spray flying up from the tyres, to pull up by the terminal building. I let out the long breath I discovered I'd been holding, and tottered out to collect my pack and suitcase from the Twin Otter's luggage hold. Yes, agreed the girl in the terminal office, I could certainly leave my case there for a few days. But would I please let her know where I was staying – just in case it blew up.

Back on the mainland temperatures were in the high eighties, but here at the foot of the Outer Hebrides low grey clouds scudded across Barra's hills on a chilly wind. Ten steps away from the air terminal and I was straight back under that Hebridean island spell – a narrow sheep track across a thick wedge of machair stippled with buttercups, daisies and clover; a backdrop of grey-green, lumpy hills with the hard underlying rock poking through the turf like bones through skin; oystercatcher pipe and wheatear chatter the only sounds competing with Atlantic waves sighing on unseen beaches a stone's throw away. Just an hour before I had been jostling with the crowds in Glasgow airport.

The cliffs beckoned along Barra's western coast, but the three-sided house of Suidheachan stopped me in my tracks. Perched on the edge of the machair overlooking Traigh Mhór, Suidheachan ('Soo-yeckan') was half hidden behind banks of white cockle sand, mechanical grinders and rows of freshly-moulded concrete blocks. Barra Shell Ltd crushes the

175

sweepings of Traigh Mhór at Suidheachan, turning the cockle-shells into harling, a cohesive grit for coating the outer walls of houses. Cockle dust and chippings blew into my eyes. How far Suidheachan has fallen from its great days before the Second World War, when Barra's most famous publicist and celebrant held court here in his billiard room for the great men and women of his day. His writing had already made Compton Mackenzie's name when in 1935 he built the house on Traigh Mhór. Here he entertained musicians, writers, politicians, actors and historians of Gaelic culture, as well as local crofters and fishermen. Here, turning the wartime wreck of the freighter *Politician* on the neighbouring island of Eriskay to good account, he wrote *Whisky Galore*. Embroidering local people's accounts of the washed-up whisky cargo, its rescue by the Eriskay islanders and the ensuing high jinks with police, army and excisemen, Mackenzie pushed the people and customs of the Outer Hebrides into the public eye. Suidheachan in its wonderful setting stoked his fires. Now it stands in a dusty desolation, sinking in a desert of cockle-shell chippings, carrying no outward sign of its former glories. Any self-respecting mainland tourist authority would have fallen over itself to buy up this literary landmark and mount a Whisky Galore exhibition, a couple of hundred yards from Barra's airfield and the incoming tourists. Land On Our Cockle Beach And Walk Straight Into The Land Of Whisky Galore! Purely selfishly, I was very glad that hadn't come to pass.

The way along the western coast of Barra was unmarked by any footpath. I followed my nose over flanks of hillside, under sheer faces of rock and across slit-like gullies where green waves turned to black as they charged inland under my feet. I joined the island's one circular road a mile or so along the coast and trudged south, immersed in the stark images of the Barra landscape – ruined croft houses standing deep in flowery machair, roofless since their occupants were ruthlessly cleared in the 1850s by Colonel Gordon of Cluny; abandoned cultivation strips bright with yellow flags and purple orchids; small churches as dark and grim as Lancashire milltown chapels under the clouds, turning to shining white as stray shafts of sunlight found them; tiny fields of shell-sand ridges blooming with potato leaves; black headlands enclosing white beaches without a human footprint on them.

By late afternoon, when I topped the final rise of the road a good ten miles from Traigh Mhór and came down into Castlebay, exhilaration was long gone. I had had enough. It must have been the long day without food or drink that made the scattered houses of Barra's chief town and ferry port seem so drab and depressing. Even the sight of the ferry from Oban surging proudly into the bay past Kisimul Castle on its tiny island rock failed to lift my spirits. It took a good hot bath and a heroic dinner at the Clachan Beag Hotel to do that. Don and Elizabeth MacNeil run a hospitable house, filling their bar with traditional music and their dining-room tables with Elizabeth's home-cooked food. In the corner of the bar a woman slept peacefully from early evening until closing time, snoring like an old retriever after a hard day in the field. A group of Castlebay youngsters gathered round a table to swap tall stories and laughter. By the time I got to bed the cure was complete.

When I mentioned to Don that I was keen to go to the island of Mingulay, a dozen miles south of Barra, he offered to take me there himself in his boat. But a party from the Isle of Barra Hotel had planned a trip for the following day, so Don fixed me up a place with them instead. Barra is the southernmost inhabited island but one of the 150-mile Outer Hebridean chain. Vatersay with its few dozen people lies just across the sound from Barra, followed by a whole group of empty islands – Sandray, Flodday, Lingay, Pabbay, Mingulay and Berneray. South of Berneray, or Barra Head as local people call it, there's nothing but the open sea. Lingay and Flodday are little crags of rock a few hundred yards across, Sandray and Pabbay islands a couple of miles in diameter with rough hills, cliffs and sandy bays whose erstwhile populations left when life became insupportable, so far from any centre of civilization and cut off for months at a time by winter gales. But it's Mingulay that everyone wants to visit: not because of its wild mountains, enormous sea cliffs and untrodden white sands, but thanks to a sentimental song written to go with an alien air. Sir Hugh Roberton, founder of the Glasgow Orpheus Choir back in 1906, liked the way that Mingulay's three syllables fitted a Western Highlands air he'd unearthed, and borrowed the island's name to create 'The Mingulay Boat Song':

> Hill you ho, boys; let her go, boys;
> Bring her head round, now all together.
> Hill you ho, boys; let her go, boys;
> Sailing home, home to Mingulay.

It wasn't only the Glasgow Orpheus Choir that benefited from Sir Hugh's inspiration. Countless thousands of primary school children in choirs and recorder groups still hack their way through 'The Mingulay Boat Song' in classrooms up and down the country – 'Da-da-*dee*-dee, da-da-*dee*-da-dee' – their heads filled with the same pictures of the Minch white with waves, the chanting oarsmen and the island women waiting on the beach to welcome home the catch. I know it had this effect on Derek Cooper; he said as much, and a lot more, in his book *The Road to Mingulay* (1988). I took the book along with me as good relevant reading on the trip to the Outer Hebrides, but soon wished I hadn't. Splendid and enlightening though Cooper's writing is, it rapidly became a barrier to my own freedom of thought and reaction. The man had done it all already – landed by Loganair on Traigh Mhór, seen Suidheachan and enlarged on the Compton Mackenzie connection, stayed at the Clachan Beag, got to know Don MacNeil, been out in a Force 6 to Mingulay. I was turning out to be a Cooper clone, dogging his footsteps. Once I had extracted the above information on 'The Mingulay Boat Song' from *The Road to Mingulay*, I shut the book and shoved it to the bottom of my suitcase. Better to enjoy it on the flight back from Stornoway to Glasgow.

It took a good two hours of slow and steady motoring to cross the twelve miles of sea between Barra and Mingulay. The sky was cold and grey, and in the Sounds of Pabbay and Mingulay the Atlantic swell, rolling through at the end of 3000 unimpeded miles, furrowed the sea into hollows where the boat smacked and hurled up spray. In the wheelhouse, with the windscreen wipers going, Archie Campbell and Alastair Baird drank tea from their thermos and chatted to me. Alastair, a young man with a grin of epidemic proportions, was filling in time waiting to go off on a six-week deep-sea diving job in the North Sea. He'd already done four years as a clam diver around the islands, and wanted to get on and put his skills to better use. 'A lot of us young people leave Barra to get our qualifications, though you can get work straight from school at the creel fishing if you want to. Once young folk have left, many of them stay on the mainland for the jobs and wages and the city life. But lots want to come back to the island, and they keep a look-out for job vacancies on Barra. Local employers will usually give preference to an islander. The deep-sea diving is bound to take me away a good deal, but I know when it's time to settle down, maybe raise a family, then I'll be looking to come back here. Barra's a great place to grow up in. Island people tend to be a lot more knowledgeable than city people, and they seem to get a lot more out of the place they live in.'

Archie Campbell, about forty years older than Alastair, also had to leave Barra when he came to the end of his schooling. 'I joined the Merchant Navy, as all the island boys did back then,' he said. 'I was away forty-odd years, all over the world. When I came back five years ago, Barra had changed. My word, it had. For the better, too, there's no doubt about it. When I was a boy, there was no electricity in those little croft houses, you know – no toilets, no running water. Those things are taken for granted now, but they have made the world of difference to the islands.'

Both Alastair and Archie were suspicious of some of the recent improvements to the islands, however; in particular the construction of a causeway between Barra and Vatersay, due to be started the following month after years of delay. The accidental drowning of a bull, while his owners were swimming him across the narrow Sound of Vatersay, hit the headlines and seems to have been the catalyst. The causeway and its attendant road would make life a whole lot easier for the elderly crofters and handful of young families on Vatersay. But Alastair was dubious about who was behind the funding. 'It was put through the House of Lords in ten minutes, so I've heard. I thought it took them that long to even *think*. We are all wondering why the government is suddenly okaying a brand new school on Barra, new housing, a causeway that's bound to end up costing five million pounds. Is it all because the Ministry of Defence are planning a new base here? They've got plenty on the islands already – look at Benbecula, that rocket base, and the tracking station on St Kilda. Vatersay could be next. We certainly could do without them here.'

Ahead through the spray Mingulay appeared over the shoulder of Pabbay; three green peaks rising from a shore of cliffs where a tiny bay of pale gold sand lay clasped between the headlands. Above the bay a hollow apron of smooth green ground, sectioned by stone walls, showed where the people of Mingulay once grew their oats and potatoes. Two substantial stone houses stood out against the hillside, the schoolhouse and the priest's house. The rest of Mingulay's clachan or village lay low behind the beach, so drowned in sand drifts and bracken that I couldn't make it out until I had jumped from Archie's inflatable on to the slippery rocks – the only way of landing on Mingulay – and made my way round to the beach. Square stone walls stood a few feet high, still complete with door lintels, hearths, chimneys and window frames, some made of concrete as a reminder of how recently this village was evacuated. Mingulay's people hung on here until the early years of this century, existing on a diet of seabirds' eggs, cereals and boiled cormorants, puffins and guillemots, sending their sheep off to the mainland markets, fishing the waters round the islands in treacherous weather conditions, inter-marrying and interbreeding, bearing the long winter months of isolation as best they could. A trip to Barra in winter meant twenty-five miles of rowing in an open boat through mountainous seas in the sounds. Ignored by the owner of the islands, Lady Gordon Cathcart, 150 people lived like this in complete poverty.

Then in 1910 a group of Mingulay islanders landed on Vatersay to exercise what they believed to be a right established in law. Island custom said that you were entitled to any land on which you could build a house in a single day. Trespass, said Lady Gordon Cathcart, and some of the raiders were jailed to prove her point. The crofters of the Highlands and islands were soon to have some of their wrongs redressed as the Crofters' Commission, spurred by the return of thousands of men after the Great War, tried to make more land available. But for Mingulay it was the end of the road. The families packed their few belongings and left their village to the nettles and sand drifts. Nowadays, only the two big houses remain roofed and habitable. The priest's house has been recently abandoned by the Englishman who lived there in the summer months. I walked up the hill to peer through the windows. The ceilings had fallen in white heaps of plaster; the rooms were full of tables and chairs knocked together out of fish boxes. Up the grass track from the village the old schoolhouse had been newly roofed in corrugated iron. It's used as a bothy by the eight Barra men who run their sheep on Mingulay, and come across occasionally to shear and to take sheep off to Oban and the market. These two houses, with their evidence of continuing use, only emphasize the collapse of the clachan and the absence of its people.

'Two hours ashore, now,' Archie Campbell had warned the landing party by the rocks. How to make the most of Mingulay in the hour I still had left? I climbed the hill behind the bay, over squashy grass tussocks, orchids and cotton-grass, to where it fell away 800 feet down sheer cliffs into the sea. Kittiwakes screamed far below in a square-sided gully too deep and narrow to let in the sun that was at last trying to break through the clouds. I stood for a few minutes looking north over the abandoned islands and dark blue sounds to Barra, where the white houses of Castlebay looked like a few grains of sugar sprinkled across the feet of the hills. Then an orange dot crept away from the blue and white blob of Archie's boat down in the bay, making for the landing rocks. I made for them, too, leaping downhill over the grass clumps and sending puffins whirring away from their burrows. Back on the boat, I stared over the stern at Mingulay until the three peaks were hidden again behind Pabbay and Sandray.

Ashore on Barra, walking up the road to the Isle of Barra Hotel, I fell in step with an elderly man limping along, his right arm clutched in his left hand. He spelled out his name for me – Ican Mhór, or Big John. Ican Mhór had damaged his arm in a fall into a boat on the Clyde. He'd endured years of pain and sleepless nights before asking the surgeon to cut the arm off at the elbow. '"It's just a painful, useless tail end, no good to me," I said to him. He said to me, "If I take off your arm, Mr Maclean, the nervous pain you feel will jump into some other part of your body. But it's up to you." I thought about it for two days, and decided I could put up with it.'

In spite of his dangling arm and his 72 years, Ican Mhór had set out this afternoon to walk the sixteen miles round Barra's road, visiting friends on the way. We came to a crest of the road and looked down on the shining sands of Halaman Bay. 'That's the North Atlantic, yes. I was torpedoed half-way across that water during the war. I was on board a cargo boat, the *Empire Dew*, and a German submarine got us. We were eight days drifting back towards Ireland in the lifeboat, twenty-one or twenty-two of us in an open boat. The greasers from the engine room, they were very badly hurt in the explosion. We lost about eight men in that lifeboat, just laid out dead in the bottom of the boat. It was just a case of lifting them up and chucking them overboard. Damn, yes.'

Ican Mhór looked calmly out at the Atlantic where his 25-year-old self had drifted in that lifeboat. 'We were picked up by a Norwegian destroyer at the finish of it, and they landed us at Gourock. In the hospital they had to teach me to walk again. I'd lost the use of both my legs through eight days of sitting in that boat.' He chuckled, dismissing the experience with a little shake of the head. At the Isle of Barra Hotel he shook my hand – crosswise, left hand to left hand – and limped away on his private pilgrimage.

'I've never heard a single good word about this hotel,' muttered the Brummie courier in the cocktail bar, fed up to the back teeth after his twelve-hour stint of eulogizing the islands over the tour coach intercom. Next door in the lounge his elderly English clients were tittering over a video showing of *Whisky Galore*, delightedly pointing out features of the Barra landscape they recognized. The film was shot on and around Barra in 1948, and many of the sprightly young islanders who danced in the wedding scenes and rowed boats piled high with cases of whisky are still around today, identifiable despite wrinkles and white hair. Some of the whisky from the wreck of the *Politician* is still around, too, according to local tales, cached in secret hides in the caves and dunes of Eriskay and Barra that the salvagers omitted to mark in the heat of the moment.

The courier's remark wasn't the only disparaging one I heard about the Isle of Barra Hotel. Built in the 1970s on a prime site over the beautiful white beach at Halaman Bay, the hotel was a tourist board dream, funded by the Highlands and Islands Development Board to entice classy visitors to Barra. There's a colour TV in every room, bathrooms and oil paintings scattered throughout. The corridors are carpeted in tartan, and smiling girls in tartan soothe you through your stay with whispered attentions. But the hotel's grim grey slate cladding and block-like architecture sit uneasily among the croft houses that blend so naturally with the rocky hills. In February a great storm had whipped holes in the roof, only now being patched up. The coach parties file in and sit in stifling central heating, gazing at the cold seascape through smeary picture windows. Locals prefer the less polished pubs of Castlebay. Unlike all the little hotels and farmhouses I stayed in all over the islands, the Isle of Barra Hotel slipped out of sight and entirely out of mind the following morning as I emptied the central heating out of my lungs and filled them with mountain air on a hard tramp across Barra's bare back.

The scattered houses of Borve ran inland from the shore, a haphazard mixture of old croft houses, bungalows, mobile homes with bay windows and harled walls. The post office was a rusty tin shed. 'There are very few old people working the crofts on Barra now,' Ican Mhór had said to ne on the road from Castlebay, and here at Borve was the evidence – elds behind the croft houses full of nettles and weeds, once-productive round boggy and waving with rushes. Lapwings and snipe were nesting where the oats used to grow. A young girl with a satchel picked her way o school across the bogs and over tumbled stone walls. Inland rose a great amphitheatre of hills, running down from left and right to a notch n the skyline, the pass I was making for. Beul a' Bhealaich, the map named it. 'Oh, the Beul, we call it – the Pass,' said the pleasant young man at his croft gate. 'I don't know what that other name would mean – Bhealaich. Years and years ago that was the main road that people took o the east coast of Barra. You might find the old road up there still.'

The old road had disappeared under grass and heather, but I used the burn coming down from the pass as a marker and climbed up to that high saddle of ground and a truly memorable view. Behind to the west the hills swept down into the green valley, falling away to the white dots that were Borve's houses. Beyond them the Atlantic stretched flat to the horizon. Turning round and facing east, I looked down a narrow cleft to a far wilder prospect, a valley of dim browns and greens of peat and wet moss, plunging away to the rocky east coast of Barra, another sea and another horizon where the Small Isles and Scotland's west coast lay too distant to be seen. All round the ridges and peaks climbed up and away, grey rock patches showing through the sodden peat, coarse grass and heather. Sheep were nibbling wherever they could find a foothold; but nowhere, except down in the lush Borve valley, was anything to give encouragement to builder, businessman, shopkeeper or arable farmer. Standing in the middle of all this high, inviolate ground, I was struck again by how precariously – and how tenaciously – man clings on to the outer fringes of Scottish islands, winning all his living from far less than one per cent of the land. I remembered the green fields and neat woodlands of the Isle of Wight, entirely in thrall to the farmer, the forester and the tourist industry – a long world away.

Down on Barra's east coast road after a tortuous descent from the pass by sheep tracks and bog squelches, I turned north and came across a scene of island industry. At Ardveenish, on a low headland above a jetty, an unbelievable smell came wafting from a big grey factory shed. 'I wouldn't go in there if I was you,' warned the young man in the office. 'You've no idea what fish meal smells like when it's being dried, if you get close up to it. People phoo up when they have a whiff of it. And everyone can tell where you've been for days after. We've had complaints from Eriskay, and even from Uist, when the wind's been strong in that direction.'

I put my nose inside the door against his advice, and wished I hadn't. There was a glimpse of large cylindrical driers and reeking vats over which workers were bending, apparently unconcerned. Then the stink drove me out, gagging. An excremental, thick, warm smell, mealy and putrescent, that reached its finger deep down my throat and wriggled around in my stomach. The factory takes anything it can get in the fishy line – Argentines, blue whiting, sand eels, pout – all the sweepings of the sea bed that no one wants to eat. No one human, that is. The terns have an interest in the sand eels: they are their staple food. Over-fishing of sand eels around the islands is decimating the tern population. Terns, however, don't figure on balance sheets. The fish are brought in to the quay at Ardveenish in loads of up to 1500 tons, and stored in vats. Then they are sucked out and into the process. Squeezed dry of oil and water, dried and dried again, they end up as mounds of yellow powder and lakes of oil. These go out by ship, the meal for animal feeds and the oil for a variety of uses from pharmaceuticals to margarine. Next door the Barratlantic filleting and freezing company has its own shed where more edible fish – scallops, prawns, monkfish, dogfish – are cleaned, freeze dried and packed for the French and Spanish markets. The two factories employ between them more than fifty Barra people, most of them youngsters not long out of school, all glad to have the work and philosophical about the appalling smell. I asked Flo in the Barratlantic factory how they coped on bad days. 'Ach, we don't really notice it,' she said, with a wry smile that cancelled out the claim. 'We just close the door when it's bad. But it can be terrible – just terrible. I went through there one time, just to have a look, and as soon as I came out I was sick. Terrible – hooh!'

At Northbay House, an old school converted for bed-and-breakfasters, Mrs Galbraith was listening to Gaelic singing on her radio, sad songs from Stornoway women. She ran her finger up the map to Beul a' Bhealaich, frowning with concentration as she looked for the right translation. 'Beul a' Bhealaich – now, that would mean – hem, let me see . . . yes, ah – the Pass of the Sand Dunes.' I was puzzled. No sand up there in that boggy slip of high ground. Then I thought of the westbound travellers breasting the pass with the sombre peat valley behind them, their first sight over the ridge the long white sands curving on the edge of the Atlantic, a streak of brightness in an oppressive landscape. A sweet moment, then as now. Next morning Donald Galbraith courteously put his wife right. No – he thought 'Bhealaich' must mean a resting place. That figured, too.

The island chain of the Outer Hebrides, populated by just over 30,000 people, runs north from Barra, with narrow sounds and water passages separating the main islands as they process in line ahead – South Uist, Benbecula, North Uist and Harris, with Lewis at the top of the string. It's a twenty-minute hop from the cockle-shell beach of Traigh Mhór to the airfield on Benbecula. The island lies squarely between the Uists, all three linked by causeways to form a continuous road system forty miles long between the ferry ports of Lochboisdale on South Uist and Lochmaddy on North Uist. Looking down from Loganair's Twin Otter, the eastern coast of South Uist rose in high peaks, then fell away in a curve to Benbecula's extraordinary, lunar landscape. Benbecula is an almost-archipelago, a maze of peat-brown blocks of land pock-marked and knitted together by a thousand little lochs, looking from the air like giant shell holes in a Great War aerial photograph. The island stretches flat for mile after mile, as much water as land. Croft houses sit at the end of many miles of snaking trackway, surrounded on three sides by lochs and on the fourth by the sea, so isolated that you wonder how their economies can possibly work out. Causeways run out on stilts to offshore islands, but these islands are indistinguishable from the loch-encircled mounds of peat inland. Benbecula looked just as the map had suggested it would – infinitely strange and unchanging, completely indifferent to the influence of man. Then we touched down at the airport, and the 20th century came jarring into focus.

Soldiers in camouflaged fatigues were everywhere, their issue boots clomping on plastic tiles and concrete, their wives and children sitting impassively in the departure lounge. Young men with hair cropped up the backs of their skulls sat smoking and chatting with the airline hostesses. Outside, fat-bellied Hercules transport planes with blacked-out windows revved their engines beside the tarmac of the runways. A red coastguard helicopter came drifting in over the control tower and settled to earth in the car park. Two men in orange overalls leaped out and

185

sprinted across to a waiting army ambulance. Blue and red lights flashed. For the first time in my life I understood the magnetism of the armed services: the endless arrival and departure of large and impressive hardware, the constant activity, all that orderly bustle, the chumminess of a club with its own secret proceedings, impenetrable to the outsider. On the coach from the airport we drove past the army township at Balivanich. It exuded the same sad conformity as had the prison warders' ghetto on the Isle of Wight. The same small grey houses faced open squares of rank grass, the same young wives trudged slowly from one long grey road to the next.

The army has had a long time on Benbecula to develop its closed society. The airfield at Balivanich and the causeway to South Uist were built during the Second World War. In 1961 a rocket range was established on the machair in the north-west corner of South Uist, and since then the money, men and materials have gone on pouring in. The Benbecula garrison normally numbers about 500, but when visiting units fly in from Germany for a couple of weeks' training, as on this day, there are thousands of soldiers on the move through the airport and all over the island. This was the spectre foreshadowed for Vatersay by Alastair Baird on the boat to Mingulay. 'God forbid,' thinks the newcomer, reacting instinctively to the brutal contrast between immemorial landscape and overwhelming military display. But local people have a far more pragmatic idea of the camouflaged invaders. I questioned the first natives of Benbecula I came across about their view of the army presence on their island – three roadmenders, leaning on their shovels and staring ruminatively into the distance.

'I'll tell you this,' said the bearded foreman of the gang, 'if it wasn't for the army there'd be bugger-all here. They bring a lot of employment to the island, put money into these roads, give jobs to the school leavers. They came here – when was it, Neil?'

Neil removed the grass stalk from his mouth to spit with deliberation into the ditch he'd been digging. '1957, was it?'

'Aye, 1957. It was the Russian sputniks that brought them here – kind of competition, I believe.'

Were the local girls interested in the soldiers, I wondered?

'Ach, yes, some go with them and then marry them, and some go with them and don't marry them, do you know what I mean? It's not like in

my young day – though we did get with the girls on the QT.' The foreman winked and shook his head. 'There are a few fights at dances over the girls, between soldiers and the island boys, but it's just the beer talking.'
'It's a lovely island,' I said.
'Ach, you would not say that if you were here in February. It's bitter cold then, and the gales we get – Jesus Christ!'
The thirty or so square miles of Benbecula lie almost as flat from the ground as they do from the air. Entirely treeless, open to the weather from all sides, rocky brown ground and peat-brown lochs form a cratered tableland. There's just one upsurge of any size, Benbecula's 'mountain' of Rueval. Up on its 400-foot summit, sheltering from the wind in the lee of the triangulation pillar, I looked over the watery plain of Benbecula to the neighbouring islands of North and South Uist. Both islands share similar topographies: flat machair on their western seaboards leading inland to plateaus of peat that curl dramatically up as they near the Uists' east coasts into stark, primeval mountains with the concave shapes of breaking waves. These rock bastions, together with the far taller and lumpier mountains of Harris miles away across North Uist's lowlands, hemmed in Benbecula's tremendous flatness all the more strikingly by contrast. Out across the Minch were misty reminders of volcanic activity – Canna's low wedge, Rhum's tall peaks, the flat tops of Macleod's Tables in Skye, the Cuillin Hills hidden, like Rhum's mountain tops, in cloud. In all Benbecula there was nothing to hold the attention like these distant acquaintances – until I spied the old trackway curling below between loch and peatland.
The old road formed a dotted line on the map, running for a couple of twisting miles to Scarilode Bay, a splatter of islets and skerries whose channels looked unnavigable. 'Shieling' was marked beside the square box of a house down at the bay: a shepherd's summer dwelling, out on a coast where it didn't seem possible to squeeze in a boat. The trackway proved a reliable guide in that inland wilderness of rock and water, running in broad curves as wide as a two-lane road, gently cambered, drained on each side by broad ditches, held together with a core of stones, cunningly using the lie of the land to thread the miniature rock canyons where deep peat bogs fluffy with cotton-grass lay in wait for a straying sheep or shepherd. It was as purposeful and evocative as a disused railway, calling up images of the droves of sheep and cattle that must have walked

for centuries along the old road to Scarilode Bay. The path fell away to a tiny crescent of hard landing on the bay. A few sheep stood staring at me from the hillside, but there was no other sign of the hand of man except the overgrown old track dipping to the peaty brown water of the bay. Beside a loch on the way back I looked up as a Hercules throbbed and roared its way in to Balivanich airport. Across the loch on a rise of ground stood an abandoned shieling, its roof timbers gaping. Other days, other ways.

There wasn't a bike for hire anywhere round about the Creagorry Hotel on the south end of Benbecula, where I was staying.

'Well, I could always lend you mine,' offered the receptionist. She gave a deprecating smile. 'It's small – a folding bike, and a ladies' model.'

I told her I wouldn't be insulted by the lack of a cross-bar. Next morning the bike was waiting behind the counter. Small was the right word. I assumed a monkey crouch and pedalled off along the causeway that joins Benbecula to South Uist. A strong wind was blowing right in my face, and it took a lot of effort to force the little bike along. The hard work cleared my head, which was still full of cotton wool from the previous evening. On the way to climb Rueval I had been passed by an open truck-load of hilariously hooting girls trailing clouds of white balloons and coloured streamers. 'She's getting married in the morning,' they had yelled, joyfully catcalling me down the road. In the evening they were in the bar of the Creagorry, singing and shouting. A group of soldiers sat at my table, excited by the flushed faces of the girls. 'See if fifty pounds will bring them over here,' shouted one of the soldiers in a voice for the girls to hear. They looked round, giggling, and shrieked back – 'Take a running jump' – in Gaelic. I drank and chatted with the soldiers into the early hours, hearing about their base camp at Dortmund and the home towns they had left as sixteen-year-old boys: Newport, Glasgow, Stoke-on-Trent. As the evening lengthened, the beer and whisky set free the innocence of decent men from the armour of tough manners and loud, cursing voices.

The causeway pavement was littered with shards of glass from carry-outs thrown empty out of car windows. I swerved cautiously between them, mindful of the receptionist's tyres. On either side of the causeway the water rippled a delicate jade green in shallows over the sands. This was the fording place between Benbecula and South Uist where travellers faced being trapped between two channels of water. Here during the clearances Benbecula men had been transported like so many sheep, piled up in carts with their hands and legs bound, south to the emigrant ships at Lochboisdale. As the cartwheels ground across the sands of the ford, they knew they would never see Benbecula again.

South Uist stretched away southwards, flat on the west and mountainous on the east, blurred grey by approaching rain. The islands of the Outer Hebrides change their religious complexion as they go north, moving from the Catholic strongholds of Barra and South Uist through Benbecula's balance of faiths to the Presbyterian sternness of North Uist, Harris and especially Lewis, where the Wee Free church still closes shops and pubs on Sunday and frowns on any form of singing, dancing and labour that might stir the traditional Sabbath inactivity. The first thing I saw in Catholic South Uist was a roadside shrine, a little glassed-in sentry box of concrete from which a blue-robed Madonna smiled out, her Son in her arms and a vase of plastic chrysanthemums at her feet. The Norsemen had left a lasting influence on the island, too, in the flaxen hair and sturdy build of the red-cheeked children running to school at Bualadubh, where I turned off the main road and headed slowly against the wind into a flat country of machair and sea inlets.

The ties that bind the present life of these outer islands to the past were stronger here than anywhere I had yet travelled. Wooden carts piled with peat blocks stood by the side of the road; plastic bags of peat were piled beside the houses from whose chimneys drifted the sweet, heavy reek of peat fires. The wind blew snatches of Gaelic conversation from doorways and croft yards as I cycled past. Men in blue overalls moved slowly across fields white with daisies. The stillness and silence of this landscape were enormous. The houses along the road and out on the shore were modern one-storey buildings with cars in the driveways, but dotted among them were the old stone black-houses with thatched roofs weighted down by a fringe of stones. Some had glass in the windows and TV aerials on the chimneys, still lived in by old folk; others had been turned into barns and storehouses. I pulled up to stare at one thatched house whose front wall was covered with varied patterns made of sea shells. There were rosettes of cockle-shells, starbursts of purple mussels with central bosses of a single limpet shell, swathes of fan-shaped scallop-

189

shells stained pale green. They had been glued to old paint-tin lids to get the circular effect, and cemented on to the house. In the back yard stood an ancient bus, headlights spiralled with winkles, radiator lined with inside-out limpet shells, sides and window pillars swirling with a mass of shells. I longed to ask the occupier about these fabulous shell dreams made reality, but the door under the grassy thatch was locked.

'Aye, that's Mrs Johnstone,' said the woman at the house opposite. 'She stays on the mainland with her family half the time. She hasn't been keeping too well lately, so she's not been home this year. She did the whole thing – the house and the bus.'

In all my journeying through the other Scottish islands I only ever saw the traditional black-houses in ruins, roofless and tumbling, victims either of modern plumbing or of the clearance evictor's torch. Here in South Uist was my first chance to find out whether the inside of these timeless houses, on this island superseded but not yet entirely supplanted by their modern neighbours, was as unchanged as the exterior. All the thatched black-houses at whose doors I knocked happened to be empty this day, but a mile up the road from the house of shells stood an ancient one under a roof of slates. An old man in a stocking cap answered my knock. I asked if he could let me have a glass of water. 'Ah, you must have been drinking all last night if you're that dry – I know, I know,' he smiled gently, waving me in. There were two rooms in the house, one with the door half shut, through which I glimpsed a wooden box bed against the wall like a doorless cupboard, hung with stained curtains whose pattern had faded to a pale brown. In the other room, where the old man dipped a coffee-smeared mug into a bucket of water for me, two sheepdogs snored on a greasy old sofa. There were a couple of wooden chairs in front of a blackened grate. The floor was dark with damp stains, the walls and ceiling panelled with wood planks whose green paint had cracked and blistered with age and peat fire heat.

'It is not very good as insulation,' said the old man when he saw me looking at the wooden ceiling. 'In summer it lets out the heat, but in winter it lets in the cold.' He pointed out of the window. 'I stay over there in that new house, but I come and spend every day here. Why? Well, this was my father's house. It was the first white-house built in this area, well over a hundred years ago, I should say.'

I wondered how to tell the difference between a white-house and a black-house. He took me to the door and put a hand on my shoulder. 'Look over there – see those old thatched houses? Those are black-houses. The smoke from the peat fires would make the thatch and walls all black. Houses like this one, with a slate roof and a chimney for the fire, didn't get stained black, so we call them white-houses. And that's the reason of it.'

I bicycled on towards the sea, where the road ended. An MOD notice stood by the fence – 'Range Not Active'. Over the barbed wire the machair ran out in a flat green wedge under a yellow haze of buttercups. If the red flags had been flying the machair would have been closed to outsiders. Here the army has its ranges where Rapier missiles and other weaponry are tested. Hundreds of millions of pounds' worth of deadly technology operates in this ancient landscape; thousands of soldiers infiltrate it with their multitude of English accents. If I had been able to eavesdrop on the Gaelic conversation of those Benbecula roadmenders, instead of being treated to their English-language formality and politeness, would I have unearthed disillusionment and anger with the military presence and its effect on island culture, rather than hearing what the men had perhaps thought that I wanted to hear – stories of economic advantage?

I left the bicycle propped against the notice and climbed the gate in the wire. The machair was wonderful to walk on, thickly compressed shell sand many feet thick, carpeted with herbs that gave out a heady smell as my boots crushed them. The ground had been roughed up in places by gigantic wheel tracks of army vehicles, but the orchids, blue spikes of vetch and buttery, luminous yellow drifts of birdsfoot trefoil grew on regardless. Oystercatchers and lapwings circled overhead, complaining at my nearness to their nests, and rabbits scurried for their burrows in the sand. The wind poured over the flat ground in a solid stream. I trudged into it, head down, past observation towers and bunkered ranges, to a gate above the beach, flanked with more warning notices in red: 'Do not pick up anything. It may explode and kill you.'

I didn't want that to happen. I was content to lean over the gate, watching the terns beating up into the wind and gazing out across the explosive beach to a whitened Atlantic spattered with rain. The machair of South Uist runs south for twenty miles at the feet of the mountains, but this spot was good enough for me.

In the Creagorry Hotel that night, three young soldiers, seeing me scribbling, beckoned me over to their table to find out what I was up to. We opened the conversation in the usual way by exchanging names – Terry, Jason and Del-Boy. Jason was from London, Del-Boy from Inverness, but Terry wasn't too keen on revealing his home town to a stranger. No offence, mind; but you couldn't be too careful. I might be anyone, after all. Leeds was the nearest he would place himself. What were they working on? 'Oh, we're Telecom,' Terry said. This turned out to be an economy with the truth. They were in the Signal Corps, all of them lance-corporals, providing emergency repairs on field exercises in the South Uist range. Permanent staff like them, they said, got on well with the locals. It was the visiting units who made trouble, fighting with island lads and stealing the girls, able to cause all sorts of mayhem in the sure knowledge that they would be away from the scene of their crimes and virtually untraceable in a couple of weeks.

As we chatted and they sized me up, the three soldiers began to tell me stories of life as recruits on basic training and in barracks. Terry was scornful of what he called 'little boys', recruits who ran sneaking to officers after the initiation ceremonies they all had to undergo. One had even sold his story to the tabloids, and left the army with £5000 in his pocket and the undying contempt of his former colleagues. Hair-shaving, genital-painting and ritual bullying had been the gateway to acceptance in that strange, inward-looking club. Those that couldn't take it weren't worth a second's pity. These three young men, fit and self-confident, loved their army life, the camaraderie and sense of self-worth, the good groundings in trades. 'You just wouldn't understand, as a civilian,' said Terry. 'How can I put it? We're part of a team. You can rely on your mates. They would go down the line for you, and you would for them.'

Towards me they couldn't have been friendlier. They urged me to come along in their taxi to the Dark Island Hotel, the 'DI', where Jason thought he might have a girl lined up. When I said I'd stay, they shook my hand, Terry and Jason with hard bone-crushers and slaps on the shoulder. Del-Boy, half drowned in a sea of lager, aimed a limp set of fingers at mine, but missed. His eyes swam slowly around in their red sockets, searching unavailingly for shore. He lurched out of the bar, bumping the tables. I couldn't see Del-Boy making it to the taxi, let alone to the girls in the DI.

In the morning there was a gale blowing across Benbecula, raising white waves on the island lochs and streaming the wool horizontally from the sheep. It was Sunday, and nothing stirred in the landscape. I had planned to hitch a ride to Lochmaddy in North Uist, where the Wee Free elders were opposing recently introduced Sunday operations by Caledonian MacBrayne's ferries. I wanted to talk to the North Uist fishermen, who had intended to mount a blockade against the ferries with their fishing boats until they realized that by so doing they would themselves be breaking the Sabbath. A fascinating tangle of conscience, but the gale and the complete absence of public transport on a Sunday kept me confined to Benbecula. I walked out, and was whirled by the wind along the road to Peter's Port on the east coast of the island.

The ditches beside the winding road were crammed with empty carry-outs, evidence of the formidable drinking that is the modern islander's disease. The cans – McEwan's Export, Tennent's Lager, Guinness – were losing their bright colours, bleached into whiteness by wind and rain. I paced out a hundred-yard stretch and counted the carry-outs in the direction that cars would drive from the hotels through the pub-less settlements by the road. From the passenger windows along that short stretch, 16 beer cans and a half-bottle of whisky had been thrown: from the drivers' side, 59 beer cans. There were no cars in the ditch, a tribute to the hard heads or alert guardian angels of Benbecula drivers.

At Peter's Port at the end of the road, ferries and cargo boats did thriving business until they were replaced by bigger vessels that couldn't negotiate the rocks and islets of the little bay. The pier had gone, and a lone concrete slipway ran down into the empty water. South Uist's mountains were blanched out in opalescent flurries of rain. I was glad when Iain Macleod stopped his car and offered me a lift. Iain was just driving around the narrow roads in the rain, killing off two or three hours of the interminable island Sunday, before returning to his croft house to twiddle his thumbs through the long evening. Wet and windblown as I was, I represented a few minutes of extra relief from boredom. We began talking about Gaelic – how it was faring, especially here in Benbecula with nearly half the population English-speaking army personnel and their families.

'We're all Gaelic speakers in my family,' Iain said. 'When I went to school only twenty years ago, I couldn't speak a word of English. Of course, in those days we weren't *allowed* to speak Gaelic at school. Even in the playground you would be told off if the teacher overheard you. But the children here now are not speaking Gaelic at home, though they are taught it in school! Maybe their parents will talk to them in Gaelic, but they'll answer back in English. I can't really see it dying out, though. At least I would hope not.'

Crofting, Iain told me, was no kind of a living. He had no cows and no sheep, though a neighbour grazed his own sheep on Iain's ground. The sixteen acres of the croft yielded enough peats for Ian's needs, and a few rows of tatties, but it was his full-time job as an electrician, working with the army at Balivanich, that actually paid the bills. 'I had the house built new, three bedrooms, for £30,000. That does not compare with mainland prices, I believe. What would that build down in England?'

'It might pay for a builder to turn up and have a look,' I said.

Iain laughed. 'It's the loans and grants that let us build new like this. The Development Board gave me a grant of £8000, and I got a loan of £13,000 at seven per cent interest. You can't go wrong. But we have problems with the Comhairle nan Eilean, the Islands Council, being situated in Stornoway. For example, the new school they spent millions of pounds on over at Liniclate. That's a community school, so the locals are supposed to be able to use it in the evenings for sports, dances, meetings and that sort of thing. You can see for yourself' – he gestured through the steamed-up windows of the car at the rainy, empty landscape – 'what a Sunday here is like. This is when we would be glad of using the school. But on Sundays it's closed to everyone, locked up, because of the Free Presbyterians from Stornoway on the Council. They insisted on it.'

A whole crop of boards and councils has sprung up in recent years to give the Scottish islanders some practical help and encouragement to stay put and make a living. The Highlands and Islands Development Board was set up in 1965, to back with its grants, loans and advice any and every useful idea for creating jobs and a bit of enterprise. Comhairle nan Eilean came into being ten years later to administer all the islands of the Outer Hebrides from its base in their biggest town, Stornoway in the Isle of Lewis, instead of the previous rather impersonal and out-of-touch administration from mainland County Councils. The Co-Chomunn or island co-operatives were started in 1977 to allow individual islanders to club together their money and initiative on an even more local level, setting up shops, small industries and craft enterprises. And five years after that the EEC took a hand, aiming its Integrated Development Programme (IDP) mainly at improving the living and working conditions of the crofters. All these organizations, initially at any rate, were more than happy to channel money out across the Minch in amounts which the islanders had only dreamed of. It was a latter-day *Whisky Galore*.

The grants and loans keep the crofts going these days, and enable people like Iain Macleod to use them as a welcome supplement to more regular jobs. But not all the money, to put it mildly, has been used wisely. Millions of pounds have vanished in schemes that turned out to be badly conceived or badly run – fish farms that failed, forests that wouldn't grow, knitting workshops that unravelled after a year or so. And the crofters, fingering their cheques and looking around their dilapidated crofts, often and unsurprisingly went bald-headed into reckless improvements. I had learned about all this chatting to Roddie Johnstone in his little knitwear shop near the Creagorry Hotel. Roddie is a community man to his fingertips, a believer in the strength of pooled resources that was such a feature of the traditional Hebridean township – now disappearing, to his dismay.

'I'm on the committee of the local Co-Chomunn,' Roddie said, leaving his knitting machine for a talk. 'But the trouble is, people just won't take the responsibility. They'll be the first to criticize you round the fire, but will they come on the committee and stick their own necks out? Huh!' Roddie snorted. 'The IDP only lasted five years. They certainly pumped a lot of money in, but most of it was wasted. People spent thousands on bits and pieces of fencing, buying expensive great tractors – twenty crofts side by side, and twenty tractors. Now if they'd pooled their money, got together to buy one tractor, one cutter, one loader, and used them in rotation, they could have spread that money round properly and all benefited. That's the way things used to be done here. Everyone in the township would turn up to help you cut your peats and get them down to the house – then you'd go along and help them. But I'm afraid we just have not got the old community spirit as we did. There are too many people wanting to be individuals in the islands these days, working in their own way, on their own and for themselves. The incomers haven't helped things. They come here as individuals; they're used to thinking of themselves like that, not as people with a responsibility to their community.'

In the Sunday afternoon lethargy of the Creagorry, Iain Macleod dropped me off and drove away with accordion music streaming out of the windows of his little car. The wind battered the doors of the Creagorry and sent empty beer cans clattering round in the yard. I wondered whether even Loganair's intrepid pilots would be able to get off for Stornoway tomorrow. But it dawned fair and calm, one of the by now familiar quick-change acts of island weather. In a field beside the road to Balivanich a young crofter was having trouble rounding up his sheep. Led by an evil-eyed old ewe, they kept breaking out and galloping to the opposite end of the field. With the confidence of a Ramsey Island veteran I shed my pack and hopped over the fence. Ten minutes' running and shooshing had the sheep cornered in a mesh of wire netting. The young man gasped out thanks. And where was I going? Up to Lewis, I said. 'You're going to a bad island, then,' warned the crofter, without a suspicion of a smile. 'If you aren't an alcoholic, you soon will be.'

The reputation of Lewis among the other Western Isles as a bad island, or at any rate a sad one, lies heavily on the visitor. People on Barra and Benbecula look at you in a pitying way when you announce your intention of going there. If you really want to forsake all this, they are saying, for *that* place, then . . . so be it. Don't say we didn't warn you. Different strands make up this Lewisophobia – a natural antipathy towards the seat of local government, from which all regulations flow; the general view, in the Catholic southern islands, of the Free Presbyterian Church as a dead hand crushing the joy out of life; the perceived dourness and gloom of the people; their widespread reputation as desperate drinkers. More than anything, though, it's the landscape of Lewis that oppresses the outsider. From the Twin Otter I looked down on North Uist and Harris wrinkling and smoothing out, rising and falling in mountains and lowlands. Groups of houses lay isolated on the shores of seemingly inaccessible sea lochs. The Shiant Islands, below in the Minch, turned under the banking wings of the plane in humps of sheer cliff and green back. All this looked rich and enticing, bleak and rocky though most of it was. But ahead through the dipping cockpit windows the badlands of north Lewis stretched out into infinity – brown, low-lying, interminable, unrelieved – peat and water on a scale unequalled anywhere else in the islands, or for that matter in Britain.

I turned to the map on my knee. There were the badlands, filling the entire sheet: unScottish, alien white spaces ringed over by harshly angled contour lines rising a few hundred feet at best, flecked across by too many tiny lochs to take in. A couple of roads ran round the edge of the map, a single one across the middle. A few lines of houses were strung out at long intervals along the roads. Only in Stornoway were they gathered in any numbers, and Stornoway was only the size of the smallest of English market towns. All the rest was peat – peat and water. Of the 700,000 acres of land in the Outer Hebrides, Lewis accounts for just under a quarter. It's more than three times the size of Harris, nearly three times that of North and South Uist put together, seventeen times bigger than Barra. You could fit twenty Benbeculas into Lewis, and still have space in hand. Lewis measures at least 40 miles in length. It's bigger than South Yorkshire. But only 20,000 people live there, a quarter of them in Stornoway. On the rest of Lewis's empty acres the spread is very thin indeed; almost all of it, in the usual island fashion, squeezed out to the minimal fertility of the coastline. Somewhere in the south of the island – it's hard to decide exactly where – Lewis becomes Harris without the sea barrier one expects to find between islands. In these southern parts the mountains of the two islands heave together, and their two identities blur. But every inland aspect to the north is dominated by that deadening, life-repelling blanket of peat.

If Kenneth Mackenzie is anything to go by, then the people of the other Western Isles have sadly misjudged the people of Lewis. Kenneth overflowed with friendliness and hospitality from the moment I met him in Stornoway. He invited me up to his flat for coffee. Seeing that I was interested, he spread old maps of the town across the floor and pointed out the changes he'd seen in his own short lifetime. He dug out newspaper clippings of the wreck of the fishing boat *Providence* on which he'd been a crew member. He insisted I borrowed his maps, his books, his little spyglass for my ramblings around Lewis. 'I'll see you on Thursday; you can give them back then. No, it's no bother,' said Kenneth, waving away my thanks. His kindness made rainy Stornoway glow.

Looking for accommodation in the tourist centre's brochure, I spotted among the Macleods and MacDonalds the name of Taj Mohammed, and booked in with him purely on the strength of his name. What on earth was a Muslim doing in the stronghold of the Wee Free? During a delicious meal of spicy Punjabi food, eaten with the fingers ('You're the first guest who has ever asked to eat with us,' said Taj with wonder), I learned about his job selling fabrics door-to-door round Lewis and Harris. Taj Mohammed had come to Stornoway twenty years before, following his uncle who had pioneered the business before the war. Trade had been so bad in Glasgow that the Outer Hebrides came as a relief. The isolated crofting communities were glad to see these latterday packmen at their doors. It was a reasonable living, though the weather was bad. There were seven other Pakistani families in Stornoway now, and more down at Tarbert in Harris. The locals had been pleasant to them. There was no racial prejudice, Taj said, and the children were getting on quite well in school. They were being brought up strictly as orthodox Muslims.

'Do you speak Gaelic?' I asked his eleven-year-old daughter, Shazia. She hid her face shyly behind her long black hair and whispered 'No.' The television was on in the corner of the room, relaying an Australian soap opera to these Hebridean Pakistanis. Nazia, four years old and perky with it, bounced up and down on her chair. 'Kylie Minogue!' she shouted. Taj smiled tolerantly. 'They are bright children,' he said thoughtfully. 'I don't know if they will stay here in Stornoway when they grow up.' I'd like to think so. Stornoway would be the richer.

Rain in the evening, rain in the morning. I pulled on all my wet weather gear, with twenty miles of tramping in front of me. It began outside the arched Gothic entrance to Lews Castle, for centuries the home of the Macleods of Lewis, who were famously inhospitable to intruders, especially the English. They were happy to turn their swords on the Fife Adventurers, too, when towards the end of the 16th century King James VI (later to become James I of England) gave *carte blanche* to this hotchpotch private army to carry out as much 'slaughter and mutilation' as they could in the troublesomely independent Hebrides. The Adventurers made three landings, and on each occasion were beaten up, robbed, slaughtered and mutilated by the clansmen of Neil Macleod, the chief of the day. The Lews Castle of the Macleods has long gone, replaced in 1847 with a mock-Tudor pile built by Sir James Matheson. Sir James had had a finger in the Chinese opium trade, and bought the island of Lewis from the Mackenzie family for £190,000 on the proceeds of that and other profitable dealing out east. Matheson was not a despotic, grabbing laird-come-lately, though. He and his wife really seem to have done their best for Lewis. They spent a quarter of a million or more on a whole multitude of schemes – lobster and whitefish enterprises, new harbours, new roads, new building; an attempt to reclaim the vast acreage of peat moor by using seaweed as a fertilizer; tree-planting in various sheltered spots; a Destitution Fund to which they contributed half the money; as a last resort, paying the emigration costs of 1800 islanders to Canada.

When Lord Leverhulme, of Sunlight Soap riches and fame, bought Lewis in 1918, he also had a great scheme in mind: to create a fishing industry that would give the island financial security into the foreseeable future. He extended the harbour and fleet at Stornoway, initiated others, set up a line of supply from Lewis to his Macfisheries outlets on the mainland. But nothing really worked out. As a fishing base Stornoway was fine, but as a trading centre it wouldn't take off. Local fishermen preferred to take their catch over to the mainland markets and haggle their own prices. They were not (and, according to Kenneth Mackenzie, still are not) very keen to venture out deep-sea when there were fish to be caught nearer home. The peat reclamation failed through lack of manpower – transporting the seaweed across miles of trackless moorland and then spreading it by hand proved far too labour intensive. Almost all the trees died, flayed by salt rain and wind, except those round Lews Castle which had been bedded on soil brought from the mainland on Lady Matheson's orders. And, more frustrating to progress than anything else, there was the reluctance of the islanders themselves, perhaps implanted by family memories of ruthless evictions and suppression by earlier lairds, to be the tools with which rich outsiders could build a brave new world in Lewis. All new methods and trades foundered on the rock of their traditionalism.

When Lord Leverhulme left Lewis in 1923, after five years of growing disillusionment, and took his money and his ideas off to Harris, he was a disappointed man, but not a vindictive one. Lews Castle and the Leverhulme properties in Stornoway were made over to the town, and the whole of the island to the Lewis District Committee – apart from the land already being crofted, which he offered to the crofters as a gift. This was parting generosity – coals of fire, perhaps? – on the grand scale. The majority of the crofters, however, weren't interested in taking on the burden of land ownership. Lewis was split up among a host of private owners, most of it used these days for sporting and speculative purposes. Rusting piers and fish sheds, roads that go nowhere and pathetic patches of starveling trees, litter the island as sad memorials to all the energy and optimism of the Matheson and Leverhulme eras. The trees round Lews Castle still grow tall and green, though, a bizarre but welcome sight in these treeless islands. They lined my road out of Stornoway until the peatlands closed in on both sides, to dominate the long day's march.

It was the kind of rain that shrivels the hopes of holidaymakers, rain that drives people off the peat banks and into the bars. Not really rain, in fact, but a fine, spitting mist that swirled in bands across the moor. Outside work in this sort of weather is out of the question. Even walking becomes a purgatory. The rain brushed contemptuously through my waterproofs and turned my shirt into a sopping winding sheet. Every so often a hole appeared in the gloom overhead, revealing a heavenly vista through the rift: a blue sky over the Minch, full of enormous white cumulus clouds lit by a sun that I never saw. Next moment the veil would be drawn across again, as another insidious, miasmic drift of vapour slid down over the ridges of grass and heather. A few miles out of Stornoway the tarmac road veered off into the mist, and I went on along an endless, stony track in the sodden silence of innermost Lewis. Water trickled and plovers pleeped in a landscape scarred like a battlefield by the ramparts of the peat banks and their chequered lines of cut peats awaiting collection. The only colour apart from a blur of grey, brown and green came from the white plastic bags of peats and the primary blues and reds of the peat-cutters' tin shacks beside the workings.

The track ran ahead straight and clear, a positive slash through this landscape of negatives. 'Pentland Road' it was marked on the map (slowly dissolving in a slowly hydrating map case round my neck). Thanks to the efficiency of Bob Eaves, the Stornoway librarian, I had teased out a few facts on its poorly documented history the previous evening. A phone call from Benbecula and a taxi dash from the airport, and I found Bob waiting in the library with a copy he'd unearthed of the Report of the

Congested Districts Board for Scotland, 1897–8, and back numbers of the *Highland News* for 1912. Together they told a sorry story. The road had been started in 1891 to bring fish from Loch Roag, near Carloway on the west coast, to Stornoway on the east. It would cut seven miles off the only alternative route, and get the fish to market in a fresher condition. No native of Lewis could be persuaded to put his hand in his pocket and back the venture, but the Minister, Lord Pentland, had enough influence with the government of the day to raise a Scottish Office grant of £15,000. Things went wrong from the outset, however. 'This work has been unsatisfactory from the very beginning,' noted the 1897–8 report. The local engineer had grossly underestimated the work involved, and had been sacked. So had the two local contractors. Drainage along the road was appalling. Only a couple of short stretches had been completed, and there was just £1500 of the grant left. A light railway might be laid along the route, perhaps, and the venture revitalized. But that would cost a further £92,000. The report wasn't hopeful.

Fifteen years on, the *Highland News* was jubilant over the long-delayed opening of the road that September by its benefactor, Lord Pentland. By this time Pentland had served as Scottish Secretary for many years, and was about to be replaced. There were treasuries of praise from Stornoway big-wigs – the very men who had refused to invest in the road in the first place – for the noble lord after whom the route had so fittingly been named. 'This is a gold-lettered day,' wrote Neil M. Macleod in his column on 28 September. But Macleod still felt a light railway would have been a better bet. 'For the development of fishing in the west of Lewis,' he observed drily, 'the Pentland Road, all said and done, is little better than a cart without a horse.' A cart without a horse it has remained, a rutted track winding across the moor, incapable of use by anything other than tractors or lorries. But down in a dip half-way along its fifteen-mile length I came across a mechanical grader pulling stones together on the surface. Yes, said the driver, it was being improved. Tarmac would be spread from end to end, and the road opened for light traffic. Half a million pounds, it was going to cost. Why? Well, he didn't know. Lots of money about these days for schemes like this. Like confetti, the way they threw it around.

From the road the peatlands rose in gentle curves to a long skyline. The rain had eased up for the moment and was hanging in tattered black curtains from lines of cloud. I wanted to get at least one high-level view over the whole immensity of the badlands. The brown back of Stacashal showed between two shoulders of moor, a couple of miles north of the Pentland Road, 450 feet at the summit. I plunged out among the heather, saturated moss and coarse grass. The top of Stacashal was a maze of peat hags seven or eight feet deep, in which I floundered in a welter of sweat. The summit took on the dreamlike quality of the surrounding moor, an ungraspable goal that suddenly arrived under my feet. A tremendous prospect burst into view, twenty miles of lowland streaked with sheets of water. Peat and loch, peat and loch, all the way to the Butt of Lewis. Behind me the mountains of south Lewis and Harris bulged, melting under rain on their distant horizon. On Stacashal I stood lord of fifty miles of emptiness. Peat, peat and peat again. I grubbed up a handful of the stuff and spread it out on a rock – twigs, roots, delicate leaves that crumbled at a touch, all compressed into a brown, fibrous block.

The changes in climate 7000 years ago that blanketed Lewis with peat also wiped out the pine trees, the birch and hazel that had spread all over the island during the warming-up period after the end of the last Ice Age. Warm rain replaced cold snow, washing away the mineral-rich soil down to the acid gneiss rock, among the oldest in the world, that forbade all growth of trees. The new scrub vegetation squashed down, layer upon layer of it, unable to rot into productive soil because of the acidity of the rock. Instead it formed peat, twenty feet thick in places. Meanwhile the basins in the gneiss that had been gouged out by Ice Age glaciers – millions of tons of ice dragging inch by inch across the rock – filled with water which could not drain away through the iron-hard gneiss. The bogs and lochs came into being, and came to stay. What patches of forest remained soon fell to the axes and fires of islanders and invaders. The timeless sterility of the Lewis peatlands was launched on a reign unbroken to this day.

The only benefits of all this barren progression have come to local fireplaces. Back on the Pentland Road in driving rain, I passed the mounds of peat blocks cut from the moor by the inhabitants of Carloway at the end of the road. Each garden and back yard held a long mound of peats, to be slowly burrowed into during the winter months. Brown peat dust powdered the track, and stray peats fallen from carts lay on the verges. The rain thinned and died off, and crofters in blue overalls began to drive past on tractors, making for the peat beds. I squelched on into Carloway, where young Morrison and his stout friend Beanie were rebuilding a house. Morrison (I never learned his first name) and Beanie were men of Ness, the northernmost district of Lewis and tip of the entire Hebridean chain, proud of their homeland and its continuing customs. The eating of gannets, to name but one.

'Did you know that we folk from Ness eat gannets?' Morrison asked, taking off his hard hat and digging his hands deep in his pockets as he set himself by the cement mixer for a chat. 'Oh, yes, they're fine eating, you know. We catch them each year on Sula Sgeir.' He took my map and opened it. Sula Sgeir was in a boxed frame at the top of the map, 'about 65 km or 41 miles N of the BUTT OF LEWIS', a narrow slip of cliffs climbing out of an empty sea. Morrison pointed out the house marked on the rock. 'That's the shieling where the men stay. They go in September to catch gannets on Sula Sgeir. They still use the same thing as they always did, and that's a long pole with a noose on the end. You get the noose over the gannet's head, then pull the string – k-k-k-k! There's a lot of climbing to be done. No one has been killed by falling in my memory, but old men sometimes die of heart attacks on the cliffs. It's all kept in families. If your father went, then you'll go when your time comes. I've never been asked, but how I'd love to go!'

'The night the boats come back to Ness with the gannets,' Beanie put in, 'it'll be Ness men waiting on the quay. The next morning there'll be a thousand visitors there, but the best of the gannets will be already gone. I stood in the queue for two hours last year, but this young man here did not. He has connections, you see.'

'The gannet grape-vine,' said Morrison with pride. 'They cook very well. You boil them, then split them open and quarter them. A real good eater might manage – what do you think, Beanie? – about two quarters at the most. We eat them with potatoes and a pint of beer.'

I thought of the Bass Rock gannets, their enormous beaks and green-striped feet, their fishy stink. Was it tradition or taste that kept the men of Ness eating gannets?

'Oh, they taste beautiful,' Morrison said dreamily. 'Have you eaten very, very, very salty mackerel, raw? Well, they taste something like that. We send them to wherever people from Ness have emigrated to –

Canada, mostly. Yes, there's plenty Americans and Canadians would be very disappointed not to have their gannet every year.'

Beanie grinned. 'A gannet ready for eating looks like an old dishcloth – very bad. And they smell terrible in the pot. You can't imagine from the looks of it what a fine taste it has. I still have one that I've kept over to eat before the next lot come back. They are even better when they've kept a while.'

Next morning I hired a car and drove up into Ness to see the country of the gannet-eaters. The A857 runs north from Carloway for 25 miles to the Butt of Lewis, a mile or so inside the coastline all the way. It undulates in a long straight line over the edge of the peatlands, ribboned every mile or so with a small settlement of widely scattered, low grey and white houses, each township with its large, stark Free Church building and tin shack post office and stores. These communities – Shawbost, Barvas, Five Penny Borve, Swainbost – in their open, bare surroundings, have a look of the mining villages of north-east England, raw and exposed, superimposed on rather than sheltered by their landscape. But there are no companionably close brick terraces here. The houses sit alone on their green patches or on the roadside, with their peat stacks and clutter of rusty car bodies, old fridges and children's bicycles. They look too widely dispersed for neighbourliness. Yet Ness is famed throughout Lewis for the closeness of its community life, the strict adherence of its people to the rule of family and church. Traits of individualism and competitiveness, the lifeblood of the favoured towns and villages of England, are liabilities in this self-regulating and virtually classless place. The potter of Borve, a native of Burnley who came to Ness sixteen years ago, cast round for an illustration of his neighbours' reluctance to stand out from the crowd.

'People have been allotted sections of the moor recently, to improve the grazing or do whatever they want with. Now, that moor is fifteen miles across at least. I've no doubt that anyone could take as much as they liked. But everyone has ended up with a piece exactly the same size as everyone else, no matter what their plans might be, or what their needs are. I can see the point. In a small community like this, in a very isolated place, the last thing anyone wants is to look different.'

It's a hard life for the potter, waiting month by month for the rare good weather that might tempt the tourists up the long road to buy his jugs, plates and bowls with their beautiful, swirly red and blue glaze. He speaks no Gaelic, and sometimes finds himself standing uncomprehendingly by while his neighbours chat. But he wouldn't swap the sunsets, the easy pace of life or the friendliness of his adopted homeland for anything – certainly not the noise and crime of the Burnley streets. 'I can leave the shop open,' he said as he wrapped up the bowl I'd bought, 'and my house, without any fears that anyone will pinch anything. The locals say, "Oh, you should lock your doors. You never know who may come in." They're far more concerned than I am. I'm never going to lock any doors again, and that's that.'

Up at the Butt of Lewis the lighthouse tower was closed for painting, but the keeper gave in to my disappointment and fetched his keys. From the platform 200 feet up the peatlands of Ness ran away in brown folds. The townships lay dotted across the landscape to the south. To the north, nothing but sea. Sula Sgeir lay over the horizon. Beyond Sula Sgeir stretched empty seas to the Arctic ice.

I got back in the car and drove south again through the townships, idly wondering which of the houses I was passing had a gannet in the freezer.

As I headed south from Lewis and down into Harris the landscape changed, became lumpier and rockier, swelled higher as the gneiss climbed free of the peat and reared into mountains. In two hours I was over that unplaceable Lewis/Harris border and juggling the car over proper mountain roads on ledges hundreds of feet above the floors of valleys. Peaks hung 2000 feet up against the sky, their heads in cloud. The mountains of Harris were scabbed with pale grey; naked flanks of gneiss only touched with green in their crevices and round their feet. Trying to bring these eastern heights of Harris into cultivation has always been a waste of time. They forbid human influence. There is so little soil on the east of Harris that bodies used to be transported right across the island for burial on the west coast, where there is machair and a little fertile ground. The mountains and the gneiss outcrops have the final say on the internal arrangement of Harris. Roads creep and snake where they can find a way, depositing houses in ones and twos in the remotest spots where crofting or fishing can be sustained. Where all the mountains squeeze together into an isthmus only half a mile wide lies Tarbert, a tiny village whose few shops, hotels and ferry pier make it the capital and social centre of the island.

If West Loch Tarbert and East Loch Tarbert were each 300 yards longer, the isthmus would be a sound and Harris would be properly islanded. Thank goodness it isn't. Tarbert is a great place, a meeting point of travellers, a marketplace for news and gossip. All Harris roads lead – eventually – out of the hills and down to Tarbert, the Samarkand of the Hebrides. As I pulled up by the bridge, a party of clergymen in smart suits and dog collars came laughing and joking down the steps of the Tarbert Hotel after what had obviously been an excellent lunch. The jetting rain wasn't going to dampen *their* spirits.

Back home a few months earlier, preparing for my island journey, a story in a newspaper had caught my eye. Headlined 'School may be at end of road', it gave just enough details to tantalize. The tiny township of Rhenigidale, eleven miles from Tarbert, had hitherto only been reachable by boat or by a hill path four miles long. Now, after decades of campaigning, the crofters were to get their motor road. But Rhenigidale school would probably have to close as a result. The school had just one six-year-old pupil on the roll, Duncan Mackay, being taught by his mother, Moira. The new road would enable Duncan to get to school in Tarbert and, according to the chairman of the local council's education committee, 'enjoy all the facilities which he hasn't got at Rhenigidale, like gym and sports facilities'. I grabbed the map of Tarbert and looked for Rhenigidale. It took me ten minutes to find it, a couple of houses at the head of a sea loch, a tortuous footpath wriggling to the township from the nearest road four miles away. I longed to write about it – the little lad and his mother at their lessons, the handful of crofters still clinging to an isolation long abandoned everywhere else, the cruel modern world slicing its way towards them with its tarmac, tourists and 'facilities'. I decided then to walk in to Rhenigidale and spend a day with the Mackays in their lonely schoolroom.

'The school at Rhenigidale? Oh, it's closing today,' said the manager of the Tarbert Hotel. Too late! I dialled the only telephone number in the township – Rhenigidale I. Mrs MacInnes answered. She sounded tired and cross. 'Well, I'll see if I can whistle her for you,' she said reluctantly. Several blasts followed, on what sounded like an old-fashioned police whistle. Mrs MacInnes came on the line again. 'No, I'm afraid she's tied up with that television crew. We've been pestered, you know. Who are you, anyway?'

I can't imagine now why I ever thought I would have the Rhenigidale story to myself. The fight of the townspeople for their road, the expense of it (nearly £1,000,000, I was told), the little boy in isolation – these, of course, were gold dust to TV and newspaper journalists. Rhenigidale had been under the media spotlight for the past two years, ever since the road had been approved, said the hotel manager. Cameramen and interviewers were thick on the ground. Some had been pushy and intrusive, annoying the people who lived there. Rhenigidale had had just about enough of them. All they wanted this day was to be left alone. I didn't blame them one little bit.

Next day, though, I was climbing hard along the track by mid-morning. The green path curled away from the road, dodging up through the heather and rocks to vanish over the skyline. The enormous amount of work that had gone into its construction – bridges of stone slabs over the burns, a hard core of compacted stones, edges of shaped blocks of gneiss – astonished me, until I remembered that this wandering way had been (and still was, until the new road would be finished later in the year) the one and only lifeline joining Rhenigidale with the outside world. A stiff climb up, and a supremely dramatic one down the other side. The hillside steepened suddenly to a gradient of less than 1 in 2, and the path began a series of short zig-zags, each zig folded tightly on top of the zag below, like the half-closed bellows of an up-ended concertina. Each hairpin bend was a scuffle of loose scree, with an almost sheer drop waiting for a false step. A rocky bay cut between opposing slopes 600 feet underneath, and on the far side the path mounted again in green half-diamonds to another ridge. Across the hillside beyond that ran the rough line of the new road, lined with orange and yellow cubes – the diggers and drillers creeping imperceptibly towards Rhenigidale, still hidden by a long headland. As I stood and stared, a puff of stone dust shot out of the hillside and the delayed crack of the blasting explosion came shakily across the two ravines. The sense of distance, of giddy height and plunging depth, gripped like vertigo.

It took me a good hour to get down, up and over and round the ridges, but at last I stood looking down on Rhenigidale. Seven or eight houses were grouped around the head of a tiny, stony bay, a few trees sheltering them. The diggers on the new road were out of sight round the corner of the hill, though not out of earshot. Rhenigidale looked out between the jaws of its bay to the hills of Skye, faintly in view twenty miles away across the Minch. At the back of the township the Harris hills rose 1500 feet to the sharp crown of Toddun. Sea and mountains held Rhenigidale in complete isolation.

The first house I knocked at was Moira Mackay's. I was prepared to be met with hostility as another nosy outsider, even to be sent off with a flea in my ear. But Moira, now the TV crews were gone, was happy to chat. We leaned over her gate, one each side, in the first honest sunshine I'd seen in the Outer Hebrides. She'd come to Rhenigidale from the mainland ten years before as a teacher, the only job going at the time. She hadn't really expected to stay long, but then she met Kenny Mackay and things went on from there. Kenny's family had been in Rhenigidale for generations. Back around the turn of the century the settlement had been a busy one. People had been cleared in the past from poorer land elsewhere in Harris to do the best they could down here on the coast, and there were about 100 inhabitants, crofting and fishing in the usual way. But they had gradually drifted away. The returning servicemen of the two world wars had been offered more land over in Skye, crofts with better prospects. Young families had gone, unable to cope with the roadlessness and the isolation, the difficulties of transport, the lack of modern amenities. Recently they'd had the electricity, but it hadn't halted the slow death of Rhenigidale. Now there were a dozen people left, most of them elderly, all waiting to see what changes the new road would bring. Would it just siphon away those that remained, and replace them with moneyed Englishmen crazy for a holiday home in a romantic spot?

'I don't know what difference the road will make,' Moira said, and grinned. 'We'll be glad of it here. This place would certainly die without it. There's only a few of us now, and when anyone dies there's no one coming in to take their place. Of course, there's always interest from outside in a place like this. As soon as the papers started making a fuss we had people on the phone – "Are there any houses for sale?" A couple of the houses belong to English people already, but I don't think Rhenigidale could ever become a tourist place. In winter it's . . .' Moira smiled again. 'Well, it's not easy.'

No, not easy. With gales blowing and blizzards sweeping across the township, the mountain track impassable and the sea too rough to launch a boat, it's as hard as anywhere in Britain. Moira had wanted the education authority to reprieve the school for a year, to see how the new road would stand up to a mountain winter. But they'd taken their decision. Moira had accepted their offer of redeployment to the school in Tarbert where Duncan would be going when the new term started, but she was still sad to see the end of the school which she'd run – often with only two pupils, from time to time with none at all – for ten years.

'Yes, we had the breakfast television people in yesterday. They spent all day here. Duncan became a bit upset, because everyone kept talking about the school closing. But he's looking forward to going to Tarbert, making new friends. There's only his cousins here to play with, and they're older and stay away in Tarbert for the week. I wouldn't say, though,' Moira said with defiance, 'that he's missed out in any way in his schooling. Well, talk of the devil!'

Duncan had wandered up from the beach in red wellies and a duffel coat. From the safety of its hood he looked sideways at me. Another strange man asking questions. 'Is your father still on the beach?' Moira asked him. Duncan's freckled face was still averted. 'Yes, actually,' he said in a small voice.

'And did you see anyone you didn't know?'

'No, actually.'

I left Duncan to his lunch and went down to the schoolhouse just below the Mackays. Through the windows I could see a computer, video equipment, a blackboard on an easel, plants in trays on the windowsill. Duncan had obviously had a whale of a time in school. On the beach his father was wrenching nails and bolts out of a plank. Kenny Mackay's face was lined with weather and topped with a thatch of black hair. 'Would you be a reporter?' he asked carefully after we'd helloed each other. 'Every second person we've had here over the last two years has been a reporter.' He laughed ruefully. 'They seem to think we're some kind of freaks.'

Fishing nets were spread to dry over the pebbles, brilliant white in the sunshine. I said what a lovely walk it had been over the path in the sun. 'Aye,' said Kenny, 'it's lovely in the summer, right enough. But in the winter, that track – well – I don't want to remember just what that's like then.' Kenny should know: he had done the job of Rhenigidale's post-man for years, making the two-way journey of eight leg-aching miles in all weathers on a path where any burden could become a fatal un-balancer.

Back at the house there was a midday ceilidh in progress. Friends had made the long walk over, and were gathered in the sitting room over tea and sandwiches, exchanging genealogical details, family news and agreeable gossip.

'Now, would that be the Murdo who was cousin to your sister's husband?'

'No, no, that was Murdo Mackenzie. This was Murdo Macleod – you remember, he stayed at Rodel in that house at the end there.'

Duncan left his comic to pass round the sandwiches, while Kenny Mackay told me of the struggle they'd waged to get the new road approved. When the islands were run from Inverness, no one there had lifted a finger. The townsfolk of Rhenigidale had had to wait until the islands' council, Comhairle nan Eilean, was well established in Stornoway to make the breakthrough; and even then it had taken them ten years of lobbying. 'We had to pester and pester,' said Kenny, 'year after year, going back and back to Stornoway each time we'd been turned down. We wouldn't take no for an answer. Luckily there are young people on that council who will make a bit of a fuss to get what they want. I think we wore them down. In the end they got sick of the sight of us, and said yes.'

Time was prodding me to my feet. I had to leave – back to the hire car at the foot of the track, the drive to Stornoway and next day's flight to the mainland. This phase of the journey was over. I said goodbye to the Mackays and walked away up the new road past the tarmac spreaders, the workmen who all shouted 'Grand day, ah?' and the blasting engineer tamping fresh explosive into the rocks. Looking across the two ravines I saw the faint green zig-zag of the mountain path climbing a thousand feet to the pass above the Tarbert road, and thought of the centuries of Rhenigidale folk who had laboured to build their lifeline and had trodden it in sun and rain, gale and blizzard.

'Och, it is a bloody waste of money, that new road,' growled the crofter who gave me a lift back to the car. 'They should never have built it.

There's just a couple of stubborn old folk down there, you know. Two-and-a-half million, or whatever it is – shocking! There'll be nobody there at all in ten years' time.'

13. Mull, Iona (second bite) and Skye

INVADERS AND DEFENDERS

Standing in bright sunshine on the upper deck of the ferry *Isle of Mull* as we moved slowly out of Oban harbour, I looked ahead to see snow lying in patches on the peaks of Mull. Soft blue shadows moved across the flanks of the hills. Early April, and the second year of my island travels about to begin. Ahead lay the two largest Inner Hebridean isles, Mull and Skye. I paced the deck impatiently, made itchy by the sunlight and nine months away from the other British isles.

All round the deck, fruity English accents boomed and brayed under tweed caps and headscarves. Self-confidence oozed from every hairy inch of their plus-fours and thick heather-mixture stockings with green garter tabs. 'Roddy will be waiting for us, darling – now *stop flapping.*' These were Mull's well-heeled new aristocracy, retired couples coming back to their Hebridean haven from Easter visits to England. All the way up the Sound of Mull they kept up a running commentary on the rocky marriages of their sons and daughters south of the border, the lack of manners of their grandchildren, and the *hellish* discomfort they had suffered in guest bedrooms in Surrey and Hampshire, while the *Isle of Mull* ploughed a powerful furrow through the narrow waterway between Mull and the mainland. Here last year Don and Mike had watched with quiet amusement while we stumbled and fumbled our way around *Lorne Leader's* unfamiliar gear. I was looking forward to seeing Tobermory again.

The Tobermaries and their Gaelic exuberance were missing from the Macdonald Arms, but the lady behind the bar remembered that riotous evening of mixed music. 'I thought I recognized you,' she said, smiling like a beacon. 'That was a night, yes. *Lorne Leader* has been out in the bay a couple of times this week. Maybe you'll be seeing your friends?' I kept an eye out for the blue hull and gaff-rigged sail after that, but *Lorne Leader*, like the Tobermaries, failed to materialize. Tobermory felt just the same, though, friendly and relaxed, its single waterside street so quiet that a pair of shaggy dogs dozing in the gutter stayed scratching and yawning undisturbed all through the afternoon.

Up till now my island travelling had been done slowly, most of it on foot or on shaky old bicycles, with all the little insights this kind of leisurely progress gives into the small areas one can cover at a stretch. This time, though, mindful of the size of Mull and Skye, their hundreds of miles of winding road and deeply indented coastline, I had brought my car over on the ferry. For the next few days I followed the writhing roads of Mull, changing gear every few hundred yards, never even touching 40 mph. Mull's roads snake over passes and round sea lochs, single-track affairs on which the sheep mount roadblocks round every corner. It's no good at all being in a hurry when you drive on Mull. Long and winding roads they certainly are, but in the hundreds of thousands of empty mountain and moorland acres they make only the slightest of marks.

Mull is a great layer cake of basalt, overspill from the gigantic volcano whose petrified outpourings form the surrounding islands – Eigg, Muck, Coll, the Treshnish Islands and the rest. From the crests of the Mull roads the basalt layers marched away on every side, dipping into glens and stepping up in sharply angled ledges one above another towards the long, bony ridges of the hill tops. Elongated lochs lay among the folds of the hills, grey and steely cold this early in the year. For every immensity of basalt seen from a high point in Mull, five times as much lies beyond one's range of sight. The roads creep modestly round and round these enormous wastes, linking up the little villages and single farms sprinkled on the margins of a great swelling sea of rock. The towering mountains of Skye shrug off all human influence as they turn their remote faces to the sky, but Mull's lower, more accessible landscape feels emptier and more desolate. More than any other Hebridean island, Mull seems to miss its vanished people, cleared with as much ruthlessness as anywhere in Scotland. From a 19th-century peak of over 10,000, the island's population was reduced in a couple of generations to less than half that amount. Down on the shore at Calgary Bay I came across the sad remains of two of these cleared settlements, tumbled stones marking out the ground plans of Innie Vae and Arin. Their handful of houses occupied a splendid eyrie high up over the long arm of the bay, on a little plateau tucked in below a tall basalt cliff, looking out west towards the shelves and blades of the Treshnish Islands and beyond to the Atlantic and the new world their people were all forced to seek.

After dinner on that first evening I got out the car and drove over to Dervaig for an evening at the theatre. Mull's Little Theatre is reckoned

213

to be the smallest professional theatre in the world. Housed in a converted cowshed, it seats just 43 people at one end on proper tip-up seats in tiers, crowding down on the ten-foot stage. The rough, whitewashed stones of the old byre walls grazed my elbow as I tried to peer round the Medusa curls of the girl in front. Five actors, all local amateurs, put on two plays in the course of the evening, one of them a murder thriller, the other a Harold Pinter psycho-drama. Lit by spotlights from above, the actors themselves changed props between scenes by simply standing still and reaching out. Coffee and home-made cakes came with the price of the ticket. It was an excellent evening.

The Little Theatre gets professionals in during the summer season, and even mounts its own tours through the Highlands and islands, and further afield; but these actors were doing it for love and to raise much-needed funds. The enterprise was started back in 1965 by Marianne and Barrie Hesketh, two young professional actors bent on marrying up their twin passions for Mull and the stage. They did it expertly, too, with sophisticated lighting equipment, producing and acting a range of plays that would put most provincial repertory companies to shame. When Marianne Hesketh suffered an early death from cancer, Barrie left Mull. But local groups from different parts of the island are quite determined to keep both spirit and substance alive and well, in spite of reduced grants and the loss of their two guiding stars. I came to the Little Theatre expecting, rather patronizingly, to have to make allowances, but left in admiration. This is the positive side of incomer influence at its best.

The involvement of incomers in Mull has been steadily on the increase in the past twenty years or so. Beautiful, wild, remote, yet less than an hour's ferry ride from the mainland, the island is both a romantic and a practical lure for outsiders. The tweed-jacketed, knickerbockered elderly settlers parading the deck of the *Isle of Mull* are one manifestation. Island nicknames are revealing – Mull is known to locals as the Officers' Mess, the 'officers' themselves as the Green Wellies. Their new bungalows can be seen springing up round Tobermory, handsomely built on land bought at prices that leave plenty in hand from the sale of ridiculously inflated property in the south of England. A story I heard more than once was of the couple who sold in the Home Counties, bought and built in Mull and retired comfortably on the income from investing the residue. The down side of this picture comes, as always, with the diminishing prospects for young native islanders of ever being able to afford a place of their own to start a family; a problem compounded, here as in every other remote country district of Britain, by second-home owners and their nine-months-empty properties. Then there are the young outsiders, some of them rich beyond dreams of avarice through rock music or city dealing, setting up fish farms and planting forests on Mull's great open hillsides. Though treated with due caution by the islanders, enterprising incomers – those that actually come to visit and take an interest in their possessions – are far from being resented. They have brought jobs and a new vitality to the island. Mull's population, in contrast to almost every other Scottish island, has actually increased in the past decade, moving well past the 3000 mark. 'We could do with more, too,' said the young builder I gave a lift to, as he nodded at a long slope of empty hillside. 'I personally wouldn't mind a bit if that braeside was covered in twenty thousand new houses. Mull needs a big influx of new blood, in my view. Since the population's been rising the shops have improved no end – more variety, more of them. There's more going on all round. It's a nice feeling.'

Before this recent immigration boom, the island was in danger of becoming a sterile network of sporting estates and Forestry Commission corduroy battalions. The sporting estates in particular, many thousands of acres each of bare deer forest, posed a problem of modern-day absentee lairdship. Great tracts of country were only visited by their owners for a week or two in summer and autumn, the owners themselves too strapped for cash to keep things up together, lowlands reverting to bog, uplands thronged with an exploding population of red deer – more than 5000 at the last count – whose old and sick beasts were left to limp miserably on; no gamekeepers, no vermin control. These days the landowners, encouraged by grants and tax concessions, are beginning to take their affairs in hand again, led by the biggest among them, the Forestry Commission.

I was determined to have at least one good walk in Mull, to work off some winter weight, to leave the road for the vast interior and get myself in the exploring groove again. Before setting out, I filled up on facts and figures at the Forestry Commission's office at Aros, a few miles down the road from Tobermory. John, a young forester with a full day's workload drumming at his conscience, found a few minutes to give me a clipped resumé – a rather rose-tinted one – of what the newly conservation-conscious Commission is doing with its 40,000 acres in Mull.

'The thing is,' said John, drawing hungrily on a thin roll-up cigarette and glancing at his watch, 'the Forestry Commission is very, very aware of the bad image people have had of it. We made mistakes when we started back in the thirties – too many conifers, too many hillsides in straight lines, no interest in the wildlife. Nowadays we plant mostly Sitka spruce, a bit of larch and Douglas fir. Seven per cent broadleaf for contrast, using only native species – oak, ash, warty birch. Ploughing lines are changed every fifty yards to stop erosion and break up the long lines. We work very closely with the Nature Conservancy Council and the RSPB. They're consulted and involved all along the line. We use professional landscape architects, too. Look at these plans.'

The plans were pinned on the office wall, half-a-dozen versions of the same hillside blocked in with different colours. Each colour represented a tree species. In one picture conifers climbed a stream bed: too ugly. In the next, larch made spoke-like lines among the Sitka: too regimented. At the end of the row of rejected plans hung the approved one, a varied, subtle blend of colours and textures.

'We try to make the broadleaves follow the course of the burns. Use much less phosphate fertilizer, too, and apply it by hand instead of the old spraying by plane. We keep archaeological sites clear, cull deer, leave nesting sites for birds, tracks for walkers. Okay? Got enough?'

John sped off, leaving a sheaf of leaflets in my lap. Full of facts, I kept one eye on the forestry blankets swaddling the hillsides as I drove down the west coast of Mull. They still looked just like blankets, though, smothering the lower landscape in drab conformity, for all their acreage just dark green strips at the feet of the sweeping, sloping mountains.

This west coast road is the most dramatic in the island, weaving its way around deserted bays and sea lochs, creeping on narrow ledges under hanging curtains of basalt 500 vertical feet overhead. Fallen boulders the size of the car lay littered along the roadside. Out across Loch Keal, the islands rose in their varied steps and hummocks – snub-nosed Eorsa, craggy Ulva, tiny Inchkenneth under whose low green shoulders lie the bones of Scottish kings, buried on the island when storms barred the way to their rightful resting place on Iona. Below the central crag of Inchkenneth stood a tall mansion house where, locals told me, Adolf

Hitler stayed before the war as the guest of Unity Mitford when her family owned the island. One of those apocryphal stories firmly believed by many. Out beyond the sea mouth of the loch were more stirrers of *Lorne Leader* memories – long-backed Staffa and the low wedges of the Treshnish Islands, grey and indistinct in cold, drizzling mist. Gazing greedily seaward at the feast of islands, inland at the snow-powdered hills, it was all I could do to keep the car on the road and away from the sharp drops on each corner.

Down at last in the long and lonely peninsula of the Ross of Mull, I drew up a few miles short of the westernmost tip and rummaged for scarf, gloves, an extra sweater and a woolly hat. Wrapped like an Eskimo, pushing hard into spitting rain and an icy southerly wind, I punished my boots through fifteen miles of hill and headland, feeling better with every step. At one point in the march, following a locally-written booklet's recommended route, I was pulled up by a polite Englishman who stepped out from behind a Land Rover to block my path. 'Oh, God,' he said, smiling whimsically, 'not another walker trying to follow that blasted booklet, are you? That thing was written out of pure malice. Six or seven landowners are up in arms about it, you know. The authors never bothered to check up. I'm afraid their route goes right across our land. We're lambing just now, shooting hoodies and black-backs, and a rifle bullet carries an awful long way, doesn't it?' The Englishman smiled again, pleasantly. His level glance said, 'My land, not yours. Beat it.'

I took the hint and struck out anew. Strips of ancient runrig farming on the headlands, black cliffs plunging down to white sand beaches, skerries offshore made of thousands of upturned rock needles; marshy, tussocky miles working my way round the backs of hills; an abandoned graveyard by the shore of a loch where a medieval grave slab dense with interlaced carving lay on the grassy floor of a tiny, ruined chapel. Then a stony track mounting through private forest where red deer clattered away from their drinking places in the burns; buzzards planing above the trees, and near at hand some invisible bird in the spruce tops calling '*Sweet*-ie, *Sweet*-ie'; a viewpoint over thousand-foot cliffs and dark basalt ridges. Back on the track a mile short of the car, I watched a dozen rooks swaying head to wind, loudly cawing the rest of the colony home to their newly built nests at the tops of the beeches around Assapol House. Tomorrow was earmarked for the Isle of Iona. Just now I was content to watch the rooks, and feel that virtuous stiffening at the back of the thighs that told of an inactive winter exorcized by exercise.

A remarkably large number of young islanders are over-qualified for their jobs. Coming back to their home islands after college or university, they often find that the only work available is the sort of thing they would have ended up doing if they had started in straight from school – crofting, fishing, council manual jobs. The young man I chatted to in the bar of Mull's Salen Hotel had a PhD in archaeological studies; not much use to him in his job stringing wires and checking equipment for British Telecom. In the course of the evening he gave me chapter and verse on brochs, duns and standing stones, as well as the sphagnum mosses of the Islay peat bogs and a run-down of the Dalriadic kings. Hearing I was intending to revisit Iona, he laughed. 'Saint Columba, ah? Not quite the saint he's made out to be. Do you know the reason he came from Ireland to Iona? It was a game of hurley that went wrong. Columba's team started an argument over some disallowed goal, and the thing got out of hand, developed into a pitched battle with a thousand killed. Columba was running away for shame at what he'd done. Made a decent job of his atonement, though.'

There had been a pitched battle, as I found out later; but the game of hurley turned out to be a bit of fun at this gullible Sassenach's expense.

Iona was a closed book to me, in spite of *Lorne Leader*'s call there last year. Full of the joys of Staffa, I had brushed unheedingly through the tourist part of the island with my head still swirling with basalt columns and caves full of music, seeing almost nothing and feeling even less. Now, I hoped, a full day and night on the little island would get me closer to the spell Iona had continued to cast so potently for 1500 years.

A prosaic start to the trip, though. It was dustbin day on Iona, and it was raining. Down at Fionnphort jetty at the end of the Ross of Mull a yellow rubbish lorry inched backwards aboard *Coll*, the tiny, rusty ferry that plies all day back and forth across the mile-wide Sound of Iona. The dustmen sat phlegmatically smoking and reading the *Sun* in the stuffy little saloon while the ferry pottered across the water. They spared never a glance for the charms of Iona as they winched the waiting skip on to the lorry and backed back down the slip and into *Coll*, duty done.

The rain spotted down, a gradual but complete soaker, as I splashed off along the shore. 'Tee-oo! Tee-oo!' called a woman in a waxed coat from the field next to the Abbey buildings. Sheep came running from all directions. 'Jeanetta Tyndall,' she introduced herself as the sheep barged round in a circle. Peeping out fearlessly from the middle of the woolly stampede were her two little sons, both under five, Colin and Graham, wrapped against the biting spring wind into a pair of pantomime goblins, cheeks glowing crimson. 'Tee-oo! Come on, there.' Jeanetta walked up the field, spilling pellets of concentrated feed along the ground from the paper sack in her arms. The sheep jostled after her, gobbling the pellets like a flock of shaggy seagulls after the plough. 'Two weeks until these lamb,' said Jeanetta, 'so they need the extra nourishment. We've had a pretty good season so far.'

Jeanetta, like her husband, was born and raised on Iona, but she's glad to have gone away for a few years into the wider world, teaching and living a different sort of life. 'You need to get off and live a bit away before coming back to the island. Otherwise you get dissatisfied later on. No, it won't break my heart to see these two go off to school in Oban when they're eleven. There's a good wee school here, just fourteen children, but they need more.'

The Tyndalls run one of the three-mile-long island's two farms. There are about a dozen crofts as well, eking out with the usual mixture of farming, fishing and sidelines for the tourists. Second-home owners have bought up many of the houses in and around the little village, leaving them untenanted through the winter, returning in the balmy summer to find themselves spending most of their holiday repairing the damage done to their empty nests by the winter weather. The summer day-visitors don't bother Jeanetta, except when they break down her stone walls by standing on them to take photos of the Abbey. Most come across on three-hour trips – lunch, the Abbey, the gift shop and away – seeing only one tiny strip of the island. The Abbey itself, though, is the focus of another community entirely, a remarkable one, that lives a fluctuating, hard-working, joyous life side by side with the islanders. The girl from college in Loughborough who was serving lunches in the Abbey coffee shop was coming to the end of her six-week stint as a volunteer helper, baggy-eyed with exhaustion. 'I've swept floors, washed dishes, baked cakes, sung in choirs, pilgrimaged out in the rain, taken services, all day every day. I'm knackered!' But she glowed as she said it.

The Iona Community believes in rolled-up sleeves. It was founded in 1938 by the legendarily strong-minded George MacLeod, to bring together in a common purpose people of widely differing religious, political and social connections. They started by restoring the Abbey buildings from the ruinous state they had fallen into after four centuries of neglect. That took them thirty years, and cemented an ecumenical, evangelical feeling that has gone on growing. There are 200 members all over Scotland who come in groups of twenty or so to live on Iona for several years at a stretch, running and maintaining the Abbey and the MacLeod Centre where guests refresh body and soul with discussion, prayer, ceilidh, drama, song and celebration. Everyone mucks in with the chores. The enthusiastic young volunteers who come to help out, usually students on their holidays, throw themselves without reserve into this holy stewpot of effort. Girls and boys sing and skip as they pass you in the corridors, shouting to friends, joshing the guests. Such overflowing commitment would melt the ice round the deepest-frozen heart. Whether the dozen original companions of Columba were so full of joy, of up-and-at-'em drive, I don't know. But I suspect the saint would have grabbed with both hands at such cheerfully malleable clay.

It wasn't a disputed goal at hurley that forced Columba out of his native Ireland in 563 AD, but an infringement of copyright. Columba's transgression, copying out a set of gospels for his own use without permission of the monk who had brought them to Ireland from Rome, boiled up into a tremendous row. It culminated in a condemnation by the High King of Ireland, incensed factions taking sides, bloodshed and slaughter, and a self-imposed exile for the appalled Columba. The middle-aged man who steered his boat into Port a' Churaich, the Harbour of the Coracle on the southern coast of Iona – already a commanding figure in the Church of Ireland, founder of monasteries and an influential leader – brought with him a burden of guilt that spurred him on to unequalled deeds of missionary zeal. Here on this slip of an island, with Ireland out of sight and therefore out of mind, he set himself and his companions to take the Word through Mull and on through the mainland of Scotland. The Celtic Church which he established, a simpler and less hide-bound offshoot of the Roman mother church, attracted converts wherever its messengers went. Iona was holy ground, the centre of a mighty religious system under whose yoke bowed kings, queens, chieftains and ordinary men and women from Scotland, Ireland and Scandinavia. Norsemen with older fires burning in their bellies came to raze the buildings and slaughter the monks from time to time, but nothing could stop the flow of craft and artistry, religious influence and moral leadership of the community on the little island off Mull. The Celtic Church, though Roman authority eventually began to bring it closer to heel, ploughed its own rich furrow for more than a thousand years, until the 16th-century backlash against Catholicism by the new, dour Presbyterian Church in Scotland brought despoilers over to scatter the Iona Community and destroy its idolatrous symbols – illuminated manuscripts, carved crosses, bells, glass, statues.

On my previous visit to Iona I had bought in the little bookshop a battered copy of one of the greatest travel books ever written, Martin Martin's *Description of the Western Isles of Scotland*, published in 1703. In his chapter on Iona, Martin tells of visiting the island only a few years after the latterday Vikings of Presbyterianism had settled with the monastery, and finding the buildings standing empty but complete, together with the tombs of the forty-eight kings of Scotland, four of Ireland and eight of Norway. Martin also saw the carved grave slabs of numerous Lords of the Isles and lesser chieftains, all brought here to be buried in the most sacred ground they knew. When Dr Johnson and James Boswell made their journey to Iona about seventy years after Martin, the buildings had gone a long way downhill. Johnson found the floor of the Abbey church so thick with mud and rubbish that he could not read the grave-slab inscriptions, and the chapel of the nunnery (established on Iona in 1203) in use as a cowhouse. That would have been double displeasure to Columba, a sexist chauvinist if ever there was one, who allowed neither cows nor women on to the island, holding that where there was one there was the other, and where there was either there was mischief. Dr Johnson noticed that the roofs were all gone, pulled down for their valuable timber, so scarce on Iona. Johnson found this dilapidation inspiring, musing on 'that illustrious Island, which was once the luminary of the *Caledonian* regions, whence savage clans and roving barbarians derived the benefits of knowledge, and the blessings of religion . . . Far from me and from my friends, be such frigid philosophy as may conduct us indifferent and unmoved over any ground which has been dignified by wisdom, bravery, or virtue. That man is little to be

221

envied, whose patriotism would not gain force upon the plain of Marathon,. or whose piety would not grow warmer among the ruins of Iona!'

Boswell, usually the more lively commentator by far, must have slept badly in the haybarn he had shared overnight with the Doctor and Sir Allan McLean, since the best he could do by way of commentary was to repeat his friend's 'sublime passage', with a footnote on the admiration it had excited in the President of the Royal Society. Boswell's own remarks are mostly peevish ones. 'We were both disappointed, when we were shewn what are called the monuments of the kings of Scotland, Ireland, and Denmark, and of a King of France,' he complains like any surfeited tourist. 'There are only some grave-stones flat on the earth, and we could see no inscriptions. How far short was this of marble monuments,. like those in Westminster Abbey, which I had imagined here!'

There is a marble monument imposing enough to satisfy the grandest of Boswell's expectations, in the beautifully restored pink and grey stone body of Iona Abbey today: the white, aristocratic figures of the 8th Duke of Argyll and his wife. The Duke presented the ruins of Iona to the Church of Scotland in 1899, in hopes that they would take on its restoration, as well as continuing his practice of allowing ecumenical services to be held there. To ensure this, the Duke prudently added a clause to his Deed of Trust, expressly denying the parish minister any say in the running of the Abbey. As I set out into the rain, a young girl from the Iona Community was softly playing 'The Water of Tyne' on the church piano.

The rain did not let up all day – just rang the changes between a soft drizzle and a proper downpour. I made my way round and across the island, tramping through sodden peat bogs cratering the back of Iona, wandering along the white shell sand beaches and over the springy wedges of machair. The beaches on the seaward side lay deserted, dotted with otter tracks and speckled with multi-coloured pebbles. Fifteen hundred years of spiritual magnetism play their part in giving the island its special atmosphere, but geology takes a hand as well. Standing 300 feet up on the highest crag, Dun-I, I looked across the Sound of Iona to the pink granite of the Ross of Mull standing up in blocks all round Fionnphort. But the rocks under my feet, and those jewel-like pebbles on the shore, were made of far older stuff, outcrops of immensely ancient gneiss. Iona is a distant geological clansman of the Outer Hebrides, far from home, surrounded by an alien tribe of granite and basalt. The beach pebbles shone in startling colours – round buttons of salmon-pink granite mottled with white quartz like chunks of German sausage, green blades of serpentine, swirls of delicately banded brown. It looked as if some wild artist had dipped a paintbrush in every colour on his palette and flicked it over the sands. Down at the southern end of the island, glassy green pebbles of Iona marble lay like cats'-eyes among the stones. Here in the Harbour of the Coracle where Columba landed I looked out towards the black hummocks of the Torran Rocks lying low to the south in a dark grey sea against a light grey sky, bleakly beautiful, as remote from mainland complexities as any fugitive saint could wish.

Next day, as I was driving back through rain-soaked Mull to Craignure for the Oban ferry, a teenage boy standing by the road flagged me down. Lank black hair was plastered each side of a hungry face. Beyond him, other people were waiting – three bedraggled kids and a pinched woman who could have been any age between 35 and 70. They crowded into the back seat of the car, sitting gingerly on my maps and cassette boxes. 'D'ye knaw the time o' the last fairy fer Oban?' asked the woman. Her speech was unplaceable, but strongly reminiscent under the Scottish overtones of an accent I'd heard before in travellers' caravans in Somerset. There was a burst of conversation between her and the children, completely unintelligible to me. The kids peered over my shoulder, bright blue eyes in three filthy faces. A rank, sour smell of wet fox arose from all five passengers. The car windows fogged up. I asked where they were from. 'Glasga,' said the youth in the seat beside me. He rubbed the window with his sleeve and stared morosely out at the rainswept mountains. We drove on for a few miles in silence.

'Ha' ye seen a white Ford Transit van roond th'eeland?' asked the woman behind me suddenly. In the driving mirror her dead white face was set in iron creases from top to bottom, monkey-like and ageless. 'No,' I said, 'friends of yours?'

'It's ma husband,' said the woman. 'He assaulted us and pushed us oot.' The children sniffed and squirmed cautiously like mice on the plush car seat. When I dropped them off near the ferry jetty, the smallest, a six- or seven-year-old girl, piped, 'Goodbye, and thank ye, please.'

'Nice manners,' I said, and her dirty face broke out in a smile, the only one on offer. Their feral smell and silent tension lingered long in

223

the car as I drove it north from Oban towards the Kyle of Lochalsh and the ferry to Skye.

Arriving in Skye, the Misty Isle, was rather an anticlimax. What place could possibly live up to such a billing as one's imagination gives Skye? Here in 1746 Bonnie Prince Charlie had landed in an eighteen-foot rowing boat from the Isle of Benbecula, accompanied by the quintessential Highland heroine Flora Macdonald, on his desperate and romantic escape from the aftermath of Culloden. Here is Flora's later house, and her grave. Here are the craggy, towering Cuillin Hills, so often seen on the horizon on my island wanderings, that put love on Harry Lauder; the famous weather changes that glow and glower from glen to mountain. 'The Magic Isle' said the tourist brochure.

In fact, so impressive were the mountains and glens along the mainland road to Skye that the island appeared ahead quite undramatically, one more sweep of brown hills behind rain curtains. Loch Alsh, separating Skye from the mainland, is only a mile wide. I drove in ignorance along the shore, wondering when the island would come in sight even as I was looking at its rainy hills: expecting, I suppose, a neat island shape romantically distant in the middle of the sea. Such is the power of the myth of Skye. But the map told a different story – an enormous piece of land, fifty miles long, thirty miles wide, cut by sea lochs into five great peninsulas, in each of which you could fit all the Small Isles. Just to explore a few corners of those peninsulas took me all of five days' hard driving, walking and talking. If it hadn't been for the overwhelming, fatal island hospitality, I would have seen a lot more of Skye. Time and again I found myself glued to conversations, raising another glass at the start of another story, my impossibly long schedule of things to do and people to see lengthening all the time. In Skye I filled a whole fat notebook from cover to cover.

The weather put on a fine display as I drove up into the Trotternish peninsula on the north-east corner of Skye. The great Red Cuillin hills, rearing away towards the middle of the island, soon gave way to a stupendous wedge of basalt, nearly twenty miles of sheer inland cliffs several hundred feet high, under which the road ran. The wind came icily from the west, dropping rain as if from a sieve as it hit the Cuillins, plastering the flat top ridge of the basalt cliffs with drifting bands of

224

cloud, letting brilliant shafts of sunlight through to light up their flanks. I went up and up, stopping to get out of the car and take photographs, for thirty miles under the basalt, until a couple of miles short of the tip of Trotternish the road gave an extravagant wriggle and fell away to the front door of the Flodigarry Hotel.

In a country famed for hospitable welcomes, Gavin and Myrna Scott-Moncrieff and their family are right at home. Gavin and Myrna came to Flodigarry in 1988 to try their hand at the hotel trade after years of farming. They live in a modest cottage at the back of the hotel, yet a historical one. Here Flora Macdonald lived after her marriage, and brought up her children. The Flodigarry Hotel, a solid house built by later Macdonalds shortly before they sold up in Skye at the beginning of this century, stands in a superb position in one of the island's few and precious groves of trees, the sky-high cliffs of basalt at its back, looking out over the sea to the mainland hills. I arrived to find the hotel officially closed, its season not yet begun, mattresses in the corridors and new carpets being nailed in place. But nothing was too much trouble to make me feel welcome. Late that evening I found myself by a good fire with a dram at my elbow, strumming a guitar while a large American from North Carolina sawed through Scottish reels on Myrna's fiddle. Later still, in the hotel bar at two in the morning, I learned a good deal of Macdonald history from the Carolina fiddler. Seumas Domhnallach (Jamie Macdonald to the non-Gaelic listener) was over in Edinburgh studying Gaelic at the university, and had come up to visit the land of his forefathers and practise his Gaelic in an area of Skye where it's the main language. Jamie's phone call earlier in the evening had secured him and his friend Barbara beds for the night at the Flodigarry, and here he was chatting away in his hard-learned Gaelic, ten miles from the place which his ancestors had left for Carolina two centuries before, a Coke in his hand and pleasure all over his earnest face.

Next morning I went with Jamie and Barbara to the Gaelic service at the Free Kirk in nearby Staffin village. Gaelic has been a dying language for many years, though children are nowadays taught it in school. At home each afternoon the children watch television that pumps out soap operas in the accents of Australia, America and the East End of London. The few programmes in Gaelic are on around midnight, or later. Many parents won't speak the language at home, believing that their children's best interests will be served by cutting their links with a tongue they'll never meet outside the Highlands and islands. These remote areas are its last stronghold in Scotland, the Trotternish peninsula in Skye being one of the strongest. The Free Kirk's church in Staffin was a large, plain room panelled in wood, rows of virtuously uncomfortable pews facing the minister's high pulpit. All the men wore dark suits and ties, all the women smart hats. The three strangers in their jeans and bare heads may have looked conspicuous, but no one gave even the flicker of a disapproving glance.

A couple of old men led the psalm singing, keening the first few words of each verse in a nasal moan before the congregation joined in with a long, flowing mode of singing in which people shifted tone to create subtle harmonies like the drone of pipes. Prayers were said standing. The sermon was formidable, forty-seven minutes by the clock on the wall, delivered by the frock-coated minister with great energy. His rich voice modulated between a seductive, consoling murmur and a biting, admonitory clarion call. At the start of the sermon I was intrigued by a subdued crackling that seemed to come from every corner of the church. My neighbour, a lovely freckled girl in a black leather skirt and red coat, reached across towards me with a smile. I held out my hand, expecting a sisterly embrace in the Lord, and received a toffee éclair. All round us respectable women and sober-suited men were furtively unwrapping their tedium-relieving sweeties. Half an hour into the sermon my neighbour reached across again with a peppermint and another ravishing smile. If only I had had a bag of barley sugar in my pocket, this could have been the start of a beautiful friendship. At the end of his stint the minister paused, picked out the three aliens among his flock with eagle eyes, and with great courtesy gave a précis in English of the chief points of his exhortation – not a short précis, either. Gaelic speakers will invariably switch their conversation into English the moment they spot a stranger, considering it the height of bad manners to exclude him. Here was the same thoughtful custom in operation, even though every bottom in that church must have been aching on the narrow wooden seats. At the end of the service nearly every member of the seventy-strong congregation shook our hands and wished us well. From first to last, apart from the minister's translation, I had understood not one word; but the warmth of the Free Kirk of Staffin needed no interpretation.

226

Back at the Flodigarry Hotel, Gavin Scott-Moncrieff was waiting in walking boots. Knowing I was keen to get up on the top of that basalt ridge, he had decided to give up his afternoon to accompany me. I couldn't have had a better companion. We struck up over heather and bogs, working our way up the contours through a hanging valley a thousand feet above the sea where pinnacles of rock stood clear of their parent cliffs, fifty feet tall, their profiles weathered into outlines of faces like totem poles. Any valley in England so remote, high and full of fantastic rock shapes would be a major tourist attraction, signposted and car-parked to the hilt. Here in the flanks of the Quiraing ridge there was no evidence that anyone had ever come this way – no paths, no signs, no litter. We scrambled up scree and boulder slides to reach the crest of the basalt, where at 1700 feet the snow lay in drifts and the wind pushed hard. A golden eagle came planing overhead, the first I had ever seen, riding the air currents along the cliffs and out of sight. Gavin and I stood on the brink of the lava curtain, looking over great shark's teeth of basalt with appropriate names: the Prison, the Needle, the Table. Below them the coastal plain of Trotternish lay spread out for twenty miles. The basalt cliff stepped south, its seaward face sheer for hundreds of vertical feet, its grassy inland back sloping dramatically down and away. A view glimpsed, gasped at and immediately blotted out. Mist came across in a solid grey pile, collapsing the enormous prospect into a few yards of grass and heather. We went on, up over the ridge summit and down into sunlight and rain, across hillsides where dislodged stones went bouncing all the way to the foot of the cliff.

The talk flowed, turning on a hub of Scottish politics, music and manners. At the hotel the previous evening Gavin had lent me a book, *The Scottish Islands*, written in the 1950s by his father, George Scott-Moncrieff. Quirky and evocative, the book attacked industrialism and shabby architecture, the fading of traditional island life and the influence of shoddy modernism, all mingled with intimate descriptions of the islands. George Scott-Moncrieff had made his home on the island of Eigg and brought up his young family there, so he knew very well what he was writing about. Just the same passion for an active, independent Scotland spiced the opinions of his son, brought out for discussion on that glorious scramble along the spine of Trotternish. Gavin felt strongly that Scotland had had enough of an unsympathetic Westminster, and

227

was in the mood for severing ties and governing itself. He couldn't see how such widespread absentee landlordism, especially in the islands, could be tolerated much longer. By the time we had dropped down to the road we had worked up a fine head of indignant steam. The top of the Quiraing is a great place for putting injustices right.

Several times on the road back to Flodigarry I thought my final moment had come. We made the journey in the open back of a pick-up truck that had stopped to pick us up, bouncing wildly over the potholes, swerving round blind corners, hanging on for dear life while the truck's spongy brakes squealed as roadside sheep and cows wandered out into our path. Steep drops loomed and vanished, all in a second. The slipstream chilled our wet bodies to the bone. But at the hotel there was a warm invitation from Myrna to join the family at their evening meal. The talk never stopped flowing, sweetened with joking and outrageous stories. All too soon I found myself back in the car, pushing on across the sunlit Trotternish peninsula towards the west coast of Skye, out of Macdonald country into the land of the Macleods.

In the hotel at Dunvegan, where the twin peninsulas of Vaternish and Duirinish join up, I came across the only episode I saw in Skye of the melancholy drunkenness which has become a modern curse for the Scottish islands. A skinny, middle-aged man sat at the bar – just about sat, clutching at the bar top to stop himself sliding from his high stool on to the floor. The bar was sticky with spilt beer, the whole room cheerless and utterly unconducive to pleasant, sociable drinking. The drunk's eyes popped, swimming lazily at random in their grey sockets, the irises green as gooseberries in pink pools of veins. Their owner did his best to ask me a question: 'Ha' ye a sh -- sh – a shnae . . . a sh – sh – sh . . .?'

'He's from Barcelona,' wisecracked the kilted barman. The landlady sighed. 'He came through that door at midday, out of his brains,' she muttered, 'and he's *still* here.' By the pool table a black coat had been thrown across a corner of the bench. A pair of legs protruded from under the coat. Pool cues and ashtrays rested on the motionless heap. 'Drrrrunk,' explained one of the pool players when he saw me looking. 'Really?' I said. 'Aye, really,' said the pool player solemnly.

'The name of highest dignity is Laird,' recorded Dr Johnson in his *Journey*, 'of which there are in the extensive Isle of *Sky* only three,

228

Macdonald, Macleod and *Mackinnon*.' Macdonalds held Trotternish and parts of the south of Skye, Mackinnons the southern ground, while the Macleods were most influential in the west of the island. Here they had their stronghold on the rock of Dunvegan, a mighty castle that stands proudly today, a mish-mash of architectural styles where seven centuries of Macleod chiefs have held sway, longer than any other clan leaders. This has a lot to do with the clan's well-attested ability to trim sails to the prevailing wind. No Macleods of Dunvegan were to be found out on the heather in 1715 or 1745. Not that there were many milk-and-water Macleod chiefs in the days when the clans had and held their land by the sword. Efficient acts of terrorism to be laid at the Macleod door include that frightful massacre of the entire Macdonald population of Eigg by suffocating them in a cave, and another atrocity shortly beforehand, in 1557, when it was the Campbells' turn to suffer.

Iain Dubh, or Black Iain, tenth chief of the clan at the time, was a real bastard. Iain was the illegitimate son of the ninth chief, John, and secured his doubtful inheritance on the death of his father by slaughtering some of his rival claimants on their return from the chief's funeral, and throwing the rest into the Dunvegan dungeon to starve to death. Campbell of Argyll, legal protector of one of the prisoners, became involved when he tried to have them released. Black Iain invited eleven Campbell chieftains over to Dunvegan to discuss the situation, which he had already decided to settle in his own inimitable style. With everything apparently signed and sealed, the prisoners' release agreed, Iain put on a banquet to celebrate the amicable settlement. At the end of the feast the Campbell chiefs raised their goblets to drink a toast to success and the triumph of sweet reason. Not until the cups touched their lips did the Campbells realize that they contained not wine, but blood. As the guests sat there aghast, Black Iain's retainers rushed forward to plunge their dirks into the helpless Campbells. The tenth chief had entered on his inheritance. Strong stuff indeed.

The dungeon where Iain's victims rotted is still to be seen through a hatchway in the floor of one of Dunvegan's towers. A hole less than three feet square leads to a drop of thirteen feet into a clammy stone chamber hardly big enough for a prisoner to turn round in. Once the stone slab had grated into position over the hatchway, there was no possible escape from the oubliette under the guardroom. There's no knowing the number of innocent or not so innocent victims starved or frozen to death in the dead silence of that pitch-dark, grim little pit. Spring tides washed into the dungeon twice a year, taking away with their receding water the grisly remnants of forgotten feuds and jealousies. Only a few feet away, their captors feasted in the castle's banqueting hall.

Macleods were invincible, so clan superstition ran, while their precious Fairy Flag remained in their possession. The legend of the flag is one of the most famous in the islands, a tale which most Macleods even today don't like to discount absolutely: one of those skeins of fact and fiction that no one wants to see clinically disentangled. The fourth chief, the story says, was happy with his fairy wife until their son was a year old. Then the fairy was summoned back to her people, but left her husband the Fairy Flag by way of compensation. Twice already unfurled to snatch victory from defeat – or, some versions say, to heal clan cattle of a terrible disease – the Flag will bring disaster on the Macleods if brandished a third time. That's unlikely to happen, as the Flag is now stretched flat under glass and hanging on one of Dunvegan Castle's walls, looking as if a touch would crumble it into dust. It's a tattered piece of wafer-thin material, veined with the red seams of darning repairs, jagged at the edges where clansmen have snipped out bits over the centuries as talismanic charms. The strangest thing about the Flag is what experts have discovered to be the one attestable fact about it: the material predates the fourth chief of Clan Macleod by nearly a thousand years. This frail bit of cloth was woven in the Middle East as early as the 4th century AD. At one period in its history, some say, it was used as a battle standard by Harald Hardrada, the Norse prince killed at the Battle of Stamford Bridge in 1066. One wonders what snippet of 700-year-old material could have been invested with such magical powers that a tough Norse warrior believed it gave him invincibility. The shroud of a very early saint, perhaps? Harald certainly had faith in the protection afforded him by his standard, and fell at Stamford Bridge without its sheltering presence – it had been left on board his ship by mistake. Who knows the truth at this remove? It makes a good story, to be numbered with all the other good stories that swirl around the other British isles.

Dunvegan Castle holds many other treasures – ancient inscribed goblets, Jacobite relics given by the Bonnie Prince to those who helped him in his escape, great head-scything claymores of bloodstained Macleod chiefs. The lot of a clan chief these prosaic days is not to sweep the heads from the shoulders of his visitors, but to star as kilted and sporraned narrator in videos that introduce them to the clan history. Though you can buy Macleod whisky and Macleod knick-knacks in the Dunvegan gift shop, clan membership is not to be trivialized, especially for those most ardent of clansmen who burn with Macleod zeal in Canada, America and Australia. Thousands of them make their way back over the sea to Skye and Dunvegan, land of their fathers and very real focus of their deepest dreams. At such times the thin overlay of success and sophistication melts away in the powerful twin stream of emotion and malt whisky, and Macleod business barons from the ends of the earth dance reels around Dunvegan and bristle up against all comers.

Among the visitors at these hot-blooded gatherings of the clan, the name of MacCrimmon gets special glory. The MacCrimmons were hereditary pipers to the Macleod chiefs, musical magicians whose inspired fingers could make the clan laugh, weep or swing the claymore. One thing I was determined to do before leaving Skye was to have a go on the bagpipes, and the Piping Centre at Borreraig, MacCrimmon country to the last sprig of heather, seemed the ideal place to do it. The Macleods gave the MacCrimmons free tenure of a large tract of flattish, productive land on a broad finger of the Duirinish peninsula across Loch Dunvegan from the castle, and here they established a famous school for pipers. It ran for three centuries until a squabble with the rent-greedy laird put paid to it at the end of the 18th century. The present Piping Centre, funded by a Canadian branch of the MacCrimmons, was opened in 1976 and has every right to be the bagpipe Mecca of the islands. But in spite of its displays of dismembered pipes in all stages of construction, its carefully laid out chronology of the pipes and its annual piping festival, it lacks authority and a live feel. Surely, here of all places, one could reasonably hope for a well-signed approach road and a full-time, handsomely paid, well-informed curator who can actually play the blessed things, rather than a bored girl operating a taped orchestral recording of 'The Skye Boat Song'?

Luckily, the young man who followed me in was a piper to the fingertips, albeit from Edinburgh. Having followed the custom of all experienced but amateur musicians by modestly murmuring, 'Ach, I haven't touched these in years – let's see, now,' he picked up the demonstration chanter and let fly. The motive power of the pipes is a skin bag, the harmonic accompaniment a pair or two of drones that hum a constant note; but it's the chanter pipe with its holes for fingering that actually gives out the tune. That city boy knew what he was doing. Blowing directly into the top of the chanter, he wailed up a storm. When he had finished 'The Flowers of the Forest' and shaken out his spittle, I took over. The MacCrimmon ghosts must have had a horrible half-hour. I gave my lungs a rebore, but that was about the sum of it. Chanter-blowing is not as easy as it looks. Smiling thoughtfully, the Edinburgh pipe-player repositioned my fingers on the chanter holes. The sheep on the hill outside were still producing more melodious sounds, blow as I did. Had drones and bag been attached, I might well have screeched down a curse on Dunvegan.

Legends of the MacCrimmon pipe experts rival those that surround their Macleod lords. The first MacCrimmon piper, for example, was blinded by a malevolent banshee and granted his musical gift in compen-sation. The best story, though, is of Patrick Mór MacCrimmon, Big Patrick, the greatest piper that ever lived. Patrick Mór was born in 1595 and lived to be seventy-five, when, as one version of the legend says, he went to join the fairies. As a young man, Patrick was so skilled on the pipes that his Macleod chief backed him to blow eleven other pipers off the stage in a great contest at Dunvegan Castle. But Patrick, in common with more than one musician, had a fatal weakness for the bottle. Taking Dutch courage with the other contestants before the competition, he loosened up so disastrously that he couldn't blow a note when show-time came round. Thoroughly ashamed, young MacCrimmon went off to have a good sulk by himself. A fairy woman appeared, and offered him the choice of three wishes – to be a great scholar, a victorious warrior or a brilliant piper. Patrick settled for the music, and found himself the recipient of a magical silver chanter. 'When you dance,' promised the fairy, 'all shall dance; and when you weep, there will be lamenting all over the island.' But there was the usual fairy catch. When she might please to call him away, MacCrimmon must come. Also, the magic chanter must be treated with respect, or the MacCrimmons would lose their gift for ever.

With the silver chanter under his fingers, Patrick Mór MacCrimmon became chief piper to the Macleods of Dunvegan, and a great man in his own right. At last the fairy call came to him in his old age. Giving his set of pipes to his eldest son, Patrick Mór walked off along the shore and into a cave, playing the fairy chanter and followed by his faithful terrier. His sons traced his progress beneath the island, guided by the sounds of the chanter, until they came to the Fairy Bridge where the fourth Macleod chief had received the Fairy Flag from his departing wife. Here the sounds underground stopped; but the sons, listening above, could still hear the barking of their father's terrier. They went on across to the other side of Skye, where from the mouth of the Golden Cave emerged the little dog, stripped by the fairies of every hair on its body.

Another version of the tale has the silver chanter in the possession of the MacCrimmon family until the time of the 24th chief of the Macleod clan, John Norman. Rowing across to the island of Raasay, the chief's party was caught by a sudden storm. Macleod commanded his MacCrimmon piper to keep up everyone's spirits with a tune. The piper, unable to play properly with cold, wet fingers, forgot the fairy's admonition and cursed the magic chanter, which promptly slipped out of his hand and overboard. It's impossible to say, and unsuitably workaday to try to establish, just how much fact lies at the back of these legends. They are best left shrouded in island mist. But strands of them still persist. Today's expert pipers – none of them, sadly, MacCrimmons – compete for a silver chanter in an annual contest in the drawing room at Dunvegan Castle.

It wasn't in the sumptuous surroundings of the castle drawing room that I met John Macleod of Macleod, 29th chief of the Clan Macleod, but in his cramped little kitchen well behind the scenes. The chief, brightest star in the Macleod firmament, warmed up the last of his lunchtime coffee for me and sat down at the kitchen table, not sorry to be dragged away from his dutiful penning of yet another speech. Deciding how to refer to a clan chief when talking or writing of him is a delicate matter. Dr Johnson notes: '. . . none but the Chief of a clan is addressed by his name. The Laird of *Dunvegan* is called *Macleod*, but other gentlemen of the same family are denominated by the places where they reside, as *Raasa*, or *Talisker*. The distinction of the meaner people is made by their Christian names. In consequence of this practice, the late Laird of *Macfarlane*, an eminent genealogist, considered himself as disrespectfully treated, if the common addition was applied to him. Mr *Macfarlane*, said he, may with equal propriety be said to many; but I, and I only, am

Macfarlane.' The present chief of Clan Macleod is certainly not a man to consider himself disrespectfully treated by the common addition, but the elderly gentleman whose advice I sought at the castle gates was very definite on the point: 'You may write of him as John Macleod of Macleod, chief of the Clan Macleod, in the first instance, and thereafter as Macleod.'

Macleod, therefore, gave me a fascinating hour's ramble through his family's history and on out into the wider aspects of what it means to be a clan chief in the modern world. The chief of Clan Macleod is a calmly spoken man in his early fifties, warm and approachable, possessed of a window-rattling laugh; though when he was speaking of clan dispossession after the '45 Rebellion I was very conscious of thunder and lightning being held only lightly in check. In his stocky frame and dark colouring, strong features in a square face, was a striking resemblance to the portraits of his ancestors on the Dunvegan walls. Dark, strong Macleod men seem often to have chosen dark, strong Macdonald women, in the intervals between the two clans trying to wipe each other off the face of the isles. The potent thousand-year brew of different bloods, nomadic Norse and more settled Scots, has given the chiefs of Clan Macleod a propensity both for deeds of tremendous bloodiness and for political astuteness – after all, they are the only clan to have lived in their ancestral home in an unbroken line for 750 years. Impulsiveness and a bent for self-destruction are in the mix, too.

'The awful Red Man, Norman, the 22nd chief, backed the Government in the '45, but he still died owing £45,000,' Macleod told me. 'His grandson, the General, inherited from him, and was £38,000 in debt when he died. And the next but one chief, another Norman, pretty well destituted himself trying to relieve his tenants at the time of the potato famine of 1847–51. That was a true disaster, as terrible here as over in Ireland. It devastated this part of the country. The Highlanders had come to depend on the potato in a very short time, so when it failed four years running the effect on this community was colossal. My ancestor's efforts on behalf of his people are still remembered here; they're probably the reason why the Macleods of Dunvegan escape the vilification that most landlords seem to get these days.

'When I succeeded at Dunvegan in 1965, our affairs were in a terrible mess. Family pride was strongly against turning Dunvegan into a tourist

234

attraction, and it took me twenty years to realize that that was the way I would have to go if I wanted to preserve the castle and keep us going here.'

More rigid members of the clan still don't at all like it, but a tourist attraction is what Dunvegan has become. The tens of thousands of visitors every year help to pay the bills and spread publicity by word of mouth. Macleod has been giving speeches and donning his kilt to shake clansmen's hands all over the world since he was a teenager. 'At sixteen I went to Nova Scotia with my grandmother, Dame Flora Macleod; at eighteen for three months to the United States. It was a wonderful experience for a boy of eighteen, but I began to dread putting on the kilt for yet another arrival at another airport. I still don't much care for that side of it, but it's my duty. They got me to narrate the video on Dunvegan for the overseas market, and that was another breakthrough. I'd say that my main role as clan chief is to be available.'

Macleod well appreciates the ritualistic need of every clan member to see and touch the chief. Behind all the careful marketing, the public relations and income-generating ploys lies a great well of emotion, partly that universal 20th-century desire to be in touch with deep-reaching roots, partly the pleasure of belonging to what is still plainly a powerful hierarchy.

'I've always regarded power as an illusion. Someone once said to me, "Remember, my boy, those who have influence can only use it once." There were checks and balances operating just as strongly in the clan system as elsewhere. The other chiefs in the clan had plenty of ways to rein in the power of Macleod of Dunvegan. But I do experience a time warp sometimes, when I'm talking with one of our people round here. I suddenly realize that we are talking and listening exactly as our ancestors would have done 400 years ago. But it's a power of the emotions nowadays. The land that gave my ancestors their power has mostly gone out of clan ownership. At one time Macleods owned land all the way from Harris down through Skye. In terms of communications by sea it made sense, but after the '45 Rebellion everything changed. This part of Scotland was devastated.' Macleod's well-rounded, restrained voice darkened, and he made a crushing movement with both hands on the kitchen table. 'There was nothing left for the clans – *nothing*. Everyone suffered. The fact that the Red Man had backed the winning side counted for nothing.

235

Dunvegan was virtually a ruin. People thought of the Highlanders as I was taught to think of the Mau-Mau when I did my National Service in Kenya – as barbarians. We were vermin, to be exterminated.'

The tale of that extermination, and of the rise and fall of the Lords of the Isles, is told through the display at the Clan Donald Centre in the old Macdonald stronghold of Armadale Castle, down in the Sleat peninsula at the bottom of Skye. Wandering there a few days after talking to Macleod, I was moved again by the pride of the clans in their history, the tremendously strong and enduring links with a distant past; and, above all, by that sadness for a deliberately destroyed culture that the Scottish islands can awaken in the most unsuspecting visitor. Just to read the beautiful words of the Gaelic poets brought home to me, poignantly, how rich and expressive was the culture closed to me as a non-Gaelic speaker. I'm sure that the English side-by-side translations provided in the Centre were as good as they could be; but, as the curator said to me, if you haven't the Gaelic you'll never quite have the proper picture.

> O Children of Conn of the Hundred Battles,

chanted the Clan Donald hereditary poet, Lachlann Mór MacMhuirich, to the waiting warriors before the Battle of Harlaw in 1411:

> Now is the time for you to win recognition.
> O raging whelps,
> O sturdy heroes,
> O most sprightly lions,
> O battle-loving warriors,
> O brave, heroic firebrands,
> The Children of Conn of the Hundred Battles –
> O Children of Conn, remember
> Hardihood in time of battle!

The Gaelic poets did not just use their talents to whip up their clansmen to battle. In his poem 'The Message of the Eyes', the 17th-century poet Niall Mhór MacMhuirich touched on the subtlest of tender feelings:

> Silence gives meaning to the swift glancing of the eyes.
> What matters the silence of the mouth
> When the eye makes a story of its secret?

236

And a century later, Alexander MacDonald's 'The Song of Summer' catches the colour and movement of a salmon as only a man who had spent many hours watching patiently could do:

The swift slender salmon in the water is lively, leaping upside-down, brisk, in the scaly white-bellied shoals, finny, red-spotted, big-tailed, silvery lights clothing it, with small freckles, glittering in colour; and with its crooked jaws all ready it catches flies by stealth.

Henry Williamson would have enjoyed an afternoon with Alexander MacDonald.

In the kitchen at Dunvegan, Macleod was looking to the future of the islands. Clan Macleod still owns land in Skye, of course – Macleod is proud that the clan's possessions include the savagely beautiful Black Cuillin hills. But this cultured, artistic man – he and his wife are both musicians, and hold an annual festival of chamber music at Dunvegan – feels beleaguered and belittled by what he sees as governmental neglect of the islands. 'I don't think it's a deliberate policy, but the product of government by people with such a narrow cultural vision. It's a very English government, an Anglo-Saxon one, and becoming increasingly so. A small example is their cutting off of the subsidy that allowed Loganair to fly a Skye–Glasgow service. Not an important route, but a useful link all the same. No one bothered to let us know it would be withdrawn; I only found that out by chance, when I booked on the last flight. We simply don't figure in their scheme of things.'

Macleod saw me to the castle door, but he couldn't hang around chatting. A briefcase had appeared in his hand. That chief's speech was waiting on his desk, along with the letters of twenty clansmen.

Travelling south through the island, I travelled through Macleod country. The long brown heather hills rose higher, while behind them black teeth of rock began to slice the sky: Macleod's revered Black Cuillins. The road twisted and turned, heaving itself up on to hillsides and falling away to the feet of the mountains. They stepped closer, seeming to press the brown foothills flat under their wrinkled elephant skins. Knife-edge ridges stood sharply cut, 3000 feet up in a dark grey sky. Yellow slides of scree funnelled down from the ridges like powdery rivers. All the tops, weathered into that special volcanic jaggedness, rose into snow-covered points somewhere in the cloud. They were immense, physically overwhelming things, dominating their landscape with a black-and-white clarity I found frightening. I could no more have climbed up the flank of one of those Black Cuillins, or gone along one of those ridges, than I could have piped for a silver chanter.

I was heading for the Strathaird peninsula, where Macleod country gives way to Mackinnon territory, to meet a Mackinnon, though not *Mackinnon* himself. In Strathaird, I had been told, a new laird was bringing some optimism and some jobs into the island, setting an example to less energetic estate owners. The Strathaird estate, for many years a run-down sporting concern, was now making a go of hill farming, of forestry, of deer farming – and, above all, of fish farming. I found out when I got to Strathaird that the deer had not been much of a success, and the hill farming was just about ticking along on a break-even basis. But the fish were going swimmingly. Fish farming became something of a trend in the 1980s. All you needed, it was said, was a salmon hatchery, some netted cages and a bit of water. The potential profits were good, it created employment for local people, it was simple and very suitable as a small-scale, manageable industry for the islands, with their great numbers of fresh and sea water lochs. Several local people tried their hands at fish farming, only to discover the snags once their money had been invested. What you need, above all else, is a good training. And money, lots of money.

The new laird of Strathaird has the money, and Gordon Mackinnon has the training. A thickset, freckled young man with dark red, curly Scots hair, Gordon runs the Strathaird estate's fish farm at Loch Slapin, a cold sea loch under dark, conical outposts of the southern Cuillin Hills. First making sure I had a lifejacket on, Gordon took me out in a boat into the middle of the loch to show me the salmon in the cages. We landed on a lattice-work metal raft, with gently rocking catwalks bobbing on polystyrene floats. Inside each fifteen-metre-square cage sagged a nylon net, in which the salmon swam freely. Gordon scooped up food pellets and sprayed them out over one of the cages. As soon as the pellets hit the dark green water, up flickered the salmon to grab them. Alexander MacDonald's lovely description of salmon in the water fitted them to perfection. Some of the fish skidded across the surface; others leaped clear to splash back again, showering water all over me. Now I saw why Gordon Mackinnon was wearing thick yellow oilskins. One or two of the

238

salmon had dull white patches on their noses. 'Sea lice,' explained Gordon. 'The lice stick to their heads and necks, burrow in and suck the blood. That's one of the diseases. There's another one that brings them up in pus blisters. Disease can wipe out a whole batch of salmon. That's one reason why a whole lot of small fish farmers have gone bust. You need to be able to write them all off and start again from scratch if you have to.'

Another thing salmon suffer from is stress. I found that amazing at first, thinking of the human stress victim, the workaholic in a screaming city. But salmon are sensitive creatures. When they are taken out of the water and sent down chutes to be graded for size, they suffer stress. Overcrowding brings it on, too, and so does the proximity of predators such as herons or seals. The Loch Slapin farm has a seal scarer, not a very effective one, that makes underwater bleeps. The seals like to come up the loch and do a little window-shopping around the nets. Salmon can die of stress, sometimes in hundreds, said Gordon. Of course, they are destined to die anyway, when they reach a weight of between two and six kilos, either from a blow with a 'priest' or loaded stick, or a painless but lethal dose of CO_2 in a sedation tank. Then they are bled, steeped in fresh water, counted, packed in ice and sent away to Inverness – many of them to another Strathaird venture, a processing plant and smokery. Life for a Strathaird salmon before that journey to Inverness must be pleasant: coddled from an egg onwards, getting a gleaming silver coat after a year or so, driven or airlifted like a VIP to the seawater loch when they're ready, as much food as they can eat, regular medical check-ups – then bang! and it's over. If it wasn't for the aggravation from seals and sea lice, I think I'd like to be reincarnated as a Strathaird salmon.

The estate's fish farms employ altogether about fifty Skye people, more than half of them born-and-bred locals. More than a hundred people work at the Inverness plant. 'English incomers work for the fish farms,' Gordon said, 'but they're mostly on the freshwater side and in the hatchery. It's the locals who work out on the sea lochs. Why? Well, it's harder work, you see.' He grinned. 'The English are tolerated in Skye, though some don't mix socially very well. Of course, every time there's any bother it comes down to the same old thing – "Ach, it's the bloody English!"'

One thing tends to weary the fish farm workers – the number of television crews that come up to film their every operation, except the killing and bleeding which are reckoned to be bad PR. 'We get a lot more attention than other fish farms,' I was told in the office, 'because of who owns us.' That new-fashioned laird is Ian Anderson, rich through his twenty years of slogging round the concert stages of the world as singer and flute player with the rock band Jethro Tull. Many were the head-shaking forecasts of disaster, of pot-smoking hippies with more money than sense playing at being landed gentry, when Mr Anderson bought the Strathaird estate. But he did what he sensibly announced at the outset that he would do – he spent as much again, if not a lot more, on making those hills and lochs work for him and for the community he'd bought into. The hill farm may not make much profit, but he keeps it going because it's part of the local way of life. Not so with the fish. They have been his justification in the eyes of local people. You won't hear many grumbles about the laird in this district. Unlike other rock zillionaires who buy up island estates and soon forget they own them, Mr Anderson lives a good part of his life at Straithaird. He keeps himself informed, attends fish farming conferences, knows his employees and his business. Starstruck fans who turn up unannounced to see their idol are unlikely to gain an audience; but those who strike lucky are likely to come away a lot more knowledgeable about allevin, fry, parr and grilse. He couldn't meet me that day, as he was nursing the memory of four recently-departed wisdom teeth. But Gordon Mackinnon made a good stand-in lecturer. I nearly froze my fingers off on that floating farm, aligned so cunningly with a wind-funnelling gap in the snowy Cuillins. But I wouldn't have missed a word of it.

Before I left Skye, I had two walks which for very different reasons stayed in my mind, still vividly there as I write. One walk was around the tip of the Strathaird peninsula, on yet another cold morning that froze my fingers and filled my eyes with tears. The road through the peninsula came to an end at the scattered community of Elgol, a few houses spread across the cliffs. Down on the shore was a primary school with what must be the best classroom view in Britain. I could tell from a glance through the window that Elgol children get an excellent, lively education. A flaming Piper Alpha oil rig toppled into the sea on one wall, its undersea pipes and wells done in 3-D cardboard tubes, a large helicopter swinging to the rescue from the ceiling. On the other wall were mountains, but the painted plain was full of tepees and the grotesque totem pole in front told me they weren't Scottish ones. All the same, I wonder that any work gets done at Elgol Primary. Those lucky children look out on a complete collection of Small Isles – the cloud-capped mountains of Rhum, tiny rocky Muck, Canna turned sideways on and bulged out of its customary wedge shape, Soay like a long rising pudding, Eigg curving so sharply round its bay that it looks like two islands. And to the right, a view into Camasunary Bay that literally took my breath away: great black ridges in the sky, dominating the brown hills in front of them, which in their turn towered over a wide green bay where two specks of white houses stood at opposite sides like neighbours after a quarrel.

To reach Camasunary Bay from Elgol meant a scramble of three miles along forty-five-degree slopes a hundred feet above the rocks, the only path a muddy sheep walk twelve inches wide at best, in places directly over sheer rock faces. Loose boulders, slippery rocks and rain-greased mud made this a tricky proposition. Canted over sideways and grasping heather roots in the hillside for dear life, I still couldn't keep my eyes on the path with that mind-boggling view in front. Down at last in Camasunary Bay, though, there was an antidote to all this exultation. The entire bay from end to end was littered with plastic, bright primary-coloured blobs like a field of exotic flowers. There were scarlet cartons, yellow squeezy bottles, coils of green twine, boxes and crates in every rock cranny and on every patch of heather, thrown far inland by winter storms. Into Camasunary had drifted the detritus of three nations' ships – bright blue milk crates from Dublin dairies, a green box from Burtonport Co-op, a brown one from the Foyle Fishermen, a white one from what must have been a Lowestoft trawler, to judge by its name: *Suffolk Endeavour*. How long does it take a plastic box to become biodegraded? How long before a rubbish skip makes it over the mountain track to Camasunary Bay?

The other walk I will not forget came about after I had said goodbye to Macleod at Dunvegan and found my way by ever-narrowing roads to the western end of North Skye. I left the car at the remote farm of Ramasaig, the only building in a wide, rocky valley which rose to the lips of cliffs 700 feet high. From the farm a rutted track led away, beaten into the surface of the moor by the hoofs of cattle, up across a shoulder of hillside with a view out to the humps of the Outer Hebrides islands across the Minch. The track climbed, concealing what lay ahead until I was right at the top. Then I stopped short, staring ahead into a hidden valley. From far up in the head of the valley a river came crashing down through flickering white falls to wind gently the length of the wide green strath to a pebbly beach. On each side of the river lay the ruins of at least thirty houses, each marked out in the grass by a rectangle of stones. Climbing down to look more closely at the ruins, I found chimneys still standing, hearthstones in place, doorways complete. Cattle pens stood half their original height, still plain to see. Drystone walls ran round and through the ghost township. On every side the green ground stretched up towards the hills or the cliff tops, still ridged with old runrig strips where a few sheep were nibbling.

It was yet another of those silent, eloquent clearance townships that remind Highlanders and islanders of their terrible personal family histories. Emotions felt at the site of any historical tragedy are usually a bit suspect. One comes there prepared to feel indignant, sad, misty-eyed. But this was a hidden place, far from any road, about which I had known and supposed nothing before stumbling on it. The green grass acres were so obviously fertile and productive, the township supplied with fresh water on its doorstep, the runrig well drained, sea fishing right there at the bottom of the valley. I walked from the falls down to the beach, hearing only the roar of falling water and the suck of waves on the pebbles, and saw no natural reason for the valley to be so achingly empty. Just how and when the factor's men came to burn the thatch, throw out the furniture and evict the tenants of the township at Lorgill I didn't know, and never learned. But all the peaceful, sunlit beauty of the day did nothing to lift the shadow from that abandoned valley.

14. Shetland

A LANDSCAPE IN MUSIC

My island dream of Shetland, northernmost outpost of Britain, was of ogs and fiddle music; misty isles in a remote, cold sea. The Shetlands, een on the map, had none of the solidity of Lewis or Skye. They were hin, tattered rags of islands. Through Shetland Mainland, Yell and Jnst, from toe to top, the Shetland chain measured seventy miles, yet io point in the islands was more than three miles from the sea. The Norse place-names – Hamars of Houlland, Swarta Skerry, Grunnavoe, Haggersta – suited the remoteness of Shetland, a hundred miles further north than John o'Groats.

Looking at Lerwick on the map, neatly huddled on its nose of land half-way up Mainland, I'd formed a mental picture of a sweet little town, a plump bird on a cosy nest with never a feather out of place. This romantic image shouldn't have survived what I had read about the place. Lerwick, above all, is a working town, the capital of the Shetland Islands, rich in fishing, oil and industry. The town was forced into being through rade and war with the Dutch in the 17th century. It grew as circumstances demanded, expanding from a garrisoned fort into a settlement of huts, then into a thriving, lively town for deep-sea fishing boats and the Greenland whalers that would set off for their months of frozen hardship with twenty or thirty Shetlanders apiece making up the crew. By the urn of this century Lerwick had grown to be Britain's chief herring port, crammed with gutting and packing sheds, stinking and prospering. It attracted boats from as far south as Lowestoft in Suffolk, as far west as the Hebrides and Ireland; east as far as Norway and Finland. Lerwick also supported its own fleet of anything up to 500 steam drifters. Slump came when the herring went their mysterious way between the wars; boom followed during the 1970s when North Sea oil began to pump through Shetland's economic arteries.

These days Lerwick boasts one of Europe's most sophisticated and successful fishing fleets, modernized and equipped on the surge of a flood of oil wealth. What that meant in terms of fish docks, fish markets, fish merchants, fishing boats and fishermen I began to appreciate as I wiped the rainwater off a dockside bollard on Lerwick's waterfront and sat to

243

eat a paper of chips. None of the inactivity and semi-silence of other British fishing harbours here. Norwegian and Shetland trawlers were in, as tall, long and stately as international hotels. Inshore boats rimmed with old car tyres, their decks cluttered with orange netting, no bigger than the Twin Otter that had flown me in an hour before, nipped in and out under the trawlers' great steel flanks. Hammers clinked on rusty metal plates, engines puttered, generators whined, crew members swore and whistled. Lerwick was fully alive, untidy and energetic. Seagulls know a thriving fishing port when they see one. In Lerwick there were thousands of the cold-eyed, asbestos-throated opportunists, planing around and sauntering along the edge of the harbour. They nonchalantly gobbled my blistering hot chips, and came up to peck resentfully at my shoes when I tried to mark a reserve on my supply.

Later on, wandering around Lerwick's tangle of paved, narrow roadways and foot passages, I found the Norwegian Welfare Centre. An atmosphere that had been elusive all afternoon clicked into focus. The dark-skinned, black-browed Shetland face slots into a Celtic image, but up here one is far nearer to Scandinavia – 200 miles from Aberdeen and the same distance from Bergen in Norway, as the Shetland guidebooks all say. Where the Dutch were once as familiar in Lerwick streets as the Shetlanders themselves, nowadays it's the tall, blond Norwegian fishermen who buy provisions in the shops, drink in the bars and push the boat out with the local girls. Ties with Norway are far stronger than those of English towns with their French or German civic twins. Lerwick street names look east, not south – Saint Olaf Street, King Erik Street, King Harald Street. There's a well-supported mutual friendship society, which meets in the snug, wood-panelled Welfare Centre. Norwegian fiddlers come across to Lerwick to swap tunes and techniques. A contingent of Norwegian families has settled in the town. It's good neighbourliness, and good business.

Astrid Vetvik, who runs the Centre with her husband, has been in Lerwick fifteen years, fielding phone calls across the North Sea, dispensing coffee, cakes and good advice to Norwegian fishermen, some of them lonely young boys in a town they haven't yet learned to think of as a home from home. 'Her ken du ringe hjem' says the notice in the window. Astrid can put you in the way of a trip on *Norrøna*, a Faroese boat plying the remote North Sea and Atlantic routes. £300 buys a week on board

244

MULL
Left: incised grave-slab in the chapel ruins on the shore of Loch Assapol in the Ross of Mull

RHUM
Below left: Iain and Kathleen MacArthur, guardians of the bizarre grandeur of Kinloch Castle

MUCK
Below: the settlement at Gallanach Bay. Tides potentially useful materials lap around the wall of Hebridean houses

Opposite above: the MacEwen family burial circle, looking out to the mountains of Rhum

CANNA

right: sheep barge after the feeding sack, fuelling up for lambing time

SKYE

Left: the author at the Bo
reraig piping centre, find
out the hard way that he
not a drop of MacCrimm
blood in his veins

Below: Trotternish basalt
ridge with the Old Man of
Storr standing clear on th
right, all bathed in Skye'
wonderful stormy light

Left: Gavin Scott-Moncrieff at the Quiraing

Below: once home to a whole community, now entirely deserted – the fertile valley of Lorgill

Above: Gordon Mackinnon on the salmon cages at Strathaird Estate's fish farm on Loch Slapin

FAIR ISLE
Top: plunging cliffs of
the island's coastline

Above: Bob Macleod of
Loganair all but fills the
cabin of the Islander

Opposite above: seen
across the sheltered
South Haven, Sheep
Crag rears up and away
from the cliffs like a
green tongue

SHETLAND
MAINLAND
Right: Statsraad Lehmkuhl
making ready for sea in
Lerwick Harbour

FETLAR
Right: Mark Wilson, volunteer warden, on Stackaberg, with Unst's long brown back lying across the Sound

ORKNEY MAINLAND
Centre right: the Ring of Brodgar

UNST
Below: Vesta Skerry, Rumblings, Tipta Skerry, Muckle Flugga and finally Out Stack – the lonely full stops that close off Britain. Next landfall north from here is the Arctic Circle

Norrøna. Food is not included, but a large helping of empty sea is. You make a pitching round that includes the Faroe Islands, Shetland, Denmark, Norway and Iceland, in flexible order. The boat doesn't linger at these stopping points. It sounds like a pretty stern treat.

Joan Whyte, the owner of Kumalang Guest House in Lerwick, was bursting with enthusiasm and suggestions. I liked Shetland fiddle music, did I? Well then, I should just have been here last week when the folk festival was on. They'd had a group of Irish boys, over in Shetland to play, staying at Kumalang. Wonderful evenings that stretched into nights round at Trevor's house – 'Trevor's Nightclub', he'd renamed it – the Irish fiddlers coming home with the milk each morning, played out. Joan put on a tape someone had made of that back-kitchen music, the tunes racing along to a background of laughter and clinking glasses. An enormous plate of pie and potatoes was shoved in front of me, along with the teapot. And did I play, myself? Honesty fought with wish-fulfilment, and won. Well, no – not in that kind of company.

In the pale twilight of a Shetland early summer's night – ten o'clock, and still bright in these far northern latitudes – I strolled along the main Lerwick thoroughfare of Commercial Street. In any other British seaside town Commercial Street would be pedestrianized and lined with gifte shoppes. Its twisting, constricted course, full of corners and edges, runs between tall stone-built shops offering market town goods: upholstery, electrical gear, meat and groceries. Dawdling in the middle of the street, I was parped out of the way by motor bikes and hoarse old cars tearing up, down and round as their teenage joyriding occupants shouted obscenities at each other and at me. Lerwick's teenagers, barred by age from the pubs, suffer in the long, quiet evenings.

'Hi.'

'Hi.'

'How are you?'

'Bored.'

Upstairs in the plushly respectable bar of the Queen's Hotel, three Norwegian fishermen in white plimsolls and sweatshirts with 'Trondheim' logos sat around a table heaped with empty beer glasses, taking on board their eighth or ninth pints of lager and chasers of whisky. Deep-throated laughter and yawns of boredom chased each other in time with the whisky and beer. One of the Norwegians began to bend forward from the waist, racked by hiccups, until his forehead rested on the table. His mates urged him to drink out of the far side of his glass. The beer blurted out across his knees.

'Hic! Huc! Bjørden een ut – hic! – fockin' snjarden voe. Hic!'

In the morning there was a crowd along the waterfront, full of excitement. *Statsraad Lehmkuhl*, an enormous three-masted sailing ship, had come into the harbour on a weekend visit from Bergen, packed with Norwegian families out on the spree. She was a stirring sight, her three gently raked masts rearing over the fishing boats, a pale grey sausage of sail lashed to the top of each yard, ratlines like strands of cobweb running aloft among a maze of standing and running rigging from which three long lines of flags fluttered out some message of friendship for Lerwick. Under her polished teak taffrail the curve of her stern was embellished with carvings in red and blue, and with curlicues of gold. A fleet of small sailing boats had come in with *Statsraad Lehmkuhl*, racing for a prize between Bergen and Lerwick. Elderly Lerwegians in beards and blue caps had turned out, alongside flocks of children and smart-suited businessmen, to shove their hands in their overall pockets, gaze and ask technical questions of the crew. The streets of Lerwick were suddenly loud with Norwegian talk and laughter, emphasizing again Shetland's remoteness from everyday life of the mainland variety.

Richie Simpson of LHD met me for a pint at lunchtime to talk about Lerwick's fishing industry. The 'L' in LHD stands not for Lerwick, as one might imagine, but for Lowestoft – the Lowestoft Herring Drifters company, legacy of the golden age of herring fishing here at the turn of the century when boats from the south of England were a common sight in Lerwick harbour. Nowadays LHD handles most of the business side of fishing in Lerwick; an industry which, in contrast with most harbours further south, is doing well at the moment.

'We have about fifty small and medium size boats here, going after white fish for the processing plant over on Bressay Island,' Richie told me in the smoky fishermen's bar. 'These are almost all boats from the islands of Burra and Whalsay – there's only five or six Lerwick families still fishing. But a hell of a lot of Lerwick people are in fish processing, making fish meal, cleaning and filleting. There's maybe a dozen small boats after the shellfish, and then the big purse-netters cleaning up – about ten of those. A purse-netter can take two thousand ton of herring

246

year by the quota, and about double that of other kinds. That's quite
a lot of fish. All these boats are owned by the people who work them –
you'll usually find it's kept in the family, and all the crew members have
a share in the boat. So it's worth everyone's while to keep going. Since
the oil's been on, the Shetland Islands Council has been giving grants
to young fishermen to get them started in shares in their own boats.
Things are going quite nicely.'

Not quite so nicely for the tern population of the Shetlands, however.
The terns have been decimated in the last few years, as a consequence
of their chief food supply, the little silver sand eel, being fished by island
and other boats almost to the point of extinction. The Bressay fish
processing plant, like the one at Ardveenish on Barra, can make good
industrial use of the sand eel. Boats come from all over – from Norway,
the Faroes, Iceland, Denmark, Ireland, France and Germany – to fish
the waters close inshore and sell their catches into the Bressay factory.
The Russians make a different use of the harbour, bringing their big
4,000-ton factory ships into Lerwick and anchoring just offshore. East
German, Romanian and Polish ships come in as well, all these Iron
Curtain arrivals known to Lerwegians as 'Klondykers'. They stay from
the end of June until September, the purse-netters emptying up to 250
tons of herring a day directly into their Moloch mouths. By the time the
herring arrive in Eastern Europe they are all ready for the store shelf or
table. Richie Simpson sees dangers for the future in all this intense
activity around Shetland's waters.

'Shetland boats have the EEC quotas on, that's true, but there's no
proper international agreement about net sizes. With a big mesh you
could guarantee only taking big fish, but the boat skippers know that all
the other countries' boats are taking up every size of fish, no matter how
small. So they think – why should we be the first to lose out? If the others
don't worry about what they bring in, neither will we.'

Underpinning the success of Shetland's fishermen is the lucrative black
sludge that has so convulsed the islands' economy and way of life. Before
1972 it was crofting, fishing, some knitting and a bit of tourism that kept
Shetlanders solvent. Life had gone on up to then with the same even
tenor of long centuries. Unemployment was less than three per cent.
Most Shetlanders shuffled by on their traditional mixture of occupations.
Shell UK blew most of that out of the window with their announcement

247

in August 1972 of the discovery of the Brent oil field a hundred or so miles out to the north-east beneath the North Sea. Shetland, placed so conveniently near to the new field, was first in line to provide a terminal where the oil could come ashore. What took place over the next few years was an invasion of the islands. Money, men, materials, hopes, expectations – alcoholism, too, and debt, and deep resentment – came flooding into Shetland. Many of the islanders feared their familiar way of life would be swamped beyond recall. That hasn't in fact proved the case, but change has reached out on the back of the oil wave to touch every life in Shetland.

The SIC (Shetland Islands Council), to give them due credit, have tried their best to think ahead, to plan for and assimilate the effects of the oil boom. Sullom Voe, a wide inlet up in the north-west corner of Mainland island, was the obvious choice as a site for the new terminal well away from Lerwick, near to the North Sea, with deep water close inshore and width enough to allow the great supertankers, some of them half a mile long and over a quarter of a million tons in weight, to manoeuvre in and out. Hot on the heels of the announcement of the Brent discovery came the speculators, snapping up land all round Sullom Voe, buying or taking options on tens of thousands of acres of peat moorland and shoreline. Some of the local crofters were set to get rich quick, while others sold their birthrights for a mess of empty promises. The SIC moved in quickly to put a stop to the speculation, alert to the damage being done to the islanders by greedy outsiders while at the same time sniffing an enormous potential advantage to Shetland as a whole. The Council itself bought up Sullom Voe, leased it at handsome rates of return to the oil companies and took on the running of the newly created Port of Sullom Voe, creaming off more revenue in fees and tolls. This was island hard-headedness at its most effective; as was the use to which the money was put. Hospitals, community halls in out-of-the-way settlements, grants to the fishing fleet, to crofters and craftsmen, fish farms and tourism – these were just a few of the benefits. The business of servicing the terminal has added to the prosperity of the islands, too, with improvements to roads and airfields, new schools, new hotels, new housing. The oil companies also paid vast sums of disturbance money into a charitable trust which is approaching the £100 million mark.

But then, as always, there was the other side of the boom coin. To

248

ild a terminal capable of handling one-and-a-half million barrels of
ude oil a day meant an influx of construction workers in numbers not
en in Britain since the great days of Victorian railway building – never
en, of course, in railway-free Shetland. These tough, footloose navvies
ere known to the islanders as 'bears', and 7000 bears were at Sullom
oe at the peak of activity, housed in two purpose-built 'construction
llages' which catered for their inhabitants' every need. 'Build villages,
ot camps' was the order of the SIC, and these places were equipped
ith TV rooms, cinemas, laundries, bars, squash courts, gyms, concert
alls, canteens, libraries, banks, surgeries. Not even Lerwick could
rovide facilities like these. Shetlanders flocked to Sullom Voe to be
ken on as workers, often husbands and wives both after the lucrative
il jobs. Child neglect, hitherto a rare event in such a close-knit society,
egan to figure on social workers' case lists. So did abandonment of the
lderly, whose peats remained uncut, gardens undug and firesides un-
isited by offspring dazzled by the bright lights of Sullom Voe. Shetlanders
ere reeling around with hundreds of pounds in their pockets and nothing
o spend them on except drink. Alcoholism got a grip in many a
ousehold. Other bodily and emotional needs of the lonely, well-off and
rustrated bears needed catering for, too, resulting in many a broken heart
nd head. And when the bears came roaring out of their isolated lair for
 night on the town, they often brought trouble with them, to packed
erwick hotels where locals couldn't get to the bar, or village halls built
or a dancing tradition that admitted few incomers. Somehow Shetland
oped with the influx, and sighed with relief when Sullom Voe's terminal
as complete and the bears moved on.

But what then? Oil began to come ashore in 1978, but by that time
he main job market had already been sold out. There were posts for the
ucky few in the oil companies, and a few more in the hotels and the
ervice industries. Most Shetlanders appreciated the weight of heavier
allets, the more efficient road and air travel, the oil-backed refurbish-
ment of their livelihoods, the bright new community halls. But expec-
ations of a better – or at any rate a more affluent – life, once raised,
on't obediently lie down again. New money had revolutionized the
slands' economy, and the islanders' view of their way of life. Shetlanders
ow expect as their right a little jam on the basic bread of existence. In
he wake of all the oil upheaval, about a thousand permanent jobs

have come to Shetland. But so have furious drinking, family tensions, impatience among the youngsters, a need for a car and a night out – not all attributable directly to the oil boom, but all exacerbated by it.

The oil isn't expected to flow much beyond the year 2000, though the SIC hopes it may trickle on until the middle of the next century. Those prudently invested funds aren't likely to dry up in the immediate future, either. But one day – sooner than many islanders realize – the chill winds of reality, shut out for a couple of generations by oil cosseting, will blow through Shetland again. When that oil-funded fishing technology has sucked dry the North Sea fish stocks, and the charitable trust has bestowed its last benefits, it will be back to the basics of peat, croft and family boat. Whether the old acceptance of those limits to life will reassert itself is quite another question.

Now came a treat: an all-too-short trip to Fair Isle, the lonely blob of an island set in the sea half-way between Shetland and Orkney. Bob Macleod, a large, cheerful, ginger-haired native of Lewis, was our pilot. He approached me in the departure room at the Tingwall airfield like a man with a treat up his sleeve.

'You're the chap who's interested in the islands, are you? Okay – you come and sit up front with me. We'll go down and make a little detour over the Pictish broch on Mousa, and then take a turn round Fair Isle so you can get some good camera shots. Okay? The windows aren't too clean, mind.'

The eight passengers filled every available inch of the Islander plane. Up in the co-pilot's seat, headphones on and microphone adjusted so that I could talk to Bob Macleod, I quickly re-assessed my ideas of small plane flying as we arched up from the runway, bumping in air pockets across the crofts and hillsides below, then banked extravagantly over the Isle of Mousa. The double walls of the broch, a forty-foot defensive tower, slanted in a forty-five-degree slide across the windows of the tiny plane. Bob brought the Islander level before swooping down to buzz low over Sumburgh airfield at the southern tip of Mainland. As he swooped up again, pressing my back into my seat and my heart into my throat, a laconic voice from the control tower said in the headphones, 'Ah hairrd that, Bob. But Ah saw nothing, ye'll be pleased to know.'

Bob Macleod's approach to flying is an attractive one – get some fun out of it. We flew at 500 feet over fishing boats, getting waves from the crews, as Fair Isle grew larger ahead, a low grey bulk with the sharply angled blade of Sheep Crag rising on the corner. More generous banking brought the tilted strata of sheer 400-foot cliffs wheeling up across the windows as we flew round the island, Bob leaning across me to point out the two lighthouses and the dark crater of a blowhole. Then we were dipping down to touch, bump and touch again on the short airstrip.

'I'll do you a fly-past,' Bob promised as he handed me out my pack from the Islander's hold. 'It'll be low, so get your camera ready.' I stood up by the windsock and watched him bank round like a Spitfire after an ME109, then come slanting right down at me. It was low.

Jerry and Ingirid Eunson's small house at Leogh, near the southern end of the island, was full of twitchers. They came in from twitching to the evening meal, went out twitching afterwards until it grew too dark to twitch any more, and were out again twitching before seven o'clock next morning. Talk around the Eunsons' table was all of twitches, great and small, achieved all over the country. Dave had been to China just to twitch. Twitching is bird-watching, but that's hardly an adequate way of describing the complete slavery in which the twitcher's pastime binds him. Pastime is wrong, too. Twitching is a way of life, a grand obsession with its own tightly-structured procedures and customs. Twitchers will drive crazily from Suffolk to Shetland, charter a helicopter from Sumburgh to the Scillies, for the chance of adding a bird to their lists. There are personal life lists, season lists, year lists, UK lists, world lists. John spoke with modest pride of his father's Shetland list: well over 300 ticks (birds spotted) and growing all the time. Twitchers have the same emotional relationship with the objects of their passion as gricers have with steam locomotives. Fair Isle, smack in the middle of the track of great autumn and winter air movements across the top of the world, is a staging, resting and nesting post for birds unequalled anywhere in Britain. Twitchers come on pilgrimage to stay at the bird observatory at North Haven for weeks at a time. If that's full they bed down with any islander who'll have them. This May the observatory was booked solid. Every bed at Leogh held a twitcher, or two. The Eunsons, after some thought, managed to squeeze me in on a mattress on the sitting-room floor.

A warm, hospitable welcome is the hallmark of island people in general, of Shetlanders in particular and of every Fair Islander without exception. At about eight o'clock in the evening I went out for a walk in the soft half-light of Fair Isle's early summer night, four or five miles in a drizzling mist squelching round the square-cut, towering headlands and great, plunging geos or wave-worn clefts of the island's coastline where puffins sat calmly at their burrow entrances right under my boots. Towards eleven I got back to Leogh, chilled and soaked through. The Eunsons' enormous, matter-of-fact kindness was even more warming than the second supper, the wet gear whisked away to dry on radiator and stove, the hot coffee and the unstinted dram.

Fair Islanders have always had to rely on their own resources to keep going on their thinly-soiled chunk of rock nearly 25 miles south-south-west of Sumburgh Head. The island is only about three miles from north to south, and about half that across. In ten minutes you can stroll across the southern half, where the fertile land lies and where the houses are dotted across the fields, all facing south. The further north you go, the wilder the surroundings become. The airstrip lies across a saddle of high ground in the centre of Fair Isle, and you walk north from here into an upland swell of heather and peat moor where the bonxies or great skuas nest in enormous numbers and defend their territory in dive-bombing attacks that will scare the most macho of twitchers – or walkers. All the land in Fair Isle, north and south, falls off a knife-angle edge straight down into the sea; hundreds of feet down in parts of the western side. There's a feeling of being floated in a green and brown blanket somewhere between sky and sea. Stand on any of the cliff edges and you look out over many miles of sea: to the horizon most of the way round the circle, to a smudge of Foula Island in the north-west. It's as far to Orkney in the south as it is north to Shetland's other islands.

Until the airstrip was opened in the mid-1970s the only way to Fair Isle was by sea, a sickening journey of three hours or much more coming south from Shetland across the tide-rips of Sumburgh Roost where the Atlantic and the North Sea meet head-on and try to push past each other. The Fair Islanders run their own ferry, *Good Shepherd IV*, from Grutness near Sumburgh across those long miles of sea into the sheltered cove of North Haven by the bird observatory. When mist and strong cross-winds combine to keep Loganair's tiny planes away, *Good Shepherd* comes into her own. She's a tough little boat, built like a trawler and handled expertly by the Stouts, Sinclairs and Thomsons – all long-term Fair Isle family names – with her motley cargoes of barrels, stores, farming equipment, cars, wool, oil and passengers. But even she can be defeated by the battering seas that fill Sumburgh Roost during ferocious winter gales. At such times Fair Isle's community of sixty-odd people slips all tethers to the outside world.

Jerry Eunson's Scandinavian forebears look out of his face, round-nosed and blue-eyed. He can trace his family back on Fair Isle through seven centuries to a disreputable ancestor, a turncoat Norseman who reneged on his duty of lighting the beacon on Ward Hill, so letting in the rival gang. The Norwegians' Island of Sheep stayed in their hands until the 15th century, when King James I received it as part of a dowry paid over by the King of Norway. As in the rest of Shetland, the Norwegian influence is still strong in faces and names on Fair Isle. Jerry's father left the island at fourteen, never to return. Jerry himself was drawn back here to live after coming over to help put up the TV mast in 1974. Ingirid Eunson, an Orcadian by birth, arrived in Fair Isle to cook at the observatory and met Jerry. 'From then on,' he says, 'things went downhill.'

Living in the tiny Fair Isle community is not quite the incestuously cheek-by-jowl affair it might seem. The houses are well spaced out, each on its own plot of ground and mat of green fields of coarse grass. People are drawn together far more than in most mainland communities; to church, to the island dances, to help each other out. But the constraints of those three square miles of available space make it necessary to give everyone else plenty of room, too.

'We don't crowd each other,' Ingirid said. I was sitting barefoot at the table, sipping whisky as my sodden socks and raingear steamed dry by the stove. The generator had packed up for the night, but a battery light shed enough of a glow to talk by. 'You just have to get on with everyone else here. You can step on their toes, but you make sure they have their steel toecaps on first.

'Everyone takes part here, especially at the dances. The Thomson family band provide the music. There might be three or four members playing normally, but when film crews are over in Fair Isle making documentaries it's amazing how many band members suddenly want to join in! We have our own dances – quadrilles and waltzes. Visitors pick up the hang of them quickly – they're not left to just stand around if they come to a dance. Church is another strong meeting point. Everyone goes, to church and to chapel on alternate Sundays. Many of us probably wouldn't go if we lived anywhere else.'

Fair Isle is heaven for twitchers, and it's paradise for knitting buffs. Fair Isle sweaters look wonderful, keep out the coldest winds, cost a lot and are worn all round the world. The distinctive banded patterns in squares, zigzags, diamonds and crenellations were handed over to the islanders, legend says, by the crew of the Spanish Armada galleon *El Gran Grifon* when she made abrupt contact with Fair Isle in 1588. The 300 occupants were rescued, ate the winter-bound islands to the point of starvation and were then taken off by a kind-hearted Scot. Other tales say that the Fair Islanders gave a beach party for their unwelcome guests in a cliff-enclosed bay, climbed inland as the tide came up and left the Dons to drown. Whatever the truth, the patterns are still passed on from mother to daughter and to women coming from outside to settle in Fair Isle. The dyes are no longer made from island plants, though the recipes still exist. There's a thriving market for Fair Isle knitwear, fed entirely by garments produced on knitting machines these days. But Fair Isle women spend weeks over sweaters, scarves and hats for their own families, knitting them by hand with thin needles known as 'wires'. The tiny Fair Isle museum, just opposite the Eunsons' house, displays samples of the art that go back 150 years, the stitching twice as fine as commercially produced knitwear, the vegetable dyes of red and blue still glowing vividly.

Other livelihoods are got in a variety of ways. Most people do some form of crofting, and add other jobs as they feel competent to take them on – operating the great three-bladed wind generator, running the boat, fishing, making, mending. Jerry Eunson looks after the island's water supply. Ingirid does bed and breakfast. Jerry and some other men make up and tar the island road. Ingirid knits for the tourist market. Jerry mended and re-set the damaged winch shed of the *Good Shepherd*. Ingirid drives the tractor to disc-harrow their few acres of grassland. And so on, an always lengthening list of jobs done and jobs still to do, in a style very reminiscent of Harry Hawkes of Skipper's Island all those hundreds of miles away. The Eunson house is marked with earth stains, sheep smears, scratches and dents. Around it lie planks, rolls of wire, tools, fish boxes.

air Isle life is measured out in fish boxes, according to Jerry. Very little ndeed is wasted, very little has no use. This isn't twee self-sufficiency; 's everyday life sharpened up by lack of easy alternatives.

Such practical resourcefulness forms one of the basic strands of Fair sle life; another is that instantly-seen, hospitable friendliness. Both spects came together when Ingirid found out that my birthday was due next day. Nothing further was said, but later on she presented me with little box containing seven candles – rather stringy, warped and misshapen birthday cake candles of yellow and orange wax, still service-ble after fifty years' immersion in the steely waters of the Pentland Firth. Paraffin wax in barrels had been part of the cargo of the 5500-ton *Johanna Thorden* when she was wrecked off Swona in 1937, in the narrow race between southernmost Orkney and the northern coast of Scotland. Thirty people died in the disaster, and the cargo went to the bottom. Now, half century on, the barrel staves have all rotted away; but their barrel-moulded contents are rolling out of the wreck as she breaks up on the sea bed, rolling north round the Orkney Islands to fetch up on remote beaches and rocks. Several came ashore on Fair Isle, three feet high and barrel-shaped, amber-coloured paraffin wax still fit for reshaping into enough candles to bless the birthday cakes of Fair Isle children – and visitors – till the skies fall. The Eunson girls had added the colours to their own batch of candles by melting some of their crayons into the salvaged wax. 'That ship was also carrying a load of Model A Ford cars and some tractors,' Jerry told me. 'We're still waiting for those to turn up.'

It was Eve Eunson's birthday, too, her eighth. Eve and her young sisters, Rachel and Polly, had been hanging over the fence when I arrived, watching the new-born lambs and getting them to suck their fingers. I hung over the fence, too, had my finger sucked – and nipped (inexperi-ence) – and heard about the Fair Isle school with its fifteen pupils, single teacher and multitude of volunteer helpers who come in to teach anything from recorder playing to ballet. Eve, jumping on to the shed roof to deluge her sisters with water bombs, brought the conversation to an end. The water flew back and forth, and so did the insults. You couldn't say that island life stultified the Eunson girls.

'Lovely girls, full of life, a blessing to the island,' said the other islanders. But not for much longer. At secondary school age all the Fair Isle children go off to the big school in Lerwick, boarding at the hostel there and coming home once a month. To picture them as innocents primitives out of the wild, would be a misconception. Television, radio newspapers and visitors to Fair Isle bring the outside world into ever island house. All the children go to the mainland from time to time some of them frequently, to see Grandma and Grandpa, to holida abroad, to visit friends and relations. Children arrive in the Lerwick school from other remote Shetland islands, to mingle with Mainland' boys and girls. It's a cosmopolitan meeting place. But it's also a slackening of the cord that has anchored them up to now to their native islands When they leave the secondary school, the world and its jobs – or dole queues – beckons them further afield. Some of the Fair Isle youngster may already be set on returning home; others may drift back one way o another, through marriage or, like Jerry Eunson, by chance. For many though, that step away to school is a final one.

Depopulation has been the Scottish islands' biggest problem down the years, by clearance, hardship or desire for wider horizons. Since the National Trust for Scotland acquired Fair Isle in 1954 there has been a big measure of stability in the island. Grants from the Shetland Island Council, the EEC and the Highlands and Islands Development Board have raised the standard of life well above the subsistence level of the last century, when land was parcelled out by the laird and long, dangerous fishing trips in the stormy seas out towards Norway were the only way to keep the wolf from the door. There are no second-homers on Fair Isle buying up crofts at prices the islanders can't hope to match. Anyone prepared to plant their feet firmly on the bedrock of community effort hard work and good neighbourliness can fit in. Jerry Eunson doesn't see much point in trying to look too far into the future of Fair Isle.

'You can't predict what there will be here for our children in twenty or thirty years' time. It's not profitable to think in that way. The SIC are very good about encouraging young families, or young couples about to start a family, to come and settle: people with something to contribute to the island. The question to ask is not really, "What is there here for the children to come back for?", but "What was it that brought their parents here in the first place?" It was their parents' sense of adventure that brought them here, away from whatever situation they were in; and it's the same sense of adventure that will take today's children away from Fair Isle.'

By seven o'clock next morning I was jolting in the back of an open lorry down to North Haven to see off a party of twitchers on *Good Shepherd*. Well wrapped up, binoculars around their necks, sandwiches and tick lists in their hands, they were off for a day's sponsored twitch from one end of Shetland to the other. There was a good sprinkling of pale faces and of jokes about the waiting pleasures of Sumburgh Roost, visible between the narrow, rocky jaws of the harbour as a dark bar of tumbled water on the skyline. As the bright blue hull of *Good Shepherd* slid away from the jetty, one of the crewmen called down to me, 'I wish you a very pleasant day and a good walk.' That piece of courtesy carried me joyfully over the headlands to Sheep Crag, one of the most spectacular pieces of sea-sculpture in Britain.

A great upward-curving tongue of rock, Sheep Crag rears from a knife-edge connecting bridge 500 feet and more into the sky, a green-backed pinnacle daunting even to look at. On the cliff edge opposite the crag you look dizzyingly down on to the backs of the fulmars planing on stiff wings above the water, but you still have to crane back to see the topmost point of Sheep Crag. Up those sheer sides of fractured rock where fulmars and gulls roost in tens of thousands, Fair Isle men would climb each year by chain and boot-tip on one appointed day in September to shear the sheep pastured on the summit. Catching the sheep, completely wild after their year-long isolation, was a ticklish business. One careless lunge and you could be rolling over the edge. Bales of wool and sick or elderly sheep were lowered on a rope's end to waiting boats. Only necessity, and pride in tradition, could have led the men to such extremes of effort and danger. The pasture on the back of Sheep Crag is said to be the best in the island, and goes with the tenure of Fair Isle's shop. Not surprisingly, Sheep Crag has seen neither sheep nor shearer for some years now. Intrepid explorers go through the wave-worn caves and arches that undercut the rock, and one twitcher bent on glory crossed the razor-backed rock bridge recently to roost with the fulmars half-way up the face of Sheep Crag. Rather him than me.

From Sheep Crag I set off to walk across the island. The fulmars were already nesting, and not keen on intruders. I almost put my foot on one female, invisible in the shadow of a stone wall. She opened her beak wide, spat half a pint of bright yellow fish soup at me and hobbled into take-off, leaving the large white egg she had been sitting on to fend for itself. She circled round, close enough for me to hear the air hissing over her wing surfaces, until I had cleared off. The bonxies, though, were different matter. The spread of the great skua is one of bird preservation greatest triumphs. Only a couple of pairs were known to be in existenc at the turn of the century, but they have multiplied to take over man areas of moorland and sea coast in this part of the world. Up on the moo slopes above the airstrip they were getting ready for their own nestin, season, and made me most unwelcome. The Fair Islanders would hav been ashamed of the bonxies' bad manners as they swooped down showing pale patches like landing lights on their dark wingtips, dive bombing raiders that just missed parting my hair. I was lucky to be walking here in mid-May: a month later, with chicks on the groun(to defend, the anger of the disturbed bonxie parent is somethin; to see. Steve, ardent twitcher and fellow-guest at Leogh, told me o expeditions he'd made when bonxies were diving down at half-minute intervals to smack his head with beaks and wings until he got out o their territory.

Climbing up to the 700-foot crest of Ward Hill was a sweat, unrewarded by the spectacular view I'd been hoping for. Mist had crept in again from the sea, swirling into hollows and hiding the ground ahead. From glimpse: I took before the white curtain came sliding across, a long unbroker slope led down the cliff tops all the way. But no walk in Fair Isle i: straightforward. Rims of geos and blowholes appear unexpectedly, hun dreds of feet down and right under your feet. I went down into sunshin(again through Bonxie Alley to inspect the remains of the Heinkel bombe that crashed on Fair Isle during the Second World War. Two crew members were killed; two survived, including the pilot. The Fair Islanders gave him a tremendous welcome a few years ago when he dropped ir again in less dramatic circumstances. The wreck lies on Vaasetter below the airstrip, a snapped-off section of tail and tailplane up-ended in a pea ditch. There were figures moving around the little tangle of twistec aluminium; a TV cameraman, a girl with a clipboard in yellow tracksuil trousers, a couple of men. One of these turned out to be Leslie Thomas, author of *Some Lovely Islands*, the book that had first focused my imagin- ation on Fair Isle. He had come to the island to make a television programme, but was not too busy to tell me a funny story about a Russian armed trawler wrecked off the island of Unst, the weapons-laden crew

258

stumbling across the most northerly field in Britain to scare the life out of the farmer as they appeared in the middle of his ploughland.

The mist shredded away from Ward Hill, and there was a pearly glow in the sky and on the sea as the Islander came whirring in from Orkney. Eve Eunson's birthday party was just getting under way. Supper at Leogh that evening was being cleaned and filleted by her father, two freshly caught fish, a present from the neighbours. The Thomson family band was tuning up for a dance in the community centre that night. I could hardly bring myself to board the plane.

On Sunday the stately *Statsraad Lehmkuhl* sailed out of Lerwick for the voyage back to Bergen. At nine o'clock in the morning a small crowd waited on the quay to watch the sails being set. Crew members of both sexes, some entirely new to the job when the ship had left Bergen, climbed up the ratlines like commandos to the topmost perches, then spread sideways out along the yards; a row of denim-clad bottoms seen from a hundred feet below, bending over the sail sausages to loosen the bindings and shake out the crumpled, untidy bundles of sail. The canvas hung awkwardly from the yards, awaiting a proper tightening by deck-hands at the winches. No deep-sea hails here – the mate spoke his orders crisply and calmly into an electric megaphone, and the captain clutched a walkie-talkie. *Statsraad Lehmkuhl*, far bigger than I had imagined her, slid away from the quayside under engine power, turned and slipped smoothly out to sea past Bressay Island, honking three long blasts on the klaxon as she went, by way of farewell to Shetland.

In the unbelievably hot, smoky, crowded bar in Lerwick known as The Lounge, musicians were packed in one corner, hammering their way through a series of traditional Shetland tunes: a girl from Minneapolis on fiddle, a young man on banjo, a middle-aged Aberdonian on accordion, an old man at the piano dressed like a prosperous farmer or auctioneer in tweed jacket and flannel bags. The music cut completely across all social and age barriers. Sitting squashed against the banjo player was Willie Johnson, tapping time with a packet of fags on the table – a famous man in Shetland, 'Peerie Willie' or Little Willie to one and all, a guitarist who began playing in the twenties and developed a whole jazz-flavoured style of chording to accompany the racing, exhilarating fiddle tunes of the islands. Peerie Willie's wide, down-turned mouth and thick white hair swept back from a square brow are a familiar sight wherever traditional music is playing in Lerwick.

'It's all in the bass, you see,' Willie explained, accepting a pint. 'I use the thumb a lot – no barres – and I play well up the neck of the guitar. Gives it that rhythm. It's really jazz I'm playing behind the tunes. It gives it that lift.'

Willie had left his guitar at home this night, but when he slid into the piano seat the tweed-jacketed accompanist's polite parlour plunkings gave way to a strident walking bass all the way from St Louis. Frank appeared, large and well lubricated, to sit and play his harmonica. Then he began to sing – not traditional Shetland songs of fishing and peat cutting, but American 1930s songs of love and betrayal. 'Ach, that fucking shite,' mouthed the young banjo player in disgust as Irving Berlin came sliding out of the woodwork, all purist tradition thrown to the winds. At closing time, downstairs in the grand tiled echo-chamber of the urinal, Frank sang ever louder and with more tremolo while his wife outside tried to urge him home with coos and threats through the doorway. At midnight, idling on the quay under a northern sunset glow and a bright chip of new moon, I saw Frank tacking down the street towards one of the visiting Norwegian sailing boats, arm in arm with its crew, bound for a night's drinking and cross-cultural fertilization.

In the 1930s Willie Johnson's partner in music was Tom Anderson, a man set throughout his life on a single-minded crusade. Tom's whole being has been channelled into prodding, coaxing and persuading Shetlanders to preserve their heritage of music and culture. Shetland fiddle music holds powerful excitements. Listeners gather round the performers in clubs, pubs and dance halls, urging them on from one virtuoso display to the next. Young children have a fiddle pushed into their hands along with their spelling books. It's a tradition passed on from father to son, from teacher to pupil. Girls, these days, are turning out to be even better than the boys. Tom Anderson is generally reckoned the greatest living teacher and authority, a man respected and loved throughout the islands. Mention his name to any crofter, publican or school child from Fair Isle to Unst, and you'll open a box of tunes and stories. Tom Anderson's most celebrated pupil is Aly Bain, fiddle player with the Boys of the Lough, who has taken Shetland's music far and wide into concert halls and television studios all over the world. I first met Aly on a dull night in Bognor Regis when beer and whisky drowned out the dissatisfactions of a half-empty concert earlier in the evening. From Aly I'd heard, then and on subsequent occasions, enough about Tom Anderson to encourage me to call on him in Lerwick and hear first-hand about his work.

Waiting for our meeting, I spent an hour at evening service in the Baptist chapel near Tom's flat, enjoying the powerful harmony singing welling from the congregation of sixty or more. Strong preaching from a visiting minister on Nicodemus and new birth, warm and impassioned, was surrounded by this wonderful all-out harmonizing and by two equally stirring songs from 'da young folk'. At the chapel door five or six people who'd noticed the stranger in their midst shook my hand, told me what a pleasure it was to see me there, and hoped I'd have an enjoyable holiday and fine weather.

Tom Anderson's upstairs flat was filled with photographs of his students, clean young faces smiling over their fiddles. There were little drawings and loving messages propped on the chimneypiece and hanging on the walls. Tom, a tall and well-set man nearly eighty years old, sat me by the fire. I put my foot in it straight away, referring to 'folk music'. Tom sat forward and glared. 'It's not *folk* music, man. It's *heritage* music, Shetland's heritage. Nothing to do with *folk* music.' I trembled for the outcome of the evening, hearing the scorn in Tom Anderson's voice, but I needn't have worried. Once the talk was under way my gaffe was forgotten, and Tom began to take me back to the first stirrings of what he cheerfully admits to be an obsession with Shetland's music. Born on a croft at Esha Ness in the remote north-west corner of Mainland, he learned to play the fiddle in an era when Scandinavian, German and Dutch seamen were bringing in tunes to complement the home-grown ones. Cutting peats, fishing and croft husbandry went hand in hand with the young Tom's fiddle playing, a background close to the heart of island existence that has enriched all the music he has played throughout his long life. In those days the church minister was the enemy of the 'devil's music', and when he was spotted approaching the house the fiddle had to be whisked out of sight. Perhaps it was this association of traditional music and ministerial disapproval that gives so many of Shetland's older generation an attitude to that home-grown culture that comes near to shame.

By the success of his career Aly Bain has proved to today's young

Shetlanders that their traditional music can be appreciated far beyond the islands, but there were no such influential exponents when Tom Anderson began to collect fiddle tunes nearly half a century ago with one of the first tape recorders to make its way this far north. Tom found himself up against stone-walling from the old men and women. 'Ach, you don't want to hear that old stuff. I don't quite mind that tune, you see. And I haven't played in years, ye ken. The old fiddle's not just properly in tune, anyway.' Tom soon learned to carry a good fiddle with him, and to talk his way patiently through the barrier. Eventually the tune would be gone over, at first on the family fiddle with its slack strings and terrible tone, then more willingly on Tom's own instrument. Gradually he began to put together a collection of the old, unregarded tunes on tape, a slow business that filled the following forty years.

'Would you like to hear some music?' Tom asked when we had talked into the subject. We moved next door into his music room, where a photo of Yehudi Menuhin hung on the wall – Tom met and played with him, one of his proudest connections. The reels, waltzes and slow airs came slipping out of the tape machine. I drank them in, along with the first of several drams. Old books of fiddle music piled up on the couch at my elbow as Tom brought them from their shelves below the stack of tapes. He played me a slow air, 'Da Slockit Light'; one of the 600 or so tunes he has composed.

'There's a story behind every tune, you know, and I always tell the story to my students. They are the ones who are now passing on this tradition down the generations, after all. You cannot play this music properly without having the story in your mind. I composed "Da Slockit Light" in 1969, at midnight one night up at Esha Ness. I was standing on the side of the voe looking across at the lights in the houses going out one by one. A slockit light is one that has been put out. My wife had just died, and I was thinking of her, and of how few houses there were around Esha Ness compared with when I was born there. The tune came to me as I stood on the hillside. I went back to the car and sat in there, writing down the tune in sol-fa on the back of a cigarette packet, by the car's interior light.'

The talk turned to the colours of music, a notion which has haunted Tom for years. What came as a drug-induced revelation to psychedelic musicians in the 1960s has been Tom's experience through music alone.

262

Each key has its own colour, and the tunes he writes are each coloured differently for him. G is green, B♭ is blue, E is purple. A is the red of the sun, A minor is pink and F is tinged with silver. From the colours of music we drifted out into abstract physics, mathematical theory, the electrical frequency of the aurora borealis, extrasensory messages passed between musicians. Arthur C. Clarke had been a wartime colleague of Tom's, and some of his theories were brought out and speculated upon – by Tom, while midnight became two o'clock and I blinked over the whisky, left hopelessly behind by this razor-sharp octogenarian mind.

As I stumbled back through Lerwick's streets to bed with the dawn, I wondered hazily what Tom Anderson's course through life might have been had he not lived all his life in Shetland. A fruitless question. As well as being the most influential teacher of Shetland's music alive today, a man who has earned the MBE and an honorary university doctorate, he has pulled together an unrivalled collection of the music that still lights him up. Most of it lies in rooms of controlled humidity and temperature at Stirling University, fragile old tapes in ever-increasing danger of crumbling and fading away. One day, Tom Anderson hopes, it may come back to stay where it belongs, if a suitable place can be provided in Lerwick. Shetland owes that to its passionate archivist.

Next morning I caught the eight o'clock bus to the Northern Isles with five minutes to spare, and sat in a daze looking out at rolling brown hills in a low, treeless landscape while we drove north to the ferry at Toft. The other passengers all had their heads buried in newspapers, the wide scenery outside being familiar unto contempt to them. The man in the opposite seat woke up to cough his way through a roll-up cigarette before settling his head back against the bus window to resume his snoring. Peats were stacked in neat walls along the sides of excavations in the hillsides, and there were drifts of new houses facing across Firths Voe to the ruins of old crofts as we approached the oil metropolis of Sullom Voe, whose flares burned an unearthly brilliant orange on the far side of a hill.

At Toft the bus drove straight on to the little ferry for the short crossing to the island of Yell. Black peat moor lay on both sides of the road during the eighteen-mile drive from bottom to top of the island. Yell is almost entirely made of peat, lying fourteen feet thick in parts, forming a sombre landscape in which the peat cuttings of centuries have made hardly a scratch. The dark little post office at Gutcher yielded up a couple of postcards and a bottle of pop before the bus lurched on to another ferry and crossed over to Unst, Britain's most northerly island and my destination the following day. The bus drove away north with its load of yawning passengers, leaving me on the ferry to be cut by an icy wind as we reversed away from the island and butted our way out to the steep cliffs and rock stacks of Fetlar.

The island of Fetlar, a few miles east of Yell, suffered as much as any during the clearances of the 19th century, the lairds in this case being the Nicolson family. Arthur Nicolson of Lochend had bought a good portion of the island from the Bruce family in 1785, and built the fine mansion of Brough Lodge at the western end. In 1815 he inherited more of Fetlar, at about the same time that landowners all over Scotland were comparing the rents they were getting from their tenanted crofts with the income that could be theirs if the crofters were evicted and the fat, hardy Cheviot sheep brought in to graze the empty land. 'Fetlar' means fat land, and on some of the most fertile soil in Shetland the tenants had made a reasonable living by crofting and fishing. But at the beginning of the 19th century the Cheviot was champion. Seven years after his inheritance, Arthur Nicolson decided on a rigorous clearance programme. The south-western side of Fetlar runs down into the long, blunt-tipped Lambhoga peninsula, the islanders' only source of peat and an area on which they held the scattald or hill grazing. Nicolson annexed the scattald for his Cheviots, leaving the Lambhoga crofters scratching for a living. That was only the first of a series of annexations, take-overs and evictions that drained the life-blood from Fetlar's community. The population table for the island gives the story in bare statistics:

Year	Inhabitants of Fetlar
1836	859
1851	658
1871	517
1891	363
1911	279
1931	217
1951	161
1971	. 90

What the Fetlar clearances meant in real terms for individual families lay plain to read all round me as I humped my pack from the ferry and walked off along the northern shoreline of Fetlar. At Urie the ruined crofts still raised their gable ends and low stone walls on the banks of the little burn. Fetlar men had subsidized the basic produce of the croft by 'da haaf fishing', deep-sea trips in their six-oared sixareen boats. The stone jetty and couple of buildings on Urie Ness were crumbling away below the ghost township of Urie by the burn. Urie was just one of the score or more crofting townships cleared by the Nicolsons in the western part of Fetlar, sixteen of them in one ten-year stretch between 1847 and 1858. In one year alone, 1839–40, all thirteen crofts in the Gruting district of east Fetlar were emptied. The croft houses were pulled down, and their stones used to build a round, tower-like summer house at Gruting itself, for the pleasure of the laird. Such an act tells everything about the laird's opinion of his evicted tenants and of those who were still there to see the tower and its constituent stones every day of their lives.

From Urie I wandered down into the wide, marshy valley of Gors Geo among more charred gable ends and square ground plans in the grass slopes. Families evicted from such places had a stark choice: starve, or leave the island. The terrible grief of the old people, the anger of their sons and daughters and the bewilderment of the children at having to leave house and home, built up and maintained through generations, still stained these derelict townships of Fetlar, as they had done everywhere I had been in the Scottish islands. It was impossible to stand among their stones and not be gripped by sadness. The loveliness of the view out over the small islands in the sound to Unst's green, brown and purple hills only added to the poignancy of the dead, half-buried crofts. Such sadness still lies over Fetlar, stimulated by the evidence visible in every valley. 'The Nicolsons? Ach, that bloody family,' growled the man who gave me a lift later in the day: 'D'you ken what they did?' and he told the story of the round house at Gruting built of croft house stones with as much contempt and venom as if it had happened last week rather than last century.

Down at Funzie (pronounced 'Finnie') Beach at the eastern end of Fetlar there was no sign of the thriving fishing haven that once launched the sixareens out to the haaf fishing. But the fulmars dispelled the gloom of ruined townships as they came cutting past on rigid wings, glancing at me with their bright black eyes. The fulmar was a rare bird only a few years ago, but you wouldn't know it on Fetlar. The coastline was cut by deep geos, bays and cliffs, and thousands of female fulmars sat in the crevices defending their eggs with an impressive exhibition of vomiting, spitting orange juices like old salts with a quid of tobacco in the cheek. I spent an hour admiring their defiance and the air mastery of their cruising mates before making inland to St Rognvald's Guest House, where Mrs Jane Richie filled me in on life in Fetlar today.

The island's chief difficulty has always been the lack of a safe harbour. Harald Fairhair, King of Norway, arrived in Fetlar back in 880 AD to sort out a group of renegade subjects of his who had settled in Shetland and begun to mount raids back across the North Sea. But the shallow water under sheer cliffs couldn't accommodate his ships, and he sailed on to Haroldswick in Unst to start a campaign that eventually put all of Shetland and Orkney in his power. What stymied Harald Fairhair has defeated attempts at sea communication down the ages. Until the roll-on-roll-off ferries were established in the early 1970s, Fetlar relied on a thrice-weekly visit from the steamship *Earl of Zetland*. She would anchor offshore and transfer passengers and goods to small craft whose operations were neatly summed up by their local name of 'flit-boats'. Loganair planes began to fly in to the island's tiny airstrip at about the time that the ferries arrived, but Fetlar's population of 94 proved unable to supply the two or three able-bodied men needed to crew the mandatory fire-tender. Shortly before I arrived Loganair had discontinued their service, though in an emergency they would do their best to get a plane into Fetlar.

That population level of under a hundred threatens the future of Fetlar's community as surely as ever did the clearances. The Nicolson family connection with Fetlar was severed in 1987 by the death of their last descendant to own land here; the other landowning family in the island, the Cheynes, only visit from time to time. The Nicolsons' Brough Lodge is semi-derelict, sliding slowly the way of the clearance croft houses. Meanwhile, Fetlar's school serves just nine children. Three-year-old George Richie is the only child of his age on the island, destined for a lonely schooling unless things change. As in the other Shetland islands, youngsters leave at eleven to go off to Anderson High School in Lerwick, few of them to return. A high proportion of Fetlar islanders are advanced in years, the old croft houses standing empty as their elderly owners move into the small clutch of sheltered housing at Fetlar's main village of Houbie. The Fetlar shopkeeper says he won't be able to carry on if the population drops any further.

Jane Richie inherited the family croft and came back to Fetlar after several years away; but it's only the guest-house business, coupled with a lorry-driving job that keeps her husband Kenny away in Unst six nights of the week, that makes it possible for her to stay. She was realistic about winter in the island.

'Winters here are very, very harsh. We get gales up here to Force 11 and 12. You should just see the waves coming crash! crash! over that cliff on Lambhoga. We advertised for couples to settle in Fetlar a few years ago, but those that came had no idea what they were coming to. I sometimes get fed up with it in winter, and think – what am I doing here? You sicken for a sight of the sun, some warmth, for the wind to die off. But you have to have optimism. When the summer comes, with our long days and short nights up here, it's just beautiful.'

In the morning I set off early from St Rognvald's. I had a date with a local bird, though she didn't know it. Up over the rocky back of Stackaberg I tramped with Mark Wilson, a wiry young man from Ollerton in Nottinghamshire who was up in Fetlar for a stint as volunteer warden on the RSPB reserve that takes in moorland, marsh and mountain habitats in the centre of the island. On my walk across the northern half of Fetlar I'd seen curlews and whimbrels trilling over their half-completed nests among the sedges, an oystercatcher pursuing and seeing off an over-inquisitive bonxie, and a raven rolling in the sky, carking and cronking to its mate in the rocks below. I hadn't seen, and couldn't have named them if I had, the red-necked phalaropes, rarities whose breeding sites in the Fetlar marshes are a secret that Mark Wilson would rather have lost his life than reveal. The old lady I was hoping to visit was in a different category, a once-and-for-all ornithological freak now on the verge of disappearance into history. I followed Mark's energetic course over rock and heather, crouching and sidling from cover to cover as we neared the trysting place among the rock outcrops on the crown of Stackaberg. The wind tugged, jerking flashes of grey and brown across my binocular lenses. 'Steady the bins on a rock,' suggested Mark. Still the bare hill top showed a blank face, fifty yards away. 'See that dark bit?

She's just left of there,' Mark prompted, pointing over my shoulder. Still nothing. A patient smile from Mark. 'In that light patch. Just looking towards us now.'

She was sitting hunched up in the lee of the rocks, a magnificent snowy owl, a bundle of grey fur rather than feathers, staring in our direction from black slit eyes. I was transfixed with admiration at the sight of her, especially at her size: three feet tall with wrestler's shoulders and a great round head which turned abruptly away to stare north over the bay at Gors Geo. 'Probably looking for a mate, poor thing,' Mark murmured in my ear. 'Not that one'll be along for her, of course.' The snowy owl continued to look out to sea, every now and then revolving her head to keep us under surveillance. As far as I could see, her body moved not a muscle in the ten minutes I lay gazing at her through the binoculars.

On every Fetlar pamphlet or booklet you pick up, snowy owls feature in drawings and photographs. Visitors come from all over Europe, twitchers and holidaymakers alike, to lie out on that bleak hillside and look their fill. Snowy owls are Fetlar's Big Attraction and their fans contribute significantly to the island's economy. The RSPB wardens, accustomed to taking parties up to see the owls several times a day in spring and summer, walk in a matter-of-fact way straight to the best viewing places. Snowy owl-watching on Fetlar takes only one hour out of a visitor's schedule, the maximum of efficiency with the minimum of fuss. These strange arrivals from the tundra blew in in 1967, a pair ranging far from their natural haunts in northern Scandinavia. A shortage of lemmings, their usual food, may have been the cause of their extended journey that year. Perhaps too many potential victims had rushed over too many cliffs. Fetlar's snowy owls were luckier than the Tengmalm's owl on Cramond Island. They survived the winter on a diet of rabbits, mice and whimbrels, and stayed on to breed.

But the miracle didn't repeat itself with the offspring. In 1975 the last brood of the elderly pair was hatched, and the numbers of snowy owls, like those of Fetlar's human inhabitants, began a steady decline. The specimen I was watching this day was one of a pair of spinsters. The previous year a clutch of eggs, probably infertile, had been laid. A week ago this owl had shifted her ground to the breeding area where she had been hatched – in futile hopes of mating, Mark guessed. But even if

Hollywood had been controlling events and a handsome young fellow was at this moment skimming his way into the last reel, it would have been no go. Thirteen years is the limit of fertility in snowy owls, and this bird was at least that. From now on she and her sister can look forward to a few more years on their lone sentry duty. Then Fetlar's snowy owls will be over the hill of history.

'It's ma first visit tae the islands,' shouted the young Glaswegian who gave me a lift into Unst from the ferry in his rattling old furniture van. He looked uneasily out of the window at Unst's long brown back. 'Ma last visit as well, Ah hope and pray. Tae much fresh air and open space.'

Unst is full of air and space, everything running north and south in long valleys and moorland hill spines. From the van I looked down into voes whose banks were patched at close intervals with the skeletons of crofting townships. Only a hundred years ago the landlords in Unst were still putting people out of the door. But the island was lucky in the number of livelihoods it could offer for people to turn their hands to. There were haaf fishing stations dotted round the coastline, and when the herring boom came to Unst at the turn of this century it brought prosperity with it. The drifters packed into the long harbour at Baltasound on the east coast, sheltered by the Isle of Balta which all but fills the mouth of the voe where 700 boats at a time lay jammed together, a solid causeway of decking across which a fisher girl could walk from one side of the harbour to the other. Unst's rock bones are rich in minerals for mining, too – iron chromite in past years for hardening steel, talc today for packing as a lubricant in rolls of roofing felt. After the peatlands of Yell and the green fertility of Fetlar, it was strange to see heaps of mining spoil, open roadstone quarries and grey mountains of piled talc.

People diversify in Unst. Sullom Voe brings work into the island; the RAF station at Saxa Vord employs a lot of Unst people. At Clingera, my night's lodging, Tony Mouat runs a croft, helps neighbours with their sheep, does a bit of fishing, works on the tugs that bully 400,000-ton oil tankers into and out of Sullom Voe. Tony also built his own house from his own plans, laid his own drains, watched the electrician wiring the top storey and did the rest himself from what he'd picked up. He showed me a photograph of his infant sons laying the first block of Clingera, struggling to get their twenty fingers all together on to the handle of the trowel.

'You're interested in the fiddle music, are you?' Irene Mouat asked when I mentioned Tom Anderson of Lerwick. 'There's an old man over yon who might play you a tune or two. Just a minute till I phone him up.'

Gibbie Gray was not at all put out to find me at his front door. Almost eighty years old, short and bespectacled, with a strongly curving nose and chin, Gibbie wasn't in any hurry to bring out the fiddle. Sitting on the couch, he balanced a chocolate biscuit a couple of inches above the slavering chops of his dog. 'Say nyem-nyem,' Gibbie commanded. The dog's straggling moustaches twitched, and little white teeth appeared. 'Nyem-nyem,' said the dog. 'Now the cat way,' ordered Gibbie. 'Nyem . . . nyemmmmmmmm,' miaowed the dog, rising to a tremulous whine, and the biscuit vanished under the moustache. Three more bribes went the same way before Gibbie began to edge his way into something more musical.

'All the old tunes had names, ye ken. I'm afraid I can't mind them now as I used to. When the Unst fishermen went to the haaf fishing in sixareen boats, the fiddles would go along with them. Some fiddles were made out of tin – these were rough trips. The fishermen would play and compose out at sea. The tunes were named after places they could see on the shore, landmarks that would tell them where they could find fish. If I can mind the names, a picture of the place comes into my head, and then the tune's there. But I just canna catch the names now.

'Every house had a fiddle in those days. People would come visiting in the evening, and out the fiddles would come. Well, let me see' – Gibbie got up to fetch his fiddle case from the corner of the room – 'I haven't had the fiddle in my hands for months. Rheumatism in my shoulder and fingers . . .' – he brought out the fiddle, its varnish cracked and blistered – 'We had a fire in the house, and I damn near lost this fiddle. I lost the best one I ever had when I was torpedoed off Aberdeen during the war.' Gibbie sat down and struck the bow across the strings. 'Now, let's see if I can mind any tunes for you. The memory's going, ye ken. I'm seventy-nine, after all. Now, then . . .'

As the tunes came to mind, Gibbie played them: Shetland reels, airs, jigs, waltzes, strathspeys. His fingers were stiff with lack of practice, but they soon loosened up. He retuned the bottom string to a drone, and played a Highland pipe tune. Mrs Gray put down a cup of tea on the table, along with a photograph of Gibbie walking beside the bride and groom at a Baltasound wedding, playing the same tune. After half an hour Gibbie's shoulder began to pain him and he'd had enough, though I hadn't. The visitors' book was brought out for me to sign, full of signatures from America, Australia, England, New Zealand – people who'd come to Unst to meet Gibbie and hear him play. 'One more,' Gibbie said as I got up to go. 'This was the one the fiddler would play at the end of an evening when the visitors went. "Come Again, You're Welcome", it's called.'

Early next morning thin grey rain came sheeting horizontally across Baltasound. 'Indoor jobs today,' said Tony Mouat. But by ten o'clock brilliant sunshine lay over Baltasound. I laced the boots and walked north over the rounded face of Hermaness to stand on the forehead of Britain. You can't stand any further north than Hermaness, unless you can negotiate a helicopter ride out to the little group of skerries slanting up out of the sea beyond the cliffs. Vesta Skerry, Rumblings, Tipta Skerry and Muckle Flugga – names that stick out like elbows, for bare blades of rock splashed with seabird droppings, the dark stains of storm waves reaching nearly to their peaks, canted all at the same not-quite-vertical angle one beyond another. They close off Britain like a little row of full stops. On top of Muckle Flugga the short white tower of the lighthouse sprouts straight out of the rock. Relieving those keepers in pre-helicopter days during winter storms was out of the question. They just had to stick it out until wind and sea had let up. One more rock humps out of the water north of Muckle Flugga, the very end of the very end – Out Stack. From here it's all wind and waves to the edge of the Arctic Circle.

Looking down from Hermaness I couldn't imagine how Jane Franklin in her billowing Victorian skirts had ever managed to scramble up on to the slippery sides of Out Stack from a pitching boat. The story fits the place, outlandish almost beyond belief. Poor Lady Franklin, praying on Out Stack and breaking her heart for a husband she must have known she would never see again. Sir John Franklin had disappeared in the summer of 1845 somewhere north of Hudson's Bay, commanding the last great expedition in search of a North-West Passage over the top of the New World. The prize that beckoned was an uninterrupted sea route for

271

trade with China and India that would avoid the great gales of the southern capes. Europe had been fixing its eyes on that prize for more than three centuries. Nothing was too good or too expensive for the fitting out of the Franklin expedition. On 19 May 1845, 134 men set sail from the Thames in their ships *Erebus* and *Terror*. Both ships were centrally heated by steam pipes, their bows reinforced with iron against the pack ice. Nearly 70 tons of flour went with them, 3000 gallons of liquor, 8000 tins of meat, soup and vegetables; candles, soap, wolfskin blankets, lemon juice against scurvy. What they didn't take in the way of technological equipment hadn't been invented. There was even a camera on board, to record the jowly face of Sir John Franklin and the stern seamen's frowns of his two captains. They were, to all appearances, fully set for three years in the wildest place in the world. But time ran out well before then.

Two whalers met them in Baffin Bay at the end of July, and then the ships, stores and men were swallowed up in mystery. Lady Franklin poured out her grief and her money, funding four separate rescue missions which came to nothing. The public couldn't get enough of romantic Lady Franklin, her broken heart and her pilgrimage to pray on Out Stack, the nearest she could get to her vanished husband. It took nine years for the pathetic bits and pieces of Franklin's expedition to begin to come to light – an Eskimo report of white men starving to death, a boat discovered with skeletons inside, a scribbled message left in a cairn telling of ships locked in pack ice for years on end, of Franklin's death and a last hopeless crawl away by the survivors. Other tales came in, too, as time went by: tales of cannibalism among the starving explorers. Victorian England didn't care for these at all, but they turned out to be true. Forensic science of the 1980s finally brought out the terrible facts when the bodies of members of the expedition were exhumed, perfectly preserved, from the makeshift graves dug for them by their comrades 140 years before. Some of the bones displayed clear evidence of gnawing by human teeth. But breaking through that ultimate taboo hadn't been enough to save the eaters.

Why did things go so wrong for the best-equipped expedition ever to set sail? Tired leadership from a 60-year-old commander, mistakes in judgement, bad planning and slow reaction to the increasing hardships may all have stemmed, in a fatal irony, from the very technology that made the whole venture so viable. Those 8000 tins of preserved food were each sealed with lead solder. Forensic examination of the bodies found enormously high lead levels. As the men ate their way into the stores, they were eating their own damnation through lead poisoning, dulling their faculties until they were too sick to save themselves.

It was too windy on Hermaness to stand and stare for long. Unst is the windiest place in Britain – a gust of 177 mph was recorded here – and most of it was coming straight at me. So were the great skuas. Hermaness has an enormous colony of bonxies, and they were keen to show me what they could do. One in particular kept appearing over the shoulder of the hill, a meaningful dark blob slung low between quickly flapping wings. He soon found out he was dealing with an idiot. I kept a lookout on the port bow, and got torpedoed from the starboard quarter. While I was scanning the moorland to starboard, he was doing Stuka impressions from above. His webbed feet fascinated me. I had plenty of chances to observe them as they swept past the end of my nose. He stank, too; a musty, musky, fishy aroma. I got out of his target area as quickly as I could. I had a plane to catch at the Baltasound airstrip, out of Shetland on the last leg of my island journey.

15. Orkney

THE END OF THE DANCE

Jimmy Wiseman, the taxi-driver, was apologetic about the £15 fare from Lerwick to Sumburgh airfield. When we got to Sumburgh he pulled out a plastic bag from the boot of his car: 'A couple o' things for your journey.' In the bag were a Mars bar, a can of lager and two paperbacks – Jimmy's own form of discount.

'We may overshoot the runway at Kirkwall due to low cloud there,' announced the British Airways captain laconically as we were taxiing out across the tarmac. 'We took half an hour or so on the last run-in, going up and down looking for a break in the cloud. If we do happen to overshoot, it'll feel like a rather sudden take-off, steeply up without touching the ground.' He paused, as if considering the effect of this statement. 'But *don't worry*. Just sit back and *relax.*'

As a guarantor of a white-knuckle journey, this took some beating. The landing at Kirkwall turned out to be as smooth as silk, however, and the man in the next seat offered me a lift across Orkney Mainland – the somewhat strange name of the biggest island in the Orkney archipelago – to the little harbour town of Stromness. After the peaty hills and moors of Shetland, Orkney looked green and tranquil, well-ordered farming countryside where every acre is made to work for its living. Orkney lies on sandstone, which gives warmth and colour to the landscape and yields readily split plates of stone for building and walling. Here the farmhouses are solid, strong stone boxes, standing in the middle of lush green meadows where fat cows graze. The land sweeps away from long aprons of greenery by wide bays, up to hills cultivated nearly to their tops. Prosperity shines from farmsteads and fields, in contrast to Shetland's air of crofting struggle. People own their own farms, and run them confidently.

All around the farmsteads, in the middle of cornfields and on the ends of headlands stand the monuments of Orkney's pre-Christian settlers in the shape of burial mounds, single standing stones and stone circles. You can't escape the distant past in Orkney. Down in England, even in such prehistorically well-favoured counties as Dorset or Wiltshire, it often requires a leap of faith to square the tumulus or standing stone posited on the map with what's visible on the ground: a just-visible hump of earth, a slight swell in a field edge, a knob of eroded stone too low even to trip you up. In Orkney these things stand ten or fifteen feet tall in a virtually treeless landscape, breaking the skyline and claiming attention. Every turn in the road delivers a new excitement.

Stromness, where my neighbour dropped me off with a handshake and broad grin, lay spectacularly round its harbour of Hamna Voe, more than a mile of waterfront full of ferries and fishing boats behind which the houses rose up narrow, cobbled alleyways to the top of the town under Brinkie's Brae. The main street was even narrower and twistier than Lerwick's Commercial Street, the old-fashioned shop doorways more crammed with shrinking pedestrians as cars and lorries claimed the entire width of the paved roadway. From every hotel bar and lounge came the by now familiar racing tunes of fiddles and accordions as the town limbered up for the long wet weekend of the Orkney Folk Festival. I drew a deep breath, and plunged in over my head.

I'd planned to travel far and wide among the Orkney islands, hopping from one to the next by Loganair stepping-stones, garnering pieces as I went to make a comprehensive jigsaw picture. The folk festival would be just a pleasant episode in this, my last great chapter of exploration. Good intentions, but they didn't survive that first hour in jolly, jumping Stromness. Hello! Come for the festival, eh? Have you met Willie, Donald, Fay, Bridget, Phil? Going to the concert in the Town Hall tonight? So are we! Come back afterwards and we'll have a tune. And what are you drinking, by the way? Questions like these are the sort I like. The four or five days opened up and swallowed me, the most unresisting of victims.

Images of that long weekend blurred and ran together, a patchwork of singing, dancing, laughing, walking, talking, bicycling, exploring early and drinking late. Certain highlights pop out of the general mist as I look back. One is of Aly Bain sitting foursquare in his chair on the little stage of Stromness Town Hall, fiddle tucked more under his ear than his chin, face red and streaming under the spotlights, tearing with absolute mastery into a set of reels. His playing bounced off the throwaway brilliance of Phil Cunningham's accordion, both players driven further and further by the piano underpinning of Violet Tulloch from Lerwick, her whole frame twisting in response to the music as she played. Every

275

face in the audience was rapt, every foot tapping time. Another snapshot in the mind is of the wide, wide, delighted grin of the guitar player with Groupo Bolivia (Orkney's nod to internationalism) as he entered the club room of the Royal Hotel to find a beautiful, black-haired Irish dancer kicking up her short skirts six inches from the end of his nose. Groupo Bolivia were the great hit of the festival, roared back for multiple encores wherever they appeared. The Orcadians' generosity even extended to the bloody English. It was not only possible, but after a time seemed almost obligatory, to leave all one's possessions wherever one might happen to be, wander off to do some shopping or chat to the fishermen, and expect to return hours later and find everything untouched – camera, cheque book and money included. As in Shetland, no one locked house doors, put away lawn mowers or bikes, or demanded a booking deposit. The Orcadians' pleasure in the music filling their islands seemed boundless. The one act of churlishness I witnessed during the whole festival – a chubby Glaswegian with a braying voice and drink-sodden, purple cheeks, viciously swearing at the barman who had refused him his tenth or eleventh pint – stuck out like a sore thumb.

The only Orcadian to fall from grace in my eyes came hurtling out of a farm gateway as I trundled past on a hired bicycle, and tried to remove my left leg from the knee downward. It was the second day of my stay, a peerless morning of enamel blue sky and fresh, cold air; just the day to hire a bike from the Baby Linen Shop in Stromness and go off for a long pedal around some of Orkney's prehistoric monuments. I was still trying to get on the right side of the bicycle's ancient and rusty Sturmey-Archer three-speed device as I passed the entrance to the farm. The black and white sheepdog was level with my leg in a couple of leaps, and stayed right there as I tried to accelerate away. The treacherous gears slipped and spun backwards as my snarling outrider did his best to self-destruct beneath my front wheel. His teeth clicked as he snapped at my ankle. My efforts to make it a contact sport by kicking the dog into the roadside ditch all but put me under an oncoming lorry. At last the gears caught, and I legged it away in a standing position for maximum momentum, leaving the sheepdog apparently defeated in a panting bundle on the grass verge. A good mile further on – I measured it later on the map – I stopped and dismounted to inspect the slipping gears and to get my breath back. Before my heart had had time to stop pounding there was a clatter of claws on tarmac, and round the bend of the road came racing that single-minded dog, shoulders hunched high above his head. One look at those black lips writhed back from red gums and a hedge of white teeth, and I was in the saddle again and praying to the God of Gears not to let me down. As I gasped along with my pursuer right at my heels, the front wheel of the bike began to wobble. No time to worry about that. A long downward slope gave me a moment's advantage, but through the sweat stinging my eyes I could see the corresponding upward climb getting closer. We must have been at least two miles from the farm gate by this time, and my enemy showed no slackening of lust for my leg. Abject fear gripped me, turning my pedalling muscles to jelly. At the bottom of the hill I jammed on the brakes and squealed to a stop, prepared to risk everything in one almighty kick at the brute. This was obviously the 'Game's over!' signal the sheepdog had been waiting for. He, too, skidded to a halt, sheathed his fangs, turned round and trotted unconcernedly away back down the road. Just before disappearing round the bend, he paused and lifted his leg to spell out his contempt in a nonchalant squirt of urine.

I biked on, past a farm longhouse where hens stood in rows on the ridge of the grassy roof. A very old lady in blue trousers and knitted hat came hobbling out to scatter scraps for the hens, calling them down with a piping little tune out of the side of her mouth. The house stood alone on the shore of a loch that emptied into the wide and beautiful Bay of Skaill, all silver sand and low, rocky headlands. Up among the dunes I came across the Incredible Fling Band, accompanied by what their fiddle player referred to as 'the wives and sweethearts', taking time out from the folk festival to visit the buried neolithic village of Skara Brae.

This tight little group of stone-built huts looks as if it was built underground. The minute houses are interconnected by short walled passageways. You walk around the grassy dunes at roof level, looking down into rectangular rooms where stone beds, stone tables, stone chairs, stone doors and walls stand just as solidly as they did when sandstorms wiped the place out and covered it over about four-and-a-half thousand years ago. During excavations, two female skeletons were discovered lying huddled together in one of the stone beds, and beads were scattered in a passageway as if the wearer had caught the string on some wall projection in headlong flight. These details suggest that the last sandstorm to hit Skara Brae may have made a miniature Pompeii of the village. Certainly the inhabitants were resourceful, making remarkably delicate furniture out of the sandstone slabs available to them, and employing the heat given off by the settlement's refuse heaps in a form of cavity wall heating. Many a mountaineers' bothy and hikers' lodge offers less comfort than the little rooms of Skara Brae – though all that stone must have been damnably cold in winter. The current notion is that many of the households may have been occupied by teenagers setting up together and being edged by the community into the early responsibility demanded of dwellers in that harsh prehistoric world.

That tradition still continues on Orkney's farms, where from an early age youngsters are expected to lend a hand. As we stood listening to the curator of Skara Brae, a cow in the next field began to moan. What looked like a half-unfolded artist's easel was slowly emerging from her nether regions. A burly boy in a T-shirt came down the field to her, wound a rope around the protruding legs of the calf and began to haul. Soon another boy joined him; then a woman came out to help. They strained and gasped, the cow bellowed and the curator's audience either drifted away to goggle over the fence, or fixed its eyes desperately on his face, according to strength of stomach. The grey bag containing the inert calf came out suddenly with a loud *schlooop!* and spray of fluids, landing on the grass with a thump that I thought would break every bone in that baby's body. Mother knew better, licking and nuzzling at the motionless lump until a bleary eye opened and an ear began to twitch. As I left Skara Brae the calf was on its knees, beginning to investigate the drinks supply.

Five miles further on, and starting to ache around my own nether regions, I ate lunch – Jimmy Wiseman's Mars bar and can of lager – under the great standing stones of the Ring of Brodgar. About half of the original sixty stones still stood in their enormous circle, more than a hundred yards across. Some were angled sharply at the top like giant Stanley knife blades; all were wafer-thin and straight-sided. The largest stone was man-shaped, brooding over the rest. There's no telling their precise age, or even guessing at the original purpose or function of the Ring of Brodgar: nor of the four Stones of Stenness standing a mile down the road. Brodgar could date from around 2000 BC, Stenness probably from several hundred years earlier. Cultural differences between the two sets of builders can only be hazily surmised. Theories of worship, of megalithic calendars, of lunar or solar observatories have been put forward. All that can be said for certain is that it was no idle whim that drove primitive men, already fully stretched in subsistence living, to undertake these vast labours. On the contrary; their reasons must have been overwhelming, central to their very lives.

Burial seems to have occupied an equally important place in such men's minds. Less than a mile from the Stones of Stenness, the twenty-foot mound of Maes Howe lies like a green, grassy upturned bowl in the fields. Maes Howe may have been built around 3000 BC, perhaps a little before the Stenness Stones were erected. Five thousand years of weathering have had almost no effect on its symmetry. It has an unyielding core under the grass and earth, a great stone burial chamber filling the centre of the mound, with massive corner stones rising from floor to roof. The chamber walls are of stone slabs, superbly measured, cut and fitted, some of them several feet long and weighing as much as three tons apiece.

Rousing the guide from his conversation with a friend took some time; waiting for him at the entrance to Maes Howe took much longer. At last he came bicycling along the field path, and unlocked the iron gate. Bending double, I squirmed along thirty feet of narrow stone passageway into the main chamber. The guide delivered his recitation in a toneless chant, breaking into a rich Orcadian sing-song whenever I interrupted him with a question. Standing in the dimly-lit great chamber, consciousness grew with every passing minute of the crushing weight, the coolness and power of that enveloping mass of stone. Openings in three of the four walls led into burial recesses. Once again, the monument raises questions but answers none. The Vikings who broke in through the top of the mound were returning Crusaders, according to the guide. Before learning this, I'd always pictured Vikings and Christians as being at opposite ends of the spiritual spectrum. Were these Vikings returning from *raiding* Crusaders, perhaps? The guide gave me a look, half plea and half threat. If this had been Canvey instead of Orkney, that look would have translated as: Clever little sod, aincha? I don't bleedin' know, do I? So don't ask stupid questions, all right?

Someone had certainly cut a Christian cross deeply into one of the stones. Hakon found treasure in Maes Howe, so the runes scratched in

279

the walls say, and carried it out by himself. Another set of runes tells of a treasure that lay in the mound in times past, and other inscriptions describe how yet more treasure still lies buried nearby. 'Happy is he who might find the great treasure.' Blither spirits than these treasure-seekers were in that Viking party, or in another that came along later to find the tomb empty. 'These runes were made by the Number One Rune Maker,' boasts one graffitist. 'Ingibiorh is the most beautiful,' scratched a lovesick swain. There actually was an Ingibiorh living locally at the time, wife of a warlord, so perhaps this was only a bit of unsubtle buttering-up.

All these runes, branching delicately like crinoids on the stone walls, called Tolkien irresistibly to mind, although Maes Howe was far too heavy and solemn a place for hobbitry. I came out blinking into the clear afternoon sunlight and forced my aching bottom on to the bike saddle for the six miles back to Stromness, surfeited with ancient stones and shadows.

That evening I caught a bus crowded with fiddlers to the southern end of Orkney Mainland. The village of Holm (pronounced 'Hame') was hosting a ceilidh of wonderful proportions – nearly 300 people squashed into the community centre, regardless of fire regulations, to enjoy a concert that lasted the best part of three hours; and then, fuelled by reeling music and strong home brew, to dance the night away. Before the ceilidh I wandered down to the brink of Scapa Flow to have a look at some of the leavings that war has scattered across the islands. Sited where they are, at the northern extremity of Britain and blocking a vital passage between two seas, both Shetland and Orkney have been fair game for radio masts, concrete War Office blockhouses, gun emplacements and other war detritus, some of it removed after the fighting was over, some left behind to crumble in its own slow time. Everyone in Orkney knew the story of the penning-up of the German High Seas Fleet in Scapa Flow at the end of the First World War, its scuttling and the subsequent long-drawn-out salvage for scrap. Three great battleships and four light cruisers are still down there on the bed of Scapa Flow. Their scrap metal becomes more valuable, the older it grows, thanks to its lack of radioactivity. Since 1945 it has become ever more difficult to find non-irradiated metal for such delicate items as surgical instruments. The ships on the bottom of Scapa Flow, sealed in pre-Bomb purity by the protecting waters, represent a fortune lying idle. What I'd come to see hough, is very much in use: a practical memorial to men of uncrushable pirit.

Scapa Flow, fifty square miles of deep water, is surrounded by islands - Orkney Mainland on the north, Hoy on the west, Flotta on the south. To the east are the islets of Lamb Holm and Glims Holm, leading south o Burray and South Ronaldsay. The gaps between these eastern islands ire very narrow, a few hundred yards at most; and, choked as they were with the wreckage of ships, no one at the beginning of the Second World War doubted that Scapa Flow would serve as a safe deep-water anchorage or the British fleet, impossible to penetrate from the east. Eight hundred sailors in the *Royal Oak* paid for that misjudgement with their lives on 14 October 1939, when Kapitänleutnant Prien slipped his U-boat in on a freak high tide and torpedoed the battleship.

This catastrophe led to the building of four barriers, the Churchill Causeways, that linked up the eastern islands of Scapa Flow and sealed t off completely. A foundation of rock had to be laid first, in water up to ten fathoms deep; then enormous numbers of concrete blocks were swung into place – 66,000 of them in all – until the causeways rose clear of the water and a continuous roadway, leapfrogging the intersecting channels, could be built from Mainland across all four islands. According to local people, the Churchill Causeways have done the islands nothing but good. The water west of them is calm enough for salmon hatcheries to have been established there. The causeway road has enabled people to continue to live on Burray and South Ronaldsay 'nae bother', only a couple of minutes' drive from Orkney Mainland. And Scapa Flow itself s well protected from easterly storms.

Low sun was lighting the jumbled concrete blocks as I strolled over Churchill Causeway No. 1 on to Lamb Holm islet. To get such a striking, cubist effect of opposed angles and patches of light and shadow from the work of a peacetime architect, you'd pay millions. In wartime, however, a group of Italian prisoners-of-war at Camp 60 on Lamb Holm did the job for free, or helped to do it with as good a grace as they could muster. The validity of making a roadway as an exercise in civil engineering was sufficient justification for getting the POWs involved with assisting the war effort of their enemy.

Devout Catholics, the Italians then set about creating their own chapel out of the barest of bones, a couple of standard wartime Nissen huts.

281

Creating is what literally happened. Every single piece of work in that little chapel on Lamb Holm was handcrafted by the prisoners. The elaborate, crow-stepped concrete façade leads into an interior of such vision and skill of execution that some visitors find themselves weeping as soon as they set eyes on it. Even on this lovely sunny evening the chapel hummed with the frustrations and dreams of the men of Camp 60, poured out on the elaboration of that tunnel-like interior; a little slice of Italy laid with immense effort over the bare surrounding table of grass and water. The Spam-tin light fittings, painted plaster-board tiling, driftwood tabernacle and wrought scrap-iron rood screen speak more about the resilience of the human spirit expressed through craftsmanship than any masterpiece sponsored by a Renaissance princeling. The chief architect and artist of these humble glories, Domenico Chiocchetti, stayed on to finish his work even after his fellow-prisoners had all gone home in 1945. In 1960 he came back to Lamb Holm to revisit the chapel and repair some of his original handiwork. 'It must be judged a work of ingenuity rather than of art,' opined my guidebook. A work of pain and yearning, rather, transcended by a faith as much practical as spiritual.

I lingered in the chapel and on the grass outside, looking over Scapa Flow and picturing those 550 homesick Italians hauling at the blocks of the Churchill Causeways, until a faint thumping came across the water from the direction of Holm's community centre. It was time to get over to where things were livening up. The Bobby Harvey Trio were booked to provide music for dancing. Bobby, well past his youth, was a dapper little figure in a smart tartan dinner jacket, a great purveyor of smoothly professional wisecracks. '. . . Mr George MacDonald on pee – yano! Thank you! And that reminds me of why a woman is like a pee – yano. When she's no' upright, she's grrrand.' Bobby swung his snake hips as he sawed at his fiddle, delighting the ladies of Holm. I fully intended to dance with the best of them, but somehow the evening got hijacked by home brew and rambling conversation. It didn't matter. The wives and sweethearts of the Incredible Fling Band didn't allow my feet to touch the ground, once they had me properly cornered on the island of Shapinsay.

I'd signed on for the Shapinsay ceilidh as a fitting farewell to my journey round the islands of Britain. The following day would be for the plane out of Kirkwall, the train ride through the Borders back to England

and everyday life. This night was ticketed and set aside for celebration, a night to remember. It turned out to be just that, though the chances had looked slim at Kirkwall harbour earlier in the afternoon. The kind lady in the tourist office at Stromness had given me a ferry timetable on which all my Shapinsay plans were based. 'Kirkwall – 3.00' it said, quite clearly. At three o'clock nothing was in sight anywhere around the sea horizon or tied up at the quayside that looked even remotely like a ferry. I studied the timetable in my hand more closely. It was the brand new summer timetable, with a line of small print at the foot announcing the date it would come into force. Tomorrow's date.

No one on the Kirkwall waterfront could tell me if there was an evening ferry to Shapinsay. The island lay low a mile or two across the sound. It looked as if I would have to give the whole thing up. Then Iain sauntered up; a tall, slim young man with a manner so relaxed I felt ashamed of my anxious, fragile over-planning. No ferry, ah? Well – jump down here into my little sailing boat and I'll take you across. No, no – nae bother. I'm just killing time, anyway. The wife's expecting a bairn this afternoon. The third, yes. I mustn't go far away. There's a couple of Shapinsay lads here want a lift as well. Plenty of room. Just grab hold of that tiller, will you, while I get the jib up. Steer for that white house, low down there on the shore. Okay?

A skeleton from my personal cupboard leaped out and grinned, derisively: an inner vision of myself as a lumpen, seventeen-year-old member of the school sailing club, hopelessly at sea in the middle of Poole Harbour, hauling red-faced at the wrong ropes as the sail of the tiny Enterprise flapped admonishingly and a shrimp three years my junior (but a Cox'n to my Ordinary Seaman) yelled a string of incomprehensible orders from the sternsheets. Iain's little boat heeled over and dashed along, unresentful of a stranger's hand on the tiller. We bumped into the String, a skein of tangled tide-rips, and my young companions in the cockpit began to look green. Iain stared forward from the scrap of decking, apparently content with my steering. Shapinsay grew steadily larger ahead. I began to see that there might be something to be said for small boat sailing, after all. By the time we had swooped into the island jetty and tied up, I could have given Sir John Franklin a pointer or two.

The pub where we went to wet the as yet unborn baby's head was in the gatehouse of Balfour Castle. Balfour is a name that calls up a curious mixture of responses on Shapinsay – amusement, head-shaking dismissal: from older folk a guarded deference. Balfours began buying land in Orkney back in the 16th century, and eventually got their hands on Shapinsay. John Balfour made a fortune in 18th-century India; and his great-nephew David, inheriting most of it, set up in tremendous, princely style in the castle he built in the 1840s. Balfour Castle overlooks Shapinsay's harbour, everyone's dream image of a dominating baronial pile encrusted with bulges, points, pinnacles and battlements. It looks like one of those conglomerate fungi to be left well alone if spotted in the woods. While Victoria ruled Great Britain, David Balfour reigned in Shapinsay, single-mindedly set on fulfilling a role as well-loved, unquestioned father to his people.

Those who dared to question got a very dusty answer, like the New Kirk elders in 1847 who had the audacity to reprimand members of their flock who had been kicking up their heels at Mr Balfour's newly-instituted Harvest Home supper. This was Balfour's first year at the helm, and he was determined to show who was boss in Shapinsay. The elders soon found themselves evicted from their crofts: but they didn't go alone. The laird was fired by zeal for agricultural improvement, and put out sixty of his tenants in the course of his radical reforms. These involved squaring off the surface of the entire island into exactly similar ten-acre fields, to achieve uniformity of supply and production among all the tenant farmers. As I wandered around Shapinsay that afternoon, progression was in a series of straight lines and right-angle bends. On the horizontal plane, there's hardly a curve to be found in the island. David Balfour's experiment has to be judged a resounding success; nearly 150 years on, Shapinsay is still, for its size, the most productive island in all the Orkneys. Even though most of the evicted families (but not the elders) were reinstated when the squaring was complete, at the time of the changes the tenants were deeply suspicious and resentful. Island people told me that, when Balfour Castle's home farm of Balfour Mains was being laid out, tenants were required to bring the best soil from their own fields and spread it on the newly created farmlands by the castle.

Such wounds to pride, even if probably mythological, survive tenaciously in so many parts of clearance-affected Scotland. Apart from his eviction of the Shapinsay elders, however, there's no evidence that David Balfour was anything more extreme than what he set out to be, a

284

benevolent and forward-thinking despot. At least he didn't put Cheviot sheep before his people. He died in 1887, after which the Balfour line continued in a gentle downward curve for another seventy-odd years, spending its money and strength until it petered out in 1961. It left its mark on Shapinsay in the form of a salt-water douche tower, an eccentric gas works, a neat model village and that bristling castle; but most of all in the military neatness of the well-drilled farmsteads and the chessboard regularity of their fields.

The villagers of Holm had tasted the talents of their visiting folk festival concert party with delight: Shapinsay gobbled them up, and raved for more. Shapinsay stamped and whistled more loudly, sighed more sentimentally and laughed more unrestrainedly than any other island community that roaring weekend. When the tiny mites of Shapinsay school stood forward and scraped out their rigid, expert little fiddle tunes, real tears flowed. Packing away the trestle tables for dancing took a long time due to the press of bodies in the community centre's hall, but once the floor was clear there was no holding the dancers. Literally no holding. During 'Strip the Willow' contact was missed more often than made, as kilted youths alight with beer and excitement went hurtling out of the lines to crash into the onlookers. Young boys went round between the dances, sprinkling chalk on a floor slippery with spilt drink and trodden trifle, little Herculeses in the Augean Stable. It was all the fault of the Incredible Fling Band, strung out on the stage belting out the dances at a hundred miles an hour. With music like that, even David Balfour's disapproving elders might have got up to cut a rug or two.

I got into conversation with Michael, a freelance copywriter who'd moved to a rented estate house on Shapinsay from Derbyshire with his wife and three small children the previous autumn. 'We moved up here to get away from the rat-race, suburbia, the whole nuclear thing, dirty air. Now we don't have a TV, or a telephone – not even a car. That's down in Derbyshire, along with our house. Who needs them? I can take my children for a walk here, and see no one and everything. But I must admit, as one Englishman to another, that we've met a certain amount of resistance from the locals. A bit suspicious, if you know what I mean. Rather watchful.'

A hand tugged me briskly to my feet. It was Fay, no-nonsense figurehead of the wives and sweethearts. 'Come on, you.' I trotted obediently after her, to be swept into some unnamed whirlpool of beating music and blurring movement. 'Ach, he's no bluidy good,' was Fay's verdict on me to her next partner as I stumbled away, defeated. But other wives and sweethearts were waiting on the sidelines to catch, turn and re-educate me. An hour later, sweating like a cottage cheese, with a deep ache in my lungs and a step pattern shakily on hold in my cerebral computer, I carted Fay off for a Boston Two-Step that earned a stern nod of approbation. 'I see you've learned something, at any rate,' Fay said judiciously as she wheeled smartly into yet another swain's arms. I felt as if I'd just graduated, with honours.

Few of Shapinsay's 300 residents had dared to stay away this night. The youngest dancer I saw was a tot hardly out of nappies, kilted and bow-tied; the oldest couple must have been well over eighty. They danced neatly, heel and toe, with sublime expressions, miraculously escaping collision with the charging young bulls around them. It was these youngsters that caught and held my attention, while I was bumping up against their hard elbows in the dances, and afterwards as I sat out, dripping, and watched them plunging up and down the hall. The girls had come giggling in at the start of the evening, in their tightest short skirts and highest heels, dressed as if for an evening's disco pouting in the city. But here they were at midnight, shoes kicked off and hair tangled, passing partners in the Dashing White Sergeant and Eightsome Reel with young children, grandparents and middle-aged folk as well as boys and girls of their own age. You'd need a hydraulic press to get fourteen-year-old boys and girls to dance like that with each other anywhere in mainland Britain.

'Yes, they're good boys and girls,' said Ivan Houston, the Shapinsay boatbuilder, when he saw me sitting out and watching. 'That's our seed-corn dancing there, of course. They give this island some hope for the future.'

That phrase was in my mind when my head finally hit the pillow at Balfour Mains farmhouse with dawn well under way. And later that day, flying out of Kirkwall airport with Shapinsay's geometrical green face not far below, I thought again of those seed-corn boys and girls, unburdened by anything so solemn as the future and its responsibilities, deliriously dancing my island adventure to a close.

286

Looking Back

Travelling through the other British isles took me the best part of eighteen months, on and off. I visited them as and when tides, times and opportunities allowed; not exactly in the neat clockwise succession in which this account is arranged, though I tried to keep to that basic framework as far as possible. While it was all happening I never really found time to sit back and sort through this tremendous, diverse experience. It was always rush and bustle, chat and move on, catch the plane or boat to the next destination. Each island obscured a clear view of the previous one. As soon as the journey was over, though, the picture began to balance up.

Islands exert a pull on the emotions of practically everyone. The 'Mingulay Boat Song' isn't such a well-loved song just because of its words or tune – it's because it is about an island. Islands are romantic, in most people's minds: dreamlike places on the edge of reality, neither quite of land nor water. Stepping on to an island, you step out of the everyday world, no matter how narrow the gap between mainland and island. Islands are seen to offer solitude, relaxation and a safe retreat, a womb of security. People talk – visitors very keenly, islanders more circumspectly – of their sense of privilege at being there. Visitors and islanders both feel this precious and fragile joy in their island, like a shared secret, no matter whether it be a flat, cold, grey slab of mud and marsh on an East Coast estuary, a granite block miles out in the Bristol Channel or a basalt extravaganza of ledges and caves in the Hebrides. Islands come in an infinite variety of shapes and atmospheres, some – like Canvey – unattractive, even repellent, to those not besotted with them. But I failed to find or hear of even one without any admirer at all.

Of course, there were many islands that for one reason or another I never got to. The sharpest disappointment among these was St Kilda. I'd be a rich man if I had a penny for every person I met who urged me on no account to miss St Kilda, the remote outpost 40 miles further into the Atlantic than the Outer Hebrides, the lonely island of towering cliffs 1000 feet high, of gannets and fulmars. I heard so much about the unique poignancy of the atmosphere there, where the islanders had clung on to their traditional ways and suffered incredible hardships until they gave in at last and asked to be evacuated in 1930. But I suspected from the outset that I would never get out to St Kilda. One needs a week at least to do that, allied to fine weather for landing and departing. Even then one can be stranded for days by a sudden storm. I couldn't risk it – not with all the populated islands, the conversations and explorations nearer at hand. There was a moment on the island of Benbecula when it looked as if I might be able to talk my way aboard an army helicopter going out to the St Kilda tracking station. But that window closed as soon as it opened, and the 'ultimate island', as someone put it, stayed out of reach.

The islands round the British coastline have been many things to many generations – farms, rabbit stores, battle spoils, gambling counters, drying-out havens for alcoholics, chemical weapons testing grounds. Of all the varieties of use and abuse they have been subjected to, it is their function as military bases that has left the ugliest and longest-lasting scars. Some, like Inchgarvie in the Firth of Forth, were turned into complete arsenals, concrete-covered from end to end in the two world wars. Others were studded with searchlights, guns, barracks. No one has cleared all these leavings away. Far too many of the small islands groan under this blight of concrete, historically important though the buildings may be. Where the MOD is still active on the islands, the feelings of the inhabitants vary. Foulness people like the exclusion of the outside world imposed by the army; Benbecula people like the money and the jobs, but don't much care for the soldiers; Vatersay people look with dread to the possibility of anything of a military nature coming over their new bridge.

History is writ plain on island landscapes; far plainer than on the mainland, as fewer people come to trample, build over and obliterate Iron Age fields, standing stones, ruined medieval chapels, incised Celtic crosses. Some island history has been terrible in the extreme, clan atrocities in the Hebrides that wiped out hundreds at a time – in Eigg's case an entire island population. The Scottish islands were hit as hard as any mainland area at the time of the clearances, when the houses were being pulled down around their occupants' ears to make way for the more profitable sheep. History in the islands is more mingled with the present than elsewhere. Real anger and bitterness are still expressed towards the Nicolson family in Fetlar, and towards Colonel Gordon of Cluny and his

290

wife Lady Gordon Cathcart in the Outer Hebrides, even though these harsh landlords have been dead for many decades. Islands with artificial communities composed entirely of incomers doing a job, such as Lundy and Rhum, have no shared history to bind their populations together, no old folk to keep old flames of allegiance and hatred alive. In conse-quence, they lack the vitality that hums through the populated islands.

While the larger islands all have their own community life, continuing from a bedrock of history through the present into the future, many of the smaller ones are given over to conservation and have been turned into nature reserves. Thinking back over the amazing breadth of wildlife I either saw myself or heard of, I give three enthusiastic cheers for this. The first landfall that migrating birds make is more often than not an island – Fair Isle, the Hilbres, Fetlar, Ramsey, Barra. Birds, plants, insects and animals like the islands for their quietness, their safety and the thinness of human influence on them. Humans can occasionally make helpful decisions, too. Horsey and Osea are not to be ploughed, in spite of the profits that might accrue to their owners. Alpine plants of the Ice Age will continue to grow undisturbed on the mountains of Rhum. The rare plants and moths of Skipper's Island, the roseate terns of Coquet, the gannets of the Bass Rock, the wild peonies of Steep Holm; the Manx shearwaters of Skomer and Skokholm; snowy owls of Fetlar, red deer of Jura, bonxies of Shetland – all refugees, all in safe haven.

But a journey through the other British isles is really a journey through the lives of people, first and last. At the start of my wanderings I couldn't imagine what characteristics might possibly be common to the Essex mud islanders and the crofters of Harris, the fishermen of Lerwick and the monks of Caldey. I had still to learn, too, the great and often glaring differences between the born-and-bred native islander and the incoming island settler. Gradually, though, the figure of 'the islander' became a little clearer – though I can hear all my island friends saying, as they read this: 'That's nothing like me!'

Born-and-bred islanders are hard workers. Fey self-sufficiency and airy-headed romanticism don't last long in the face of winter gales and unpaid bills. Islanders have to diversify to keep going, often taking on several jobs at once. The bus driver runs a croft and sees to the water supply; the shopkeeper is also the island musician and the roadmender; the crofter is a fisherman is a taxi-driver. This hard work can be deceptively masked by the island attitude to time: do the job until it's done, then relax until the time is right to start the next one. The pressures of nine to five, of deadlines and self-erected hurdles of unnecessary toil, melt away out in the islands. Island life is by and large classless, too, especially in Scotland. There are no McJoneses to be kept up with. Many an island croft looks scruffy to the uninitiated beholder, window-deep in fish boxes, rolls of wire, plastic bags and piles of peats. Islanders have little truck with neatness for its own sake. They are practical people, making use as their forebears did of whatever wind or wave brings their way. Rubbish disposal is an enormous problem, in these days of plastic. The all-pervasive heaps of old, discarded or exhausted materials can be either monuments to energy and inventiveness, as with Harry Hawkes of Skipper's, or the fruits of lethargy and despondency, as on certain islands of the Inner Hebrides.

Maybe it's this ever-open eye for discarded items turnable to account that gives islanders their reputation as eccentrics. Eccentricity can be a positive blessing – on the East Coast islands below sea level, for example, where the inhabitants agree, apparently quite calmly, that one day soon a catastrophic sea surge will probably wipe their islands and themselves out of existence. This fatalism, a strongly-marked characteristic of islanders, makes it hard to plan for the future, especially when so many islanders feel betrayed and ignored by the government. Scottish islanders feel passionately that a Westminster government of well-off southern Englishmen and women can never begin to appreciate or be effective in solving the problems of Gaelic-speaking, storm-lashed, thinly soiled, remote and utterly un-English places like the islands. The Highlands and Islands Development Board, Comhairle nan Eilean and the local co-operatives are much closer to what the islanders want, in spite of the notorious cases of misspending of grants and loans. There's the feeling, too, that island communities are too small to be able to make the necessary waves in order to get improvements carried out; though the story of the Rhenigidale road shows what a handful of determined people can do if they won't take no for an answer.

When islanders feel threatened, they unite with a snap against the enemy. They don't at all care for woolly-hatted or woolly-minded conservationists, for outsider experts coming in to tell them what to do, even though they may be utterly in the wrong and the experts incontrovertibly in the right. A wholesome bloody-mindedness sustains them. Neither do they relish the prospect of their islands changing hands, or changing style or direction. Developers looking for potential holiday playgrounds arouse the fighting hackles of islanders. All this, of course, goes dead against the wonderfully active and evident tradition of hospitality that I never failed to find in any of the islands. It ranged from cups of tea at croft doors to drams of whisky on wet nights; from meals and beds to evenings of chatter and music round peat fires. I found warm hospitality in the churches, from the Catholics of South Uist to the Presbyterians of Staffin in Skye and the Shetland Baptists: an important aspect of island life. Islands fill spiritual voids with their space and distance from the everyday world. It's what drew those early saints to set up base on so many of the other British isles. Islanders need this inner strength when trouble arrives in their small communities. Tiny Muck had suffered three deaths in a few months, hammer-blows on the heart of the island.

Old people in the islands looked back to their young days as a time when life was harder, but better. There was no electricity, no social services, no tap water, none of the material benefits of modern life. But, they said, there was more laughter, more community spirit, camaraderie and mutual help; more time to chat, to sing and play. Individualism was the problem today. People wanted to fulfil themselves nowadays, and hard luck to the old ones or those in need in the community.

What native islanders think of incomers varies remarkably little from island to island. Everywhere there is an undercurrent of caution, of wary amusement as they wait for the rookie to take a pratfall. Often they seem to distrust the incomers because it is they – brash, loud and over-enthusiastic – who spot cracks in the social fabric that have been comfortably papered over for generations. They leap brightly in to 'get something done about' making an airfield, establishing a theatre group, running a roster for visiting old folk. Often the incomers hold up a mirror to the natives in which they see, to their outward indifference but secret shame, lethargy and laissez-faire, two endemic island diseases. The White Settlers, the well-heeled Green Wellies of Mull and the near-destitute Caravan Crew of Eigg, all suffer more or less from island romanticism. So do the retired couples settling with a grateful sigh into the Isles of Wight and Man. They can seem to the born islanders unbearably smug and insensitive; responsible, too, for inflating house and land prices to levels that young islanders can't possibly hope to match.

All sorts of people try their hands at island life – escapers, evaders, people with a past, people in flight from the rat-race, people in search of the simple life, or the good life. Some fall in love with their chosen islands, head over heels, and invest them with personalities. Some flap and bray in their own closed circle, never touching their island-born neighbours' lives at all. Others come with their heads in the clouds – 'Two goats in tow, and she thought she'd be a crofter!' – and leave miserably, disillusioned by poverty, bad weather and seemingly indifferent neighbours. Some forge their way by patience and good nature into island society, and slowly learn how to contribute to the work and leisure, the social and emotional life of their island. None ever quite gets to the heart of the native community. As a defensive measure, well-spoken and fluent incomers usually find themselves voted into the position of spokesman on this and that committee. Let them be the ones to stick out their necks and get them chopped off. It's a hard row to hoe, being an island settler with a social conscience. Things were easier for that past generation of dictatorial overlords who bought up islands – the Bulloughs of Rhum, the Balfours of Shapinsay, the Smiths of Tresco – and did what they liked with them in mailed-fist philanthropy. Easier, too, for their successors, the absentee City men, rock stars and faceless financial institutions who own so much of the islands and seldom, if ever, visit their investments.

For incomers and natives alike, island life today is fraught with difficulties. Bad weather can plunge any of the islands back into the inaccessibility of the pre-aeroplane world. It's impossible to overestimate the value of *Oldenburg* to Lundy, the helicopters to Scilly or *Lochmor* to the Small Isles. Everything costs more than on the mainland – goods and people coming in, produce and people going out. Everything takes twice as long. Planning and forethought are second nature to islanders. If you haven't got that essential medicine and a Force 10 suddenly blows up . . . Old folk, sick people, mentally and physically handicapped people can all go short of the support they would take for granted on the mainland. Above all other problems looms the worst one, no matter where one looks among the islands – the running sore of depopulation. Island populations are still falling, as they have done since the kelp peaks of nearly two centuries ago. Young people with drive and ambition are still obliged to leave the islands, to seek their fortune in the wider world. This is not a phenomenon peculiar to the islands. Ambitious youngsters from every part of the country leave their small home communities for travel and adventure and to broaden their horizons. But the call back home for native islanders is painfully strong, and many have nothing in the way of work to return to. There is a great, aching dearth of talent and energy in the islands between the ages of twenty and forty.

Drink and depression are island diseases, going hand in hand with the state of the seasons and the weather. There's a claustrophobic paranoia that gets a grip on many islanders in the winter months when gales batter the islands for weeks on end. At such times the victims of island depression would do anything to escape their remote little prisons in the water. Drink is an effective if deadly escape route in a place where most drinkers can defer until tomorrow what a thick head won't let them do today.

There were some sad elements to my journey through the islands: the miserable jails on the Isle of Wight, the TT deaths on the Isle of Man, the once populated, now empty islands like Samson and Mingulay. Saddest of all were the clearance villages – Urie in Fetlar, Grulin in Eigg, Lorgill in Skye – where the ground itself seemed stained and impregnated with the weight of vanished people. Better to look back over the pleasures of the adventure – the remarkable people I met, the transfixing landscapes and the tunes and tales that went with them, the glimpses into lives so utterly different from mine. The other British isles and their islanders hold steadfastly to their own particular ways and attitudes of life, even while the modern world, for good or ill, invades them. Like a flotilla of little ships they head towards an uncertain future through an unpredictable, contrary sea of grants and self-help, protection and marketing, native tradition and incomer energy, independence and vulnerability. In the end their well-being rests with those seed-corn boys and girls dancing so blithely in community halls all round the islands. That's why I dedicate this book to them.

Index

Index

Index

Armadale Castle: Clan Donald centre 236
Camasunary Bay 241
  flotsam and jetsam 241
clans originally holding 229
clearance township of Lorgill 242, 295
Cuillin Hills 161, 164, 187, 224, 237, 238
disillusionment with government from Westminster 227–8, 237
Domhnallach, Seumas (Jamie Macdonald) 225
drunkenness 228
Dunvegan 228, 241
  castle 229, 230–1, 232, 234, 235, 237, 238
  dungeon 229–30
  Fairy Flag 230, 233
Duirinish peninsula 228, 231
Elgol 240
  primary school 240–1
Flodigarry Hotel 225, 227
  Macdonald, Flora, house behind hotel 225
  Scott-Moncrieffs 225, 227, 228
Gaelic language, state of survival 225–6
Loch Dunvegan 231
Macleod, Black Iain, 10th Chief 229
  Dame Flora, 28th Chief 235
  Norman (The General), 23rd Chief 234
  John, 29th Chief 223–6, 237, 241
  Norman (The Red Man), 22nd Chief 234
Macleod atrocities 229–30
  clan feeling, strength of 231
Macleod's Tables 187
piping 231–3
  Borreraig Piping Centre 231
  legends 232–3
  MacCrimmon, Patrick Mór 232–3
  MacCrimmons, hereditary pipers to Macleod chiefs 231–2
potato famine (1847–51) 234
Quiraing 227, 228
Sleat peninsula 236
Staffin Free Kirk 225, 226, 293
  Gaelic service 225–6
Strathaird Estate 238
  Anderson, Ian, rock star and laird 240
  Loch Slapin salmon farm 238–40

Mackinnon, Gordon, manager 238–40 passim
Strathaird peninsula 238, 240
Trotternish peninsula 224, 225, 226, 228, 229
  basalt spine 227
Vaternish peninsula 228
Somerville, Christopher, Britain Beside the Sea 105n
South Glamorgan County Council, backing of Flat Holm Project 59
South Ronaldsay, Orkney 281
South Uist, Isle of, Outer Hebrides 185, 187, 188–92
  army ranges 186, 191
  black-houses 190, 191
  Catholic influence 189, 293
  causeway to Benbecula 188–9
  machair 191, 192
  traditional pattern of life 189–90
  white-houses 190, 191
Staffa, Isle of, Inner Hebrides 144–7, 217, 218
  Am Buachaille (The Herdsman) 145
  basalt formations 144, 145, 146
  Fingal's Cave 146
  flora, beauty of 146
  Mendelssohn, Felix, Hebridean Overture 146
  shags 145
Steep Holm Island, Bristol Channel 55, 56–9
  gull colony 61
  Kenneth Allsop Memorial Trust 57, 58, 59
  Legg, Rodney, warden 57, 58, 59, 61
  military remains 55–8 passim
    problems posed by 58
  ownership 57
  wild peonies 55, 291

Thames Flood Barrier 21
Thomas, Leslie, Some Lovely Islands 258
Tiree, Isle of, Inner Hebrides 140
Torrey Canyon disaster (1967) 46
Treshnish Islands, Inner Hebrides 140, 144, 175, 213, 217
  Dutchman's Cap 144, 175
  Lunga 144

Ulva, Isle of, Inner Hebrides 144, 216

Index